Leslie Page Moch
East Lansing
337-7058

P9-CCC-493

COERCED AND FREE MIGRATION: GLOBAL PERSPECTIVES

LPM

THE MAKING OF MODERN FREEDOM

General Editor: R. W. Davis

Center for the History of Freedom
Washington University in St. Louis

COERCED AND FREE MIGRATION

GLOBAL PERSPECTIVES

Edited by David Eltis

Stanford University Press
Stanford, California
2002

Stanford University Press
Stanford, California
©2002 by the Board of Trustees of the
Leland Stanford Junior University
Printed in the United States of America

Library of Congress Cataloging-in-Publication Data

Coerced and free migration: global perspectives / edited by David Eltis.
p. cm. — (The making of modern freedom)
Includes bibliographical references and index.
ISBN 0-8047-4454-8 (cloth : acid-free paper)
1. Forced migration—History. 2. Population transfers—History.
3. Emigration and immigration —History. I. Eltis, David. II. Series.

HB1951.C64 2002
325—dc21 2002001137

This book is printed on acid-free, archival-quality paper.

Original printing 2002

Last figure below indicates year of this printing:
11 10 09 08 07 06 05 04 03 02

Typeset at Stanford University Press in 10/13 Trump Mediaeval

Acknowledgments

This volume has been generously supported by a grant from the Lynde and Harry Bradley Foundation and a gift from Carolyn and Joseph Losos of St. Louis. As always, we are also grateful for the support of Washington University.

Series Foreword

THE STARTLING AND moving events that swept from China to Eastern Europe to Latin America and South Africa at the end of the 1980s, followed closely by similar events and the subsequent dissolution of what used to be the Soviet Union, formed one of those great historic occasions when calls for freedom, rights, and democracy echoed through political upheaval. A clear-eyed look at any of those conjunctions—in 1776 and 1789, in 1848 and 1918, as well as in 1989—reminds us that freedom, liberty, rights, and democracy are words into which many different and conflicting hopes have been read. The language of freedom—or liberty, which is interchangeable with freedom most of the time—is inherently difficult. It carried vastly different meanings in the classical world and in medieval Europe from those of modern understanding, though thinkers in later ages sometimes eagerly assimilated the older meanings to their own circumstances and purposes.

A new kind of freedom, which we have here called modern, gradually disentangles itself from old contexts in Europe, beginning first in England in the early seventeenth century and then, with many confusions, denials, reversals, and cross-purposes, elsewhere in Europe and the world. A large-scale history of this modern, conceptually distinct, idea of freedom is now beyond the ambition of any one scholar, however learned. This collaborative enterprise, tentative though it must be, is an effort to fill the gap.

We could not take into account all the varied meanings that freedom and liberty have carried in the modern world. We have, for example, ruled out extended attention to what some political philosophers have called "positive freedom," in the sense of self-realization of the individual; nor could we, even in a series as large as this, cope with the enormous implications of the four freedoms invoked by Franklin D. Roosevelt in 1941. Freedom of speech and freedom of the press will have their place in the narrative that follows, certainly, but not the boundless calls for freedom from want and freedom from fear.

We use freedom in the traditional and restricted sense of civil and political liberty—freedom of religion, freedom of speech and assembly, freedom of the individual from arbitrary and capricious authority over persons or property, freedom to produce and to exchange goods and services, and the freedom to take part in the political process that shapes people's destiny. In no major part of the world over the past few years have aspirations for those freedoms not been at least powerfully expressed; and in most places where they did not exist, strong measures have been taken—not always successfully—to attain them.

The history we trace was not a steady march toward the present or the fulfillment of some cosmic necessity. Modern freedom had its roots in specific circumstances in early modern Europe, despite the unpromising and even hostile characteristics of the larger society and culture. From these narrow and often selfishly motivated beginnings, modern freedom came to be realized in later times, constrained by old traditions and institutions hard to move, and driven by ambition as well as idealism: everywhere the growth of freedom has been *sui generis*. But to understand these unique developments fully, we must first try to see them against the making of modern freedom as a whole.

In the first decade of the twenty-first century, the necessity of such a volume as this in a series on the making of modern freedom hardly needs belaboring. The impact of migrations in changing societies for the bad as well as for the good is evident all over the world. In Europe, migration from the east is putting serious strains on the values and practice of freedom in Germany. Algerian migration is having the same effect in France. In Britain the two major parties are competing with each other in their advocacy of restricting the right of asylum. Indonesia is torn by the effects of migration, present as well as past. In the Balkans too they continue, in this case the result of deliberate and malevolent human contrivance.

With such examples before us, it is sometimes difficult to remember that migrations can also bring great good, and usually do in the end. Perhaps most often, they are freely undertaken by people whose labor, skills, or talents are clearly required in the areas where they are going. Neither Europe nor the Americas would enjoy today the prosperity, vibrant cultures, and variety of choices they do had it not been for migrations, some of which still continue. Unfortunately, however, initially at any rate, new homelands are apt to have short memories of the benefits they have received when adversities, real or perceived, occur, and to blame those for whose efforts gratitude would be the appropriate sentiment.

Much more has this been so, though the benefits to the host countries have been no less great, when the migration has been coerced. Such was the case with the centerpiece of the present volume, the largest of the modern history's forced migrations and the most momentous in its consequences, the Atlantic slave trade. Valued only for their labor at the time, the slaves and their descendants have had much to bear since, though their contributions over several centuries are increasingly coming to be valued at their true worth. The technically free laborers from India and China who were brought in to take the place of the ex-slaves after emancipation in the West Indies in 1834 at least started and may have continued in a better situation, but stresses and strains with the other populations in the Caribbean still exist. Russian migrations provide contrasting experiences in a very different society. In another instance, British convicts may have started their lives in a situation as desperate as any, but in Australia where they were the first European settlers they were able remarkably quickly to become both prosperous and respectable.

David Eltis and the other authors who join him in this volume have all made distinguished contributions in their earlier work to our knowledge of the impact of migrations in these several areas of the world. Their chapters in this volume represent a combination of new research, new insights, and a comparative approach which together yield a new and deeper understanding of this vitally important topic.

The Making of Modern Freedom grows out of a continuing series of conferences held at the Center for the History of Freedom at Washington University in St. Louis. Professor J. H. Hexter was the founder and, for three years, the resident gadfly of the Center. His contribution is gratefully recalled by all his colleagues.

R.W.D.

Contents

CONTRIBUTORS

Philip D. Curtin
The Johns Hopkins University

David Eltis
Emory University

Stanley L. Engerman
University of Rochester

Colin Forster
Australian National University

Richard Hellie
University of Chicago

Walton Look Lai
University of the West Indies

David Moon
University of Strathclyde

David Northrup
Boston College

Mechal Sobel
University of Haifa

Lorena S. Walsh
Colonial Williamsburg Foundation

Marianne S. Wokeck
Indiana University—Purdue University

COERCED AND FREE MIGRATION: GLOBAL PERSPECTIVES

Introduction: Migration and Agency in Global History

DAVID ELTIS

FROM THE EMIGRATION OF homo sapiens from Africa perhaps 100,000 years ago, to the Viking visits to North America, and Chinese and Arab contact with the Indonesian archipelago, migration meant in essence the settlement of the globe. In the absence of continuing exchange between old and new communities, migration resulted in continual goodbyes. Ocean-borne migration began about 1000 BC, and for a further two millennia after this, migrants very seldom returned to their areas of origin. Migrations gave rise to new cultures and societies that remained largely unaware of their place in the increasingly diverse kaleidoscope of humanity. People created identities for themselves without the aid of the "other," a phenomenon almost impossible to imagine in the modern world. The creation of land-based empires in Eurasia and elsewhere periodically slowed or reversed the process of cultural fragmentation. The steady expansion southward of imperial control in China culminating in the Chin and Han dynasties led to consolidation and integration, but these were sub-, not inter-continental phenomena.

A little over a thousand years ago the broad pattern of dispersion began to change as peoples in the far west, the far east, and then the south of the Old World launched extensive transoceanic, or at least trans-maritime, satellite communities, whose existence involved the maintenance of retraceable sea-borne connections. Viking trade with the Dorset peoples of Labrador beginning in the late ninth century, Chinese expansion to the Indonesian archipelago and beyond, and monsoon-based navigation in the Indian Ocean were predicated on return voyages thousands of miles in length.[1] While the colonization of the globe continued, indeed at an expanding rate, this was a cultural turning point comparable to the revolution that converted hunter-gatherers to settled agriculturalists. Because the problems of sailing were minor compared to overland journeys of equivalent length, reciprocal sea-borne contact began the reintegration of human societies, a process that continues today in the form of cheap air travel and the communication revolution. At some time in the middle of the last millennium it is likely that the number of languages and cultures in the world that disappeared each year came to exceed those that were created. Conceptions of self at both individual and social levels became tied to ever-changing perceptions of others.[2]

Old World expansion, especially in its western maritime manifestation, has usually been seen as a continuation of global occupation and colonization. But from the broad perspective adopted here, the diaspora of the peoples of Western Europe, western Africa, the Russian Empire, and Southern Asia was not merely an outward movement, it was rather a critical stage in the conflation and consolidation of the world's peoples and cultures. After 1000 AD, migration began to pull together once more the peoples of the Old and New Worlds, Asia and Europe, and Southern Asia and its archipelago. This was an era that saw the greatest, most concentrated, and longest mass migrations in the human experience up to that time, much of it sea-borne and swift by comparison with what had gone before. More important it necessarily constituted the first time in migration history that some continual contact with the point of departure became possible, either because of additional new arrivals from the area in which the original migrants had left, or through written communication.

Return became a possibility for many migrants for the first time. Even forced migration eventually resulted in the possibility of return, such as in the nineteenth-century cases of the thousands of Yoruba in Brazil who bought their freedom and went back to the area where they had been enslaved, and descendants of slaves who founded Liberia and Sierra Leone. Return migration of Europeans and Asians—for example Italians from Brazil and Indians from Mauritius and the Americas—was massive by pre-modern standards—some 85 percent of migrants to the Mascarene Islands electing to go back to India. And in the African case, numerically small though it was, there is a growing literature on how Old World identities, for example the Yoruba, were not just reshaped, but created, by the returning migrants.[3] None of these phenomena would have been possible in an earlier era.

While the global mixing of the world's peoples continues to accelerate in the twenty-first century, it is likely that this process is still in its infancy. Eighteenth-century German and Irish migration to North America pointed the way to the mass transoceanic migrations of the nineteenth century. In an even larger canvas, the ethnic composition of free and coerced migration in the four centuries before 1900 is a template for migration in the twentieth and twenty-first centuries.[4] No one who has taken a subway ride in New York, London, or Toronto can be in any doubt that modernity today is increasingly associated with the multi-ethnic metropolis, despite government efforts to control migration from the developing world. In the last two decades four-fifths of all US immigrants have originated from non-European parts of the world, and the equivalent ratios for most European countries are only slightly smaller. In London today, there are no less than 307 languages spoken by the 25 percent of the city's children who use a language other than English at home. In Amsterdam the figure is 180, and the New York figure is unlikely to be smaller than London's.[5] A multi-ethnic supply of labor appears far more important to the continuation of the modern global economy than to its seventeenth- and eighteenth-century rise.[6]

Intriguingly, while the process of expansion was initially led in the European case by nascent nation-states with some degree of ethnic homogeneity, it is also clear that the movement of peoples that resulted built the base of most multi-ethnic societies in the modern world. Individuals have moved around so much that there never was a time when strictly homogenous peoples formed nations, but the mixing of peoples is greater today than ever before in global history. The future of bloodlines and in the long run of religion as a basis of nationhood does not look secure at this point. Today, as in the last five centuries, mass migration and mixing is triggered mainly by Europe, and what were originally European settlements, yet most people caught in the phenomenon were (and are) not European. The end of this process—a long way off given zero natural rates of population increase and an expanding need for labor in the developed world—is perhaps a fuller integration of the world's peoples and cultures than has existed since homo sapiens left Africa. Nazi Germany and late twentieth-century Rwanda and Yugoslavia appear as anachronisms on this broad canvas, or, one would hope, the last coruscation of the most evil form of ethnocentrism prior to its expiry.

Reintegration of the peoples of the world often occurred in the face of resistance of the migrants (or potential migrants) themselves—whether against forcible movement or the much less studied related phenomenon of the struggle of people to become migrants in the face of efforts of others to prevent voluntary migration. Conquest has always been a major element in the migration of peoples, in both its initiation and its stemming. But since the rise of the nation-state in the early modern period, governments of emigrant as well as immigrant societies have frequently raised barriers of a non-military type to the movement of migrants, as well as compelled or countenanced the compulsion of others to move as slaves and convicts. A closer examination of the issue of agency and migration—a topic on which all the chapters in this volume throw light—reveals some striking patterns. These patterns are grouped and explored here around three themes. The first is the rapid expansion of long-distance mass migration in the four centuries prior to 1900 against the wider context of migration history. The second is the remarkable range of migratory regimes—slaves, serfs, prisoners, indentured or contract workers, and free migrants—that held during these centuries. The third is the similarities of the different forms of migrations. Much of the literature on migration is organized along national or ethnic lines stressing the westward transatlantic flow, but new insights are generated by breaking down these national divisions as well as by attempting to reassess the quickening outflows of Africans, Europeans, and Asians to the east as well as to the west. While no attempt is made here to match the all-inclusive sweep of the world-systems school, similarities in the eastern and western and southern movement of peoples out of the Old World since the early modern period are examined.[7]

I

Coercion and Expansion from the Old World

All migration hinges on a cultural differential between donor and recipient societies.[8] People may move to better their economic lot, or, as in the case of forced migration of slaves, serfs, and convicts, to better the lot of someone else. Such instincts regarding migration are universal and cannot manifest themselves as behavior without the emigrants or their controllers either having an advantage over those already living in the recipient society, or being attracted to such an advantage in the host society. Even the first hunters and gatherers moving into previously unoccupied areas had to develop the clothes and tools that made the move possible. After the as yet poorly understood Great Migration of Peoples in the first millennium of the Christian era, sedentary peoples tended to replace their nomadic predecessors, and migration was toward nexus points of new technologies or new opportunities for old technologies, which normally demanded concentrations of labor—whether in cities, mines, or plantations.

The westward transoceanic migration and the eastward expansion of the Russian Empire were characterized by the movement of sedentary peoples into areas occupied by peoples at earlier stages of conversion from hunting and gathering, or in the east a nomadic pastoralism, to settled agriculture. In the Americas, Australasia, and the steppes south to the Crimea and east up to and beyond the Urals (as well as the initial westward movement of the Russian Empire), migrants practicing settled agriculture found themselves in environments in which the ratio of land to labor was much higher than anything they had previously experienced. They and their descendants did exceptionally well demographically, certainly much better than the people whose lands they had successfully invaded. The epidemiological underpinning of gains and losses is now widely accepted. High-density populations of people and animals in settled societies ensure more virulent pathogens than are normal among nomadic peoples, and the ending of the multi-millennia isolation of New World peoples from the Old led to a devastating impact from the latter in the aftermath of Columbian contact.[9]

Most migration before 1500 was voluntary in a fundamental way. Most migration has voluntary and coercive elements. If the migration is sufficiently large, the immigrant society is changed forever in ways that few of its original occupants would have wanted had they been given the choice. Historians probably view most migration as forced at some level as social or ecological conditions at the point of origin might be such that individuals have no choice but to leave. Theodore Schultz makes the useful distinction between those compelled to migrate against their own perceived self-interest and those able to exercise choice over the decision.[10] Indentured servants from Europe and contract laborers from India and China were not usually forced on board ship, chained and kept behind temporary barricades so that they could not see their homeland before setting sail. Neither were they subjected to special measures to restrain suicide during the actual sea voyage. Slaves from Africa and convicts from Europe could expect all or most of these things. The distinction between free and coerced migration hinges on who makes the decision to leave, the migrant or some other individual. In the context of the twentieth century, the "fall" of coerced migration has to be spelled out carefully. One recent estimate puts the number of slaves in the modern world at 27 million,[11] though their status is clearly not a result of a slave trade and the categorization of slavery employed would be recognized by neither nineteenth-century slave owners in the Americas nor their human chattels. Moreover, we might compare this estimate with the views of Arthur Young (and many other eighteenth-century observers) who claimed that rather than 27 million slaves in the world (or less than half of one percent of the modern population), 95 percent of the world's population was then "unfree."

Schultz's view is also useful for the case of the Russian Empire, but the latter is nevertheless different in that the major restraints there were aimed at stopping people from moving. Serfs were moved when their owners decided to relocate, but given the prospect of higher agricultural yields many appeared willing to move.

Estimates of total migration, much less its free and coerced components, before 1500 are not possible. The flow of slaves into the Mediterranean at the peak of the Roman Empire or when the relative prosperity of Islam was at its height may have been considerable, but the numbers could have been only a tiny fraction of the voluntary migrants flooding into Europe from the Visigoths in the fifth century to the Slavs down to the tenth. Beginning in the sixteenth century, volition in the decision to migrate was increasingly eroded. Someone other than the migrant either forced an individual to move, as in the slave trade, or enforced regulations that prevented migration.[12] From the perspective of both users of labor and labor itself, the ratio of land to labor rose dramatically in source and target societies combined as Europeans reached the Pacific Ocean from both eastern and western directions.[13] Systems of coerced labor that had disappeared in Western Europe during the Middle Ages underwent a renaissance either in the new societies or in the societies supplying the migrants or in both, as those with land and capital attempted to obtain (or retain) access to labor. The massive development of the slave Americas was matched by the Russian enslavement of some Turkic peoples and the more gradual imposition of a second serfdom in the east—between 1497 and 1649 in the Russian case, although restrictions on serf movements continued to increase down to 1796. The convict interlude in Australia belongs in some senses to the same pattern. Down to 1800, perhaps two-thirds of the people moving both east and west out of the Old World were coerced (either slaves, convicts, serfs, or military recruits, which in the Russian Empire often presaged a forced and permanent move).

Despite worsening conditions in the Russian case, some of the new serfs and slaves escaped or successfully resisted, though there were always more escaped serfs than escaped slaves. The flights of serfs and deserters to both sides of the shifting and imprecise line defining the limits of Russian imperial control were paralleled by four centuries of flight (the so-called grand and petit marronage) in the slave Americas. But escape for some always meant enserfment or enslavement for others, as the massive expansion of the slave trade to the British and Spanish Caribbean in the aftermath of the St. Domingue revolution indicated. In addition to the imperatives of expansion, negative natural rates of population growth in most of the slave Americas ensured an increasing flow of labor into these systems, the labor often originating thousands of miles distant from the place of its ultimate use.

There were some exceptions to this pattern of increasing coercion. European expansion actually interrupted some major traffics in slaves. To the west the inflow of slaves into the Aztec empire—many of them used for ritual sacrifices—came to a sudden halt with the Spanish conquest. In the East, effects were even more striking. The centuries-long depredations of nomadic raiders in the Russian borderlands that directed thousands through the Black Sea to Mediterranean slave markets had once been extensive enough for Western Europeans to drop the old Latin word for a chattel laborer—"servus"—and replace it with "esclavus," derived from "slav."[14] A similar shift from "slave" to a derivation of the Latin word for black, "negra," might have occurred later if Latin had retained its preeminence into the nineteenth century. Nevertheless, the net impact of European expansion on freedom (however defined) of non-Europeans was strongly negative, and the scale of the new labor systems in both east and west was such that European expansion was associated with a sharp increase in the coerced component of migration.

In the Atlantic, the dominant migratory regime for most of the period after 1500 became the slave trade from Africa. Convicts and prisoners of mainly civil wars were always sent overseas in much smaller numbers than slaves, perhaps one exiled white for every 40 black slaves as long as the convict traffic lasted. It is interesting to note, however, that convict departures had a temporal profile similar to that of the slave trade, though somewhat delayed. They began in earnest a century later than the slave trade, peaked in the mid-nineteenth century some 70 years after the traffic in slaves, and petered out first in the West and then in the USSR some hundred years after the last slave ship crossed the Atlantic. In the East, while there is no evidence of a significant organized long-distance traffic in serfs (that is, serfs being moved for the specific purpose of sale), no precise estimate of numbers moved by their owners south and east is possible. Western observers have tended to exaggerate their volume, but there is little doubt that Russian governments sent far more prisoners into exile than all the western European governments combined between 1500 and 1914.[15] When movements of military personnel are factored in, coerced migration was, as noted, perhaps double its free counterpart down to 1800. There was no equivalent phase of coerced labor for Chinese and Indians in the earlier part of the period—the worst excesses of the contract labor trade to the Spanish Americas, where the parallels with slave trade were closest, not coming until the mid-nineteenth century. Nevertheless, between 1600 and 1820 it seems likely that human migration from both the east and west of the Old World was less "free" than ever before, and less "free" than it was ever subsequently to become. After 1850, by contrast, only one in eight of the six million arrivals in Russian Asia could be classed as coerced (all political and criminal exiles), and to the west the slave and convict component of transatlantic migration was much less than 1 percent.

The rise of coerced migration may well have been inevitable in the sense that large-scale migration (several million people over a period of say a century or less) could not have occurred in the pre-1800 world unless it *was* coerced. That China did not share in this pattern of increasing coercion is no doubt in part because it was easily capable of resisting European expansion and its effects at this time. Yet the Chinese pattern supports the above generalization for a different reason. Chinese overseas migration of all kinds was of small volume during the seventeenth and eighteenth centuries when enserfdom and slavery were peaking in the West (including the Russian Empire). Thus, free migration was small, or at least very gradual, particularly when expressed as a percentage of source populations. In the Atlantic, the Spanish averaged 2,000 migrants a year in the sixteenth century, the Portuguese, 3,000 a year in the eighteenth century, and the English, 5,000 a year in the 60 years after 1630. In no period before the nineteenth century is it likely that European migration—including indentured servants—exceeded a five year annual average of 10,000. The white populations of the Americas were not only still small by Old World standards in the mid-eighteenth century despite two and a half centuries of migration, they were also overwhelmingly native born. Apart from the slave Caribbean and Brazil, these were not migrant societies before the eighteenth century. After 1820, by contrast, free migrants from Europe averaged 50,000 a year to the US alone.

The same pattern holds for the Russian Empire with the turning point (that is the onset of mass free migration), like its counterpart in the Chinese case, coming later in the century. But whereas the absence of mass free migration in the Americas prior to 1820 largely reflects the choice of Europeans, its absence in the East was in part because government restrictions meant that the migrant was not entirely free to move. Dense voluntary migration of the scale that appeared in the Atlantic after 1820 developed in the Russian Empire only in the late nineteenth century, though free migration in the last century of Tsarism was still sufficient to make the numbers of inhabitants of the Russian Empire crossing the Urals the third largest long-distance migration in history after the transatlantic movement from Europe and the slave trade.[16]

The standard explanation for modern mass migration usually has two parts. The first is per capita income differentials that favored the target country, and the second is falling transportation costs. In other words, migrants (or their controllers in the case of slaves and prisoners) could do better materially by moving. But these factors do little to explain the dramatic shift over time in the number of voluntary migrants and the collapse of the coerced component of migration. It seems very unlikely that income differentials between Europe and America, or between the Russian heartland and beyond the Urals, or China and the rest of Southeast Asia and the Americas suddenly increased severalfold after 1820. In addition, it is now clear that while passenger fares fell between the mid-eighteenth and mid-nineteenth centuries, presumably because of falling transportation costs, they did so by only 40 percent.[17] A decline of this magnitude is not likely to have had much to do with a fivefold increase in the volume of passengers.

An alternative, or more accurately a supplementary explanation, has psychological roots. Massive voluntary migration to even the temperate "neo-Europes" in Crosby's phrase[18] required some certainty of connection with the source society (or at least other migrants). Migrants hungered for land, higher income, and control over their lives, goals that were not necessarily compatible. But before such factors could trigger a transoceanic or transcontinental population movement on a modern scale of intensity there had to be reliable communication, a sense of ultimate military security, and the possibility that collective identities could retain characteristic elements of what had been familiar to migrants prior to moving. Perhaps technology could not widely guarantee a threshold level of physical and psychological security until the nineteenth century, although the speedy return voyages and the circulation of written matter, especially newspapers, clearly pointed the way in the late seventeenth-century North Atlantic.

An important initial element in the ability of contract labor schemes to attract labor from Asia was the promise of a return passage. While earlier forms of indentures from Europe did not have this feature, distances across the Atlantic were less than those across the Pacific and freedom dues paid at the end of the indenture provided at least the appearance of an escape hatch. In the nineteenth century, railroads made a major contribution to this sense of connectedness. The closest parallels between eastern and western expansion come after the construction of the trans-Siberian railroad, when settlers poured into the far east in the two decades before the Revolution. Indeed, while war (and civil war) disrupted the pattern in the East, mass voluntary migration continued into Siberia for about as long as it continued into western Canada—to the later 1920s—though the reason for its termination was Soviet policy rather than the closing of the arable frontier. The beginning of mass migration to Siberia might be compared with the great upsurge in free transatlantic migration originating 80 years earlier. In both cases the potential income gains from moving had been in place many years, and while transportation costs undoubtedly declined, this decline must have had as much effect on the migrant's sense of continuing links with the familiar as on the economics of the decision to move.

Generally, large-scale and systematic coerced migration began with European expansion and ended when free and contract migrants became more willing—or in the Russian Empire were allowed—to replace slaves and prisoners. In effect the predominance of slave, serf, and prisoner migrants was sandwiched chronologically between long periods when voluntary migration was the norm. For three centuries labor would not move into new territories at a rate deemed appropriate by the state—especially in the Russian case—or by landowners. The few that did move tended to do so unofficially and usually squatted or at least avoided the kind of labor that the propertied elite wished them to undertake. Coerced migrants accelerated the development of the territories to which they were sent, sometimes paving the way for free migrants.

In the Americas, the free migration that did occur before 1730 (mainly indentured servants) headed overwhelmingly to the plantation areas. And while after this point, free migrants tended to bypass the plantations to which slaves and convicts were sent, slavery clearly contributed to higher income in all parts of the Americas as well as to the stronger commercial and communication ties between Europe and the Americas that made mass voluntary migration to the Continent more likely in the long run. In Australia, the connection between coerced migration, development, and a subsequent mass inflow of free migrants is clearest of all. Convicts created a colonial infrastructure as well as the beginnings of a staple economy that free migrants took over directly some 60 years after the penal colony was first established. The proportion of the New South Wales and Tasmanian populations who were convicts in 1850 fell between the proportions of the Chesapeake and the South Carolina populations, respectively, who were enslaved at the time of the American Revolution.[19]

After free migration became a mass phenomenon in the nineteenth century, completely unrestricted migration would have filled up the land more quickly. Unrestricted migration, however, scarcely served the class interest of the landed establishment in Imperial Russia, nor eastern industrial employers in the US. The Russian government was always torn between restricting migration (in the sense of preventing the flight of serfs) and encouraging the movement of people into new areas, preferably under government control or that of the serf owners. There can be little doubt, however, that in Siberia, the area of settlement that most resembled the North American pattern, coerced migration before the railroad contributed to an infrastructure and made mass free migration after the railroad more likely. Yet coerced migration was clearly not enough in itself to guarantee development either at the time it happened or subsequently. New Caledonia and French Guiana remained backwaters despite a steady supply of prisoners (greatly exceeding those going to French Canada, for example) over many decades. As discussed below, the major factor in the ending of the coerced branches of migration was not, however, an increased supply of voluntary labor, but rather a shift in values that permitted forced migration, or indeed any migration with coercive undertones, to be viewed as evil.

≺ II ≻

Cultural Values and Migration

The global "reintegration" of peoples was associated with a huge change in the value systems (hinted at by the changing nature of the nation-state). Growing ethnic diversity in the mass movements and mixing of peoples was initially paralleled by the diversity of migratory regimes under which the migrants moved. Conceptions of self and community—what the modern literature calls "identity"—are central to determining the form migration takes, who will become migrants, and what will be their ultimate destination. But the most enduring influence of conceptions of identity was on deciding under which of the migratory regimes a migrant would travel, what would be his or her reception on arrival, and what would be the status of the migrants' descendants. A hemispheric and very long run perspective suggests that fundamental shifts in identity lay behind the migration patterns described above. It is beyond the scope of this introduction to explain these shifts, the aim rather being merely to note that they happened and to draw some implications for one of the fields of human endeavor affected by such shifts. Constructions of others (or more generally, outsiders) both defined and determined the treatment of prisoners of war, lawbreakers, religious and racial minorities, and refugees from advancing armies. The flow of convicts from eastern and western Europe as well as part of the flow of people into the African slave trade was shaped by community morality, often reflected in formal legislation. Social mores not only ensured that the convict component of migration would be small (and thus that the demand for other coerced migrants such as slaves would be greater), but that convicts would have more rights than slaves, and that the convict trade would die out altogether over time—usually in response to pressure from recipient societies in the western case.[20] More broadly, exile came to be regarded as cruel, though in the Russian Empire it survived as a method of political repression until past the mid-twentieth century.

The most important shift in values that affected migration was not in the definition and treatment of criminal behavior or religious minorities, however, but rather in conceptions of who should be slaves and serfs. One way to think of this is as a boundary in the mind, as opposed to a geographic or political barrier. Not until the twelfth century could Western European conceptions of the larger society—a grouping of people that as a minimum could be counted on not to enslave each other—encompass most of Europe. Before this an internal slave trade still flourished as people from the North were captured by other Europeans and carried for sale in the South, many, ultimately, to the prosperous Islamic areas. This situation was little different from what existed in Africa when written records become sufficiently dense to be reliable.

In one sense the story of transatlantic migration (and eventually abolition of the slave trade and slavery) is a coda to the expansion of this sense of identity to incorporate ever-larger geographic and cultural areas. In another, the massive and unprecedented flow of racially exclusive coerced labor across the Atlantic is perhaps the result of the differential pace in the evolution of a cultural pan-Europeanness on the one hand, and a pan-Africanism on the other. An interlude of two or three centuries between the former and the latter provided a window of opportunity in which the slave trade rose and fell dramatically. For four centuries from the mid-fifteenth century to 1867, Europeans were not prepared to enslave each other, but were prepared to buy Africans and keep them and their descendants enslaved. Given that "Africa" scarcely existed as a concept for Africans in any sense before the nineteenth century, there were always some people living in the subcontinent south of the Sahara who were prepared to enslave others from adjacent or distant societies. "Pan" in this formulation refers to conceptions of who might be considered eligible for enslavement, not political and economic cohesion. Down to the twentieth century, migrant groups, especially peoples of African descent, became the enemy other in the formation of most dominant collective identities in the Americas. The "achievement oriented individualism" that has long been a major element of how all migrant groups see themselves, in the US at least, has worked only slowly to erode the rejection and hatred that such an identity has fostered.[21]

In the transatlantic case the peculiar multi-regimed pattern of migration before 1870, as well as the racial basis of the different regimes, is related to the very sudden increase in large-scale intercontinental contact after 1492. Oceans that had hermetically sealed peoples and cultures from each other sprouted sea lanes almost overnight. Cultural accommodation between peoples, in this case between Europeans and non-Europeans, always took time. The big difference was that before Columbus, migrations had been gradual and tended to move outward from the more to the less densely populated parts of the globe. After Columbus, Western Europe, Central America, West Africa, and eventually much of Asia, all with cities and relatively densely populated, were suddenly thrown into contact. Before Columbus, cultural accommodation or the emergence of a dominant culture, as with epidemiological adjustment, tended to grow with the migration itself. Columbian contact was sudden and inhibited any gradual adjustment, cultural or epidemiological. A merging of perceptions of right and wrong, group identities, and relations between the sexes, to look only at the top of a very long list of social values, could not be expected to occur quickly in a post-

Columbian world. In short, cultural adjustment could keep pace with neither transportation technology, nor the epidemiological consequences of that technology. The result was first the rise, and then, as perceptions of the insider-outsider divide slowly changed, the fall, of the transatlantic trade in enslaved Africans. If the English had taken possession of Barbados in 1024 instead of 1624, and introduced sugar two decades later, they perhaps would have found the slaves they needed (in a decision which would have been as unthinking as the move to procure Africans six centuries later) much closer at hand in the Celtic regions of Britain.[22]

The oceans may also have contributed to racial slavery in another way. Communal identity is more than the sum of individual perceptions of self. Deep-seated social and economic forces as well as personality traits that had no obvious links with these forces are basic to the formation of collective identity and the ability of an individual to integrate or accept others as full members of society. In both early modern Europe and Africa the division between the individual and collective conceptions of self was much less distinct than it was to become in North America. If transoceanic migration meant that identity became less dependent on the community it may also have come to hinge more on the invention of an alien other, many variants of which were to be found in most migrant communities in the Americas. Tensions between European and colonial constructions of identity are easily found in the nineteenth and twentieth centuries, with in most cases the construction of the colony (or more precisely that of the dominant local elite) winning out. In the British case, the Colonial Office branch of the imperial government did not gain as much as it wanted in struggle for rights for ex-slaves in the immediate aftermath of emancipation. Within the US, the contrast between Reconstruction, initially supported by the victorious North, and what came afterward is a stark parallel. In Africa, the Afrikaaner-speaking republics lost the war, and while there was considerably more at stake than race relations, the anti-British forces nevertheless imposed their own construction of race on the region. And in Australia, the British government dispatched blacks to New South Wales in the early nineteenth century—many of them slaves convicted in the West Indies and shipped via London—but with the emergence of responsible government and sugar cultivation in Queensland, the Australian government opted to exclude non-whites, despite the full realization that this policy would make their sugar more expensive.[23]

In the east, migration occurred under quite different circumstances that had fewer implications for collective identities and slavery. The Russian Empire expanded rapidly in historic terms, reaching the Pacific coast in the early seventeenth century. Except for Alaska, expansion was always land-based and the actual settlement of the newly acquired territories was both gradual and dependent on the extent of the central government's military authority. There was no sudden accession of new lands beyond the close control of the state analogous to the western wing of European expansion. Most indigenous peoples displaced by the expansion were nomadic, but given the Euro-Asian land mass, they were not an unknown quantity and were scarcely exotic in the way that Africans and American aboriginals appeared to Europeans. Indeed, Russians had been dominated by the Mongols and Tatars for two and a half centuries before asserting their independence in 1480 and initiating their own expansion process to the east and southeast.

Perhaps the crucial east-west difference was that unlike in western and northern Europe, slavery had never died out in Russia prior to its expansion, though the slaves were retainers and household servants rather than field laborers. The issue in the East was thus the expansion of coerced labor and its deployment in new circumstances when the opportunity arose in the form of newly conquered lands, rather than, as in the West, the revival of a moribund institution. Just as important, Russian imperial expansion, even to the warmer southern lands, did not bring on stream crop types that required radically new production techniques using slave labor. There was no counterpart to sugar or rice in the degree of crop disamenities. Curiously, where the tropics in the Americas were associated with the most exploitative forms of labor, serfdom in the southern Ukraine was generally reckoned to be both less extensive and less oppressive than in the Russian heartland. The eastern expansion of peoples of the Russian Empire pushed the settlement frontier toward colder, or at least more continental climates.

But again, radical changes in production techniques were not required and dependence on the labor of peoples who could be defined as alien others was not a major issue. Prisoners excepted, Siberia, like southern Ukraine, was associated with less, rather than more, oppression prior to the Revolution. From the late eighteenth century, the Russians experimented with schemes to attract migrants from outside the empire, but while the chief motive was the acquisition of new human capital, this occurred within the framework of introducing improved western technologies rather than filling up the vast eastern and southern spaces with cheaper labor.[24] The western migrants, including peoples from the Russian Empire who moved east—and it needs to be noted that for every German that moved to the Americas, nine migrated in the opposite direction—generated considerable friction, but nothing to compare with the racially charged atmosphere of the Americas.[25] The opportunity for a system of racial slavery did not arise, and in the late nineteenth century at least, migration came to be more aligned with North American values of opportunity and freedom (for whites, at least), as well as higher incomes.

Yet shifts in both values and collective identities did in the end have a major impact on long-distance migration everywhere and helped ensure the elimination of all migratory regimes that contained elements of direct coercion. It is hard to conceive of the overwhelming predominance of voluntary migration in the twentieth century—or at least the fact that coercion came to be restricted to refusing entry to a country as opposed to forcing people to move against their will—without shifts in conceptions of right and wrong, and more inclusive ideas of who should be considered full members of society. Neither expectations of higher profit nor legal precedent can explain the demise of the migratory regimes that supplied indentured servants, slave, serfs, prisoners, and contract laborers between 1792 (date of the decree abolishing the Danish slave trade) and say the 1950s (which saw the cessation of the flow of people into the Soviet gulag archipelago).

Industrialization and economic growth ensured that labor remained in high demand in the tropical and sub-tropical areas of the globe in the nineteenth century. Outside the US, a variety of migratory regimes governed labor flows into the plantation Americas over the course of the nineteenth century. Broadly, these regimes followed a chronological progression from the more to the less coercive, and each may also be viewed from a strictly productivity standpoint as a less desirable alternative to what it replaced. Prior to 1807, increments to the plantation labor force came from Africa alone in the form of the transatlantic slave trade. In every region the ending of the traffic was associated with a rise in the price of slaves and, where it was allowed, a strong increase in the intra-American slave traffic as the more productive plantation regions bid slaves away from other parts of the Americas. As slavery itself came to an end, mainly in response to pressures from outside the plantation regions, ex-slaves left the plantations, and sugar output in most regions fell dramatically.

The initiation of contract labor migration from Asia—though it should be noted that thousands of Portuguese from the Madeiras and Spanish from the Canary Islands as well as Africans also migrated under this system—was in essence a substitute for a slave trade on which planters were no longer allowed to draw. In Cuba, the contract trade began prior to the ending of slavery, but its inception coincided exactly with the first effective Cuban attempts to restrict the slave trade that sent Cuban slave prices soaring in the mid-1840s. Over its 108 year life span (1809–1917), the contract labor trade was subject to increasingly stringent regulation. Generally, if we take the movement of Chinese contract laborers into mid-nineteenth century Cuba or the early French and British recruitment of freed African slaves as marking the closest contract labor conditions came to matching conditions in the slave trade, and the movement of contracted labor from British India to the Americas in the twentieth century as least resembling the slave traffic, then there was a clear decline in the degree of coercion over time.[26]

By the twentieth century the re-emergence of voluntary migration (with no legally enforceable ties between migrant and future employer at the end of the migration) was complete. In 1770, very few could be found to question the dominance of the slave trade as the chief means of supplying labor to the Americas (or anywhere else). A century and a half later, there were even fewer to question the idea that free migration was the only morally justifiable way to organize long-distance migration.

The shift from almost universal acceptance of the slave trade to exclusive approval of free migration can be tracked through first the debates on abolition of the slave trade, then court decisions on laborers indentured to US canal companies in the 1820s, then French and British abandonment of the recruitment of recently enslaved Africans as contract laborers by the 1850s,[27] and then the reports of commissions of inquiry into Asian contract labor later in the century, leading to the broadsides of the Indian government up to and during World War I. Migratory regimes containing coercive elements were first subject to closer supervision and then shut down altogether. The infamous conditions in the selection, transportation, and work regime of Chinese contract workers in Cuba not only helped end the system, but ensured that surviving contract systems would be more closely regulated. Shipboard mortality in the movement of convicts and indentured laborers and in the legal slave trade declined at the same time that regulation increased.[28] It is intriguing that the British decision to end the system of assignment in Australia, where a convict was subject to bonded work with an employer of the government's choosing, came in 1838, the same year that apprenticeship—the requirement that ex-slaves work for their former owners for nothing—was abolished in the British West Indies.

By the beginning of the twentieth century, no amount of official supervision and regulation was sufficient to preserve contract and indentured labor migration from new sensitivities. In the 1820s, the indenture contract came to be seen as a form of slavery, even though it was freely entered into and had been operating successfully for nearly two centuries.[29] By the early twentieth century, the contract labor system for Asians had come to be viewed in a similar light, despite (or perhaps because of) the fact that there was a degree of inspection and regulation over all aspects of the business that had no parallels in the era of slavery. Yet most historians of the movement of Indian contract workers into the English, French, and Dutch Americas believe that the vast majority of indentured migrants consented freely to their contract. During the life of the contract, enforcement of terms came under criminal law, and the imbalance of power between employer and employee was even greater than that in the free labor market. The terms of labor were very similar to those experienced by convicts in Australia. By World War I, French transportation of convicts was to continue for another quarter century, but the much larger British system was a distant memory. Moreover, the British domestic Master and Servant Act, that had treated failure of a servant to meet the agreed terms of work as theft from the employer and thus a criminal matter, had been off the statute books for nearly half a century. The contract labor trade thus had no surviving parallel by 1900.

Again the pressure for suppression came not from the planters but from governments in provenance countries, who came to view the business as unfree and demeaning. Having lost the slave trade, the sugar areas now lost the traffic in contract laborers. From the late 1880s in the French Americas and from 1918 in the British Caribbean, sugar planters and mine owners could call only on free laborers or renewed indentures to augment their labor force. An intra-American traffic in cane-cutters, largely originating in Haiti, sprang up in response, though on Brazilian coffee plantations the shift to free labor had taken place as early as the 1880s in the form of a large transatlantic movement of seasonal workers from Italy and Spain. Once more, the new option, free labor, was seen by planters as a second-best alternative to contract labor. In the sugar-producing areas of the Americas, then, the move from dependence on a slave trade to reliance on free migrants was enforced by governments, usually in Europe and Asia rather than in the regions that used the labor. What from one perspective is an ever stricter definition of freedom, is from another perspective the shift outward of the line dividing those who are counted as full members of society from those who are not. Just as it was impossible to imagine European prisoners being put to work as slaves in the Americas in the eighteenth century, so it was impossible to imagine Europeans being offered, much less accepting, a contract on an American sugar plantation embodying conditions under which Chinese and Indians worked. The few that did, Canary and Madeiran islanders, signed for three years only, not the five or more common among Asian workers, and thereafter quickly moved out of the plantation sector.

Elements of the same phenomenon may be seen in the East. Making economic gain the basis for explaining emancipation seems no more promising for Russian serfdom than for slavery in the Americas. Neither trends in serf prices nor the debt burdens of owners support such an approach.[30] The movement of serfs to new lands, always less significant in the total Russian imperial migration picture than the movement of slaves in the Americas, was certainly less in the nineteenth century than in earlier times. A more important development was the tapering off of large-scale enserfments in the late eighteenth century—the transfer of state peasants to private owners by Catherine the Great and Paul being the last such meas-

Peter Kolchin

ure. The ending of this practice "represented the Russian equivalent of the end to the slave trade" in the Americas.[31]

It is thus not only in the timing of emancipation itself, but in the removal of one of the main underpinnings of the coercive systems, that parallels exist between East and West. In Russia this ending coincided with the disappearance of pro-serfdom arguments, and an increase in the laws facilitating manumissions as well as in measures to ameliorate the conditions of those not emancipated—including restrictions on sale and possible movement. As in the West, amelioration preceded abolition, and as in the West, the system came to an end long before the land frontier had closed. In 1862, migration to Siberia alone was scarcely underway and it was far from complete in 1903 when the Russian government made it much easier for peasants to leave their communities. Nevertheless, the huge internal migration of peoples of the Russian Empire (to cities as well as the borderlands) after emancipation suggests that the commune's hold on its members was limited and that there was still much land available.[32] The association of free labor with progress—and the accompanying sense of inevitability of the end of coerced labor or anything that smacked of coerced labor—came to be as strongly cemented in the Russian Empire as it was in the Atlantic World by the mid-nineteenth century. Some 70 years later, the only movement of coerced labor was to the gulag archipelago and Devil's Island, and while the inmates in both were expected to work, the primary motive for neither could be said to have been the extraction of labor.

As the above implies, the move to greater individual agency in migration in the East came about not so much through the ending of the forced movement of serfs, but rather in the gradual removal of barriers to migration. There were certainly parellels in the West. Many more Germans would have migrated in the eighteenth century if it had been easier to cast off feudal ties. The abolition of the last vestiges of feudalism throughout Europe helped trigger mass migration in the following century. In Canada and the US, there were no formal regulations inhibiting the move to western lands; but the terms on which that land became available to settlers was a key factor in determining the volume of migration, and these became easier in the course of the nineteenth century. In the Russian Empire in the same period, there was steady erosion in the responsibilities of the peasant to the community in which he lived. The government was determined to ensure that peasants paid their owners compensation for the abolition of serfdom; but peasant access to passes and passports was gradually eased through the century. There was the controlled allotment of state lands to peasants from 1889, the effective ending of collective responsibility for taxes and redemption payments in 1903, and the abolition of redemption payments themselves two years later. In the decade before the Revolution, peasants were finally on a legal footing with respect to migration similar to those in England and the Netherlands since at least the seventeenth century, and those in the rest of Europe since the eighteenth and early nineteenth centuries.[33]

≺ III ≻

Patterns and Consequences

Finally, what of the long-run consequences of the unprecedented mixing of peoples and labor regimes? The differences between electing to move across the Atlantic and being forced to move by others appear so enormous that at first sight comparisons might be expected to highlight only contrasts. The impression is strengthened when stock is taken of shipboard conditions, morbidity and mortality in slave and non-slave transatlantic passages, and the permanent loss of control over one's life and the life of one's offspring that always separated slavery from the worst conditions experienced by non-slaves. However calculated, mortality was always three or four times higher for slaves and crews of slavers than for free migrants and their crews. From opposite sides of the race and slavery divide, Frederick Douglass and Thomas Ruffin pointed out the unwillingness of free workers to escape their oppression by voluntary enslavement in the South. Nevertheless, once we set aside volition and its consequences, some intriguing parallels are apparent across migration regimes and regions—and not just in the New World where the environment faced by coerced and free was often the same.

In two of the sub-continents of origin, Europe and sub-Saharan Africa, though Turkic peoples continued to pressure the western European frontier until the battle of Mohács in 1687, the major internal migrations were probably complete by the tenth century AD, from Asia in the first case and the Bantu movements southward in the second. In a third sub-continent, China, new crops and new strains of rice made possible migration to the Szechuan basin and hitherto underexploited southern forests into the eighteenth century sufficient for some historians to discern a major southern land frontier.[34] New crops and technologies may actually have removed the impulse for Chinese overseas movement after the brilliant fifteenth-century explorations until the late eighteenth century. Setting aside the very gradual colonization of Formosa, overseas migration began in earnest in China, as in Europe and the land-based impulse in Russia and its surroundings, only when internal opportunities appeared less attractive than hitherto.

Overseas migration was forced on Africans, but it is nevertheless of interest that in all three regions the onset of overseas migration coincided with the onset of relatively stable ethno-linguistic and political divisions at home. In Europe, as nation-states emerged, movements between town and country and the circulation of people within the nation-state appear to have accelerated. Most of the growth of towns arose from migration, not natural increase, and in early modern England "mobility was so pervasive that it was seen as much a natural part of the life cycle as being born or dying."[35] Yet most migrants moved only short distances, and ethno-linguistic boundaries in Western Europe have remained unchanged for most of a millennium. In Africa, at least in West Africa after 1440, continuities also appear strong, colonialism and the seasonal movement of migrants apart. As in Europe, the boundaries of states changed markedly, but there is little evidence that this was associated with mass migration. Between the Senegal and the Cameroons River, some ethno-linguistic units have expanded and others have contracted, but none seems to have disappeared or shifted position; and of nearly 50 identified modern groups, only the Mende are not recorded before 1700.[36] Except perhaps when the Roman Empire was at its height, stability of this duration cannot be said to have existed in Europe for any equivalent period in known history. In China since the eighteenth century and in the Russian and Ukrainian heartlands, population densities have increased, but political boundaries and the distribution of language groups have been less subject to change.

One implication of this pattern is that long-distance migration, whether free or coerced, has never been sufficient to redraw the political and ethnic boundaries of the source society. The Chinese case is self-evident. By the time overseas migration became significant, the size of the domestic population was so large that no amount of migration made an impact. In the European case, the nations with the largest overseas flows of people, Portugal and England, were also among those nations having the smaller populations. In two centuries after 1540 England experienced net migration of about 1.2 million persons, many of them to Ireland rather than the Americas. This represents between one-third and one half of the mid-sixteenth-century population. During and after industrialization an even larger proportion left the British Isles—43 percent of the 1841 population in only 90 years after 1845. Gross migration from Portugal in the two centuries after 1460 was probably equivalent to the total population in that year. Yet the English population more than doubled in both of the above periods, and in Portugal the population held constant after 1460.[37] In Western Europe as a whole migration rates were much lower, but in the nineteenth century, the population grew rapidly despite huge outflows of people to the Americas. From Africa, perhaps eleven million people were taken across the Atlantic. There is necessarily much less certainty on the size of the sub-Saharan African population at the outset of this forced exodus than in the European case. But even when the slave trade was at its height between 1750 and 1850, with perhaps over eight million people forced to leave the subcontinent, departure rates must have been well below those sustained by Britain and Portugal during their peak migrations.[38]

This picture does not change much if we take into account other long-distance migrations from Europe and Africa that were going on at the same time. While long-distance migrants from Portugal, Spain, and Britain went westward overwhelmingly (though Christopher Smout argues that Scots were the largest alien group in seventeenth-century Poland), there were major movements from the Rhineland and points east that had little to do with the Atlantic. Emigration from these areas before the nineteenth century was to regions in the East. For every transatlantic migrant there were perhaps nine eastbound migrants in the seventeenth and eighteenth centuries, and in regions even more remote from the Atlantic coast than Germany, the ratio was likely to be even greater than nine to one.[39] In the Russian Empire, much of the movement was undertaken by serfs.

There is nothing approaching the quality of Atlantic ship-based data for the movement east so estimates have a weak empirical basis, but it is likely that within Europe the apparently high rates of migration from Portugal and Britain would not appear exceptional if a calculation for Germany and Central Europe that included eastern migration were possible. Indeed, France appears as an inert (in out-migration terms) and rather exceptional center in the pan-European context, with countries to the west and north dispatching millions of migrants across the Atlantic, and those to the east sending perhaps even more emigrants in the opposite direction. The counterpart in Africa to the eastern movement from Germany and points east (including serfs) was the trans-Saharan slave trade, together with, from the late eighteenth century, a traffic to India and the newly developing Indian Ocean sugar islands.[40] The numbers leaving on two of these three routes are as conjectural as those for migration to eastern Europe, but there is a consensus that together they amounted to substantially less than transatlantic departures from Africa.[41] In eastern Europe, by contrast, as already noted, it is likely that the eastern movement of peoples, at least before the middle third of the nineteenth century, exceeded those moving across the western oceans. On balance it would seem that while the peaks of departures from Europe (to both east and west) and from Africa (north, east, and west) occurred at different times, the rate of migrant departures from Europe was normally much greater than that for slaves from Africa between Columbian contact and 1880.

This is not to equate mainly voluntary shifts (for example from Europe) with the African slave trade. The social implications of emigrating under one's own volition and of being physically impelled to move by someone else are enormous. Yet the experience of early modern Europe, including the Russian Empire, suggests that the incidence of warfare, crime, rebellion, and indeed institutionalized social violence of all kinds was not dependent on the prior existence of a slave trade to other continents. The issue of the extent to which the need for slaves incited African wars has been debated since the abolitionists began to campaign against the slave trade, and it is at least clear that the slave trade was not likely to have reduced violence between African peoples. In both Africa and Europe some rather major shifts in migration were associated with wars or civil unrest. Civil war in England, then wars between England and Scotland and the English campaigns against the Irish were the occasion of the forced migration of thousands of prisoners to the English colonies as the sugar revolution gathered momentum in the mid-seventeenth century. Voluntary migration was also shaped by armed conflict in mainland Europe. Military campaigns after 1688 set the scene for the first large influx to the Americas of people from the Rhineland, and the migration flow of Germans thereafter was regulated in part by European conflicts.[42] By the late eighteenth century, however, and down to World War II, the main effect of war in Europe was to make travel across the Atlantic difficult rather than to create pools of potential immigrants through large-scale social disruption within the society of origin.

In Africa and the Russian Empire the connection between conflict and migration was more direct. People entered the slave trade in many ways, but according to one contemporary survey nearly two out of three became slaves through kidnapping or as prisoners of war.[43] The expansion of Dahomey was associated with the peak of slave departures from Whydah, perhaps the single largest point of departure in sub-Saharan Africa, and as the boundaries of that state stabilized after the mid-eighteenth century, the number of people passing through the port fell back. In another major example, Yoruba peoples in Africa have had an impact on the black Americas out of all proportion to their numbers entering the slave trade. There were in fact relatively few peoples of Yoruba descent in the Americas prior to the late eighteenth century. The dramatic reversal of this pattern appears associated with the collapse of the Oyo empire—an event, it might be added, not obviously caused by the slave trade—and the long period of civil unrest thereafter. Probably over 90 percent of Yoruba slaves entered the traffic between 1780 and 1850. In the Russian Empire, from the mid-sixteenth-century Livonian War to the late eighteenth century, civil conflict and military activity were always linked with the movement of people to the frontier.

The major consequences of migration usually played out in the areas receiving migrants rather than those sending them. Much of the analysis of immigrant communities divides over the relative importance of what migrants brought with them versus the impact of the new environment, but at least the issues have been sharpened in recent years with availability of more precise knowledge on where migrants traveled from and to, who they were, and how many there were of them. Such information is still much better for arrivals in the Americas than for those moving by land eastward from say Russia and the Ukraine. Connections between Asia and Africa to the Americas were as systematic, as significant, and as micro-specific as the better-known links between Europe and the Americas, and among the latter we now know much about the pre-1820 non-English arrivals in the English colonies. In regions as diverse as Fujian and Guangdong in southern China, the Rhineland and Slave Coast and Bight of Biafra of West Africa, there are not only single ports that dominate departure patterns (Rotterdam, Swatow and Canton, Whydah and Bonny), but evidence of particular groups and communities that dominated departures from those ports. Moreover, despite the wide range of migratory regimes under which migrants traveled, their distribution in the Americas was far from random.[44]

While the idea is at first sight bizarre given the absence of volition on the part of Africans, a kind of chain migration developed for all migrations, the full cultural implications of which have yet to be explored. Links between specific regions in the Old and New Worlds changed slowly over time. They were forged in part by shipping patterns and credit arrangements in the case of slaves, and by communications between migrants and the communities they had left behind in the case of servants, contract workers, and free migrants. But shipping patterns were perhaps even more important in establishing and maintaining such links in the eighteenth century. The Rotterdam-Philadelphia and the Chesapeake-Bight of Biafra connections emerged ultimately from credit networks and mercantile strategies of merchants in key European and in the latter case, African, ports.

All regions of the Americas have attracted a wide range of peoples over the centuries. While nodes of economic growth, especially cities, have always attracted migrants, no part of the Old World ever had a mix of peoples from far-flung places to match most places in the New by the second half of the nineteenth century. Within the New World, the Caribbean became easily the most diverse of all, with southern regions of China, separated parts of India, and a wide range of societies in West and West Central Africa represented in quite small colonies. Among regions settled mainly by those making the choice to move, it is the English-speaking North American mainland that after 1700 at least, drew on the most diverse set of societies and cultures (even apart from the significant minority that were African slaves). The share of the US population that could claim English origins was well below 50 percent even before the mass migrations of the nineteenth century, and it has continued to decline since. Except for the numerically insignificant Dutch, there was no European-claimed area in the Americas that could come close to this mix of origins among its citizens, just as there was no European-claimed area that did as well in economic terms as what became the US.

In Siberia in 1911 by contrast, after more than three centuries of settlement, most of it in the preceding half century, 87 percent of the population was of Russian origin. The freedom from centralized control that allowed the English colonies to establish the harshest form of racial slavery in history was also associated with an acceptance of different white cultures so that more Germans and Irish (and, of course, Africans) than English would arrive in the eighteenth century. Such a mix in contemporary French and Spanish colonies is inconceivable, though post-independence Argentina and southern Brazil drew on an increasingly diverse pool of migrants. Given this New World pattern, it is striking from a twenty-first-century perspective that, despite (or perhaps because of) this pattern of diversity, the major conflicts in the last hundred years where ethnicity has been an issue have taken place in the Old World—Germany, the Balkans, parts of Africa—rather than the New.

≺ IV ≻

Conclusion

Finally, does it matter for society as a whole if migration is predominantly of one type rather than another, as it clearly does at the all-important (from one perspective) personal level? In strictly economic terms, some societies clearly benefited from the flow of slaves and prisoners. A preliminary answer is that it matters for at least four reasons. Most obviously and simply, the coerced component had not chosen to be taken to their destinations, and for this there can be no compensatory offsets. Secondly, health, nutrition, and material life varied considerably within the areas of new settlement. Vital rates and nutritional status in mainland North America were substantially better than in most parts of the Caribbean, especially the low-lying sugar-growing areas. Conditions in the penal settlement in French Guiana were particularly bad. Whites and blacks together had better material conditions on mainland North America, and together did worse in the Caribbean (though blacks did worse than whites in both instances). The key point, however, is that free migrants and indentured servants could choose whether to migrate at all, and having made that decision, could decide where to go. Most elected to avoid the severe work conditions and shortened life expectancies associated with sugar cultivation and extracting precious metals, at least after the seventeenth century. Slaves and convicts did not have this option and, indeed, the decision (in other words, the free choice) of most Europeans to avoid these areas meant, in effect, that more and more African slaves would be forced into these conditions. African slaves would thus fare far worse than Europeans, whether indentured or free, because they were not allowed to move into the regions—and therefore the favorable conditions—which Europeans enjoyed.

The situation is less straightforward in the case of the Russian Empire, where serfs may have been willing to move, and the coercive element in the migratory regime was official restriction on movement. By the early nineteenth century the Russian Empire had the most severe proscriptions against migration of any country in the Old World (though not always effective and, when applied, falling short of the penalty of death exacted in early modern China). Denial of the opportunity to escape from intolerable conditions may seem indistinguishable from being forced into migration, though in practice most students of migration would not equate the two.

Third, the enormous immorality and inhumanity of the slave trade (and to a lesser degree the banishment of convicts often to dangerous locations) cannot hide the fact that in strictly economic terms coerced labor has the potential to be highly efficient. Values in human society, in this instance freedom and the virtue of maximizing economic performance, are inevitably in conflict.[45] In migration, it would seem, the greater the degree of coercion, the greater the potential increases in output in the area in which coerced migrants are put to work. Indentured servitude and contract labor were freely entered into, but had strong coercive elements during the term of the contract. The slave trade (and slavery which it supported) was by far the most oppressive of migratory regimes. It was also the most productive in the broader social sense of increasing output. The output of plantation produce rose dramatically with the inception of the slave trade and, except in the US and Cuba, it stagnated or declined when the slave trade ended. Indentured and contract labor helped offset the loss of access to the slave trade, but despite planters' ability to impose severe working conditions, it remained a second best option, probably because of the cost-raising consequences of giving migrants choice over the decision to migrate (as well as its temporary nature). From modern and humane perspectives, of course, no amount of economic efficiency warrants a slave trade or a convict trade or a trade in contract laborers from any source.

The economic advantage of the slave trade, as the above implies, derives from the fact that shipping costs accounted for a large proportion of the price of an African slave on the eastern shores of the Americas. Merchants could ignore the preferences of the migrants themselves and were able to crowd people into a vessel—within the constraints of profit maximization—so that the cost of passage was less than it would have been for any migrant who was given choice over the decision to travel. Steerage passengers from Europe in the nineteenth century never had to face conditions quite like those prevailing on a slave ship.[46] Convicts sent to Australia and the French possessions off South America and the Pacific traveled under more regulated and commodious accommodation, but the imperial government absorbed the shipping costs, and the coerced labor that convicts carried out under assignment was thus not only coerced, but heavily subsidized. But if economic growth in the Americas and Australia, conventionally measured, benefited from slavery, and the repeopling of these continents proceeded more rapidly because of the slave trade and transportation, the situation in the East is much less clear.[47] Output per person apparently did not increase for most of the period that the Russian state aggressively expanded in the fifteenth to twentieth century. Some evidence of higher productivity emerges at the very end of four hundred years of migration in Siberia, which, as noted above, was the period when migration in the East most closely resembles its western counterpart.[48]

Fourth, and most important, the migratory regime matters because migration interacts with conceptions of identity of first, migrants themselves, second, those left behind, and third, those in the receiving societies. It is hard to conceive of a society in which forms of ethnocentrism have been completely eliminated. It is impossible to conceive of one in which a racially based slave trade, or indeed a racially based traffic in contract labor, continues to flourish. As the reintegration of human societies in the world, begun one thousand years ago, accelerates in the new millennium, the apparently innate desire of humans to identify themselves with some, and differentiate themselves from others (apparently part of the same process), will no doubt continue. Despite the horrors of the twentieth century, the prospect of malevolent social consequences from this tendency seems set to diminish.

≺ 1 ≻

Free and Coerced Migrations from the Old World to the New

DAVID ELTIS

AGAINST THE BACKDROP of a steady inter- and intra-continental swarming of people since homo sapiens left Africa, transatlantic migration from the sixteenth down to the mid-nineteenth century was strikingly unusual in three ways. First, prior to this era, whether it was the initial peopling of the Americas millennia ago, the settling of central Europeans in Asia thought to have occurred three thousand years ago, or the Bantu migrations which reshaped West Africa, movement and settlement had not been accompanied by continuing and intensive contact between the source society and the migrant society.[1] Where migrants did maintain contact with those that stayed home, it was only at the level of the elite. The migration of peoples normally changed the immigrant more than the emigrant society, and unless the number of migrants was large, the region of departure would be unaffected. The Vikings who went to Skraeland and the Maoris who went to what became New Zealand could have left no qualitative impact on the lands they left behind. In the early modern Atlantic, however, for the first time in human history there appeared a hemispheric "community." Community in the sense used here means that everyone living in it had values that if they were not shared around the Atlantic were certainly reshaped in some way by others living in the Atlantic basins, and, as this suggests, where events in one geographic area had the potential to stimulate a reaction—and not necessarily just economic—thousands of miles away. Second, the migration was both ocean-borne and part of a larger expansion movement that saw Europeans and to a lesser extent Africans move east by land as well as west by sea. Tundra to the north and Islam to the south ensured the directions of the European thrust.

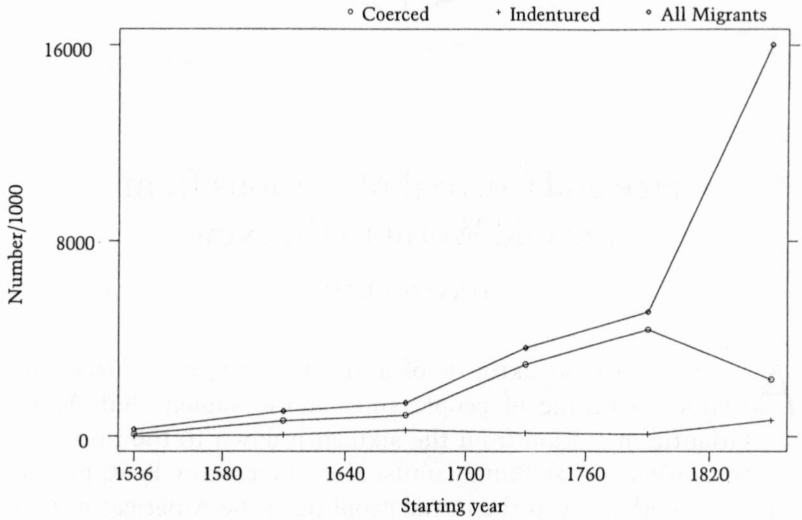

Fig. 1. Volume of Emigrants to America by Status, 1500–1880.

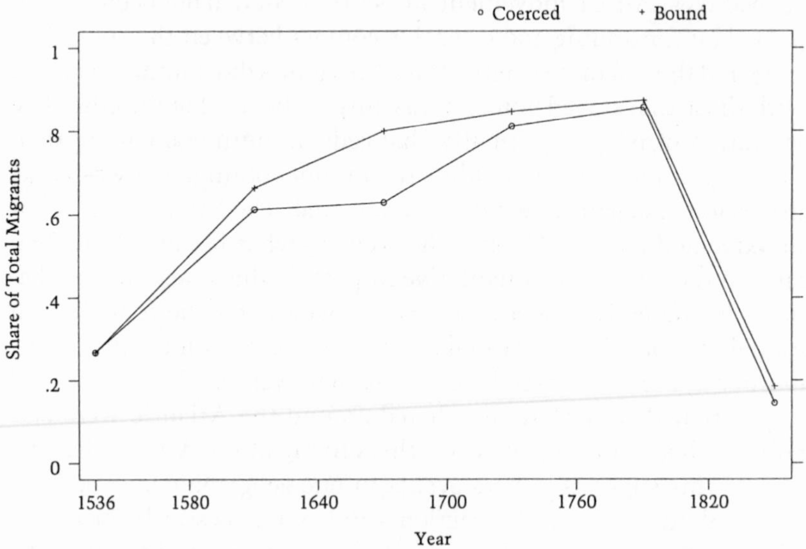

Fig. 2. Share of Emigrants to America by Status, 1500–1880.

Third, and most important for this chapter, more than half the migrants were involuntary, clearly unwilling to relocate. Trafficking in slaves is as old as slavery itself, but the size of the transatlantic flow and the fact that slaves dominated the populations of most of the receiving areas constituted an unprecedented shift in the history of large-scale migration. Of those migrants who were not forced, a very large number traveled under obligations to others that meant the migrant effectively abandoned some basic freedoms for several years after arrival. Moreover, in the eastern manifestation of European expansion a sizable proportion of those who moved were serfs, whose influence over whether they migrated was no different from that of slaves.

Recent scholarship, represented in figures 1 and 2, demonstrates the huge (and before 1850, majority) presence of either unwilling migrants, or migrants who arrived under impersonal and long term obligations to others, an aspect that sets this population movement apart from almost all others.[2] Figure 1 gives the absolute numbers and figure 2 the relative distribution of types of migrants over time. Figure 1 has three trend lines representing first, coerced migrants, which include only slaves, prisoners, and convicts; second, bound migrants, defined as indentured servants, contract laborers, slaves, convicts, and political and military prisoners; and third, total migrants, which include the first two categories together with all free migrants. Figure 2 has only two functions, bound migrants and coerced migrants, but the top axis (equal to one) represents total migration and is the equivalent of the top trend line in figure 1. It follows that the difference between the total migrants and bound migrants, or the top and middle functions of the figures, represents the number (figure 1), and the relative importance (figure 2) of free migrants. Non-coerced bound migrants (or indentured servants/contract laborers) are represented by the lower function in figure 1 and by the difference between the coerced and bound functions in figure 2.

This form of grouping by-passes the national and racial categorizations that dominate the literature. The bound category for example includes Europeans and Africans of many nations, as well as Asians—Indians and Chinese. The coerced category includes Europeans and Africans, and while the latter were the overwhelming majority, grouping in this form provides a basis, taken up below, for explaining this numerical dominance. It also points to the intermediate status of indentured and contract migrants who obtained a free transoceanic passage in exchange for control over three to seven years of their labor. Because they entered into a contract more or less voluntarily, they were like free migrants; and because they could be bought and sold and did not have much control over this process, or the work they were required to perform during the indenture, they were like slaves. The data and sources for these figures are matters of some complexity and are explained in a separate appendix to this chapter.

Free migration predominated for the first century and again after 1830. For two centuries in between—from say 1630 to 1830—coerced migration and migration undertaken under a labor debt to others were by far the most dominant regimes under which population movements occurred. Overall, migrants traveling without a labor debt, and not enslaved to others, were in a minority. Specifically, before 1820 three out of every four persons who set out to cross the Atlantic were African, not European, and four out of every five migrants from both Europe and Africa sailed with the expectation of being in some form of servitude at the completion of the voyage. At the peak of the slave trade, between 1760 and 1820, almost six Africans set out for the Americas for every European, a ratio that was dramatically reversed in the 60 years after 1820.[3]

These figures raise intriguing questions of how transatlantic migration before 1800 was for so long associated in the minds of both specialist scholars and the general public with first, Europe, and second, freedom. More substantively, they point to the need to explore the nature of freedom in the context of the large-scale movement of peoples. What did the fact that most early modern transatlantic migrants were unfree mean for the patterns and character of the migration, for migration's impact on societies at either end of the migrant route, and perhaps also for conceptions of freedom? The nature of Atlantic migration is such that we cannot begin to answer these questions without first taking into account those who did have some control over whether or not they moved—both those who migrated and those who did not—and Africans and Europeans belong to both these categories. The two main branches of transatlantic migration need to be treated as a unit, even though originating on separate continents. Coerced and free migration streams interacted with each other, as did the value systems that made them possible.

≺ I ≻

The Pattern of Coercion

The fact that transatlantic migration can be grouped according to the labor regimes under which migrants traveled is enough to separate it out from other swarmings of people. It would not occur to historians or demographers to try this kind of grouping for long-distance population movements before 1500 and after 1900, except possibly for the early Mediterranean slave trade. Indeed, it would not be necessary insofar as migrants before and after this period traveled for the most part within a common legal framework. The fact that the vast majority of migrants, 1500–1850 and into the modern era, worked for others at the end of their journey, unlike earlier migrants, helps account for the uniqueness of this period and also points to the centrality of the demand and supply of labor that formed the basis of the migration.

At one level the direction and composition of the repeopling of the Americas is a function of the relative price of labor, with the relative distribution of free and enslaved peoples (or the proportion of migrants coming from Europe and Africa) settled by wages and prices of slaves. Although transatlantic migration was the movement of labor from one area to another, economic analysis alone will not tell us why some became slaves, and some indentured servants. Moreover, even within labor regimes huge numbers of individuals were excluded from entry into a country and region (a practice that continues today) on non-economic grounds such as race or nationality. Some efforts to shape migrant flows stem from attempts of particular interest groups to gain at the expense of others in society, in which case the behavior is economically motivated, though at the level of private rather than public interest. Of considerable interest in seeking out the fundamental explanations of long-distance population movements are the cultural values and ideologies, or parameters, within which economic behavior occurs. By their nature these are so entrenched that migrants, and at times those historians who interpret the records they leave, tend to take them for granted. Examples of such shared assumptions underpinning social existence are conceptions of morality, principles of social organization, including attitudes to gender, and issues of identity. It follows that to understand migration, and more particularly the interaction between the flows of free and coerced labor which formed the basis of the repeopling of the Americas, we need to take into account the different values of societies around the Atlantic and, more particularly, the way groups of people involved in creating a transatlantic community saw themselves in relation to others. The patterns displayed in figures 1 and 2 may well make more sense if we view them through a social or institutional rather than an economic lens.

European expansion both eastward and westward put settlers into environments with which the labor regimes the migrants carried with them could not easily contend. Adjustment within the framework of what was already familiar did occur more smoothly in the East than in the West, however. In the West, expansion brought the European frontier to tropical and semi-tropical areas that for three centuries became the focal point of European expansion (as opposed to European migration). Several products that either were unknown to Europeans (like tobacco), or occupied a luxury niche in pre-expansion European tastes (like gold or sugar), now fell within the capacity of Europeans to produce more cheaply than hitherto. But while Europeans came to control the production of such exotic goods, it became apparent in the first two centuries after Columbian contact that they did not wish to supply the labor that would make such output possible. There is no implication here that a free market labor system existed in Europe in the late fifteenth century such that those working for others could choose among many employers and tasks and thus avoid unpleasant working conditions. Free labor in the modern sense of nominally equal legal (as opposed to economic) standing of employer and employee did not exist before the mid-nineteenth century.[4] A range of dependent relations, including serfdom, existed between the propertied and the non-propertied before this point, but none that adapted easily to conditions in the semi-tropical Americas and none, despite much recent literature positing a continuum between free labor and slave labor, that came close to chattel slavery.

Ocean-going technology brought Europeans into face-to-face contact with three groups of peoples who were culturally and physically more different from themselves than any other remote peoples with whom they had interacted in the previous millennium. Of two of them, Asians and Africans, they were already aware; the third, American aboriginals, were completely unknown to them. For the first of these groups contact meant little originally. Transoceanic mercantile and imperial connections by Asians pre-dated European expansion, and the ability of Europeans to establish land-based empires in Asia, albeit using indirect rule, did not emerge until the second half of the eighteenth century. For the second, Africans, neither the initial Chinese contacts in the East, nor the much more extended and intensive European counterparts, mainly in the West, led to loss of territorial control prior to the late nineteenth century—with the single and limited exception of western Angola. Indeed, African capacity to resist ocean-borne invaders was probably one of the two key factors that determined that the sugar complex moved across the Atlantic to the Americas after seemingly island-hopping down the West African coast during the late fifteenth and early sixteenth centuries.[5] The other factor was the willingness of some Africans to sell other Africans as slaves to Europeans. In effect African strength—the capacity to retain territorial integrity—helped foster the slave trade as Europeans established their plantations in the Americas instead of Africa with an elastic supply of coerced African labor. As this suggests, and as is well known, European dispossession of the third group of transoceanic peoples, native Americans, was complete. Indeed, the epidemiological impact of the European invasion destroyed not only native American power structures, but also a potential labor supply.

Figures 1 and 2 indicate that most early migration to the Americas can be very loosely categorized as free, at least in the sense that it was neither coerced nor bound. We know about the numbers and the geographical distribution of early Iberian migration, but surprisingly little about the terms under which ordinary Castilians and Portuguese came to the Americas prior to the nineteenth century. Spain conquered and then administered an existing empire, the main export of which was precious metals—first looted and then mined. It is therefore unsurprising that a high incidence of early migrants were soldiers, administrators, and artisans.[6] Spain and to a lesser degree Portugal moved into the richest and most populous areas of the New World; and Spanish America, at least, exported few commodities compared to later European regimes. It is unlikely that the few native textiles, hides, and plantation products that crossed the Atlantic in the sixteenth century from Spanish America could have justified their transportation costs without piggy-backing on the very high value to weight ratios of bullion exports—the latter ensuring cheap space for lower-value items. In Brazil, most of the slaves on the early sugar plantations were Amerindian and the greater share of African slaves shown in the figures for the 1500–1580 period arrived at the very end of the period when the gathering demographic disaster triggered the switch from Indian to African labor. Thus neither Spain nor Portugal felt the need initially for highly elastic supplies of unskilled labor from the Old World. With corvee or mita (draft) labor supplying most of the needs of the Spanish-American mining sector, overall levels of migration were small before 1600 and both the coerced and the bound components of that migration were lower than at any other point before the mid-nineteenth century.

Perhaps the most important developments for migration in the Atlantic world (certainly for Africans), and more broadly in the saga of European expansion, came in the seventeenth century rather than with Columbian contact or the Spanish conquests of the sixteenth century. Three factors reshaped the migrant flow after 1640. First, the Amerindian population reached its nadir before 1700.[7] At the same time, more intensive production techniques came to be introduced on plantations, specifically gang labor on Caribbean sugar islands, particularly those occupied by the English.[8] By 1770 sugar plantations produced about three times more (by value) than non-sugar plantations in the Caribbean.[9] The work was unpleasant, it was carried out in low-lying unhealthy environments, and, above all, it involved loss of control over the pace at which one worked. All these characteristics ensured that wages would have to be very high to attract voluntary labor. The Portuguese and Spanish who migrated in the early period were not likely to work on sugar plantations. Indeed, no one—from any continent—would work voluntarily for long periods of time under the kinds of work regimes that evolved in the eastern Caribbean in the mid-seventeenth century. For one and a half centuries, sugar and sugar products formed by far the most valuable of products exported from the Americas. And neither black nor white, neither free nor bound could at first sustain a positive rate of natural population growth in the regions most suitable for sugar cultivation.

The third development to shape migration was the growing intensity, efficiency, and falling costs of transatlantic contact.[10] The frequency and cost of travel as well as literacy rates were such that by the second half of the seventeenth century, for the first time in human history both people and cheaply produced printed materials speedily crisscrossed vast distances. It is in this sense that there appeared a hemispheric "community."[11]

The above developments facilitated several possible responses to what was, from the European perspective, a labor problem. If Europeans had simply extended the labor regimes which were prevalent in their own part of the Old World to the New—relied in other words on predominantly non-coerced labor—then labor costs would have risen to the point where sugar would not have become a common consumer item as quickly as it did, and the plantation sector of the New World would have grown much more slowly. A second possible resolution was the employment of forced labor wherever it could be obtained most cheaply—a solution consistent with what many scholars see as the dominant ethos of the merchants at the helm of early modern European expansion. A third possibility, quite different from the second, was to tap what Europeans (and some Africans) came to see as a reserve of coerced labor thousands of miles away from where that labor was to be used and from where consumers of plantation output and organizers of the plantation complex lived.

There were modest attempts to implement the first and second solutions. In 1624, William Usselinx argued that the Swedish colonies should not use black slaves, and Georgia initially prohibited slave-holding.[12] More generally, as we shall see, several European countries sent convicts and prisoners against their will to the plantation colonies where most of them helped produce sugar and tobacco, and the US Northwest Ordinance prohibited servitude *except* for those guilty of serious crimes. But there was no serious debate over adopting the third option, anymore than there would be today about using free labor rather than say a slave trade and chattel slavery to improve company profits, even though there is no reason to doubt the efficiency of the latter. The total absence of serious debate points to the existence, then, as now, of values so widely and deeply held in a community that no discussion of them is deemed necessary. Such values, as well as profit-maximizing behavior, determine the form of migration (and most other social phenomena).

Values in turn determine institutions. The contractual basis of most economic relations in Western Europe, even those between the elite and non-elite, would have been gravely threatened if the slaves sent to the Americas had been European. The transatlantic flow of indentured servants might have collapsed. The difficulties associated with impressment suggest that a widening of the coercive net would have been impossible without a revolution in local administration. The pacification and integration of Ireland and Scotland as well as bringing the English Civil War to a close would have been much more difficult if prisoners had had the prospect of full chattel slavery before them. Despite cheaper transportation costs from Europe to the Americas than from Europe-Africa to the Americas, European social structures and institutions made an Atlantic system of plantations worked by European slaves impossible.[13]

Forcing people to move thousands of miles from their homes and then work under conditions to which they would never be subjected at home was a drastic step. It was unusual for any society to subject its own members to the extreme imbalance of rights or to absence of reciprocation implied by such a step. Most societies generated potential candidates for such a move from wars with neighboring peoples, and from judicial processes. The latter in particular, arising from the breaking of laws, implies violation of community standards determined to a large extent culturally rather than on an economic basis. Convicts were one of the major groups to cross the Atlantic (and eventually other oceans) both from Africa and from Europe. The greater the transgression against community standards, the more likely the perpetrator was to be forced to do things against his or her will. Most European countries provided for permanent deportation, sometimes in the form of simple banishment and sometimes with the requirement to labor, though in no case were there implications for the offspring of deportees. The theoretical basis of transportation and forced labor for prisoners of war and convicts appeared very similar to the basis of slavery in many societies in that the status of all three was seen as an alternative to death—more precisely in the case of convicts, judicial execution. Moreover the costs of enforcing coerced labor on plantations would not have been much different if the coerced had been European rather than African.

Naval vessels were the ultimate defense against slave rebellion as well as the attentions of other European powers. In Europe transportation or banishment was reserved for the most serious of offenses. A parallel situation existed in Africa for those Africans who entered the slave trade as a result of judicial process. Some scholars argue that laws and judicial processes were adjusted in order to enlarge the flow of convicts to the New World, but in general the offenses deemed worthy of transportation (or sale) were sufficiently severe that the number of deportees, as figures 1 and 2 suggest, remained small in relation to total flows, and more importantly small in relation to the potential pool of such migrants.[14] Communities in both Africa and Europe did not exploit this pool very thoroughly despite the fact that the costs of forcing people against their will does not much depend on the ethnicity of the coerced. As there was little debate, however, it may be classed as yet another "unthinking decision."

When the demand for transatlantic coerced labor first became acute in the mid-seventeenth century, it was prisoners of war rather than convicts that formed the majority of European deportees. Typically, however, these were prisoners taken in civil wars rather than wars with other nations. Slavery frequently emerged as an alternative to death for surviving losers during or immediately after battle—a pattern that might almost be described as universal in human history. There was somewhat of an interruption in the European case in the early Middle Ages, when the practice appears to have ceased at least when the conflict was among Europeans; and there may have been similar breaks for other cultures of which I am not aware. Interestingly, in Western Europe it broke down first in wars between the western continental European powers, but including England, as well, and lingered longest in conflicts between these powers and the Celtic and Scandinavian fringes. This was, perhaps, a function, in part, of the relatively equal strengths of mainstream European powers. One would treat prisoners with a little more circumspection if one was uncertain of being the victorious power in the next conflict. Or perhaps it was a function of how "European" (as opposed to "barbaric") one might be considered. By contrast, those defeated in civil wars and internal religious struggles continued to be treated with great cruelty. In the English case, Dutch prisoners from naval battles were put to work draining the fens before being freed at the end of the conflict. Royalists and Irish prisoners from the same mid-seventeenth-century era on the other hand were sent to Barbados to be sold as servants, usually for much longer periods than foreign prisoners of war. In France, many of the Boulonnais rebels of 1672 were killed and dismembered, with the rest sent to the Caribbean as servants.

Prisoners of civil wars ceased to be sent to the colonies in the eighteenth century, by which time all deportees were the products of the judicial system; however, the practice of enslaving one's foes continued in the struggle between Christendom and Islam, increasingly as a preliminary to a ransoming that was not always forthcoming. These developments suggest further shifts in values and provide further evidence of a non-economic interpretation of migration. It is striking that as the price of coerced labor in the plantation colonies experienced its most dramatic rise—more or less continuous for two centuries after the 1680s—western European nations perversely turned away from potential sources of that coerced labor in their own nations and sub-continent.[15] Convicts went to Australia, not the sugar islands, when Virginia closed the gate. Portuguese degredados were sent to Brazil until the 1820s, but were not normally put to work on sugar estates.[16] Although figures 1 and 2 do not separate out convict and prisoner migration from slave, it should be noted that for western Europeans, the flow of convicts and prisoners peaked in relative terms in the seventeenth century. Thereafter, despite the large numbers sent to Australia before 1850, as a percentage of the whole migrant stream the flow quickly declined to insignificance and to zero with the last arrivals to France's Devil's Island in 1939, though the facility was not closed until 1952.

From the perspective of the seventeenth century, indentured migration was the most clearly identifiable western European labor regime to evolve as a solution to the labor problem in the Americas. Closely related, in England at least, to the standard annual contract by which agricultural laborers were hired, its terms varied by skill level of migrant, age, and sex, but typically for an unskilled young adult male involved an exchange of four years of work for a free transatlantic passage, and freedom dues, which initially at least might include some land.[17] None of these arrangements permitted employers to force workers to labor in gangs on plantations for a whole lifetime without any reciprocal employer obligations, or provided for the sale of an employee into a lifetime of labor for someone else. And none ensured that the offspring of the worker would have to live under exactly the same set of employer rights in perpetuity as his or her parents.

Figures 1 and 2 show, however, that the size and relative importance of indentured/contract labor was never great. It was most important in the mid-seventeenth century when it accounted for perhaps one quarter of all transatlantic migrants, but as figure 1 demonstrates, it reached its greatest absolute volume at the end of the nineteenth century. Almost all indentured and coerced migrants went to *plantation* regions, with Asian contract arrivals to western North America constituting an exception. The bimodal distribution of indentured/contract labor in figure 1 is very significant in that the first peak is entirely European in origin while the second is almost entirely Asian. The few Africans in this category traveled in the 1840s, before Asian arrivals became significant. Extrapolation beyond 1880 would bring the trend to zero during World War I.

A profit-maximizing approach is useful for explaining the initial rise and then at least part of the temporary decline in indentured servitude. Plantation owners attracted temporary servants to the Americas and then later found they could not compete with rising wages in England. At the same time (after 1660 that is) plantation owners were able to tap into the more elastic supply of African labor that became available in the second half of the seventeenth century.[18] But the disappearance of all Europeans from the bound migrant flow in the 1820s, the dramatic revival of the system with an exclusively Asian component, then the end of that system at the behest of first the Chinese in the 1870s and then the Indian government in 1917, all have explanations which are in part ideological.[19] The refusal of US courts to continue to recognize indentures in the 1820s, the rise of Asian flow after 1837—a clear substitute for slave labor—and the intervention of the Chinese and Indian governments cannot be easily explained in economic terms. Even when the system was of greatest relative importance, in the early stages of the mid-seventeenth century, there is a strong sense of a non-economic component in its rise to prominence. If European governments had been prepared to countenance the full mobilization of the judicial system in the interests of supplying labor or, less likely again, community values had allowed slave traders to go to Ireland for their slaves instead of Africa, perhaps no European (or later, Asian) contract laborers would have crossed the Atlantic. The market for servants would likely not have existed. Like convict labor, indentured/contract labor never came close to resolving the overall labor problem in overseas European colonies except possibly in the late nineteenth and early twentieth centuries.

Because it was unusual for people to subject others in their own community to slave conditions, perhaps large scale and continuous coerced migration could not begin until one society had the technological and institutional ability to get continuous access to another and move its members against their will over very long distances. In the early modern period European development of ocean-going capabilities and adaptation of gunpowder technology clearly fulfilled this requirement. But the larger and much more important question for which every society in history has provided at least an unthinking answer, is which groups are to be considered eligible for enslavement and how does this change over time? Here, too, there is no very strong economic basis to the answers in that it was always much cheaper to obtain slaves in Europe than to send a vessel to an epidemiologically hostile coast in Africa without proper harbors and remote from European political, financial, and military resources. Europeans were generally unable to overcome African states before the second half of the nineteenth century. If, after Africans had turned the plantation complex away from Africa, it was to be located in the Americas, the answer to who would provide the labor for that complex clearly emerged from a European inability to enslave other Europeans and an African ability to see other African societies as eligible for enslavement and sale into the Atlantic economy.

In contrast to Russian, Roman, and some Asian societies, early modern western Europeans and Africans would not enslave members of their own societies, but Africans had a somewhat broader conception of who was eligible for enslavement than had Europeans. As Nathan Huggins has pointed out, the conception of Africa scarcely existed in Africa before the nineteenth century. It was this difference in definitions in eligibility for enslavement that explains the dramatic post-1640 rise of the coerced component of transatlantic migration in figures 1 and 2. Slavery, which had disappeared from northwest Europe long before this point, exploded into a far greater significance and intensity than it had possessed at any point in human history. The major cause was a dissonance in African and European identities, at the root of which lies culture, not economics. Africans and Europeans could agree that some Africans—those who did not belong to the society of the enslaving groups—could be traded. Without this dissonance, perhaps there would have been no slavery whatsoever in the Americas.

The rapid disappearance of the slave trade—more rapid even than its rise—both in terms relative to non-coerced migration and absolutely, is also very hard to explain using conventional notions of profit and loss and economic self-interest. In 1860, it was possible to buy a prime male slave for thirty dollars in the River Congo and sell the same individual for over nine hundred in Cuba when the cost of ferrying a steerage passenger (always assigned more space than a slave anyway) across the Atlantic had fallen to less than thirty dollars. Scholars who argue that the plantation sector was in decline and therefore slavery died because it was no longer profitable have generally not examined the cost structure of the slave trade very closely. The slave trade was a bulwark of labor supply for planters, outside the US at least, and it continued to be profitable throughout the nineteenth century until, in fact, it was prevented from continuing. The slave trade was suppressed. It did not die a natural economic death. Nor did it die because slave purchasers acquiesced in, much less actively sought, its termination. If it had not been suppressed, the dominance of Africa in transatlantic migration streams might well have continued. With slave prices at historic highs in the US, Brazil, and Cuba alike in the mid-nineteenth century, and steamship technology evolving rapidly, it is hard to believe that, in the absence of effective suppression the transatlantic slave trade would not have far surpassed its late eighteenth-century peaks in the course of the nineteenth century and perhaps beyond.

The ending of the slave trade as well as the ending of the other two migration regimes with coercive elements—bound and convict labor—was brought about by government fiat. For the slave and the Chesapeake and Australian convict traffic, it was the government of the receiving countries (albeit with third party pressure from the British government in the case of the slave trade) that took the decisive action, whereas for contract labor, governments where the migrants originated took the initiative. Behind the intervention lay a profound shift in values. Where for four centuries there had been four different migration regimes vying with each other in the repeopling of the Americas, only one, apart from an anachronistic trickle of convicts to French Guiana, was left by the time the US imposed its post-World War I restrictions on immigration. Coerced labor, which had never been the norm in early modern Western Europe, at last disappeared in long-distance migration. From this point on, the coercion of migrants would be of a different, and despite its rapid escalation in the twentieth century, a rather more benign variety—that of denying entry on the basis of skill level, health, race, income level, and political beliefs. The impact would be to change the direction of the migration, but not to alter the terms under which it occurred.

The reasons for the rise and fall of the employment of direct coercion in migration have not received much scholarly attention, perhaps because they are easily hidden by the economic superstructure through which they play out. As the introduction to this volume argues, cultural values are at least as important as the more purely economic in shaping all aspects of migration. Conceptions of morality lie behind the legislative enactments that send convicts into exile. Communally-held conceptions of self and others determine not only who will become slaves, but where they will be sent and how they will be treated. Constructions of gender, as central to the human psyche as standards of right and wrong and identity (at the level of both the individual and society), are also central to patterns of migrations.

African conceptions of gender clashed with those of Europe and produced a demographic profile for the slave trade that was quite different from its purely European indentured servant counterpart in the North Atlantic and the purely Asian contract labor flows that effectively replaced the slave trade to the sub-tropical Americas down to 1917.[20] The strong presence of females in the slave trade and their relative absence from nineteenth-century contract labor reflect African and Asian, as well as European social norms. Given that the slave trade was based on exchange between Africans and Europeans and not generally on European raids into African territory, it was not possible for either side to impose its own values and norms on the other. Moreover, the strong differences in the age and sex of slaves leaving different regions in Africa for the New World seem to have had little to do with European constructions of gender under which, initially, Europeans were interested in acquiring only adult males.

Just as there were strong differences between early modern northwestern and southeastern Europe in marriage patterns and options for women, so there were marked differences between say the Senegambia region and the hinterland of the Bight of Biafra which were reflected in the age and sex of deportees. These differences seem to have had little to do with outside influences, by which is meant non-European in the one case and non-African in the other. The intention here is not to make an exhaustive list of cultural determinants, but rather to point to the need to go beyond the narrowly economic in the attempt to understand migration. The economic impulse is, of course, of central importance, but, as noted above, it tends to operate within cultural parameters that are not always obvious.

II

Similarities between Free and Coerced Migration

Re-examination of the patterns of transatlantic migration, as opposed to the value systems that shaped it, demonstrates further the value of treating free and coerced transatlantic migration together. The recent CD-ROM database on the Atlantic slave trade suggests that distribution of Africans in the New World was no more random than was the distribution of Europeans.[21] Vessels, by and large, did not sail along the African coast collecting small groups of slaves until the vessel was full and could thus disembark a mixture of slaves from a wide variety of African coastal regions. The traffic was highly specialized and European slave traders took cargoes of goods designed for particular African regions and even ports, which they would have great difficulty disposing of in any other region, given the specificity of African consumer tastes. This translated into a concentration of trade in individual ports in much the same way that vessels carrying European servants, convicts, and free migrants carried most of their human cargoes from single ports in Europe. It is also clear that over 95 percent of slave ships disembarked all their slaves at a single port in the Americas. Thus, while African slaves could have traveled from various regions in Africa before they reached their port of embarkation (though supply lines went into the interior rather than crossed boundaries between coastal regions), and slaves in the Americas could have entered an intra-American

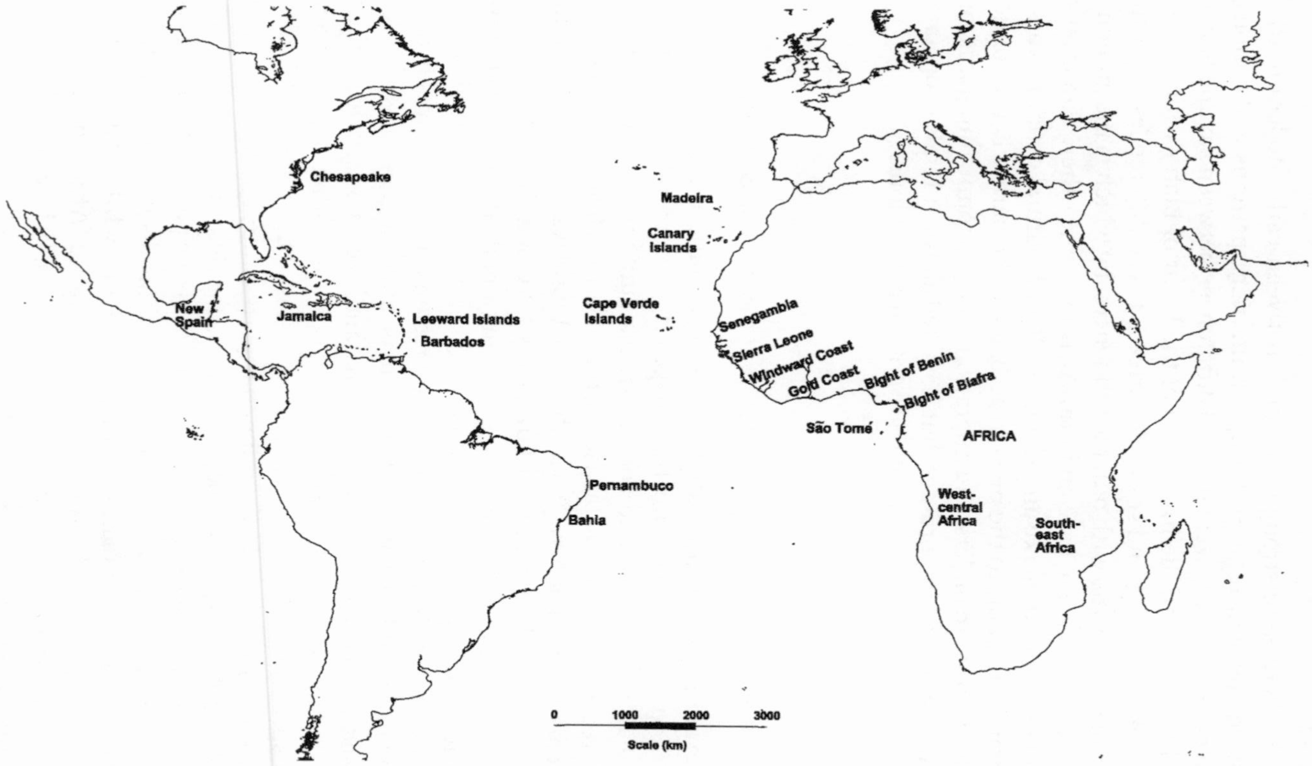

Map 1. Regions of the Atlantic Involved in the Early Modern Slave Trade.

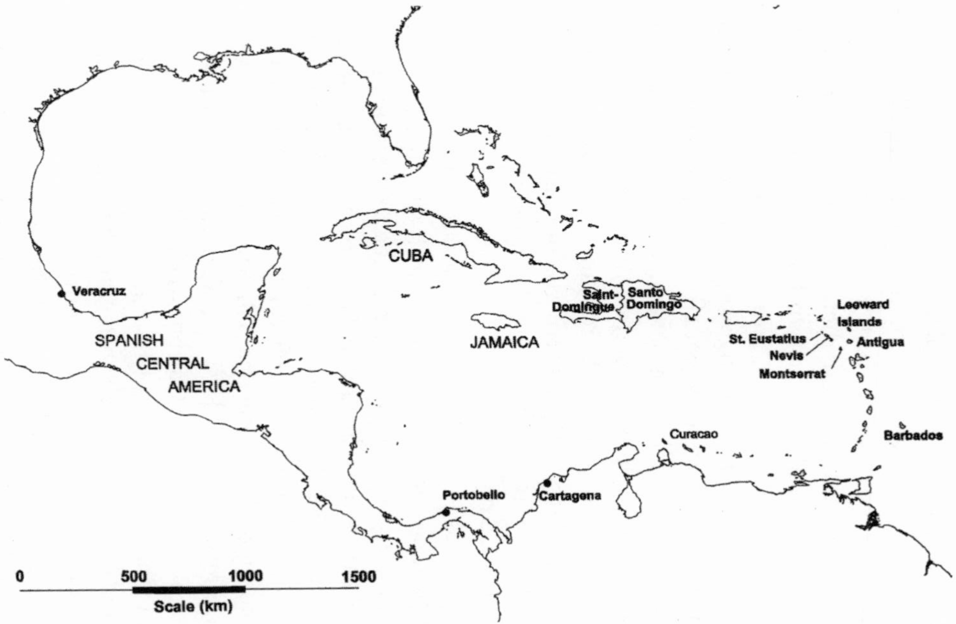

Map 2. Early Modern Caribbean.

slave trade after disembarkation, on the transatlantic portion of the voyage it is possible to map out fairly clear links between Africa and the Americas. The resulting patterns are recognizable to any student of North Atlantic migration.

It has long been a commonplace that European migration to the Americas followed a wave pattern. In broad terms, the center of gravity moved from the extreme west of Europe in the sixteenth century to northwestern Europe and then in the nineteenth century to southeast Europe and later eastern Europe. Moreover, there has always been much evidence of chain migration within these broad regions, so that the impact of migration tended to be felt sequentially rather than being distributed equally. Towns or even villages might enter the migration focus for several years before attention would shift elsewhere.[22] Likewise in the Americas there was some tendency for particular groups of Europeans to work and eventually settle in the same parts of the Americas. For reasons that are as yet unclear, a similar pattern held for the slave trade from Africa, at least at the level of broad regions.

The specifics of the European case are rather well known and need not be repeated here, but it is worth summarizing briefly their African counterparts. Readers are referred to the maps 1 and 2 for the location of the regions discussed. For 120 years after the direct traffic from Africa to the Americas began in 1519, West-Central Africa supplied 95 percent of the slaves carried to the Americas, almost all of them going to Brazil and Spanish America. Thereafter, the Bight of Benin, known as the Slave Coast, became the most prominent West African region as the Caribbean sugar sector expanded rapidly. The Gold Coast, the Bight of Biafra, and the less important Upper Guinea and South East African regions became prominent in relative terms only in the eighteenth century.

Over the period as a whole, with the exception of the Recençavo of Bahia, and probably the province of Minas Gerais for which Bahia was a conduit, the African part in the repeopling of South and Central America was as dominated by West-Central Africa as its European counterpart was by Iberians. Peoples from the Congo basin and Angola formed by far the greater share of arrivals in South-Central Brazil—the largest single slave reception areas in the Americas—as well as in northeastern Brazil, Central America, and to a lesser extent, Rio de la Plata. West-Central Africa formed the second largest provenance zone for all other South American regions. Bahia—one of the two most important points of entrance into the New World for Africans—was a major exception. In Bahia, the dominance of peoples from the hinterland of the Bight of Benin was almost complete. A large West African presence is also apparent in Spanish Central America and in the less important region of Rio de la Plata. The latter, in fact, is the only region on the continent of South America where Africans from the Bight of Biafra—overwhelmingly Igbo and Ibibio peoples—were to be found in large numbers. West Africa is also well represented in the Guianas and Surinam, but as in Central America, it is the Gold Coast, rather than the Bight of Biafra and the Slave Coast, which supplied almost half of those arriving. This is the only region in the whole of South America where peoples from the Gold Coast have a major presence.

West Africa was as dominant in the Caribbean as West-Central Africa was in South America, though generally the mix of African peoples was much greater in the Caribbean than it was further south. Only in St. Domingue did Africa south of the equator provide half of all arrivals. And only in the French Leewards and Cuba did that ratio approximate one-third. Generally, a single West African region was a clear leader in supplying each specific American region. Barbados, the Danish islands, and Spanish Central America—utilizing mainly the Dutch entrepot of Curaçao—drew disproportionately on the Gold Coast. The Bight of Benin played a similar role for the French Leewards. In Jamaica and the British Leewards, the Bight of Biafra was easily the single most important provenance zone, though in none of these cases did a single region, unlike the situation in all Brazilian regions, provide as many as half of all arrivals. In the Caribbean, "West Africa" effectively meant the Gold Coast, the Slave Coast (Bight of Benin), and the Bight of Biafra. Senegambia was of some importance in the French Caribbean, and the long Windward Coast stretching south from Sierra Leone was responsible for almost a fifth of disembarkations in the British Leewards; but generally, these regions played a minor role in the slave trade to the major American regions. The relative proximity of Senegambia and the Windward Coasts to the Americas—passages from Senegambia to the Caribbean are typically half as long as their more southerly transatlantic counterparts—suggests some factor other than geography and cost was at work.

Of all the receiving areas in the Americas, Cuba and Barbados received the greatest mix of African peoples, although the US was not far from this pattern. No single part of Africa supplied more than 28 percent of arrivals in either island and the only major regions not well represented were southeast Africa in Barbados and the Gold Coast in Cuba. In addition, the region that supplied the greatest number of slaves—West-Central Africa—covered by the nineteenth century a wider range of coastline than in earlier centuries and drew on a vast slaving hinterland, suggesting a further mixing of peoples.

Moreover, there was no regional segregation within Cuba. Almost all the arrivals moved through Havana and ports in the west of the island and for the rest of their lives worked in the sugar heartland that formed the hinterland of these ports. Large numbers of Yao from the southeast, of Yoruba from West Africa, and of Lunda from the Kasai valley in the Angolan interior intermingled on the plantation labor forces. They arrived, moreover, within a relatively short space of time in the first half of the nineteenth century, a pattern that clearly separates Cuba from Barbados and the US. Cuba, then, was an exception. An examination of shifts over time in these transatlantic links suggests that first, some American regions such as Bahia and South-Central Brazil drew on the same region of Africa throughout the slave trade era, and others such as the British and French areas may have drawn on a mix of regions, but tended to do so in sequence—a sequence moreover that in the British case was played out very slowly. All major regions of import tended to draw on a wide range of provenance zones after 1770. The picture of a confusing mix of African cultures with all the attendant barriers to establishing African influence on the New World may be valid—with important exceptions such as Brazil—but before this date may need reexamining for many areas.[23]

Geography and Atlantic patterns of winds and ocean currents help to explain some of these transatlantic linkages, particularly within the so-called South Atlantic system. But other patterns, including the Bight of Benin-Bahia and the Bight of Biafra-West Indies connections, are less easily explained by reference to geography or transport economics. European influences were also important. With the exception of the Spanish colonies, the great majority of the slaves arriving in the Americas did so in ships belonging to subjects of the colonial powers governing the territories in question.

It follows, therefore, that linkages between African and American regions reflected in part the patterns of influence by national groups of carriers over trade of specific African regions or ports.[24] But, as with the peculiar age and gender structure of the slave trade (relative to other migratory regimes) discussed above, it is the African role in these patterns that requires more attention. Why should Europeans focus first on the Bights, and later on West-Central Africa, when regions in Upper Guinea both were closer to the Americas and provided larger ratios of the males that we are told planters in the Americas wanted? Why should loading (or slaving) times on the African coast lengthen prior to the peak period of departures and then fall in the last quarter of the eighteenth century when the transatlantic slave trade was at its height? Why should some African peoples (for example, the Yoruba) have left more easily identifiable legacies in the Americas than others (for example the Igbo) even when the latter greatly outnumbered the former among forced migrants? And are parallels to this differential legacy to be found in the case of German and English migrants in North America, where even at the time of the American Revolution, after 70 years of German greatly outnumbering English migrants, traces of the former were already fading?

Experiences common to Africans and Europeans were least likely on the transatlantic passage. No recorded voyage in the north Atlantic appears to have generated the appalling conditions typical for a slave vessel, though early convict and Asian contract labor voyages may have come close. Vessels leaving both Europe and Africa did, however, tend to collect all on board from one or two ports, so that the possibilities of shared languages among captives (or migrants) were strong. On the other hand crews doubled as jailers on slave vessels; the cultural divide between jailer and prisoner was normally absolute and the journey was too short for any ameliorating human relationship to develop across the divide. Horrific violence was a part of all enslavement and shipping, and for the slaves themselves, the violence on the one in ten slave vessels estimated to have experienced a slave revolt could not have appeared exceptional.[25] Useful parallels nevertheless exist between the passage mortality of coerced and free migrants. While slave mortality was always much greater than non-slave, the distribution of mortality was highly skewed to the right for both, with the mode and median always less than the mean. More interesting, shipboard mortality in both traffics consistently differed by port, suggesting a connection between the health of those going on board and shore-based experiences of migrants, with the latter varying in both Africa and Europe, though for reasons that were no doubt different.[26]

In the Americas, the parallels between free and coerced migration are stronger in the earlier than in the later period. The areas of the Atlantic with the highest incomes and the fastest growth until the mid-nineteenth century were the parts of the Americas that produced precious metals and plantation crops, generally the semitropics. As we have seen, these areas were initially the "distant magnets" for migrants of all regimes, who went or were taken to plantation areas and mines, rather than urban areas. Indentured servants, convicts, and slaves began their lives in the Americas in such environments and most slaves ended it there. By the first half of the eighteenth century, the Germans and Irish who passed through Philadelphia avoided the plantation regions for the most part, but neither did they dwell long in such urban areas as then existed.[27] Free migrants from Europe and time-expired indentured servants may have eventually gravitated toward urban areas beginning in the late eighteenth century, but this group formed very much the minority of migrants before the mid-nineteenth century. Only a small proportion of enslaved blacks lived in cities. Before the end of the seventeenth century, life expectancy in mainland plantation areas had improved to the point where it was ahead of that in Jamaica and Barbados. In addition, there was more land available for time-expired servants on the mainland. Thus, while most migrants continued to head for the plantation and mining regions, those with choice over their destinations headed for the healthier zones, leaving the less healthy areas for those without choice.

Free and coerced migrants not only went (or were taken) to the same broad regions of the Americas; their demographic and nutritional experiences after arrival exhibited some common patterns. The white population of the Chesapeake attained a positive natural growth rate in the 1670s, several decades before their black counterparts in the 1720s. But both reached this point well before whites and blacks in Jamaica—perhaps as much as a century earlier, with the lower South mainland falling between these two extremes.[28] We cannot make comparisons with Africa, but evidence from the early nineteenth-century Americas suggests that rates of natural population increase of both free and coerced populations in the US South were high by European standards, and that slave fertility in the English Caribbean was also high. Broadly, through the many regional variations, a New World pattern of vital rates and an Old World pattern may be discerned, and, after adjusting for regional variation, the descendants of free and coerced migrants shared more with each other than with the populations that each of their forebears left behind in the Old World.[29] Similarly with nutrition, the anthropometric evidence shows that by the second quarter of the nineteenth century, free populations were better fed than slaves, but both were considerably more secure nutritionally than a wide selection of Old World populations both in Europe and Africa. For whites, at least, the transatlantic differential was greatest in the mid-eighteenth century and perhaps earlier.[30]

But it was not just in the manifestations of material life that patterns common to both free and coerced populations are to be found. Africans and Europeans alike underwent a fairly rapid and not dissimilar creolization process, which created a massive slave versus non-slave divide that closely followed the skin color fault line rather than form a cohesive society.[31] The white version of coerced labor—the convicts—came down firmly on the side of the population descended from Europeans. Both sides of the slave–non-slave divide absorbed people different from themselves more quickly than did the populations they had left behind in the Old World. Most colonial societies were more pluralistic than their metropolitan rulers, and where central control was weakest, as in the English and Dutch cases, minorities such as Jews and Irish gained rights more quickly than did their countrymen in the metropolitan center. Thus Jews obtained rights of denization in Barbados in 1650, before they were re-admitted to England. The Irish rose from a despised minority to the principal slave-holding group in Montserrat by 1729. Even the prize possession of Spain in the Americas had, by the nineteenth century, a range of slaveholders of English, Irish, and French descent that would have been unthinkable before Cuba became a substantial slave colony. Colonies such as Trinidad that changed hands were particularly diverse. Among peoples of African descent, Michael Gomez has tracked the emergence of a black identity in the Old South of the US in the eighteenth century.[32]

There were interesting parallels in the pattern of slave ship revolts. Successful revolts were rare in the early days of the slave trade and there is evidence of fighting between African groups on board slavers. Indeed, it was common for European slave captains to use so- called "guardians" from one part of the African coast to control slaves drawn from other regions. By the mid-eighteenth century this practice had become rare and in fact almost all cases of successful shipboard revolts are to be found in the second half of the century. A black-white divide that became less pronounced in Europe hardened in the Americas.

≺ III ≻

Coercion and Ravenstein's "Laws"

In the late 1880s E. G. Ravenstein laid out six "laws" of migration, drawn mainly from nineteenth-century English evidence. These have had considerable influence over migration studies and indeed might still be considered reflective of scholarly consensus.[33] They were (1) the major causes of migration are economic; (2) the majority of migrants move only a short distance, and migration proceeds by steps so that the places of out-migrants are filled by immigrants from slightly more remote areas; (3) each migration produces a compensating counter-current; (4) major migration flows, both longer and short distance, are to cities, and though the urban born are less prone to migrate than are the rural born, towns grow mainly through in-migration; (5) females are more migratory over shorter distances, males over longer, and most migrants are adults; (6) migration increases with economic and transportation improvements. How do these hold up when we take into account the interpretation offered here, adopting a perspective that includes coerced as well as free migration and the first three centuries of transatlantic migration as well as the nineteenth?

Coerced migration patterns are not as much at odds with this scheme as might first appear. Two major and several minor adjustments are necessary. First, as already noted, migration to the Americas before the nineteenth century was not to urban areas. It was to areas that exported plantation produce and precious metals. The English who flooded the Caribbean, the Chesapeake, and the Carolinas in the seventeenth and early eighteenth centuries, and the Portuguese who did likewise in the Reconçavo of Bahia and, a little later, in Minas Gerais were not moving to towns. The eastern seaboard cities in North and South America did not assume their immigrant-attracting role until the nineteenth century. This phase of transatlantic migration is best described by William H. McNeill's migration outward from the periphery of "disease-experienced" communities.[34] If we substitute "plantations and sites for extraction of precious metals" for "cities," then the above patterns (for such they are, rather than laws) hold quite well for both free and coerced—despite the fact that Ravenstein never indicates that he ever thought of the slave trade. A second major adjustment is to rule 1. The economic causes of migration, of course, are basic for both free and coerced migrant, but economics alone will not explain whether the migration will be free or coerced, and, if coerced, which groups will be regarded as eligible for enslavement. It also follows that while production functions and elasticities of derived demand for labor may be estimated, if the elasticities for free and coerced are different, and cultural factors in part determine the choice between the two, economics will not entirely explain the total quantity of labor—more specifically migrant labor—required.

Some further tinkering is required, as is a single addition. On (2), all free migration within Africa was local in that almost no free Africans crossed the Atlantic or Sahara, and ethnolinguistic boundaries within Africa did not change much over the period, suggesting minimal large-scale migration. In addition, many slaves who did not end up in the Americas were traded from group to group. On return migration (3), there is a growing literature on free blacks who returned to Africa and according to some scholars helped construct ethnic identities in the process.[35] The numbers involved must have been considerably less than among any European group, however. In (5) it is worth noting that in the last few decades of the transatlantic traffic, most slaves had not reached sexual maturity.

Finally, the 1500 to 1850 flow of people across the Atlantic, most of them slave, suggests the need for an additional "tendency," not, regrettably, as brief as the six originals. Coerced migrants must be convicts, serfs, or slaves. They will be convicts or serfs if prior to migration they were full members of the community that is responsible for their movement. A slave trade will exist only where sellers in the region of origin, shippers, and buyers at the destination all implicitly accept that the group being traded lies outside the social identity of any of the principals involved in the transaction. With these adjustments the Ravenstein tenets seem broadly applicable not just to the slave trade, but to the early modern migrant traffic from Europe as well.

Group identities are central to explaining the rise and fall of the slave trade and the slavery it supported in most parts of the Americas. The major historical lesson is that coerced migration has reinforced senses of separateness among those living in a slave society. In societies where slaves are of minor importance or do not exist, however, the opposite is likely to happen in the long run in that migration fosters more broadly conceived conceptions of self and the immediate group in which one lives. Feedback from slavery and the slave trade, as well as resistance from the slaves themselves, helped this process along in societies that were not built around slavery, until what ultimately were two conceptions of group identity faced off in the nineteenth century. The more inclusive of the two—the one shared by slaves and free blacks it should be noted—eventually prevailed. Slavery and the slave trade have produced bitter race relations, but have also created a more multi-cultural and pluralistic America than could have existed without coercion. And one does not have to believe in progress to find it difficult to conceive that coerced migration as it operated between the Old World and the New for over three centuries could ever reappear on the global scene.

Appendix to Chapter 1

Figures 1 and 2 in chapter 1 constitute an updating and an extension of my earlier work.[36] As there are competing and largely independent sets of estimates for at least mainland British North America now available from other scholars, and as the relative importance of the different migratory regimes is of central importance to the present volume, some fuller explanation of their derivation would appear called for.[37] In contrast to other recent assessments of migration to the New World, the present estimates encompass the Americas as a whole rather than just North America or parts thereof. They also pertain to net rather than gross migration. The major organizational principle employed here is the nationality of the vessel carrying the migrant rather than the nationality of the migrant or the geography of the migration so that detailed comparisons with previous estimates are not always easy. Nevertheless, before the nineteenth century, there was a large overlap between the country of vessel registration and the region of departure and arrival, at least for European migration. Organizing around vessel nationality allows a more effective tying together of the two major sources for estimates of Atlantic migration, the first being shipping records, and the second, demographic data.

Estimates of the proportion of migrants who were forced into voyaging to the Americas hinge first on assessments of the volume of total migration from Europe, Africa, and Asia, and second on estimates of the proportion of migrants from each of these areas who were slaves, prisoners, convicts, indentured or contract laborers, and free. "Free" in this context means individuals who traveled without the obligation to labor for others when they arrived at their destinations. The major shippers of both free and coerced migrants in the 1519–1880 period were the Portuguese and the British, and the strength of the estimates therefore hinges primarily on the quality of the records in these two countries and their offshoots in the Americas. For the movement from Africa and Asia, the estimates derive almost entirely from shipping records. As very few slaves returned to Africa, the volume of slave movements may be treated as a net figure. For the flow from Europe, the major source is estimates of populations in the Americas, which when combined with estimates of vital rates can be used to generate estimates of net migration or that part of population change that births and deaths do not explain.[38] For several European areas, however, particularly those sending prisoners, convicts, and indentured servants, the numbers are taken from direct counts of emigrants. In all cases, the estimates derived here are for those leaving the source society, and where the data were originally for immigrants these are converted into estimates of emigration by allowing for voyage mortality.[39] Shipboard mortality was normally several times higher for slaves from Africa than for migrants from Europe so that the ratio of Africans to Europeans leaving the Old World in a given year was lower than the ratio of Africans to Europeans arriving in the New.

TABLE I

European Directed Migration to the Americas, 1492–1880 by European Nation and Continent of Origin

(in thousands)

	Africans leaving Africa on ships of each nation (net)	Europeans leaving each nation for Americas	Africans, Asians and Europeans leaving for Americas (col. 1 + col. 2)
	*(a) Before 1580**		
Spain	10	139	149
Portugal	56	58	114
Britain	2	0	2
Total	68	197	265
	(b) 1580–1640		
Spain**	0	188	188
Portugal**	594	110	704
France	0	4	4
Netherlands	10	2	12
Britain	3	87	90
Total	607	391	998
	(c) 1640–1700		
Spain	0	158	158
Portugal	259	50	309
France	40	23	63
Netherlands	151	13	164
Britain	379	285	664
Total	829	529	1358
	(d) 1700–1760		
Spain	1	193	194
Portugal	958	300	1258
France	458	27	485
Netherlands	223	5	228
Britain***	1206	222	1428
Total	2846	747	3593
	(e) 1760–1820		
Spain	186	n.a.	n.a.
Portugal	1507	n.a.	n.a.
Netherlands	140	n.a.	n.a.
Britain***	1605	n.a.	n.a.
France	701	n.a.	n.a.
USA	186	n.a.	n.a.
Total	4325	773	5098
	(f) 1820–1880		
Spain	612	n.a.	n.a.
Portugal	1510	n.a.	n.a.
Netherlands	0	n.a.	n.a
Britain	0	n.a.	n.a.
France	158	n.a.	n.a.
USA	16	n.a.	n.a.
Total	2296	13702	15998

SOURCES (number refers to row, letter refers to column):

Column A: Calculated from the spreadsheets posted at <http://www.edu/oieahc> that accompany David Eltis, "The Volume and Direction of the Transatlantic Slave Trade: A Reassessment," *WMQ* 60 (2001): 17–46.

1B, 5B: Magnus Morner, "Spanish Migration to the New World prior to 1810: A Report on the State of Research," in Fredi Chiapelli et al., eds.," *First Images of America: The Impact of the New World on the Old* (Berkeley, 1976), 771 less 20 percent for returns.

2B, 6B, 12B: Vitorino Magalhaes-Godinho, "L'émigration portuguaise," in *Conjecture économique-structures sociale* (Paris, 1974), 254–55. Godinho's data are estimates of gross emigration. His figures are divided by three before 1700 and by two after 1700 to allow for return migration and for emigration to the Atlantic Islands, Goa, and Africa.

7B, 13B, 19B: Hubert Charbonneau et al., "Population of the St. Lawrence Valley, 1608–1760," in Michael R. Harris and Richard H. Steckel, eds., *A Population History of North America* (Cambridge, 2000); Peter Moogk, "Manon Lascaut's Countrymen: Emigration to France from North America before 1763," in Nicholas Camry, ed., *Europeans on the Move* (Oxford, 1994) and text.

8B, 14B, 20B: Jan Lucassen, *Dutch Long Distance Migration* (Amsterdam, 1991), 22–23 less 20 percent return migration. For New Netherland, Ernst van den Boogart, "The Servant Migration to New Netherland, 1624–1664," in Pieter C. Emmer, ed., *Colonialism and Migration* (Dordrecht, 1986), 61, estimates 600 emigrants before 1640 and 5,100, 1640–1664.

9B: For mainland British America, Henry A. Gemery, "The White Population of the Colonial United States, 1607–1790," in Haines and Steckel, eds., *A Population History of British North America*, 171. For the British Caribbean see id., "Emigration from the British Isles to the New World." For the pre-1620 mainland, 6,000 is added, and for the pre-1630 Caribbean (pre-1642 for Providence Island) a further 6,000 is added.

11B: 5B multiplied by ratio of America's silver production, 1640–1700 to 1580–1640. For the latter see Arthur Attman, *American Bullion in the European World Trade, 1600–1800* (Goteborg, 1986), 20.

15B: Same as 9B except for 1650–1700 migration to the British Caribbean see David Galenson, *White Servitude in Colonial America* (Cambridge, 1981), 216–18 plus 5 percent voyage mortality.

17B: 5B multiplied by ratio of Americas silver production, 1700–1760 to 1580–1640. For latter see Attman, *American Bullion*, 20.

18B: Magalhaes-Godinho, "L'émigration portuguaise," 255 estimates gross emigration. These estimates are divided by two to allow for net movements to Atlantic Islands and Goa.

21B: For the British Caribbean, Galenson, *White Servitude*, 216–18 plus 5 percent voyage mortality. For British mainland North America, Gemery, "The White Population of the Colonial United States," 71.

29B: For British mainland/US, 1760–1780, Gemery, "The White Population of the Colonial United States," 71. For the same region, 1780–1820 see id., "European Immigration to North America, 1700–1820: Numbers and Quasi-Numbers," *Perspectives in American History* 1 (1984): 315. The middle range of the three series offered for the US is accepted here. US figure increased by 15 percent to allow for arrivals in the rest of the Americas.

36B: For the US, 1821–60, Peter D. McClelland and Richard J. Zeckhauser, *Demographic Dimensions of the New Republic* (Cambridge, 1982), 113; for the US, 1861–1880, Imre Ferenczi and Walter F. Wilcox, *International Migrations*, 2 vols. (New York, 1929–31), 1: 397–98; for the rest of the Americas, ibid., 360, 539, 549–52, 566; 2: 153. All figures divided by .98 to derive departures rather than arrivals. Also included are 624,612 Asian contract laborers calculated from David Northrup, *Indentured Labor in the Age of Imperialism, 1834–1922* (Cambridge, 1995), 154–55 and divided by .96 to derive an estimate of departures of 650,638. Data for the US, 1820–60, for Argentina, 1871–80, and for Uruguay, 1897–80 are for net migration; for all other years and regions, data are for gross migration.

NOTE: Totals include trades and territories of minor participants.

* Note that the numbers of people moving to the Atlantic islands may well have exceeded those migrating to the Americas before 1580, and that including these numbers in panel 1 of table 1 might change the ratio of coerced emigration in these years.

** Spain and Portugal are treated as separate countries despite the crowns of the two countries being united between 1580 and 1640. The slave trade is treated as entirely Portuguese in this period, however.

*** Includes migrants from Germany and Africans carried on British American vessels.

Table 1 lays out estimates of the volume of people leaving for the Americas by nationality of the vessels on which they traveled. The volume of slaves carried from Africa is estimated from newly available shipping data, most of which is published.[40] The number of migrants from Europe by contrast derives from estimates based on counts of migrants in the Spanish, French, and German cases, but those for the British Americas are based on estimates of net migration calculated from demographic data. It is not clear what the Portuguese estimates are based on. Migration on British vessels to 1780 includes almost all non-British migrants to British North America to that year, and it is adjusted where necessary for voyage mortality to derive estimates of emigration.[41]

After 1780 the estimates for the British West Indies come to an end, and in the US there is a considerable mismatch between estimates of net migration from the demographic data and those implied by scattered and intermittent counts of arrivals in the 1780–1820 period. Estimates supported by population counts and plausible vital rates range from a low of 400,000 to a high of slightly over a million. Records of actual arrivals are no more reliable than the documentary basis of the net migration estimates, but what there is supports a figure at the low end of this range. The estimates used here are taken from Gemery's "probably . . . overly optimistic" set of vital rates for the period with an allowance for voyage mortality of 3 percent.[42] The resulting total is 419,000 for 1780–1820 in the US, or 508,000 including the Gemery estimates for the 1760–80 decades.[43] In the British West Indies, European migration after 1780 was minor. In the absence of other indications, the decadal totals for 1780 to 1820 are simply the means of the decadal totals between 1750 and 1780. For the whole period, 1760 to 1820, these assumptions yield 55,000. Thus, a total of 563,000 migrants (55,000 plus 508,000) are estimated to have set out for the British Americas between 1760 and 1820.

Estimates of migrations to the non-British Atlantic are of varying quality but still serviceable for the present purpose of assessing the relative importance of coerced migration. Counts of French migration to the St. Lawrence come from the best records that exist anywhere for an immigrant society in the Americas. There were just under 10,000 "immigrants who experienced a family life in Québec" between 1608 and 1760 (just under 11,000 if we allow for those embarking in France rather than disembarking in Québec), and this category is taken as a proxy for net migration.[44] Between 92 and 93 percent of those leaving France headed for more southerly climes, especially the Caribbean, but return migration was at least half.[45] The estimate for emigrants on French ships in the second, third, and fourth panels of table 1 (4,000, 23,000, and 27,000, respectively) is the count for Québec settler arrivals divided by 0.915 to allow for losses in transit and divided again by 0.2 to accommodate the rest of the French Americas. Peter Moogk's review of the evidence of departures from French ports for the whole ancien regime era suggests 100,000 passengers.[46] If return migration was half, then a net migration of 50,000 passengers is very similar to the total yielded by the above adjustments to Québec arrivals. Estimates of Portuguese emigration occupy the opposite end of the quality spectrum from the France to Québec data. Almost all of them derive from comments by Vitorino Magalhaes-Godinho in a 1974 essay on all overseas emigration, the basis for which is unclear.[47] The Spanish and Dutch estimates are described in the notes to table 1.

After 1760, the break up of old European empires and the erosion of mercantilistic restrictions on the flows of people and goods make it neither easy nor useful to group non-slave migration by nationality of carrier as table 1 does for the pre-1760 era. Unlike the slave trade, the free migrant flow generated poorer records for this period than for any other since Columbus. Wars in the Atlantic occupied more of the 1760–1820 era than any of the other 60-year panels. There is an estimate of 3,000 emigrants a year from Portugal, 1760–1800, rising to 4,500 in the first twenty years of the nineteenth century, much of the latter perhaps associated with the movement of the Portuguese court to Rio de Janeiro between 1808 and 1817. However, these figures are for gross migration and need to be reduced to allow for movement to overseas areas other than Brazil as well as return migration.[48] Halving these figures for the 60 years 1760–1820 yields 105,000 emigrants.

There are no migration estimates for Spanish America or for the non-English-speaking Caribbean, except that Spanish transatlantic migration at this time is normally pegged below that of Portugal.[49] All the major growth areas in the non-English-speaking Americas were in fact slave economies—Cuba, south-east Brazil, and, until 1791, St. Domingue—that drew on Africa, not Europe, for labor. *Petits blancs* did flood into St. Domingue after 1763, but the white population of the colony on the eve of the revolution was still less than 35,000.[50] Rapid economic growth of the temperate Iberian Americas—southern Brazil, and what became Uruguay and Argentina—and the rising attractiveness of these areas to European immigrants belong to the second half of the nineteenth, not the eighteenth century—in the Brazilian case, after the ending of the slave trade. A doubling of the Portuguese emigration figure 1760–1820 would likely accommodate European migration to the Americas outside the English-speaking areas, in other words 210,000. Adding this to the 563,000 estimated for British areas gives a total European migration during 1760–1820 amounting to 773,000. As the volume of slave departures was nearly 4.4 million, for every European between five and six Africans set out for the Americas in these years.

For non-slave migration in the final panel in table 1, there are estimates of net white immigration into the US between 1820 and 1860 computed from demographic data.[51] For the two decades after 1860, table 1 reverts to the older and widely used counts of arrivals. All data 1820 to 1860 are converted to estimates of net emigration by the addition of a small allowance for passage mortality. Outside the US in the temperate Americas, it is possible after 1820 to use a combination of counts of arrivals for some countries and net immigration for others. The share of migrants going to non-English-speaking countries before 1880 was very small (14 percent of the movement of Europeans to the Americas as a whole, 1820–80), and given the possibility of undercounting, adjustments to derive a net migration figure from these gross counts appear unnecessary for our purposes. Canada requires separate treatment because many migrants disembarking at St. Lawrence ports traveled by land to the US thereafter and are therefore included in the census-based estimates for the US between 1820 and 1860. To avoid double counting, only half the total arrivals in Québec city and Montreal between 1820 and 1860 are included in our computation and all are included for the 1870s and 1880s. European migration to the tropical Americas at this time declined to very low levels indeed, and may be ignored, even though at the end of the period a few thousand Spanish-speakers, mainly from the Canary Islands, settled in Cuba.

Of much greater significance was another branch of Old World immigration in the form of the revival of the traffic in contract laborers, this time from Asia. Fortunately, reasonably accurate counts

TABLE 2

Slaves, Indentured Servants, Prisoners and Convicts combined, and Free Persons carried to the Americas: Estimates of Volume and Shares of Total Migration, 1492–1880

(rows sum to 1, volumes are in thousands)

	Slaves'*	Servants		Convicts/prisoners		Free persons	
	share	Total	Share	Total	Share	Total	Share
(a) Before 1580	.26	0	0	3	.01	194	.73
(b) 1580–1640	.61	49	.05	8	.01	339	.34
(c) 1640–1700	.61	236	.17	23	.02	273	.20
(d) 1700–1760	.79	128	.04	61	.02	552	.15
(e) 1760–1820	.85	89	.02	34	.01	650	.13
(f) 1820–1880	.14	651	.04	20	.00	13051	.81

SOURCE: Table 1 and text.
*For slave totals see table 1.

of these migrants exist, though most of the data are for arrivals, rather than departures net of return flows. Adjustments for voyage mortality are made here, but not for return migration, but again the distorting impact of this omission on the overall totals is rather small, given that less than 5 percent of arrivals in the Americas between 1820 and 1880 came from Asia. Aggregate European and Asian emigration to the Americas between 1820 and 1880 following the above procedures is computed at 13,702,000. Strikingly, the ratio of African to European migration to the Americas was almost exactly the reverse of what it had been in the previous 60-year period.

The estimates of migration to the Americas now need to be broken down into migratory regimes. The proportion of migrants who were indentured servants varied enormously by country of origin and over time. Broadly, while many Spanish and Portuguese migrants went as dependents, they were not under formal and fully transferable indentures, and thus cannot be classed as servants in the north European sense.[52] At the other extreme were the English in the seventeenth century; their migrant streams to the Americas were over two-thirds servants. The Dutch, French, and German were closer to the English than to the Iberian model, though in the German case a form of indenture particularly suited for families became dominant. The ratio of indentured servants and redemptioners among migrants declined to close to zero by the 1820s from its seventeenth-century high point without ever having become a feature of migration from the Iberian peninsula. Table 2 presents rough estimates of flows of four different migratory regimes by the same 60-year panels used in table 1. The four are slaves, servants, prisoners and convicts calculated together, and free migrants. Columns 2, 4, and 6 are estimates of total numbers, and columns 3 and 5 and 7 are the shares of aggregate migration that these estimates represent, with aggregate migration in all cases taken from the appropriate panel of column 3 in table 1. The share of slaves in column 1 of table 2 is just the totals of slaves in column 1 of table 1 divided by aggregate migration in column 3 of table 1. Both totals and shares of free migrants (columns 6 and 7 in table 2) are residuals obtained by subtracting slaves, servants, and prisoners from total migration (or the number 1 in the case of column 7).

With the estimates for slaves taken from table 1 and the estimates for free migrants as a residual, detailed discussion of table 2 need be concerned only with servants, prisoners, and convicts—columns 2 to 5. For some periods the ratio in these columns is extracted from the literature first and is then used to compute the absolute numbers in columns 2 and 4; for other cells in the table, however—where the evidence warrants—absolute numbers are estimated first and are then used to compute the ratios in columns 3 and 5.

For indentured servants, the ratio for Spanish and Portuguese migration is set at zero for all periods. Servitude in its colonial adaptation emerged in the early 1620s in Virginia.[53] From this point to 1640, the incidence of indentured servants among Chesapeake migrants quickly increased from zero to 80 percent,[54] perhaps averaging 50 percent for the period 1607–40. In New England, a breakdown of passenger lists for the 1630s suggests 17 percent of arrivals were bound workers, and the 1630s was also the decade when the relative importance of the region as a destination was probably at its highest level ever in the history of Atlantic migration.[55] An average of New England and Chesapeake ratios yields one-third as the servant proportion of arrivals in the British North American mainland. For the very early English Caribbean and the Dutch and French Americas, there are no data. The total number of migrants before 1640 sailing to the Dutch and French possessions was very small, but in this period the 53,000 of the 87,000 English migrants in cell 9B of table 1 set out for the Caribbean, and the rest for the mainland. Given the plantation base of the early Caribbean, at least half, and probably two-thirds, of the Caribbean-bound group must have been servants. Two-thirds of 53,000 Caribbean-bound migrants is 35,300 servants; one-third of the 34,000 going to the mainland (87,000 less 53,000) yields 11,300 servants; and applying the English mainland ratio of one-third servants to the French and Dutch possessions (cells 7B and 8B) yields another 2,000. The total number of servants, 1580–1640, is thus estimated at a rounded 49,000. Dividing 49,000 by aggregate migration of 998,000 in cell 10C of table 1 suggests that 5 percent of all transatlantic migrants in these years were indentured servants.

For a half century before 1660 more people sailed to the Caribbean than to the mainland, but after 1660 the opposite held as the Chesapeake became the major attraction. On the English-speaking mainland, 1640–1700, three-quarters of arrivals in the Chesapeake were servants, and the Chesapeake accounted for 96 percent of all servants leaving for English mainland North America in these years.[56] For the English West Indies, 57.4 percent of a sample of 15,363 emigrants leaving for the Caribbean 1640–99 were in the indentured servant category, but this does not include those who signed according to "the custom of the country" after they arrived.[57]

The true ratio was likely similar to what held for Chesapeake migrants. If we accept 75 percent for all European migrants on British ships shown in cell 15B of table 1, then 213,750 servants are estimated. French Atlantic ports, especially La Rochelle and Bordeaux, sent a small but steady stream of servants to mainly the French West Indies. Detailed work on notary and port records indicates about one third of total departures before 1763 left under an indenture.[58] Applying this ratio to cell 13B of table 1 generates a further 15,333 servants. Finally, for the small Dutch contingent, 55 percent of arrivals in New Netherlands are estimated to have been servants, a share used here for the Dutch West Indies as well. Fifty-five percent of cell 14B of table 1 gives 7,150 Dutch-borne servants.[59] The total number of indentured servants of all nations 1640–1700 is estimated to have been 236,250 or 17.2 percent of all migrants—the highest proportion of indentured servants in any of the 60-year periods of transatlantic migration presented here.

During the first half of the eighteenth century, information on the proportion of English, Scots, and Welsh transatlantic migrants who were indentured servants is weaker than for any other period, and there is no alternative but to guess at the ratio based on the experience of other groups. Between 1730 and 1760, two-thirds of 29,000 Irish arriving in the Delaware Valley—the major target area for mainland immigrants at this time—were indentured. More Germans than Irish could pay their own fares. The ratio of redemptioners among the 96,000 German speakers arriving on the mainland before 1760 increased from zero in the 1720s to half after 1750, and averaged one-third for the full 1700–60 period.[60] Migration from Britain was closer in age and marital status to the stream of young and single southern Irish than the family-oriented German flow, and a guess of 60 percent is used here. Overall, 55 percent of migrants arriving on British vessels between 1700 and 1760 are estimated to have been bound to others at or shortly after arrival.[61] For the migrants on French vessels, the ratio of servants continued to average one third in this period, and for the tiny Dutch group, the ratio of the previous period (55 percent) is used. Applying these ratios to cells 19B, 20B, and 21B of table 1 generates an estimated 127,550 servants for 1700–60.

For the 1760–1820 period, it is necessary to focus only on the British Americas, and for the first half of the period, St. Domingue. Grubb's compilation of data for German servants arriving in Philadelphia, the major port in the Americas for servant migration in the later eighteenth century, suggests an irregular decline by decade in the share of servants, from 55.5 percent in 1772, to less than 1 percent in the 1820s. For the whole period, 30 percent of German migrants were servants.[62] German migration 1760–1820 totaled 49,312 arrivals, or 51,000 emigrants after allowing for 3 percent voyage mortality,[63] suggesting just over 15,000 German servants.

The proportion of other national groups of migrants who were indentured at this time is just not known. The institution of indentured servitude died in the US in the 1820s. Canal companies who had brought over English and Irish indentured laborers tried to enforce the contracts in the criminal courts in the face of the attempts of other companies to hire away the newly arrived workers. The courts no longer upheld the contracts and the system collapsed, but the relevant point here is that the evidence presented in court suggests no discontinuity in the practice of indentured servitude in the years before the 1820s.[64] Unknown numbers of English and Irish servants had apparently continued to arrive in the years prior to the 1820s. The proportion of all English and Irish servants who were indentured emigrating to the US in the second half of the 1760–1820 period was no doubt below the 30 percent calculated for Germans above, but it cannot have been zero after the 1780s for either group.[65] An estimate, probably upper bound, of 15 percent for non-German immigrants is employed here. Of the 773,000 total migrants, 1760–1820, 508,000 are estimated to have left for the US. Deducting 51,000 German speakers departing for the US leaves 457,000 mainly British. If 15 percent of these were indentured, then 68,500 non-German servants are hypothesized. Among the 210,000 non-US, Latin America brought in no indentured migrants, and the French and British Caribbean brought in at most a few thousand, including the first 200 Chinese indentured or contract workers (as they came to be called) in Trinidad in 1806.[66] The number of servant migrants outside the US is arbitrarily set at 5,000. The total number of servants emigrating to the US 1760–1820 is thus estimated at 88,900, with the ratio of servants to total migration at just under 2 percent.

For the 1820–80 panel in table 2, indentured or contract labor is simply the Asian component of departures for the Americas calculated from Northrup with an allowance for shipboard mortality.[67] The resulting estimate of 650,600 divided by the total departures for the Americas in cell 29C of table 1 yields the ratio 0.04 in column 2. Thus both the proportion and the numbers of indentured/contract workers increased substantially between 1760–1820 and 1820–1880, even though the contract share of total migration was very small.

For northwestern European countries, the basic information for prisoners and convicts is in the form of counts of departures. Generally, the prisoner and convict share of total migration in the early modern period was for many years exaggerated. The older literature often stressed that European prisons were a major source of early migrants.[68] It is true that many of the surviving records that sustained this earlier image were applications for permission to deport and expel rather than records of departure and arrival. Given the natures of the migratory regimes, it is also true that official records of convicts and prisoners are more likely to have survived than those for free migrants, with the likelihood of traces of servant migrant entering the official record falling between these two extremes.[69]

Generally, the records for the Iberian Americas have not been as systematically exploited as those for the colonial possessions of the north Europeans. A total of 50,000 degredados are estimated to have left Portugal to go to the overseas Portuguese world between 1550 and 1755, with Brazil claiming about one half, or 25,000. No precise breakdowns over time are available, but royal ordinances of 1617 opened up newly conquered Maranhão as a degredado site and then in 1717 and 1722 redirected the flow to other parts of the empire. The pace of convict departures is thus known to have increased during the seventeenth and eighteenth centuries, a pattern similar to the better-known British case. An arbitrary distribution is imposed for the periodization used here of 2,000 before 1580, 5,000 between 1580 and 1640, 7,000 between 1640 and 1700, and 11,000 between 1700 and 1755. Prisoners went chiefly to Maranhão, but also to Para, Ceará, Mato Grosso, and Colonia do Sacramento (Uruguay). From 1755 to the independence of Brazil and even a few years beyond, Portugal dispatched about 150 convicts a year to the Americas. Thus, from 1756 to 1828, a further 11,000 convicts are assumed to have been exiled to the Americas. Adjustment for the periodization of table 1 yields 11,750 for 1700–60, 9,000 for 1760–1820, and 1,200 after 1820.[70] For the Spanish Americas, there is almost no information, except that Spanish convicts were working the ferries in Havana harbor in the late sixteenth century and helped build the massive fortifications at Havana over a century later. Convicts do not figure in Boyd-Bowman's compilation of early Spanish migrants, but there would have been some among those military personnel who were dispatched to the Americas and then joined the net migrant category by remaining there. Generally, the Spanish used galleys as punishment to a much greater extent than the Portuguese throughout the era of overseas European expansion.[71] The numbers are set at half the Portuguese estimates.

For the years before 1580, the guess of 2,000 Portuguese degredados becomes 3,000 prisoners for the whole of Europe after an allowance for the Spanish. Spanish and Portuguese continued to predominate among prisoner exiles in the following period; no more than three or four hundred English convicts could have been dispatched to the Americas before 1640,[72] and French involvement began later again. Five thousand Portuguese prisoners to the Americas, estimated above, becomes 7,500 from the Iberian peninsula and with the addition of a few hundred English the total number of prisoners and convicts for 1580–1640 thus becomes 8,000.

Between 1640 and 1700 most western European maritime states, with the notable exception of the Dutch, sent unwilling citizens across the Atlantic. A data set based on the work of genealogists indicates 8,786 convicts and prisoners leaving English ports between 1640 and 1699.[73] Only two of these are identified as Scottish, and the 1,500 Scots prisoners as well as 300 Irish counted by Aaron Fogleman are supplementary to this English group.[74] The sum of these British and Irish forced migrants is 10,586 but this total is unlikely to include every deportee. French policy on transportation fluctuated and was contradictory throughout the ancien regime. The French sent no prisoners to French Canada in the seventeenth century but dispatched occasional batches of transients to the French West Indies—those guilty of more serious crimes generally being sent to the galleys or executed.[75] Two thousand is allowed for French prisoners before 1700 and the addition of this to the English total and the Iberian figure suggested above of 10,500 (1.5 times the Portuguese estimate of 7,000) yields a total for 1640–1700 of 23,000.

Between 1700 and the early 1780s, at least 53,200 convicts were dispatched to the Americas from Great Britain and Ireland.[76] Seventy percent of this total, or 37,240, left before 1761.[77] Scholars tend to assume with justification that the 1718 "act for . . . the more effectual transportation of felons" was the foundation of the eighteenth century transportation system, but as the seventeenth century records show, this legislation did not initiate the forced migration of British citizens. As it would be rash to assume that no one was exiled between 1699 and 1718, 500 is added to the 1718–60 estimate to arrive at a total of 37,740 British and Irish deportees for 1700–1760. In the French Americas, 594 convicts were sent to New France in this period, out of a net migration of nearly 5,000. A further 1,278 convicts were among the 7,020 sailing for Louisiana between 1717 and 1721, though very few of this number remained in Louisiana.[78] The French state began to take a harsher attitude toward beggars about the time that the English formalized their own transportation system. Groups of vagabonds were sent to the West Indies before 1716, but thereafter the flow increased, especially to St. Domingue, where new arrivals contributed to a rebellion of whites that broke out in November 1722.[79] As noted above, New France also felt the impact of this policy in that all 594 convicts sent during the French period arrived after 1720. If the New France ratio of approximately one convict in every five permanent settlers held for the rest of the French Americas, then a total of 5,400 convicts (one fifth of cell 19B) would have left French ports for the Americas between 1700 and 1760. Adding the Portuguese and Spanish estimate of 17,625 (the Portuguese total of 11,750 multiplied by 1.5) for this period to 5,400 French-borne prisoners and 37,720 British convicts gives a total for 1700–1760 of 60,745.

For the last two 60-year periods in table 2, convicts left Western Europe in larger volumes than ever before—30,000 to Australia before 1821, and 165,000 to Australia, French Guiana, and New Caledonia between 1821 and 1880, with the flow to Australia ending at the same time as the transatlantic slave trade. During the 1760 to 1820 period, however, 15,000 British convicts crossed the Atlantic before the newly independent US closed down the traffic, and a further 13,500 from the Iberian peninsula to Brazil and Cuba (the Portuguese estimate for 1760–1820 of 9,000 multiplied by 1.5). A further 5,000 would likely account for French convicts sent to St. Domingue before 1792, and the total for the period is estimated at 33,500. Of those sailing after 1820, the 18,000 that the French sent to Guiana are added to 1,800 Iberians, for a total of 19,800.[80] The last column of table 2 shows the fall and rise in relative terms of free transatlantic migration, a close mirror image of the rise and fall of the slave trade—inevitably so given the enormous numerical dominance of the African slave component of early modern transatlantic migration. But columns 3 and 5 also show that the rise and fall of two other forms of bound labor—overwhelmingly white and, of course, small in comparison with the slave trade—closely paralleled the parabola of the slave trade. Table 2 provides the basis for figures 1 and 2 in chapter 1, and the implications of the patterns revealed are taken up at greater length in the body of the chapter.

< 2 >

Changing Laws and Regulations and Their Impact on Migration

STANLEY L. ENGERMAN

MIGRATION HAS long been an important phenomenon in human history, affecting not only those who moved, but also residents of the areas from and to which migrants traveled.[1] Movements, whether on a large scale or relatively minor, whether organized by nations, by groups moving together, or by individuals or families, have occurred in all parts of the world, over much of recorded time.

Attempts to measure and control migration are, however, of recent origin. Detailed measuring of the magnitude of migration, other than the transatlantic slave trade, began only with the development of transatlantic movements from Europe to North and South America, the simultaneous movements from west and central Europe to eastern Europe, including from Russia to Siberia, and the concurrent movements from Europe to Asia and Africa. These efforts to count migrants accompanied the development of the powerful nation-state, when increased attention was given to the causes, consequences, and means of influencing both immigration and emigration. Earlier controls, by mercantilist states, by China, and by others, tended to be concerned with emigration rather than immigration. Whether these new nation-states were subdivisions of a larger empire or consolidations of small provinces into one political unit, control over exit and entry became one of the major components of national sovereignty. Controls over mobility, whether newly created or a substitution for the earlier limitations of migration under feudalism, serfdom, and slavery, took many forms and responded to quite diverse circumstances. External, international migration became regulated in a manner that was different from the controls over internal migration within national borders.

The nineteenth century was marked by a liberalization of flows of goods, capital, and people, both internationally and within the nation. Improvements in transportation and an ending of internal trade barriers between political subdivisions within countries increased the flow of goods; the ending of serfdom had similar effects on the flows of people, while the ending of the slave trade and of slavery meant a reduction in migration, offset, in part, by increased migration of indentured and other laborers to replace slaves. Internationally, flows of goods were increased by reductions in transport costs as well as in trade barriers, such as tariffs. At the same time international movements of people increased dramatically as a result of lessened restrictions, primarily the legal restrictions against emigration, as well as the reductions in transport costs. Immigration remained relatively unrestricted prior to the twentieth century. Although there were some long-existing restrictions, they did not attain the importance before the twentieth century that they were to achieve subsequently.

After World War I, the initial decade of recovery, and the crisis of the Great Depression of the 1930s, the period of liberalization of international flows of goods, capital, and people came to an end, and restrictions became issues of major political importance. Such restrictions often took a more extensive form than previously. Not only were tariffs on imports increased, but qualitative restrictions such as quotas on trade were introduced and enforced. Immigration restrictions now included quantitative limits, such as quotas, which went beyond the more generalized nature of earlier attempts to reduce the number of immigrants or influence the character of the migrants. The nineteenth century saw a freeing of the movement of goods and people by means of lowered tariffs set by countries in the case of goods and the removal of emigrant restrictions by sending countries in the case of people. The twentieth-century reversal of this liberalization process has, by contrast, come about symmetrically through receiving countries restricting the inflows of both goods and people. Such changing patterns reflected changes in economic ideology, demographic performance, and national politics. In particular, they raised questions about the meaning of freedom in an international context, including provisions regarding who is permitted to enter, what rights migrants would have prior to and after receiving citizenship, and the conditions under which they could achieve the rights of citizens.

Any time there were political units with some distinct geographic boundaries there were potential problems in defining who could leave and who could enter, quite apart from the set of restrictions on mobility that slavery and serfdom entailed. The greater the numbers of political states, the more international borders and the greater the number and complexity of rules regarding migration. Thus, for example, medieval city-states of Europe often granted rights to those resident there for a specified period of time, and the "free air" of the city meant freedom from serfdom, even if not always the full set of rights of citizenship.[2] Generally, however, there have been relatively fewer political or legal barriers in regard to internal migration.[3] Internal movement did not entail a change in country of citizenship or generally in the rights of the citizen. The differences between the legal and the political status of external and internal migration did not mean that internal migration was considered of lesser importance than foreign immigration or that it was independent, as cause or consequence, of foreign migration.[4]

In the antebellum United States, for example, several northern states had restrictions on free black entrance, as well as on the granting of political rights and education to those blacks admitted. Southern states required out-migration of freed slaves. Provincial (Canada) and state (US) controls on the entry of Asians provide other examples of such restrictions in the nineteenth century.[5] Policies regarding internal migration were long part of the British Poor Laws, of the derivative systems in the New England states, and of policies elsewhere in Europe. Even today in China and elsewhere, residence requirements and expulsion to area of prior residence form a central aspect of the system of relief payments. Nevertheless, such policies of constrained internal migration have been more infrequent in occurrence and impact than have regulations on international migration.

Migration is primarily an economic phenomenon, shaped by the magnitude of income and wage differentials between nations, the financial costs of transportation and communication, the time and other costs arising from geographic distance, and the temporary barriers imposed by wars and military conflicts. Nevertheless it is clear that the ability of nations to control terms of movement has had a dramatic effect on the nature and magnitude of population movements, both directly and by changing relative costs. Some of these legal and political restrictions may reflect economic considerations but, as argued below, many factors other than economic have influenced social decisions regarding immigration, resulting in economic costs on those imposing the regulations. Basic institutions such as free labor, serfdom, slavery, contract labor, and convict labor will also shape migration—but the actual timing and magnitude of movements by individuals and groups will often be influenced by benefit-cost considerations. The cultural and ideological factors that affect the nature of institutions are, therefore, not completely independent of considerations of their costs to the population.[6]

≺ I ≻

Goals of Migration Policy

Issues concerning the control of immigration and emigration pose two different sets of questions. First is the number of migrants to be let in, or out, with the magnitude being at issue rather than the particular nature of the migrants. Second is the specific composition of migration with respect to nationality, race, religion, occupation, literacy level, language skills, and a seemingly unlimited number of other characteristics that have been utilized by various countries at different times.[7] These two questions are obviously not completely independent, because concerns with composition and characteristics may lower the overall magnitude of migrants, even without that being the primary intent, while attempts to control the magnitude of migration can achieve their goal by imposing restrictions on the particular nature of the migrants to be accepted. And, as with other public policy issues, given these overlapping concerns, it can be difficult to determine accurately the major goal of policy advocates from the arguments publicly made for them.

Among the major difficulties in evaluating the benefits and costs of a nation's immigration policy (or lack of one) is the problem of determining exactly what have been the specific goals of immigration measures. Moreover, because the means, if not the ends, of policy may change with variations in economic and other conditions, allowance must be made for change over time. The nature of the political decision-making process will itself vary with changes in voting rights and relative economic power so that any decisions made by a narrow ruling political elite may have to be broadened over time to accommodate a broader range of participants, often with rather different ends.[8] Policy undoubtedly reflects compromises between competing interests rather than a simpler-to-analyze single class or group decision. Further complications in interpretation arise because the implicit (or explicit) models used by advocates to argue about long-run outcomes of population movement and economic change, not only the immediate responses to policy changes, are themselves often significant sources of debate.[9]

The most familiar, and widely discussed, of national aims is that of maximization of per capita income (or welfare). This argument draws upon the extensive literature on optimum population size, trading off the (external and internal) benefits of economies of scale against the impact of diminishing returns due to factors (particularly land) fixed in amount. Yet differences persist concerning which is to be considered the relevant population whose income is to be maximized—the world's, the nation's before immigration, the nation's including immigrants, the native-born within the nation—or whether it is to be some subset of the population: some specific races, classes, or regional interests. Are the interests of foreign populations to be considered, or only those of national residents? Should the world interest be considered or just that of the nation? Is the goal of policy based on average income per person or is it the average income of some specific group, entailing some redistribution that the governmental decision-makers might wish to achieve? Policies to achieve any of these ends vary with existing endowments and adjustments of labor, capital, and natural resources and will also depend upon the extent of the internal mobility of the already resident population as well as of the immigrants. Countries with a high ratio of land to labor have generally been more receptive to attracting, accepting, and receiving migrants, although at times with some constraints on internal mobility after arrival. This willingness usually declines as the size of the population increases and less land becomes available for newcomers. And, given the probable differing economic interests of skilled and unskilled labor, not only the magnitude but also the composition of arrivals is of importance in policy determination.

While in today's world it is usually per capita income of the native born that is considered the most relevant social goal, in the past, the ideology of mercantilism (whether seen as a formal body of economic thought or merely as a set of disparate desired policies) ensured that the primary concern was with the total population of an area, or at least the total population up to the point where an individual's net marginal product became equal to zero.[10] Higher population was seen as a basis for military and political power. Military needs or the desire to maintain artisans and other skilled labor would explain the presence of restrictions on out-migration, as occurred in areas of early modern Europe and elsewhere.[11] Other arguments for maximizing population would include a belief in scale effects, so that a larger population would mean larger per capita incomes, while the case for smaller populations would include a belief in the impact of diminishing returns or diseconomies of scale. More recently the claim for a smaller population, with restrictions on immigration and the encouragement of out-migration, emerged from the claims of ecobiology that a smaller population size will provide for greater long-term capacity for the economic survival of the nation and of the world.

A more recent political justification for enhanced immigration, irrespective of population size, has been the presumed beneficial effect on foreign relations of allowing foreigners in.[12] This would meet the preferences of those nations from which emigration might occur, who believe that immigration restrictions carry overtones of racism and inferiority. At times, the need for good foreign relations might have required restricting immigration, particularly of the more educated (to avert a "brain drain") and the more skilled in the countries. This concern could, at times, have extended to the entire population, not just the educated, if there was a perceived need for a larger military force in the country of potential out-migration.

The relation between migration and total population size is not always clear, given the correlations among population, income, fertility, and mortality, and thus between immigration (or emigration) and national population size. The point at which a population reaches a unique equilibrium had been discussed by Malthusians, as well as by policy advocates in many different nations, and by international agencies. This has been particularly the case in the United States, with an argument most famously made by Francis Amasa

Walker at the end of the nineteenth century.[13] For if immigration affects the income of residents, it is possible that within some relevant time period (the crucial point of how long this time is, however, is seldom discussed) the population increase due to immigration, by influencing incomes, would lead the population of residents to decline. Thus, Walker argued, total population could ultimately be the same, with or without migration controls, although the make-up of the population would differ. This contention became an important part of the anti-immigration argument, however incorrect.

Correspondingly, population outflows might lead to higher resident growth rates precluding any long-run population decline. Such a pattern was found in some regions of the nineteenth-century United States. This argument also featured in the debate on the impact of the transatlantic slave trade upon Africa. Natural population growth supposedly increased after an initial decline brought about by the export of slaves. It was this possibility that led to a pro-slavery argument using Malthus's attack on the impact of the African slave trade. Malthus distanced himself from the argument that, on the basis of the Malthusian formulation, the slave trade would not lead to a lowered African population.[14] Unfortunately, however, there seems at present little agreement on the short- and long-run effects of migration on overall population size, despite the pivotal importance of these effects for most policy debates on migration.

In addition to the economic and political concerns with migration, there are several other considerations that have long been central to migration debates. Restrictions have frequently been imposed, in the interests of cultural homogeneity, by race, religion, or nationality. Cultural norms might lead to a policy in which certain groups would be precluded, even at some economic cost, in order to achieve a desired culture within the nation. In the debates leading to the origin of the "White Australia" policy, for example, it was pointed out that even though restricting immigrant labor would mean higher sugar prices, it would be a worthwhile policy for the country to pursue given the Asian or Oceanic origins of immigrant labor.[15] Also, many of the attempts to restrict the slave trade to the Americas derived from a decision to reduce the numbers coming from African societies, and to replace them with non-African migrants from areas more culturally compatible with the dominant elite.[16] In much of independent South and Central America, subsidies and other benefits were provided for settlers from Spain and elsewhere in Europe to offset the effects of the large decline in the Native American population. Similar policies of attracting Europeans were pursued in the Caribbean in the endeavor to "whiten" or "Europeanize" the large population of blacks originally coming from Africa. At what level it would be considered appropriate to limit the population share of "undesirable" cultures cannot be easily estimated (presumably the preferred answer would most often be zero), and such differences led to extreme predictions as to possible future flows in the absence of restrictions. Yet in many cases the numerical presence of minorities prior to their limitation or exclusion has been quite low as a share of the overall populations.[17]

Of major importance in the nineteenth and twentieth centuries has been the question of how humanitarianism should influence the numbers and sources of migrants. An earlier example of the impact of humanitarianism on migration is the ending of the transatlantic slave trade. The adjustments made for political refugees and the granting of political asylum have been seen, by some, as a means by which to circumvent existing restrictions on the numbers of migrants allowed.[18] At what stage of political oppression, or international warfare, would opening up migration to refugees be appropriate? Should the relevant criteria be based on the direct use of force against specific individuals or should it more generally be based on the occurrence of dire economic conditions and unacceptable social problems?

The concept of asylum has widened in recent years, to cover not only the direct threat of death for political reasons but issues more generally of the treatment of people (including, for example, the prospect of female genital mutilation and spousal abuse) as well as overall political conditions. As seen in Britain today, the issue of asylum is made more complex by the decision-making process which requires a case-by-case assessment of asylum applications. How long should the waiting period be until a decision on entry is made, and what rights do those seeking asylum have during this waiting period, including the right to select where they will live? While it is political refugees who attract the most attention, refugees resulting from national disasters such as earthquakes and floods have also posed problems for nations attempting to implement a policy of humanitarianism. The choice must be made between providing aid by the process of allowing immigration and of providing aid at the place of initial location in order to deter movement. An example of situations in which such choices were required is that of European decolonization and the granting of colonial interdependence by European nations in the aftermath of World War II.

≺ II ≻

Controls on Migration and the Terms of Labor

While the goals of migration policy are often contradictory, the application and impact of pre- and early twentieth-century policy appear clear enough when we group migration by the terms under which migrants traveled and subsequently labored. For a period of nearly four centuries, free migrants formed a minority of these crossing the Atlantic and for some shorter periods a minority too of those traveling eastward by land. Slaves, serfs, convicts, and indentured servants all migrated under labor obligation to others, and government had a major influence over the direction and composition under those different forms of labor regimes.

Before the nineteenth century an important concern of many nations was limiting the outflow of its population.[19] These limits could be on the overall numbers of migrants or on migration to specific countries, or else limits on the departure of specific occupational and educational groups.[20] Limiting could be accomplished by direct measures to close borders, by requiring specific permissions and passports to leave, or by imposing taxes on, or confiscating assets of, those wishing to depart.[21] The most frequent reason to prevent leaving was the desire for labor for military manpower and the related purpose of increased national power, but there were also attempts to discriminate among potential emigrants in order to maintain the supply of skilled and educated workers, entrepreneurs, and those with accumulated capital. Other reasons for restrictions, reflecting social and legal factors, included the need to prevent evasion of judicial and legal proceedings (including debt or bankruptcy), to prevent the departure of married women without the presence or consent of their husbands, or to prevent the emigration of nationals who might have been regarded as too old to work and would have become dependent elsewhere (in China this had meant over 40) or who were otherwise incapable of earning a livelihood in the area of immigration.

Under some circumstances, however, governments have actually encouraged people to emigrate by payments in cash or in kind. Such a situation has usually arisen where it is believed that a nation is overcrowded or that some of its colonies could benefit from receiving more labor. This migration could be of some particular group or of some specific number that the government wishes to remove; or the opportunity for departure might be made available to the entire population. The British subsidized fares for "paupers" going to Australia, as well as Canada and South Africa, in the nineteenth century, and similar practices were sometimes used by other countries wishing to expel people—often the poor and destitute.[22] Subsidies were used as a means of attracting labor to countries wishing to have a large labor force, sometimes as a replacement for Native Americans or slave labor, sometimes because of a naturally low population density. To encourage settlement, aid was given to specific groups, such as females of marriageable age when the sex ratio in the areas of settlement seemed too disproportionate to generate a self-sustaining population. Specific subsidies were also offered to attract skilled labor, if needed for particular occupations.

In the nineteenth century, countries in which indentured servants were recruited operated first to control and then later to end such migration because of what were regarded as unfavorable working and living conditions in those areas where the servants labored. Both countries of origin and those of destination regulated the sex ratio of migrants at the point of either departure or arrival, or both, but it was the countries of origin, notably China and India, which ultimately ended the traffic in indentured labor.

By contrast, countries of origin did not play a major role in the endings of the slave trade. Suppression of the transatlantic traffic generally entailed decisions made by the European nations that imported slaves into the New World and not by the regions of departure from Africa. The combination of a shift to palm oil production in West Africa and bribes paid by the British to Africans did help to bring the transatlantic slave trade to an end in the Bight of Biafra and most of West Africa. African suppliers of slaves, however, often pushed to keep the slave trade open in the interests of receiving more trade goods. In some cases the closing of the slave trade within Africa was undertaken for demographic, political, moral, or economic reasons, by regions previously exporting slaves, sometimes to avoid the stigma of providing human cargoes to other parts of the world, sometimes to maintain a larger population and labor force.[23]

Convict migration ended, generally, at the behest of the receiving, not the sending, areas. Nations that sent out convicts often responded to a rejection in one receiving area by switching locations to which convicts were shipped.[24] Convict labor was used by several European countries in settling new areas, but this was seldom popular in the regions to which they were sent. Benjamin Franklin's desire to trade rattlesnakes for convicts is indicative of the mind-set that ended shipments to an independent United States.[25] In Australia, after the initial period of convict transport, the political sentiment was against continuing the shipment of convicts; it was believed this made Australia less attractive to free migrants and thus limited overall migration. By the second half of the nineteenth century most such convict movements ceased, although the French use of Devil's Island (in French Guiana) persisted until almost the middle of the twentieth century. The labor and political rights of convicts did differ from those of the free population.[26] Likewise, in a different context, there is a clear modern parallel here in that convicts and ex-convicts in the United States and elsewhere frequently have different rights regarding suffrage than do the rest of the population.[27]

III

Raising Restrictions on Free Migration

This trend toward more regulation of unfree labor was paralleled in the twentieth century by rising restrictions on free migration. These have taken many different forms, with quite different implications, and as suggested in section I it is sometimes difficult to distinguish particular motives for the restrictive immigration policies from the attempt to achieve broader national ends. Underlying these policies are a number of important issues about the meaning of national sovereignty and the rights of individuals in a society. The right to migrate was one of the earliest examples used by European thinkers to contrast individual and state rights, with the development of the idea of the need for limiting the state's power in the interests of allowing more rights to choose by individuals.[28]

The simplest regulations to interpret, although not necessarily the easiest to enforce, have been outright prohibitions and exclusions against any entry. Thus, in the recent centuries, contract laborers in the United States and Australia and slaves in the Americas have generally been legally prohibited as immigrants. The twentieth century saw the introduction of quotas or numerical maxima for specific categories of free immigrants, whether based on nationality, race, religion, skills, occupations, family relations, or other criteria.[29] These exclusionary categories may reflect some specific purpose or more frequently may be intended as proxies or disguised means for handling some ideological or cultural concerns of the resident population about which groups should be kept out or have their entry limited.[30]

The justifications offered for restricting entry of specific individuals or groups fall into three broad categories. First was the economic fear that entrants would be at high risk of becoming public charges costing the state. Restrictions based on this concern have imposed limits on age, health, physical condition, mental capacity, current pauperism and indigency, illiteracy (in the language of either the country of arrival or some other language), or absence of family relations to serve as a source of support. Alternatively, there might be a requirement to post a financial bond by the migrant, by the ship captain, or by some other party. A second concern was that entrants would impose social costs through criminal or other behavior. Thus, terrorism as well as criminality and revolutionary activities has provided the basis of limiting entry into a country. This reasoning has been applied to wartime enemies, as well as to residents and citizens of specific foreign extraction; as noted above, attempts to limit the transportation of convicts provide further examples.[31] Both the thirteen colonies and, later, Australia attempted to restrict convict immigration, once the settlement of non-convicts exceeded a certain density and the free populations were able to exert political pressure. Residents argued for the shipments to be transferred to newer areas, presently less densely settled, where the convict and non-convict populations could be better separated, the convicts more easily controlled, or both. A third argument for immigration restriction is based less on specific individual characteristics than on fear either of lowering wage rates or of increasing unemployment in the host country, due to cyclical or secular factors. Restrictions have been based on total number of laborers or else, given what is known about the patterns of wage change and unemployment, on numbers of specific occupations, skill levels, or educational achievement.

Rising restrictions on immigration have also come by laws regarding the numbers and nature of those allowed in, laws influencing the financial and other costs of transportation and entry, and laws relating to the rights of immigrants after arrival and settlement. The latter, in particular, have an impact upon the benefits after migration. Large-scale constraints on the numbers of immigrants allowed is a twentieth-century phenomenon, while laws regarding the characteristics of immigrants to be excluded have been more widespread and have existed for a longer time. The differential rates of national economic growth in the nineteenth and twentieth centuries have greatly increased the extent of inequality in income and wealth among nations, while tending, until recently, to lower the magnitude of national inequality within, at least, developed nations. Hence the increased desire in less-developed nations to emigrate, but the increased desire by those in developed nations to restrict inmigration.

Regulations purporting to control health and safety in the shipping of immigrants have also had a significant influence on migration. Laws regarding ship conditions which regulated free immigrants were introduced in the nineteenth century, after earlier regulation of slave ships and ships carrying indentured servants. There was an awareness that introducing regulations would raise the cost of shipping people, as well as reduce the numbers carried, and that regulation would serve to limit emigration.[32] Laws also provided for the regulation of fees, and, more importantly, the vessel's health and safety conditions. Health regulations might raise the costs of travel but, in addition, increase the desire to travel insofar as they were symptomatic of improved conditions, in transit and in the receiving areas. Thus the net effects of these provisions are uncertain. Another policy that raised costs of migration, this time in the transatlantic slave trade, was the use of British naval squadrons to suppress what had been declared an illegal trade. The wedge between New World and African slave prices indicated the increase in costs due to the attempts to force an end to the slave trade. Nevertheless, even if the slave trade could not be stopped, once slavery was not legally enforced in countries of arrivals, involuntary African migration drew to a close.

Passage costs for immigrants could be paid for by different parties, with quite different implications for the immigration decision. Fares could be met by the government of the area of departure (a subsidy for emigration), by the government of arrival (a subsidy for immigration), by third parties with some interest in the laborer or slave after arrival, by credits allowed to the migrant for which the legal system permitted effective enforcement, or by the migrants themselves. Indentured labor was a system of international movement for which an exchange of transportation costs for future labor time was permitted, and it was necessarily enforced at the location where work was performed. If, however, the repayment in the form of labor time worked was no longer enforceable by law, as happened in the United States in the 1820s, the system would no longer be practical and the number of migrants subject to such controls would decline. In some cases, there was an attempt to discourage immigration by a cash or capital requirement for entry, or else payment of an entry bond, in the form of cash or other assets, to offset possible costs to the public of immigrant misbehavior.

Control over the terms of settlement, which influence the desirability of migration, poses a broad range of significant issues, not only for immigration but also for understanding the policy goals of the government. Immigration might be anticipated to be permanent or temporary. The recent cases of guest workers and braceros, and the cases of indentured servants in the nineteenth century, represented contracts for a limited duration of time, with no possibility of the migrant receiving permanent citizenship. In some cases, limits were placed on time allowed in the country of immigration, under threat of punishment or expulsion. The return of non-permanent laborers might be paid for by the country of immigration, as part of the contracted arrangement, an arrangement which characterized late nineteenth-century indentured servitude; or if they failed to meet the legal requirements, the return migrants might have the individual responsibility.

The provision of subsidies took a variety of forms, depending upon the type of labor desired from migrants. Subsidies were in the form either of free or of reduced cost for passage or of particular benefits offered after arrival, such as exemptions from taxes or military service. More specific forms of subsidy, in the interests of obtaining agricultural labor, would include free provision of land or equipment to those settling on the land, or both, although a period of time of residence was frequently a condition for full transfer of the title to the asset. Such subsidies were utilized in late nineteenth-century Latin America in the attempts to induce migration of European labor. The importance of the links between land policy and immigration policy can be seen in the variety of different policies utilized. Some nations provided land free to immigrants to encourage newcomers, while land was also given to those responsible for bringing in migrants. Others tried to restrain immigrants from purchasing land, as a means of forcing them to become laborers. The success of such policies depended on the specifics of the crops grown and the land-labor ratios.

The most complex of the means of raising the costs of immigration relate to the terms under which immigrants are permitted to achieve the same legal rights as those native-born residents. Even if legal equality were to be achieved after some time, this, of course, did not necessarily mean that immigrants would achieve full equality with the native-born given public attitudes regarding race and ethnicity, as well as the time required for immigrants to raise their skills and wealth to that of the native-born. Nevertheless, it is the income relative to that in the country of origin that is critical for the migrant's decision. The time required to achieve citizenship has varied considerably, as have the rights allowed immigrants prior to becoming naturalized citizens. From the early colonial period, it was recognized that liberal naturalization terms usually granted to people with desired characteristics could serve as a major encouragement to immigration. Although not all migrants stayed and became citizens—rates of return migration were frequently high—the availability of an opportunity to become a citizen was often desired by migrants, even if it meant renouncing previous citizenship.[33] Restrictions on the ability to vote in elections at various levels of government and on the rights to receive public service benefits, welfare benefits, and public education have long been, and remain, sources of political controversy, as have various limitations on rights to own land and other forms of capital.[34] Limited rights granted to migrants meant that migrants were more likely to be deported for violations of public laws or social norms, adding further uncertainty to the migration process.

Limitations on locations where migrants could reside have been frequently discussed, but less frequently implemented. Such provisions are often difficult to enforce, although the governments can make violation of such regulations costly to the migrants, by deportation or forced relocation. Limitations on location do, however, have a long history for movements within nations. As noted, the British Poor Laws were intended to provide a deterrent to internal migration, by enforcing minimum length of settlement and requiring return (forcibly if necessary) to parish of prior settlement for those seeking relief.[35]

It is clear that the nature of immigration restrictions can take a number of quite different forms, as is also true of encouragements to immigration. Governments have been rather resourceful in selecting from among those encouragements and deterrents, using those that can most effectively achieve their desired ends, so that no simple statement of immigration policy can adequately describe the full range of its subtlety. It does seem clear, however, that most countries greatly increased their controls over immigration in the twentieth century, whether they had earlier encouraged or only permitted immigration. The twentieth-century attitudes to immigration were quite distinct from those of the nineteenth century, and these will no doubt persist into the future.

≺ IV ≻

Issues of Enforcement

In the previous sections I discussed the types of laws imposed by different nations upon immigration and emigration. A study of laws is important for describing beliefs about appropriate policies that people wish to have implemented, but, obviously, laws by themselves do not guarantee that the desired outcome will be obtained. For that it is necessary not only that laws be clear and unambiguous, but also that they be obeyed, whether voluntarily or not. Problems of interpretation, administration, and enforcement can provide loopholes through which actual immigration and emigration may exceed or fall short of desired magnitudes, as well as allow for different types of desired migrants. Thus, for example, much of the current discussion concerning asylum is based on administrative decisions made in the absence of clear legislation. In the past, the specific definition of literacy and the forms of the literacy tests in many nations left a degree of flexibility to bureaucrats to determine what precisely was meant by literacy, with the result that migration decisions were often made on a somewhat arbitrary basis.

The nature of enforcement needs is influenced by various geographical factors, such as the extent of seacoast and of the natural terrain around land borders. Costs for personnel and equipment influence the number of illegal entrants, while expenditures for search and the specifics of court decisions will also help to determine and to locate the numbers of those who have overstayed their allowed time in the country. Controls may require the use of identification procedures for immigrants, worksite verification for foreign laborers, and the establishment of legal procedures of deportation.[36]

Illegal immigration will also be affected by governmental decisions as to the magnitude and deployment of border controls to limit the extent of illegal entry, as well as by the resources devoted to seeking out (and deporting) those entrants whose visas have expired. The ability to prevent or restrict immigration may also be dependent upon relative degrees of military power. In discussing the settlement of the Americas or the movement into the Russian frontier, for example, what some might regard as an invasion and conquest could be seen by others as a large-scale immigration, with colonization of the vacant lands by the newcomers.[37] In many cases, colonization was basically the outcome of military conquest (as with the Spanish in the Americas). In other cases, however, it meant settlements, with some military component, upon lands not previously used intensively by a resident population that was too small in number to control the overall region (as was the case for the thirteen colonies, Australia, and Russia). Presumably a better ability to defend borders and to otherwise deter foreign colonists could have radically reduced the extent of immigration. If, for example, aborigines or Native Americans had been able to deter Europeans more successfully, historical patterns of migration would have been quite different. Such an ability could have had more dramatic impacts on international movements than any legislation regarding sending or receiving population. While the more familiar cases of international migration might thus seem less dramatic, these differences do serve as a reminder of the fundamental impact of differences in economic power upon international movements.

≺ V ≻

Conclusion

In summary, controls over migration have a long history but have become considerably more widespread and complex in recent years. Their broad nature suggests nations have used them to pursue a wide variety of economic, political, and cultural ends. These have included the improvement of the general welfare of the population, but also more specifically changing the distribution of income and political power and achieving greater equity in the treatment of the lower-income and less-skilled parts of the population, a group that is frequently opposed to immigration. While generalization is difficult, it would seem that fewer legal restrictions existed in the nineteenth century, and that with the reductions of the cost of international transport population movements increased in step with growing movement of goods and capital. Third-world countries participated as sources of emigration and immigration, as did the more developed nations. In the twentieth century, however, most nations introduced much wider restraints upon migrations and, for the first time, these included tight restrictions on magnitudes, either overall, or in some cases, from specific nations or of specific groups.

Stronger controls over immigration were only one among the many dramatic twentieth-century changes in the size and role of national governments. The broadening of the franchise in many countries gave more voice to groups who preferred to limit migration, while increases in income made for more effective lobbying by such groups. Thus, increased political equality within the nation may have served to widen international differences by limiting opportunities to move from lower- to higher-income countries. Changes in factor proportions and technology influenced the benefits and costs of migration policy as well as bringing about shifts in the source and recipient countries for migration flows. The United States, for example, has shifted from being a recipient of migrants mainly from Europe to a nation receiving more immigrants, legal and illegal, from elsewhere in the Americas and from Asia. Australia, long a recipient of migrants from only European nations, particularly Great Britain, now receives most of its immigrants from Asia. The shift from European migration in these and other cases has also been accompanied by a more favorable treatment, legally, economically, and politically, of the original Native American or aboriginal population of these areas. Thus, in regard to the existing national polity, the original settlers have come to be regarded as similar to immigrants in their claims to expansion of their citizenship and voting rights.[38]

While we have focused upon immigration policy, often regarded by workers and others as a way to limit competition for employment, this should not be reviewed in isolation. Tariff policy is an alternative way of reducing job competition, reducing imports produced by foreign labor. It is not surprising that in the twentieth century concern with higher tariffs and concern with limiting immigration were expressed at the same time, by the same groups, thus reflecting the broader set of social concerns that usually lies behind such policies. A "fortress nation" can be achieved either by keeping out goods or by keeping out people.

Nevertheless, it is not surprising that the mixtures of trade and immigration restrictions were also a characteristic of the nineteenth century, as were frequent discussions of the impact of migration on both sending and receiving countries.[39] As free migration to higher-income nations and regions increased, the liberalization of the nineteenth and early twentieth centuries also led to perceived improvement in the institutional terms of migration, and the flow of indentured labor and of slavery came to an abrupt end. These changes may, however, have reduced the volume of international migration at least for a time, a result also achieved by rising restrictions on free immigration after the start of the twentieth century.

The Epidemiology of Migration

PHILIP D. CURTIN

MANY NATURAL CONDITIONS have limited the human freedom to move from one part of the world to another. The land bridge across the present Bering Straits made possible the peopling of the Americas, but only briefly. The Americas were again isolated until the seafarers like the Inuit and the Norse began to use northern routes of entry from east and west, and the isolation was not definitively ended until the Columbian breakthrough across the Atlantic. But transportation was not the only physical limitation on movement. The geography of disease and human immunities to disease has also been an important background factor, even when it was not clearly understood.

≺ I ≻

Disease and Migration

It is generally recognized that migration almost always exacts a price in increased morbidity and mortality from disease. That price was much higher in centuries past than it is today, but it is still with us in attenuated form. The price in increased death and disease could be exacted in various ways—from the migrants, from the receiving society, or from both. The high death rate of Europeans moving to the tropics is a well-known instance of the price paid by the migrants. The death of the American Indians from exotic diseases is the best known and most spectacular instance of damage to the receiving society. The precise extent of the die-off is subject to continuing controversy, but we know that the American Indian population in the region of most intense contact dropped by at least half within a century.

Nor is the phenomenon confined to movement over distances we customarily think of as migration. Most urban centers before the late nineteenth century had higher death rates than birth rates.[1] Cities drew in and literally consumed people, although the combination of causes for the consumption is not precisely known. They were crowded and unsanitary, which alone could bring about an increase in death rates. Enough evidence exists to suppose that urban people who survived childhood had developed some degree of immunity to the diseases of urban life. The death rates of people newly arrived from the countryside, presumably having less childhood acquaintance with disease and lower level of immunity, were probably substantially higher. It is useless, however, even to guess at the possible rate of net natural decrease of long-term residents as opposed to that of newcomers.

As early as the sixteenth century, Europeans were conscious of the increased morbidity and mortality from disease among their own people who went overseas. Over the centuries, a considerable medical literature came into existence dealing with the problem of the encounter with strange "climates." The increase in disease and death was clear, but the cause was not very well understood. The early explanations, however, were logical enough, given the evidence at hand: differential mortality was associated with the most obvious differences in physical appearance. Physical appearance is undoubtedly inherited; it was therefore natural to assume that the different responses to disease were also inherited, and the different response to disease was put down to race.

We now know better, but over the centuries the perceived difference in susceptibility to disease became one of the most important supports of pseudo-scientific racism. From the late eighteenth century on through the nineteenth century, European thought about race difference shifted from an expression of ordinary xenophobic prejudice into a doctrine of European racial superiority. This pseudo-scientific racism is pseudo-science only in retrospect; at the time, it had the support of many of the best biological scientists of the age.

In the past, xenophobic prejudice had run counter to another European tradition, that Christian salvation was open to all humankind, regardless of wealth, poverty, or differences in the way of life. Though cultural diversity, levels of intelligence, and the possibility of salvation could be debated, by the nineteenth century Europeans came to recognize that their own kind in Africa died out at spectacular rates, while the Africans were apparently immune. In much of the Americas, on the other hand, the Indians died out, while European immigrants flourished. The debates about race followed many byways, but the point on which all agreed was that races were demonstrably physically different.[2]

We now know that the differences in immunities or lack of immunities to disease are not racial, even when they are inherited, but pseudo-scientific racism lasted far into the twentieth century. Popular racism in the United States still draws support from the assumption that every inherited characteristic is a part of a racial inheritance. Sickle-cell anemia in the United States, for example, is almost entirely confined to the African American community, and many people think of it as part of the African American racial inheritance, but it is not. The sickle-cell trait is indeed inherited, but not by all black people or only by black people. The sickle-cell trait can cause a fatal anemia, but it also carries some protection against falciparum malaria. This advantage encourages its passage on to future generations in regions where falciparum malaria is hyperendemic. At the same time, the incidence of early death from sickle-cell anemia causes the incidence of the sickle-cell trait to decline in populations where falciparum malaria is weak or absent. In the United States the sickle-cell trait appears to be racial and associated with African descent, but in West Africa the rate of sickle-cell trait varies enormously from region to region, and the supposed racial connection is no longer apparent.

The association of disease and climate is also an old and persistent error about the epidemiology of migration. If Europeans died at a greater rate in the tropical world than they did at home, the change in climate—an obvious increase in heat and humidity—was held responsible. In time, this association led to a whole body of literature about the geography of disease that came to be called medical topography.[3] Some of these studies covered a particular place with great detail, seeking to explore all relevant aspects of geography and disease; others ranged more broadly. In time, such studies were taken up by encyclopedias of medical science, like the great *Dictionaire encyclopédique des sciences médicales,* which appeared in a hundred volumes between 1864 and 1889 and contained a substantial article on the medical topography of every country for which data were available.

The medical topographers were not altogether mistaken, even though their work was swept into the background by the germ theory of disease. They tended to look for the influence of some miasma that emanated from the soil, where more recent authorities talk about disease environments. Geographical climate, of course, plays a role. Sunlight is a significant factor in many diseases; and the enforced human crowding during northern winters makes it easier for some parasites to find new hosts. Many important vectors, like those that carry malaria and yellow fever, thrive only in certain physical circumstances. As we shall see, these climatic factors lie behind many of the important aspects of the epidemiology of migration. For Europeans moving overseas, a warmer climate lay behind the reduced incidence of tuberculosis, though it increased the danger of malaria. Physical climate, however, worked mainly through its influence on the spread of disease, not on the human body directly.

Current medical theory holds that, for an individual, susceptibility to attack by a particular disease depends on a pattern of immunities that can be partly inherited but are mainly built up through a lifetime experience of disease. Survival after attack by a particular disease normally confers some degree of immunity against future attacks. The extent and duration of that immunity varies greatly from one disease to another. The common cold is actually caused by a variety of different viruses, but the immunity they confer is both brief and variable. Even a mild attack by the yellow fever virus, on the other hand, carries a future immunity that is both complete and lifelong. The immunizing quality of the smallpox virus was also great, and this quality was one key to its extermination. Most diseases fall between yellow fever and the common cold in the degree and duration of the immunity they confer on their victims, but together they produce a general pattern in human populations. Anyone who survives to adulthood acquires a range of immunities to the diseases common to the disease environment of his childhood. What earlier observers identified as the influence of race was really the result of the childhood disease environment. When it comes to the epidemiology of migration, the experience of any group of migrants is a complex result of variables based on at least two disease environments working on the immune system of individuals, and at different times in their life span.

≺ II ≻

The Emergence of Statistical Evidence

The most valuable evidence we have concerning the epidemiology of migration comes from the elaborate and careful statistical study of the health of armies that began in the 1830s and lasted until the eve of World War I. The study arose from a particular intersection in the development of statistics and of military medicine. By the 1830s, social programs of European states had come to depend on quantitative evidence about aspects of early industrial life—involving a vast span of new concerns, from the condition of the poor to the rise of industrial production. As a part of this interest, military medical departments came to be concerned with the health of armies, for humanitarian reasons as well as military efficiency. The germ theory of disease was still far off in the future, but a comparative statistical study of the health of armies seemed to promise a solution to the problems of military doctors. The variables then thought to be important—disease correlated with race and climate—were the point of departure. The earliest studies went beyond simple measures of morbidity and mortality. They tried to identify the diseases responsible, the geographical origin of the soldiers they studied, and the place where they were stationed.

The first careful statistical studies were the work of Henry Marshall, Alexander M. Tulloch, and T. Graham Balfour, doctors in the British army. They began with retrospective statistical studies of British soldiers over the period 1817 to 1836. In 1839, the initial book-length compilation of statistical tables dealt with the health of the army in Britain, North America, and the Mediterranean. Further volumes on Africa, Ceylon, and Burma followed in the next three years. India was not included at this time because it was controlled by the East India Company, which had its own army.[4] Other countries took up the challenge in short order, beginning with the United States which ordered a retrospective study over a similar period.[5] By the 1860s, statistical reporting on the health of the armies began to take the form of an annual report on the health of the British army; and before the end of the century the practice was imitated by the United States, every major European power, and Japan.[6]

The form of these reports tended toward an international standard, reached partly by mutual imitation, partly by international agreement. Each report consisted of statistical tables representing the health of each sizable military or naval unit. Soon added were articles contributed by the principal military doctors interpreting the statistical evidence or reflecting a more intimate experience of a particular problem. The several national series of reports soon developed into an important international forum for discussing the problems of military medicine.

The project as a whole involved an enormous effort of record keeping and publication. The effort seemed worthwhile at the time because the true cause of disease was still unknown. Race and medical topography—the principal variables under consideration—were those emphasized in the medical thought of the time. By the early twentieth century, as the germ theory of disease became more generally accepted, statistical reports were taken less seriously. After about 1909, those of the British army began to decline in coverage and in the care devoted to their production. They continued after World War I but with only a shadow of the attention they had received a half century earlier.

These records, though limited in duration, were far more accurate than most civilian medical records and covered a far larger sample than civilian records of the period. Formal civilian records of the cause of death, even the systematic recording of births and deaths, lagged substantially behind these military statistics. In the United States at this period, only a few states made any effort to keep track of the cause of death, and the reporting was often perfunctory. The military records on the other hand were created by medical men working in a disciplined setting for superiors who thought their reports were important. They were therefore far more accurate and uniform than those of civilian doctors. Because these military reports cover the health of soldiers who stayed at home as well as those sent to serve overseas, they provide a base for measuring the differing morbidity and mortality of the two. They thus have some of the value of experimental evidence.

≺ III ≻

Disease and Migration in the Nineteenth Century: Europeans

These reports can be used to compile tables illustrating the disease cost of migration in two periods—one at the beginning of the period of most valuable statistical record keeping, and the other at its end (tables 1 and 2). Table 1 illustrates the pattern of the period 1817–38. Its figures seem to be in line with the scattered statistical studies made earlier in time, and they measure the situation that existed before the major changes in the decades that followed, often called the mortality revolution. They can be interpreted as an approximate picture of the broad pattern of the disease cost of migration for Europeans back into the eighteenth century, perhaps earlier as well. The central comparison in the table is between the disease death rates of soldiers serving in their home country and those of soldiers sent to serve overseas, measured in deaths per thousand mean strength. The statistical surveys also measure morbidity by the number of hospital admissions per thousand, the proportion repatriated or discharged for medical reasons, and the proportionate number in the hospital at any time—called "constantly sick" in the British records. It would be possible to use any combination of these measures, but the disease death rate per thousand mean strength is the most reliable overall measure of relative health. The percentage difference between these death rates at home and overseas is a broad measure of the disease cost of migration; it can be called the relocation cost for lack of a better term.

The overall pattern is remarkably clear and consistent. The disease death rate for men in European armies stationed in Europe was within a normal range of 15 to 30 per thousand mean strength. When the soldiers were sent overseas, the rate was then normally higher depending on the disease environment of the destination. In a few rare cases, the migrants enjoyed a relocation benefit, notably in some islands in the central or southwest Pacific. This was to persist throughout the nineteenth century.

In a second group of destinations, the relocation costs or benefits were negligible. These included Canada, and presumably the northern United States, though the data do not deal with any actual migration to that destination. The group also includes the Cape Colony in South Africa and certain, but not all, Mediterranean destinations.

TABLE I

Mortality of European Troops Overseas, 1817–38

Region	Nationality of troops	Date of sample	Deaths per thousand	Relocation costs or benefits (percent)
		Pacific Islands		
Tahiti	French	1845–49	9.50	50.01
New Caledonia	French	c. 1848	11.40	21.14
New Zealand	British	1846–55	8.55	44.12
		Europe and North America		
France	French	1820–22 1824–26	20.17	
Great Britain	British	1830–36	15.30	
Northern United States	American	1829–38	15.00	
Canada	British	1817–36	16.10	
		Mediterranean Climate		
Algeria	French	1831–38	78.20	–287.70
Gibraltar	British	1818–36	21.40	–39.87
Malta	British	1817–36	16.30	–6.54
Ionian Islands	British	1817–36	25.20	–64.71
Cape Colony	British	1818–36	15.50	–1.31
		Southern United States and malaria-free islands		
Bermuda	British	1817–36	28.80	–88.24
Southern United States	American	1829–38	34.00	–126.67
Mauritius	British	1818–36	30.50	–99.35
Réunion	French	1819–36	32.12	–59.25
		Southern Asia		
Bombay	British	1830–38	36.99	–141.76
Bengal	British	1830–38	71.41	–366.73
Madras	British	1829–38	48.63	–217.84
Ceylon	British	1817–36	69.80	–356.21
Coastal Burma	British	1829–38	34.60	–126.14
Straits Settlements	British	1829–38	17.70	–15.69
Dutch East Indies	Dutch	1819–28	170.00	–1011.11
		West Indies		
Jamaica	British	1817–39	130.00	–749.67
Windwards and Leewards	British	1817–36	85.00	–455.56
Guadeloupe	French	1819–36	106.87	–429.85
Martinique	French	1819–36	112.18	–456.17
French Guiana	French	1819–36	32.18	–59.54
		Tropical Africa		
Sénegal	French	1819–38	164.66	–716.36
Sierra Leone	British	1819–36	483.00	–3056.86

SOURCE: Reprinted from P. D. Curtin, *Death by Migration: Europe's Encounter with the Tropical World in the Nineteenth Century* (New York, 1989), 7–8.

TABLE 2

Mortality of European Troops Overseas, 1909–13

	Nationality of troops	Dates	Deaths per thousand	Change from table 1 (percent)	Relocation costs or benefits (percent)
		Pacific Islands			
Hawaii	American	1909–13	1.30		50.00
Tahiti*	French	1903–6	2.30	–24.20	20.14
New Caledonia	French	1909–13	2.33	–79.56	19.10
		Europe and North America			
France	French	1909–13	2.88	–85.72	0.00
Great Britain	British	1909–13	2.55	–83.33	0.00
Continental US	American	1904–13	2.60	–82.67	0.00
		Mediterranean			
Algeria and Tunisia	French	1909–13	5.25	–93.29	–82.29
Morocco	French	1909–13	21.99		–663.61
Gibraltar	British	1909–13	2.21	–89.67	13.33
Malta	British	1909–13	2.53	–84.48	0.78
Cyprus	British	1909–13	1.66		34.90
Egypt	British	1909–13	3.97		–55.69
		Formerly malaria-free islands			
Bermuda	British	1909–13	2.21	–92.33	13.33
Mauritius	British	1909–13	4.53	–85.15	–77.65
		Southern Asia			
India	British	1909–13	14.08		–452.31
Ceylon	British	1909–13	5.49	–92.13	–115.29
Straits Settlements	British	1909–13	4.75		–86.27
North China	British	1909–13	5.09		–99.61
Philippines	American	1909–13	3.27		–25.77
South China	British	1909–13	3.81		–49.41
Cochinchina	French	1909–13	8.90		–209.03
Annam/Tonkin	French	1909–13	3.57		–23.96
Dutch East Indies	Dutch	1909–13	6.39	–96.24	–150.44
		West Indies			
Jamaica	British	1909–13	7.76	–71.91	–204.31
French Antilles	French	1909–13	4.93		–71.11
Cuba and Puerto Rico	American	1904–9	3.59		–38.08
		Tropical Africa			
French West Africa	French	1909–13	6.65	–95.96	–131.04
Fr. Equatorial Africa	French	1909–13	5.66		–96.56
Madagascar	French	1909–13	5.67		–96.74
British West Africa	British	1909–13	5.56	–98.85	–118.04
South Africa	British	1909–13	3.84	–75.23	–50.59
Kamerun	German	1901–6	41.12		–1512.63

SOURCE: Reprinted from Curtin, *Death by Migration*, 9–10.

*No troops in Tahiti in 1909–13, but annual average mortality in 1903–6 was 2.3 per thousand.

Many, at some times most, Mediterranean destinations fell into a third category in which relocation costs lay within the range of about 50 to 150 percent. This third group also would include Bermuda and the southern United States as well as certain islands in the Indian Ocean which had a tropical climate but at this time were free of malaria.

In the tropical world proper, a significant difference appears between the relocation costs for destinations in monsoon Asia, represented here by Ceylon and the three Presidencies of British India, and in the humid tropics on either side of the tropical Atlantic. The relocation costs for monsoon Asia at this period tended to be in the range of 100 to 400 percent. Those of the Caribbean tended to be in the range of 400 to 800 percent. The difference was not simply one of physical climate but one of disease. Among other things, Asia at this period was completely free of yellow fever, one of the most prevalent causes of death for newcomers anywhere in the tropical Atlantic; and the Atlantic shores at this period were free of cholera, one of the principal killers in India.

The West African samples at this period, Senegal and Sierra Leone, were to some degree unrepresentative of the situation common in that region later in the century. The Senegal sample shows a lower death rate than is usual for that region, while the Sierra Leone sample is unrepresentative in the other direction. It reflects the occurrence of epidemic yellow fever, which sporadically attacked European garrisons with devastating effect throughout the century. In this instance, the statistical analyst took pains to add a special note explaining how it was possible for one unit of the Sierra Leone Command to sustain annual losses higher than a thousand deaths per thousand mean strength. Other data scattered through the century confirm the opinion of medical authorities in the early nineteenth century that the disease death rate of European troops in barracks in West Africa could be expected to be about 250 per thousand, giving a normal relocation cost of about 1500 percent. The remarkable difference between Africa and the Caribbean was not principally disease but the vectors available to carry disease. The centuries of the slave trade brought to the Americas almost all pathogens available in tropical Africa. The slave trade failed, however, to carry over the combination of *Anopheles funestus* and *Anopheles gam-*

biae, the most effective vectors for the transmission of malaria found anywhere in the world.

Two figures for Southeast Asia in table 1 are anomalous but significant as a warning of the dangers of interpreting statistics of this kind. The figure for the Straits Settlements is low for that time and place. It represents a very small force which happened to be fortunate in the passage of epidemics. The figure for the Netherlands Indies is far higher than would have been normal for Java, because it includes part of the period of the Java War of 1825–30. This was a hard-fought rebellion against Dutch rule, and soldiers on campaign normally suffer far higher death rates from disease than they suffer in barracks.

By the period 1909–13, represented in table 2, the disease mortality of military migrants from Europe had changed dramatically in some respects, while still reflecting the fact that relocation costs persisted in spite of medical advances of the past century. The truly revolutionary change was the drop in death rates from the levels of 1817–36. The disease death rate of troops in the United States, France, and Great Britain all dropped with remarkable uniformity by 83 to 86 percent. Overseas, however, the disease death rate dropped even more—often by more than 90 percent. The only striking exceptions were scattered territories where the earlier death rates had been low to begin with, or where migrants had enjoyed relocation benefits rather than costs. At first glance, it would be logical to assign the cause of this change to triumphs of modern scientific medicine, marked most dramatically by the germ theory for the transmission of disease, that began to affect medical practice in the 1880s, followed by the discovery of the mosquito vectors of malaria and yellow fever. Later applications of germ theory led to revolutionary changes in sanitary engineering and an effective vaccination against typhoid fever in the decade before World War I.

But the advent of the germ theory was not the only factor at play. It would go far to explain the sharp drop in military mortality in the 1890s onward, but the sharpest drop in absolute death rates took place earlier—in the 1840s to the 1860s—and in Europe as well as overseas. Some medical innovations, like Jennerian smallpox vaccination and the isolation of quinine from cinchona bark, contributed to the decline, but the really important changes came from relatively small empirical improvements like better water supply and ventilation.[7]

The most unexpected showing in table 2, however, is the final column. In spite of the enormous change in mortality levels, the relocation costs continued at a substantial level, frequently in the range of 100 to 500 percent. Some additional territories now joined those with relocation benefits, but the pattern of substantial relocation cost for movement into the tropical world remained unchanged. By this time, however, the disease cost of sending troops overseas was no longer a serious concern. A rise in death rate from three to six per thousand would be a 100 percent increase, but an absolute loss of three additional men per thousand appeared to be tolerable. Even today, the probable relocation cost of movement from Europe to West Africa is in the vicinity of 100 percent, but the actual death rates are so low they attract no special attention.

≺ IV ≻

The Disease Cost of Movement in the Nineteenth Century: Non-Europeans

For non-Europeans, patterns of relocation cost existed as well. The evidence is not as good as that for the movement of Europeans, but the British army often kept track of the health of non-European recruits by place of origin and place of service. At some periods, the British recruited Africans for service in the Caribbean; at others, they recruited Afro-Caribbeans for service in Africa. The records for these troops make it possible to measure the disease cost of migration in either direction across the tropical Atlantic.

The introduction of Africa into the picture introduces another variable that is less important in Europe or in many parts of Asia. The nature of a disease environment over a large region will vary with the degree of intercommunication. Intense intercommunication tends to spread disease widely. People who have lots of contact with others, especially in childhood, tend to be infected with a wide range of diseases and hence to acquire a diverse pattern of immunity. Attention was first drawn to this phenomenon in the United States during World War I, when recruits from rural areas suffered more from disease after they entered the army than city boys did. This pattern was puzzling at first because farm boys were thought to have led a more healthy life. They had indeed been more healthy, and their immunities suffered. After they entered the army, they tended to come down with the diseases they had missed in their healthy childhood.

In Africa, the differences among childhood disease environments were much greater because intercommunication was less intense than it was in other places. In Europe, for example, by the seventeenth century, smallpox was virtually a childhood disease, so that many or even most adults had a life-long immunity. Epidemics affecting large segments of the adult population were rare. In much of tropical Africa, on the other hand, many people led isolated lives and often escaped childhood infection, so that a population of largely non-immune adults could come into existence. Such a population was susceptible to a sweeping smallpox epidemic that occasionally killed as many as 20 percent of the population.[8]

The relative isolation of African disease environments probably accounts for much of the very high mortality on slaving voyages between Africa and the tropical Americas. The African passengers were often drawn from a variety of different disease environments. As a result, the shipboard mixture of diseases was new in some respects to almost everyone. The European crew of slave ships had even less immunity to the diseases of tropical Africa, and their death rates were normally higher than those of the slaves in transit. Slaving voyages therefore had higher death rates, for passengers and crew alike, than any other long-distance voyages we know of in the eighteenth or nineteenth century.

The epidemiology of long-distance travel at sea, including the slave trade, is a separate problem from the epidemiology of migration, though migration inevitably includes travel as its first phase. Putting people together on a ship or caravan frequently exposed them to new diseases their immune systems were unprepared to contend with. The shipboard disease experience had an obvious influence on the subsequent health of migrants once they reached their destination; but that relationship has not yet been systematically studied, and data to carry such studies beyond the anecdotal level may not be available.

Between 1816 and 1836, most Africans recruited into the British army were originally from the eastern part of the Guinea coast, the Bights of Benin and Biafra. Their annual mortality there can be assumed to have been no more than that of African soldiers serving on the Gold Coast, or around 20 per thousand mean strength per annum. Those serving in the Sierra Leone Command further west, and hence further from home, died at about 30 per thousand, or with a relocation cost of about 50 percent. Those sent to serve in the Caribbean had a still higher death rate and a relocation cost of about 100 percent.[9] The mortality cost of movement within Africa was merely doubled by the further move across the Atlantic. Since, by this time, the diseases of the Caribbean were largely imported from Africa, Africans suffered less than Europeans in the tropical American environment.

Later in the century, the French navy experimented with the transport of workers and sometimes soldiers from one part of Africa to another. In the construction of the Senegal railroads in the 1880s, imported workers from Morocco sustained very heavy losses in a period of yellow fever epidemics. Kru people from present-day Liberia, also imported for the railroad construction, had losses of about 140 per thousand per annum, which would imply a relocation cost of 500 percent or more. The death rates of Kru moving eastward to Gabon, however, were about those expected in their home territory.[10]

The Dutch also systematically recruited soldiers in Africa, often by purchase in the hinterland of their trading posts on the Gold Coast. The army of the Netherlands Indies was separate from the Dutch army; it was recruited partly in Europe (largely in Germany), partly in Africa, and partly in Southeast Asian islands other than Java. Thus the army serving on Java was made up of immigrants from somewhere else. No one has yet studied the health of this army systematically through the century, and the existing data give no secure information about mortality rates in the several home countries. A normal disease death rate for healthy men of military age in any of their home countries, however, could be assumed to have been between about 15 and 30 per thousand. For the Netherlands Indies army over the period 1839–53, the published report shows European deaths per thousand at 74.1, African at 89.35, and islanders at 42.27.[11] It is significant that all three had death rates high enough to imply a relocation cost of 100 percent or more. It may appear strange that the African death rate at this period was higher than the European, given the fact that Africa was also a tropical region that might have had a similar disease environment. Similar data from the Netherlands Indies later in the century, however, reflect a pattern of European and African troops having similar disease death rates, at higher rates than those from nearby islands.

The movement of African American migrants eastward across the Atlantic also entailed relocation costs, because the return migrants had lost much if not all of their ancestors' immunities to the African disease environment. Good records of a significant number of African American settlers of Liberia between 1820 and 1843 show annual death rates of between 60 and 90 per thousand per annum, which would imply a relocation cost in the vicinity of 300 to 500 percent.[12] This same pattern emerged with troops recruited in the Caribbean for duty in Africa. On the much publicized British march on Kumasi in 1874, the proportional losses from disease among the West Indian troops were only slightly less than those of the Europeans. This small difference could be a result of some holdover of inherited immunity, or it could be a result of the fact that the West Indians had already served in Africa for several months, while the European force used on this expedition was fresh from Britain.

The available data on movement within and from monsoon Asia are based mainly on the records of supervised, indentured migration, principally from India. This migration involved more than three million people leaving India between about 1860 and 1920. The pattern of relocation costs was similar to that of movement from Europe to destinations with a similar disease environment. The relocation cost of Indian migration to Caribbean and Pacific islands was rarely as high as 100 percent, and it seems to have fallen during the second half of the nineteenth century. Indentured immigration from India to Natal at some periods even brought relocation benefits, similar to European benefits on migration to some Pacific islands. Indian indentured migration to Malaya and the Assam tea plantations on the other hand yielded relocation costs of well over 100 percent.[13] The African pattern of relatively high disease costs of migration owing to the relative isolation of their home disease environments was reproduced in some Pacific Islands. In Fiji, workers from nearby islands had a relocation cost of about 500 percent, compared with that of Indian immigrants at less than 100 percent.[14]

≺ V ≻

Acclimatization

From the early centuries of European movement overseas, observers noted that Europeans in a new environment tended to become ill early in their stay. This first attack came to be called a seasoning sickness, and those who recovered were thought of as seasoned or relatively immune to further attack. These observations led to an early and persistent belief that migration to a new climate carried with it increased morbidity and mortality, but that these costs would diminish over time. The seasoned individual was said to have been acclimatized. Investigation of the process led to a considerable literature on acclimatization—a literature which grew in the nineteenth century and spread far beyond human epidemiology, to environmental sciences generally. This development grew from increased European activity in other parts of the world, but also gained from the growing recognition of the biological sciences, epitomized by the reputation of Charles Darwin.[15]

Acclimatization studies had practical implications for European imperial policy. If acclimatization were a regular biological process, then Europeans could settle anywhere. Otherwise, some regions overseas were "white man's country," and others were emphatically not. European opinion favored some places at some periods and feared them at others. When in the 1840s, French doctors debated the possibility of European settlement in Algeria, Jean Christian Boudin was the most prominent medical spokesman in the opposition, on the grounds that a healthy life for Europeans in Algeria was, and would remain, impossible. His case was well founded on the evidence available, but an effective campaign against malaria and other North African diseases brought a decisive change of opinion by the 1870s.[16]

Even if true acclimatization were impossible, it was thought possible to mitigate the consequences of observed relocation costs by appropriate policies for disease prevention and control. Many discussions of possible ways to protect troops in the tropical world turned on the idea of seasoning. One possibility was to send troops first to a tropical environment that was only moderately dangerous for a period of seasoning, then send them on to one known to be more deadly. They could be sent, for example, to the relatively benign Mascarene Islands for a period, before being posted to coastal Madagascar. The idea was attractive, and it agreed with what was then known about immunization through vaccination against smallpox. The experiments nevertheless failed more often than not.

In the 1890s and on into the new century, the British army reoriented some of its statistical studies to focus on the seasoning of troops sent to India, Egypt, and the Caribbean. Investigators measured the incidence of hospital admissions, deaths, and repatriations for medical reasons against each soldier's age and length of service in that particular area. The results were inconclusive, showing only insignificant changes over a five-year period.[17] The original expectation was correct in theory, because victims of disease *do* develop a degree of immunity against further attack. The most important immunities, however, are those acquired in childhood, and they would rarely be substantially changed in a young adult during a five-year period like that of the army's studies.

The degree and kind of immunity acquired is also highly variable, depending on the parasite involved. Measles and other childhood diseases are often relatively benign in childhood, but become more serious for adults; and they normally confer lifelong immunity. Smallpox was not benign even in childhood, but the immunity following a first attack was lifelong. Another virus, yellow fever, is often so benign in children that it shows no clinical symptoms, yet it too confers lifelong immunity. For adults, the case-fatality rate for yellow fever could exceed 50 percent. Falciparum malaria, the most important killing disease in the tropical world, however, conferred no true immunity. Children born in regions where falciparum malaria is strongly endemic are infected early in life and fight a life-and-death battle with the disease for the first five years or so. If they survive, they are infested with the parasite, but their immune system can keep it under control so that they will normally have no clinical symptoms. Typhoid fever, cholera, and the range of serious gastrointestinal diseases are somewhat immunizing, but not to the degree of childhood diseases, smallpox, or yellow fever. Even after the effective vaccination against typhoid fever, the disease could override the immunization if the infective dose were large enough.

≺ VI ≻

Disease Profiles

Even without the relative precision of the nineteenth-century military data, the fact of relocation costs and their general level have been clear for some time. To know what diseases were responsible, and to what extent, it is necessary to compare the major causes of death among the migrants at their destination with the causes of death of equivalent people who stayed home. By providing contrasting statistical pictures of the health of troops at home and abroad, the military surveys provide this information—the equivalent of experimental evidence. This evidence can be assessed in several different ways, one of which is represented by tables 1 and 2. Another measure can be called the disease profile of relocation costs. An ordinary disease profile of a population assigns to each major disease group its percentage of responsibility for morbidity, mortality, or some other indicator. A disease profile of relocation costs is similar, but it assigns to each disease group its percentage of responsibility for the relocation cost, regardless of the importance of that disease to the overall death rate of people in the society of origin or the overall death rate of the migrants at their destination. Table 3 surveys the disease profile of relocation cost of the movement from Europe to three significant areas overseas—one in North Africa, one in the tropical Americas, and one in monsoon Asia.

Comparable data are not available for precisely the same years in the cases of Algeria, the British Caribbean, and India, but five or more years from each decade are taken to represent health conditions during the decade as a whole. The table thus presents a comparative view of the disease profile of relocation costs to these three destinations over the six decades from the 1860s to the pre-war quinquennium. The time period is significant because it includes the last decades before new medical advances of the kind pioneered by Koch and Pasteur became available. At the final period, 1909–13, the germ theory of disease had been broadly accepted by European medicine and was being incorporated into medical practice in European armies. This period was therefore one of dramatic decreases in deaths for all causes; changes are reflected in tables 1 and 2.

These disease profiles of relocation cost serve to highlight several aspects of the epidemiology of migration. One is the fact that migra-

TABLE 3

Disease Profile of Relocation Costs Between Europe and Select Destinations, 1860s to 1910s

French Algeria

	1860s	1870s	1880s	1890s	1900s	1909–13	Avg. all columns
Malaria	55	63	60	18	19	18	39
Tuberculosis	–12	9	–8	0	0	–2	–2
Typhoid	15	3	0	64	71	65	36
Digestive diseases	34	20	31	10	5	16	19
Respiratory diseases	3	–2	–13	5	3	8	1
Other	5	7	30	3	3	–6	7
Total	100	100	100	100	100	100	100

Britain—West Indies

	1859–67	1869–77	1879–84	1886–94	1895–1904	1909–13	Avg. all columns
Malaria	43	42	25	26	37	29	34
Yellow fever	46	95	68	19	39	0	44
Tuberculosis	–21	–34	–10	–20	3	5	–13
Typhoid	15	61	10	70	17	18	32
Venereal disease	–1	–9	0	4	n.a.	10	1
Nervous disease	14	17	1	1	–3	–3	5
Digestive system	6	6	9	–2	5	7	5
Respiratory system	–12	–45	–1	–18	–18	2	–15
Circulatory system	–3	–18	1	2	0	14	–1
Other	14	–15	–2	17	19	19	8
Total	100	100	100	100	100	100	100

Britain—Madras (through 1880s): India (1890s onward)

	1860–67	1869–77	1879–84	1886–94	1895–1904	1909–13	Avg. all columns
Malaria	6	4	5	8	6	10	7
Tuberculosis	–8	–9	–24	–1	2	–1	–7
Cholera	24	16	22	11	6	7	14
Typhoid	7	13	27	54	56	31	31
Kala Azar						7	7
Venereal disease	2	0	1	1	n.a.	2	1
Nervous system	7	14	17	0	1	1	7
Circulatory system	3	5	0	0	3	2	2
Digestive system	55	62	55	24	24	40	43
Respiratory system	–6	–8	–18	–4	–2	–2	–7
Other	10	4	14	8	5	3	7
Total	100	100	100	100	100	100	100

SOURCE: Curtin, *Death by Migration*, 102–3.

NOTE: n.a.—not available. Typhoid listing for the 1860s and 1870s includes other "continued fevers." Pneumonia, where listed separately, is combined with "respiratory diseases." Dysentery and diarrhea are combined with "diseases of the digestive system."

tion, in the case of some diseases, led systematically to relocation benefits, a factor disguised somewhat by the combined totals for all disease in tables 1 and 2. Some of these negative relocation costs appear in almost every sampled decade represented in table 3. These negative relocation costs are most dramatic for the West Indies in the 1870s, though negative relocation costs from tuberculosis and diseases of the respiratory system were more than balanced by spectacular death rates from malaria, yellow fever, and typhoid fever. For all three sample destinations, and over the six decades, a reduced death rate from tuberculosis was a significant counter to the otherwise dominant pattern of increased deaths following migration.

Perhaps the most striking aspect of the data in table 3 is the great difference between the diseases that account for the major relocation cost in the three areas. Yellow fever, which accounted for 44 percent of the relocation cost to the Caribbean, does not occur at all in the other two regions, and cholera was significant only in India. There, other diseases of the digestive system, mainly forms of dysentery, accounted in some decades for more than half of the relocation cost. Even in the pre-war period, 1909–13, they accounted for 40 percent at a time when European medicine knew perfectly well what pure water was and how to purify it. By contrast, the same disease group accounted overall for only 5 percent of the relocation cost to the Caribbean, and in some decades showed an actual improvement over the death rates from this cause common to soldiers in Europe. The relocation costs to Algeria show another kind of pattern. From the 1860s through the 1880s, malaria accounted for more than half the cost of migration. In the 1890s and after, typhoid fever took its place. In the first period the role of malaria was the most serious in any of the three destinations, in the second the cost of typhoid fever was the highest found in any of the three.

These striking differences can often be explained by reference to the disease history of particular places, or the changing patterns of European and overseas medical knowledge and practice. But the point here is that the broad and fairly uniform patterns illustrated by the data in tables 1 and 2 are actually the sum of far more diverse relations between humans and their parasites in an ecosystem common to them both.[18]

I have explored elsewhere the epidemiology of the African movement across the tropical Atlantic in both directions.[19] Data of the

TABLE 4
Disease Death Rates for African Troops in Sierra Leone and the West Indies, 1817–36
(deaths per thousand)

	Sierra Leone	West Indies	Relocation cost
Fevers	2.4	4.6	91.7
Eruptive fevers	6.9	2.5	–63.8
Diseases of lungs	6.3	16.5	161.9
Diseases of the liver	1.1	0.9	–18.2
Stomach and bowels	5.3	7.4	39.6
Diseases of the brain	1.6	2.2	37.5
Dropsies	0.3	2.1	600.0
Total death rate from disease	23.9	36.2	51.5

SOURCE: British Parliamentary Papers, 1837–38 xl(123), 11–12; 1840, xxx[C.288], 16.

quality represented in table 3, however, are not available for migrations by non-Europeans, and a similar table of disease profiles of relocation costs would be more deceptive than helpful. In the African instance, a comparison with the European data is complicated by the small size of the West Indian force in Africa and the fact that it was so frequently on campaign. The most reliable data for African movement to the Caribbean are also for the earliest period for which we have any data at all, 1817–36. This was a period of comparative peace in the Caribbean, though the data were reported with less detail and precision than those collected later in the century.

In reading table 4, it is important to remember that the troops stationed in the Sierra Leone Command were themselves immigrants who had passed their childhood further east. The diseases listed also need translation into more recent categories. Fevers for Africans at this time and place would be almost entirely falciparum malaria, with some typhoid fever. Most Africans had an acquired immunity to yellow fever, so that disease was not significant. The eruptive fevers would be almost entirely smallpox. Diseases of the lungs would include both pneumonia and tuberculosis, which were comparatively rare in Africa, leaving African soldiers with only a weak immunity at best. Medical men throughout the Americas commonly noted an African susceptibility to infections of this type, and this weakness no doubt accounts for the overwhelming role of diseases in this category in the relocation cost of movement to the Americas. By 1859–63, when soldiers of African descent born in the West Indies began to come into the army, however, their death rate from this cause had dropped to 2.69 per thousand and it continued dropping steeply for the rest of the century.[20] The dropsies in the table would be mainly heart disease, and the high relocation cost from this disease is best interpreted as a statistical fluke, which does not recur at later periods.

≺ VII ≻

Epidemiology and the Major Streams of Nineteenth-Century Migration

The picture of the epidemiology of migration that has emerged in the past ten years or so gives a statistical outline based on the systematic collection of data by European armies in the last half of the nineteenth century, but it is far from complete. The data cover only selected parts of the world; and the general pattern has to be rounded out far more speculatively on the basis of only scattered evidence. For the enormous North Atlantic migration of the past two centuries, the relocation cost was almost certainly lower than that sustained by Europeans bound for the tropical world. The British military mortality data for 1817–36 show that the military death rate from disease was almost the same in Britain and Canada, and American surveys show similar death rates for American troops stationed in the northern United States (table 1). The rate was roughly twice as high for American troops stationed in the South, and the Surgeon General's annual reports on the health of the army later in the century show considerable differences for troops stationed in different parts of the United States. A few sample studies of the health of immigrants also indicate the strong possibility of a significant relocation cost after landing.[21] Taken together, this scattered evidence warrants a guess that the relocation cost for European migrants crossing the North Atlantic was small, but present most of the time.

The annual reports on the health of European armies within Europe show local variations that have not been systematically studied so far, nor have the disease consequences of the westward movement by land in North America, or the eastward movement overland in northern Asia. While anecdotal evidence in the travel literature suggests that overland relocation costs sometimes may have been significant, the question must remain open until historians explore the possibility of using the annual reports of the American Surgeon General and the equivalent publication of the Russian army.

The other major stream of migration of the past two centuries was that of Chinese from south China to the Americas, the Pacific Islands, Australia, and especially Southeast Asia. The region of origin within China is significant, because north China and south China had somewhat different disease environments in the nineteenth century. The British army medical authorities recognized this difference and made a separate accounting for the health of British and of Indian troops stationed in those two regions of China. The difference in disease environment between south China and Southeast Asia could have been so slight that the relocation cost was no greater than for the move westward across the north Atlantic. On the other hand, some segments of the coolie trade from China have attracted special attention from historians for their high morbidity and high mortality. In the Americas, Cuba and Peru have been most notorious for the early death of migrants, and they were the principal destinations of coerced Chinese migrants to the tropical Americas. The enslaved Africans in Cuba had not yet been emancipated when the bulk of the Chinese arrived, and the Chinese diet and working conditions were little different from those of the slaves. Indentured Chinese in Peru were also overworked and underfed, and their mortality rate was a public scandal, but, at this distance in time, it is impossible to say how many deaths came from ill treatment and how many came from the fact of entrance into a new disease environment.[22]

Migration normally, but not always, exacts a cost from the migrants in the form of increased morbidity and mortality, but the cost is highly variable. At some times and places it was a negligible part of the broader disease experience. At other times, it can be seen as a major environmental influence on the course of human history.

≺ 4 ≻

The Differential Cultural Impact of Free and Coerced Migration to Colonial America

LORENA S. WALSH

THE EARLY MODERN Atlantic world dealt very different hands to Africans and Europeans. The circumstances that shaped the entry of the two groups into movement across the ocean, their shipboard experiences, and above all the rights they and their descendants could claim after their arrival in the New World differed so dramatically that any attempt to compare coerced with free migrations might appear doomed. Historians, except perhaps for historical demographers, certainly appear to have thought so: few have attempted to bridge the scholarship carried out on the two groups. Yet there are substantial potential benefits from making the attempt, especially in the Chesapeake colonies where Old World settlers included a mix of free, indentured, and enslaved migrants. Rather than treating European and African migrations as entirely separate movements, this chapter explores possible similarities as well as the patently obvious differences. Specifically, it asks how posing some of the same questions frequently asked about European migrants might shed new light on our understanding of the cultural outcomes of forced African migration.

≺ I ≻

The Demography of the Migrant Streams

Unlike the contemporary migrations to New England and to the Middle Colonies, in which most settlers arrived in family groups, the majority of migrants to the Chesapeake region, both free and coerced, were young males.[1] This heavily imbalanced sex ratio had profound implications for social, economic, familial, and material life in early Virginia and Maryland for black and white alike.

Free men, women, and children were always a distinct minority among Chesapeake migrants. In the seventeenth century only about one out of five (roughly 25,000 people) freely chose to emigrate. Much less information is available for the eighteenth century, but it seems likely that between 1700 and 1775, the proportion of free migrants diminished to something closer to one in ten.[2] Scant attention has been paid to sex ratios among free migrants, but one sample for seventeenth-century Maryland yields a proportion among adults of nearly two and a half men for each woman.[3] The imbalance was even greater among emigrating servants, who accounted for at least three quarters of seventeenth-century European migrants (or about 95,000 individuals). Across much of the seventeenth century men servants outnumbered women by three to one, and while the proportion of servant women briefly rose toward the end of the century, the imbalance among emigrant servants never fell below about two and a half men for each woman. English women in particular virtually ceased moving to the Chesapeake; from 1718 to 1775, nine out of ten emigrating English servants were males.[4]

The literature has placed great emphasis on the deleterious consequences for family formation and cultural continuities of unbalanced sex ratios among forced African migrants. However, the imbalance among enslaved migrants was in fact significantly less than that among both free and unfree European migrants.[5] Some slave ships arriving in the Chesapeake carried the stated ideal of two men for every one woman, but others had evenly balanced proportions of men and women. The marginality of Chesapeake planters in the transatlantic slave trade meant that captives brought to this region fell below the overall Atlantic average of 170 men to 100 women. Slave traders were more likely to send shipments with high proportions of women and children, whom sugar planters had less use for, to mainland colonies rather than to prime West Indian markets. Sex ratios of new Africans in the surviving records of sales of slave cargos range from the more typical 170 to as low as 120 men to 100 women. Similarly, although equally high proportions of adult men occasionally appear on some large tidewater plantations in the early eighteenth century, the proportion of men found in most collections of tidewater Chesapeake probate inventories for the late seventeenth and early eighteenth centuries are in the lower range of one and a quarter to one and a half men for each woman.[6]

Everything being equal, African migrants should then have stood greater chances for marrying, procreating, and reproducing Old World cultures than did Europeans. For these migrants, of course, nothing was equal. The experiences of initial enslavement in Africa, forced transatlantic migration, brutal forced labor, and an oppressive slave regime in the Chesapeake apparently obliterated the advantages that a more sexually balanced migration might otherwise have afforded. The fact that this greater balance did exist, however, raises two considerations. First, rather than relying on explanations based on sexual imbalance alone, greater emphasis should be placed on the inhibiting effects of the slave regime on biological and cultural reproduction. Second, the possibility that this more even balance may have afforded some forced African migrants, in some places and times, a chance for recreating more elements of African cultures than commonly supposed ought not to be entirely dismissed.

The age structures of the different migrant streams may not have differed much. Relatively few married European women chose to migrate to the Chesapeake; it follows that the proportion of emigrant children would also be relatively low. In a sample of free migrants to seventeenth-century Maryland, children accounted for 27 percent of the total, a proportion similar to that found among voluntary early nineteenth-century migrants to North America.[7] On lists of indentured servants leaving England in the seventeenth and early eighteenth centuries males and females under age fifteen are usually no more than 3 to 7 percent.[8] These, however, were servants who had obtained written indentures in England before embarking for the New World, and they were by no means representative of all migrating servants. In the seventeenth century many more left Britain without indentures, and served according to the less advantageous customs of the colony in which their labor was eventually sold. In one seventeenth-century Maryland county, a full third of male servants whose ages were mentioned in the local records were boys under fifteen, most of whom had no indentures.[9] Enslaved Africans transported to the Chesapeake included a similar proportion of children. Between a fifth and a quarter of the new Africans for whom sale records survive were children. Most were older youths whom slave dealers categorized as "men boys" and "women girls"; "child boys" and "small" children of either sex were less common.[10]

Exclusive concentration on adult males, the majority among all migrants, and on servants who arrived with indentures has tended to obscure the extent to which immigrant child workers were employed in the Chesapeake. Low prices made bound or enslaved children particularly attractive investments for poorer planters who could not afford higher-priced adults. Neophyte slave buyers inexperienced in extracting work from culturally alien chattels likely thought youths more tractable than adults. In addition to immigrant children, native-born youths were also part of the bound work force. Orphaned children who inherited an estate insufficient to support them and who lacked kin willing to take them in, fatherless children whose widowed mother could not provide for them, and bastard children, both white and mulatto (usually the offspring of women in service who were not free to marry), were all bound out to whoever would agree to feed and clothe them in return for their labor until they reached the legal age of majority.

As in England, local authorities had to pay householders an allowance to care for poor infants placed with them. But in this labor-short region no subsidy was required to induce families to take in children over the age of two. Mulatto children, however, were penalized for their parents' violation of laws against interracial sex, and forced to serve to age 31. All these children were particularly vulnerable. The immigrant children had been irrevocably separated from their families, kin, and native lands. Many were confined on isolated plantations where they were unlikely to form friendships with anyone who might intercede in their behalf. The African youths in addition were probably often unable to communicate with anyone around them. These traumatized children must have had to assimilate to European ways quickly in order to survive.[11]

Equally important in shaping Chesapeake society was high mortality among all Old World immigrants. All immigrants experienced a period of sickness (the "seasoning") during their first year, and as many as a fifth may have died within twelve months. Substantial numbers of Europeans and Africans succumbed to respiratory diseases in late winter, but the Europeans were much less able to survive summer and early fall outbreaks of malaria, which was endemic to the region. Malaria occasionally reached pandemic proportions and frequently left survivors in poor health, unable to withstand other diseases. In addition to newcomers, children and pregnant women were particularly susceptible. Although African migrants were more likely than Europeans to survive bouts of malaria, their overall death rates were apparently as high. This appalling wastage of people necessitated a steady flow of new laborers just to maintain the existing working population, quite apart from the labor requirements of an expanding tobacco culture. The fortunate migrants who survived their initial introduction to a new disease environment continued to suffer from both high morbidity and high mortality, resulting in abbreviated life spans, short marital unions, and few offspring. Moreover high infant and child mortality decimated the population of children born in the colonies; perhaps a quarter of the infants died in their first year, and almost another quarter by age fifteen.[12]

The social consequences for both blacks and whites were far reaching. The combination of high mortality and unbalanced sex ratios, compounded by restraints on marriage and reproduction among bound European workers and low reproductive rates among enslaved Africans, delayed the onset of natural population increase. Throughout the first century, Virginia and Maryland remained immigrant societies, subject to rapid turnovers of population, stunted family life, and social and political instability.[13]

≺ II ≻

Economy, Migration, and Social Structure

The earliest Chesapeake migrations were composed almost exclusively of either gentlemen or bound servants, and the founders initially envisioned the re-creating of hierarchical, stratified communities of landlords and tenants in the new colonies. But few of the gentlemen survived the rigors of the unexpectedly lethal Chesapeake environment or were willing to commit themselves permanently to the raw new land. Those who persisted were much more adept at pursuing private advantage than in exerting effective leadership. Because the Europeans were unable to transform the resident Native Americans into a willing or even unwilling work force, indentured servitude quickly became the means by which desperately needed laborers were recruited from England. For a decade or so after they arrived, most settlers who came without capital remained in dependent, subordinate positions.[14]

From the 1630s through the early 1660s, migration from England accelerated, fueled by favorable tobacco prices. Servants still predominated, but many of the later arrivals were free migrants of modest means who came in family groups. These new immigrants helped to transform the society into a community of households headed mostly by small or middling planters. Good times enabled ordinary planters to purchase servants to develop their plantations and also enabled many former servants who survived their terms to join the ranks of landowners and to become respected members of local communities. From the mid-1660s, with the best land in the more densely settled areas taken up, and the price of tobacco declining, fewer free migrants were willing to move to the Chesapeake. News of declining opportunities also reached those adventurous or desperate enough to gamble on exchanging four or more years in service for transportation to the Chesapeake. The number of imported servants remained stable in the 1660s and 1670s, and then fell off in the 1680s and 1690s. A decline in England's population in the later seventeenth century, coupled with protracted warfare between 1688 and 1713, led to a dramatic decrease in the supply of servants, except during the brief interval of peace between 1697 and 1702 when so many servants migrated to the Chesapeake that they again briefly predominated in the labor force. In most other years wars created alternative employments in the military, disrupted established servant recruitment patterns, reduced shippers' profits, and discouraged potential immigrants from choosing a hazardous transatlantic crossing.[15]

African slaves also labored in Chesapeake tobacco fields from the first chance landing of twenty-odd captured Angolans in 1619. Early to mid-seventeenth-century Chesapeake planters were, however, "nott men of estates good enough" to afford many slaves. This assessment was based on the high cost of slaves and perhaps also influenced by planters' unfamiliarity with ways for controlling and extracting labor from an unwilling, culturally alien workforce. Moreover, masters' property rights in bound black workers had not yet been clearly defined in Chesapeake law, and there was no regular and certain source of supply. So long as they could get enough indentured servants, planters seem to have preferred European laborers, but an increasingly inadequate supply forced a switch to slaves.[16] Regular, direct shipments from Africa began in the mid-1670s, probably rose markedly in the 1680s, and increased sharply when the slave trade was formally opened to all merchants in the British Empire in 1698. Once the price of laborers fell, from around £30 sterling for a prime hand in the mid-1650s to about £15 in the 1680s, and once planters had gained experience with slaves, their reluctance diminished. By the 1680s slaves had become close substitutes for servants. Aside from an occasional indentured artisan, by the 1690s larger Chesapeake planters had come to rely entirely on enslaved workers. Perhaps as many as 20,000 captive Africans were brought to the Chesapeake across the seventeenth century, and about 100,000 between 1700 and 1775.[17]

The conditions under which Africans labored deteriorated over time. So long as Africans were a minority in the bound workforce, Europeans and Africans usually shared both work routines and dwelling spaces and not infrequently socialized, had sexual relations, and ran away in mixed groups. But once the stream of new white servants diminished to a trickle, planters began systematically to intensify work requirements, to deny slaves any claim to English workers' customary rights to food of reasonable quantity and quality or to adequate clothing, shelter, and leisure, as well as stripping them of any significant freedom for themselves or their children. By the early eighteenth century European servants increasingly refused to live and work with slaves; those who came under contract demanded (and got) separate quarters and work assignments and better food and clothing.[18]

As life-long service and hereditary slavery for blacks became ever more firmly established in both practice and law, and as the chances for surviving a term of service marginally increased, the interests of term- and hereditary-bound servants inevitably diverged. Shirking work and running away continued to be strategies to which all bound laborers might resort, sometimes individually and sometimes in concert. But even though opportunities for eventual economic advantage were severely diminished, the assurance of eventually moving out of a debased servile status, coupled with the promise of some minimal freedom dues at the end of their terms, still afforded European servants incentives for completing their contractual obligations. Laborers relegated to involuntary life-long bondage could have no such motivation.[19] Plantation discipline became more severe and more systematic as the proportion of blacks in the total population rose—"Foul means must do, what fair will not," in William Byrd II's words. Force was increasingly required and tolerated by whites, both to extract unwilling labor and to prevent violent insurrections.[20]

The diminished supply and rising prices of servants drove many small planters out of the labor market and concentrated unfree workers on the estates of the wealthy. Disparities in wealth between rich, middling, and poor increased, accompanied by increasingly rigid disparities in social status. Consequently in the last quarter of the century the proportion of ordinary planters fell in older Chesapeake communities. This decline was accompanied by a large increase in both the size of the bound labor force and in the numbers of former servants who were unable to advance from the status of inmates into the ranks of tenant farmers or landowners. Population turnover remained high in older areas, with almost all free immigrants and up to two-thirds of former servants who failed either to secure land or to marry moving on.[21]

It is well established that among the Europeans, early arrival conveyed a distinct advantage for those men and women who survived seasoning and their period of indenture. First-comers stood the best chances to acquire good tobacco land, to marry and start families, and to garner positions of respect, if not high office, in their local communities. Those who arrived later, when the best land had already been taken up and the advantages of tilling prime virgin soils exhausted, found it more difficult to advance economically or to marry. Then, only a select few who brought either skills or capital had much chance for advancing their fortunes. It was the first-comers who acquired crucial knowledge of how to survive in an unfamiliar environment, and of how to raise export and subsistence crops and to build up herds of domestic livestock. They also established the rudiments of local and provincial government, and began to delineate the "customs of the country" to which later migrants had to conform.

By 1700 in the older tidewater counties the majority of adults in the white population were native-born, a shift that had major implications for social development. Unless a jurisdiction was among the very few where modest towns appeared, white in-migration virtually ceased. With all the land worth cultivating taken up, and opportunities for earning a good living other than by farming exceedingly limited, most European migrants chose other destinations. In the 1690s most tidewater counties still were immigrant communities in which a majority of the adults retained vivid memories of, if not active ties with, the Old World. A decade or so later, a majority of the white population had no direct knowledge of Europe. As children born in the colony came of age and formed families of their own, households and local communities became bound together through increasingly dense kinship networks. Newcomers from abroad soon came to be viewed as distinct outsiders who found it increasingly difficult to become fully accepted in ever more closely knit, inward-looking creole neighborhoods.

When significant in-migration ended, adult sex ratios became more evenly balanced, making marriage and family formation possible for an ever greater proportion of men. The proportion of children rose dramatically as creole women married at relatively young ages and so had more children than their immigrant mothers. Mortality rates improved somewhat, without the high seasoning losses associated with new immigrants, and with the slightly greater immunities to local diseases that creoles possessed. As tidewater populations approached a more normal demographic balance, society became more stable. Nearly all native-born men were able to find wives, and because natives married earlier and lived longer, their marriages lasted twice as long as marriages among immigrants. At the same time, possibilities for quick increases in wealth diminished as planters exhausted the high rates of return that could be gained by farm-building, and as the local population shifted from an artificially high proportion of productive adults toward a normal balance where about half of the people were under the age of sixteen. The early frenetic race to make a quick fortune before death intervened was increasingly replaced by more prosaic concerns about making an ordinary living, marrying and setting up an independent household, maintaining young children, building up assets to pass on to offspring, and perhaps improving levels of domestic comfort.[22]

Out-migration as well as in-migration slowed dramatically. Local connections afforded creoles advantages unavailable to most immigrants, at the same time that growing family ties increasingly bound the native-born firmly to their birthplaces. In one tidewater county, whereas in the later seventeenth century roughly six out of ten European male immigrants who failed to prosper chose to try their fortunes elsewhere, after 1700 fewer than two out of ten creoles, whatever their economic status, opted to leave. Some native-born men had inherited land and moveable assets and had little incentive to go elsewhere. Others expected to inherit a farm in future or, if not land, at least a share of the family's livestock, household goods, and, perhaps, bound laborers. Still others who could hope for little or no material assistance from their parents inherited responsibilities for maintaining a widowed parent or younger orphaned siblings which tied them to the locality. For the elite there was the prospect of advancement in local or provincial political circles or a secure line of credit with one or more English merchants. Young middling planters might hope that some of their relatives would advance enough goods or credit to enable them to set up housekeeping and to stock a farm. Even the creole poor could hope that, should they fall on even harder times, relatives or friends would provide food and shelter—a much less humiliating and restricting recourse than turning to public charity. Only around 1750 did significant out-migration resume from tidewater areas, propelled by the push of increasing demographic pressure and the pull of fresh western lands.[23]

The increasing stability and demographic balance of local white populations by the turn of the century had major social and cultural implications. Chesapeake colonists of European origin developed a provincial culture based on awareness of place and a sense of history forged from common shared experiences in dealing with a unique estuarine environment. The peculiar seasonal rhythms and work demands of tobacco culture and plantation husbandry shaped the emerging culture. A common dependence on the tobacco staple and a transatlantic marketing system centered on the major English colonial ports united Chesapeake localities, as did a widespread commitment to establishing order through the adoption of English law and selected institutions of local government.[24]

Yet, despite the many cultural and institutional similarities, Chesapeake provincial society differed fundamentally from that of England. By the 1690s the bound Chesapeake work force was predominantly African. Although in 1700 blacks were only about 13 percent of the total population, they were already a third of all laborers. A novel legal system evolved piecemeal that safeguarded planters' high investments in bound workers serving for life and denied all rights and protections to that human property. So long as there was a need to continually recruit additional supplies of temporarily bound laborers, there were practical limits on the extent to which colonial masters and legislators could curtail workers' legal rights or abridge customary privileges and still attract more immigrant workers. Once masters could count on an adequate supply of coerced labor, these limitations disappeared. Concepts of racial difference came to define both legal standing and social relations between Africans and English, relegating the former to a perpetually unfree and degraded status.

From the outset it was extraordinarily difficult for individuals of African origin to escape bondage and to establish a modestly secure place within the mainstream society. Those who arrived in the first three-quarters of the seventeenth century when racial lines were not yet rigidly drawn and Africans' status as slaves was undefined in law sometimes succeeded. This "charter generation," as described by Ira Berlin, arrived with some knowledge of the languages of the Atlantic (acquired either in homelands on the African coast or from interactions with Europeans somewhere along the rim of the Atlantic) and were familiar with Christianity and other European commercial practices, conventions, and institutions. A more cosmopolitan background and, for some, a partial European ancestry enabled them to feel more at home in the new environment and led to some measure of social integration. These same attributes also meant that Europeans saw them as not entirely foreign. Later-arriving captives, Berlin further argues, were drawn from places in the African interior little exposed to the wider Atlantic world and were in contrast to the first-comers linguistically isolated and culturally estranged. Europeans' perception of the languages, manners, and customs of these later forced migrants as totally "outlandish" helped ensure a life of unremitting regimented labor that left little scope for initiative or ambition.[25]

Four reasons, summarized by Berlin, have been advanced to account for the marked differences between the experiences of coerced African migrants in the first half of the seventeenth century and of those at its close. First, as members of the initial generation of settlers, early-arriving Africans shared with their European captors an outsiders' perspective of being fellow foreigners in a strange new land. Later captives also arrived as strangers in a strange land, but they came to a place in which their captors were at home. Second, as noted, racial differentiation and labor exploitation were less fully developed in societies where slaves were a minority rather than a majority of the subordinate workforce. Third, the charter generation's background in the African littoral better prepared them to survive and make their way in a new environment than did the provincial origins of the farmers and herders from the African interior who came later. Fourth, most of those who came first, rather than arriving directly from Africa, "had already spent some time in the New World" (presumably in the Caribbean), putting the trauma of transatlantic transportation behind them and gaining more familiarity with European languages and customs.[26]

The first two explanations, rooted in changes in the social structure of the Chesapeake, are widely accepted. The third and fourth, which posit marked changes around the turn of the century in the provenance of captured Africans, are more controversial. The apparently more cosmopolitan character of the charter generation has been widely noted, although the weights assigned to differences in individuals' backgrounds or to greater fluidity in early colonial societies vary. Recent work on the African slave trade does not reveal any pronounced shift from coast to interior in the geographic origins of Africans captured in the late seventeenth and early eighteenth centuries, nor any pronounced change in the occupations that most of the enslaved had likely pursued before capture. The final explanation, that in the seventeenth century most slaves who ended up in the Chesapeake had previously undergone a period of acclimatization and acculturation in the West Indies and hence were less linguistically and culturally isolated, seems especially problematic. If, as now seems likely, most forced seventeenth-century migrants, as virtually all of those transported in the eighteenth century, either came directly from Africa or had only a brief stopover in the islands, then the deteriorating conditions of Chesapeake slave life evident at the turn of the century cannot be readily explained by "the Africanization of slavery."[27]

≺ III ≻

Ethnic and Social Variations in the Migrant Streams and Their Consequences

The backgrounds of Europeans who migrated to the Chesapeake were relatively homogenous. The majority arriving throughout the seventeenth century, and especially in the first two-thirds, came from the south and west of England, primarily from the cities of London and Bristol and the counties surrounding them. Many came from urban backgrounds, and others who had been born in more distant places had moved first to one of these cities. Almost all shared a common language and culture (albeit with some regional variations) and a common Christian religion (divided between Anglican and Catholic, and to a lesser extent Puritan, Presbyterian, and Quaker). These early comers, who were more likely than later migrants to accumulate property, marry, and rise to positions of power, were especially influential in developing the "customs of the country" that differentiated colonial from metropolitan practices, and which became core elements in the evolving regional culture to which later comers increasingly had to adapt.[28]

Later-arriving migrants were drawn from more diverse areas—Ireland, Scotland, and the environs of Liverpool, for example—and they had a lesser impact on cultural development. Most were young, poor, and unskilled, and they included more females, more Catholics (whose loyalties were considered suspect after the Anglican takeover of Maryland in 1689), and transported convicts and prisoners of war. They were numerically too few and socially too inferior to significantly influence the local cultures into which they entered.[29] Scholars have yet to establish firm estimates of the numbers of Europeans who migrated to the Chesapeake between 1700 and about 1780. The total, most agree, did not surpass the seventeenth-century migration and likely did not equal it.[30] The eighteenth-century convict trade has received the most attention. At least 40,000 convicts, mostly young, unskilled males, are estimated to have been brought into the Chesapeake from England, Ireland, and Scotland between 1718 and 1775.[31] Other seventeenth- and early eighteenth-century European migrants—a sprinkling of Dutch, Swedes, French, and Swiss—came with the advantage of being free immigrants, but they were so few in numbers that most were quickly assimilated. It was not until later in the eighteenth century that German migrants—who came primarily in family groups and who tended to settle in sparsely populated frontier areas—managed to establish and reproduce a distinctive, separate European culture. Moreover, most later eighteenth-century migrants went to the back country and not to the tidewater, which is the focus of this chapter.

For forced African migrants, the prevailing view remains that the heterogeneity of enslaved populations—origins in many different places within a large continent, multiplicity of languages, and widespread dispersal in receiving areas—virtually precluded "a coherent transfer of either languages or cultural traits." According to a recent restatement of the argument, "however much the young Africans might fight to retain their native languages and cultures, they were slowly incorporated into a larger Afro-American culture in which their own origins only partly helped define the cultural norms and patterns of behavior . . . This outcome could be the only expected one given the multiplicity of often conflicting backgrounds these slaves came from and the power that the whites held over their lives."[32]

New evidence on the Chesapeake slave trade reveals greater homogeneity in the geographic origins of transported Africans than the preceding view suggests. First, there is little evidence to support a pronounced change from West Indian and African littoral to interior sources of supply near the end of the seventeenth century. Given the high mortality and low reproductive rates prevailing across that century, it is generally accepted that the total white population of the Chesapeake in 1700 at most equaled the total number of immigrants arriving across that century, and at worst, represented a net decrease of as many as 50,000 people.[33] The black population, variously estimated at from 13,000 to nearly 20,000 in 1700, likely required at least an equivalent volume of coerced migration, and quite plausibly an even greater one.[34]

However, the belief that many if not most early Chesapeake slaves were of a mixed lot of seasoned hands brought from the West Indies after a long period of ecological and cultural adjustment, or were perhaps even Caribbean-born creoles, remains firmly entrenched in Chesapeake historiography. Their proportion has almost certainly been greatly exaggerated, given the overall low volume of Chesapeake-West Indian trade in the seventeenth century. The few vessels regularly carrying commodities between the islands and the mainland could not have accommodated the trans-shipment of more than a fraction of these numbers as ancillary cargo. Extant seventeenth-century shipping records are sparse but reveal a pattern similar to the much better documented years after 1697, when at least nine out of ten imported slaves arrived either directly from Africa or were trans-shipped from the West Indies on smaller vessels after only a brief period of recuperation from their transatlantic ordeal. Significant numbers of seasoned West Indian slaves can be identified only in two southern Maryland counties, brought in by a handful of Barbadian planters who relocated to the mainland in the 1670s.[35]

Second, there was much less initial random mixing, after 1697, of African groups within the Chesapeake than has been commonly supposed. Across the eighteenth century, three-quarters or more of the Africans brought to the Upper Chesapeake (Virginia Potomac basin and Maryland) whose regional origins are known came from the upper parts of the West African coast, from Senegambia on the north, to a second region extending from the Cassamance River to Cape Mount (present-day Sierra Leone is in the center), and then easterly along the Windward Coast (present-day Ivory Coast and Liberia), and ending on the Gold Coast (the area of present-day Ghana). In contrast, nearly three-quarters of the Africans disembarked in the Lower Chesapeake (York and Upper James basins) came from more southerly parts of Africa, from the Bight of Biafra (present-day eastern Nigeria) or West Central Africa (Congo and Angola).[36]

These strikingly different distributions of enslaved peoples within the Chesapeake seem largely a chance result of whether London or Bristol merchants were the major suppliers. Merchants in these two ports concentrated their African trades in different places on the West African coast, as well as concentrating their slave and tobacco trading in different parts of the Chesapeake. Due to differing trade conditions in Africa, English merchants sent larger ships to the Bight of Biafra and West Central Africa than to Upper Guinea, and they then directed most of these larger ships to those Chesapeake naval districts—the York and later the Upper James—where the most buyers resided. Smaller vessels coming from Upper Guinea were usually sent to more peripheral districts. Planter buying patterns tended to further concentrate slaves from the same geographic area on individual plantations, because most large slave owners bought all the African workers they required over a span of no more than ten to fifteen years, and within this short span of time most new Africans often came primarily from only one African region. Thereafter, in marked contrast to the West Indies, in the Chesapeake the natural increase of these Africans, combined with the increase of inherited creole slaves, precluded any need to buy additional new workers.[37]

Free European settlers usually established themselves in whatever areas offered the most good unclaimed tobacco land at the time they arrived, and while immigrant servants were apparently able to exercise some choice among broad North American destinations, they had no control over the particular locality in which a ship captain might decide to market their labor. Thus migrants from different parts of the British Isles were by and large indiscriminately mixed, with no direct correspondence between particular sending regions in England and particular receiving neighborhoods along the tobacco coast. There seems to have been little desire to attempt to recreate distinct English local or provincial cultures.[38]

Did the newly discovered patterns in the forced migration stream have any effect on local slave cultures in the Chesapeake? Much of the sketchy documentary evidence suggests the answer is no, but this may be in part a result of scholars arguing from examples drawn from throughout the Chesapeake and from across a broad span of time. A more refined assessment, assisted by recent archaeological discoveries, seems to suggest major differences between Upper and Lower Chesapeake in the potential for cultural continuities with West Africa.[39]

The possibilities for much cultural continuity would seem to have been limited for those groups brought to the Upper Chesapeake. The total number of transported captives was small compared to the larger numbers imported into lower Virginia, and the proportion of all blacks in the total population was also small. The Upper Guinea Coast upon which the Upper Chesapeake drew disproportionately was ethnically diverse. The peoples of Senegambia shared a relatively homogenous history and culture, and inhabitants spoke either related languages of the West Atlantic family, or Mande, which served as a commercial and political *lingua franca*.[40] Much less is known about the peoples brought from Sierra Leone and the Windward Coast. Those living north of Cape Mount had economic and some cultural and linguistic connections with Senegambia, but practiced a rice- rather than grain-based agriculture; grouped themselves in smaller, more diffuse polities; and lived in an entirely rural environment. The majority of peoples taken from the Windward and Gold Coasts in the seventeenth century were likely coastal dwellers who spoke variants of a different language family, Kwa. Those from the Windward Coast were drawn from a multiplicity of small-scale polities and included multiple ethnicities and other collective groupings. Yet other peoples with different languages and cultures lived in the interior, and from the mid-eighteenth century, conflicts between Muslims and non-Muslims resulted in the export of captives from these inland areas.[41] The peoples of the Gold Coast were more culturally homogeneous than those of the Windward Coast, and by the later seventeenth century lived in larger, centralized states. The Gold Coast economy was based on both long distance trade in gold and other commodities and an agriculture relying on tropical root crops and recently imported New World maize.[42]

The places where slaves were embarked from south of the Gambia River east to the Gold Coast are often ambiguously specified in period documents, and exported slaves are inconsistently grouped in recent studies, adding further uncertainty about ethnic affiliations. Some scholars present separate counts of slaves exported from Senegambia, Sierra Leone, and the Windward Coasts; others combine the Windward Coast with Sierra Leone; and still others lump peoples taken from Senegambia, Sierra Leone, and the Windward Coast into a single region termed "Upper Guinea."[43] Although ships often stopped at several ports on the Windward Coast to trade for gold or ivory as well as slaves, evidence from the Du Bois database suggests that relatively few slaves were taken from this region before the late eighteenth century. Moreover, in the seventeenth and eighteenth centuries, "Windward" sometimes also referred to the western part of the Gold Coast, west or "windward" of Cape Coast Castle.[44]

Even if these ambiguities about trading patterns and appropriate regional groupings are eventually resolved, considerable linguistic and cultural diversity among Africans brought to the Upper Chesapeake seems apparent. There were linguistic and cultural continuities between adjoining regions but obvious dissimilarities between the outliers. At present there is little consensus among scholars as to the degree of cultural similarities and differences in "Upper Guinea" and the Gold Coast in the era of the slave trade. Assessments range from overwhelming multiplicity on the one hand, to, on the other, John Thornton's reduction, on the basis of language, of all the entire western coast slave-exporting regions to just three "truly culturally distinct zones."[45]

In contrast to the diversity of African groups arriving in the Upper Chesapeake, half of the Africans brought to lower Virginia whose geographic origins are known came from the Bight of Biafra, as did a majority of those disembarked on the Upper James prior to 1761. Another quarter were from West Central Africa. The Ibo, who predominated among captives shipped from the Bight of Biafra, spoke closely related dialects of eastern Kwa that were broadly understood among all groups, and shared common manners and customs. The innumerable self-contained villages in which they lived had similar social institutions and a similar root crop agriculture centered on the culture of yams.[46] The peoples of West Central Africa spoke closely related western Bantu languages, primarily Kikongo and Kimbundu, and possessed many common conceptions of religion and aesthetics. They practiced differing kinds of agriculture suited to widely varied local ecologies; in the era of the slave trade, small grains were being replaced by the new crops of manioc and maize. Early intense involvement in the Atlantic trades created high levels of political instability in the Angolan zone.[47] But overall, greater linguistic and cultural homogeneity among the main groups brought to the Lower Chesapeake is likely, and with it, the possibility of greater and different cultural continuities than emerged in other parts of that region.

Ethnic diversity among newly transported Africans increased around 1740, when Liverpool traders began sending regular shipments of Africans to the Chesapeake. Liverpool slavers bought captives in ports all along the West African coast, and unlike London and Bristol traders, those from Liverpool did not differentiate between Chesapeake destinations. They generally sent smaller ships carrying smaller cargoes of slaves to the Chesapeake, and these small numbers could be marketed in any of the region's ports. Most of these new arrivals were sent to new plantations in the west or were bought by tidewater planters or town dwellers who owned few other slaves. Those who ended up in the newer western areas may indeed have encountered the "babel of languages" and heterogeneity of African and creole cultures that inform the dominant view of the impact of African cultures on the Americas. In the older tidewater, the presence of new slaves from previously unrepresented areas added diversity to the workforce in some rural neighborhoods and in towns, but they seldom were sent to the large established plantations on which an ever-increasing proportion of tidewater slaves lived.[48]

Differing sex ratios among adult slaves brought from different parts of West Africa may have increased or diminished possibilities for forming families and socializing children in a homeland culture. Men from Senegambia faced the most formidable obstacles. Shipments from that area included the highest proportion of men, sometimes surpassing the planters' ideal labor balance of two men for one woman.[49] Many enslaved Senegambian men could not, even in the most favorable of circumstances, have found wives brought up in similar cultures. The unknown proportion who were Muslims were perhaps in addition reluctant to marry unless to a fellow Muslim.[50] Thus those who were able to marry were more likely to form unions with African women from other cultures or with native-born women. In contrast, sex ratios among captives from the Bight of Biafra were nearly even. Consequently Ibos in the Lower Chesapeake had greater chances for finding a mate from the same ethnic group and so perhaps for retaining more elements of a national culture. Sex ratios among slaves from the other main sending areas fell between these two extremes, implying a mid-range of opportunities for finding mates sharing similar backgrounds.[51]

≺ IV ≻

Gender Roles

Both European and African immigrants came from societies with gendered divisions of labor and in which gender roles informed cultural identities and underpinned social order. The predominance of men in both migrant streams precluded any quick re-creation of Old World gendered social order, European or African. Moreover, as the Chesapeake slave system evolved, Europeans imposed quite different, racially specific, gender relations upon their enslaved workers in order to increase productivity, enhance control, and categorize Africans as an inferior people. Compounding the difficulties posed by a lack of control over their own lives was the multiplicity of ideas about gender roles the Africans brought with them. Conceptions about the division of labor in agriculture, occupations appropriate for women and men, rules governing social interactions between the sexes, and systems of tracing lineage varied markedly. So long as Africans made up only a fraction of the total Chesapeake population and moreover resided in small work units with only a few other blacks, reconstitution of any system of alternative gender relations was unlikely. With time, Africans and their descendants largely adopted European conceptions of appropriate gender relations, but slave owners allowed implementation only when it suited their convenience. Contests between slaves and owners over these issues would characterize slavery up to its end.

Among Europeans, the preponderance of young men contributed to the early climate of disorder, ruthless economic opportunism, and rootlessness. Virginia Company officials recognized that if they were to establish a permanent colony, wives and children were needed "to make the men more setled and lesse moveable."[52] A sufficient number of women arrived in the migration surge between the mid-1630s and the 1660s so that an influential group of married couples of middling means emerged. These free householders were committed to maintaining local peace and order. They defined and enforced norms of proper behavior, informally through gossip, admonition, arbitration, and neighborhood watching and warding, and formally by bringing breaches of acceptable behavior to court. Servants and freedmen thus became more closely governed, but to the extent that they interacted with established families they also became more integrated into local society. Dependent men who stole, transgressed sexual mores, or flaunted authority were at greater risk of being brought into court by watchful neighbors, but the most vulnerable might also find advocates willing to report cases of flagrant abuse or unfair dealing. By the 1680s and 1690s, internal migration within the Chesapeake and economic opportunities in the newer, adjoining colonies of Pennsylvania and North Carolina siphoned off the surfeit of unrooted European freedmen who had little stake in Tobacco Coast communities.[53]

The overall shortage of women meant that many men, and especially the many bound male laborers, often had to make do without accustomed domestic comforts. Some, both bound and free, lived and labored alone in rude isolation. On larger plantations, black and white bound workers often lived in barracks-like arrangements in which the men grudgingly, and often ineptly, divided up the not inconsiderable chores of food preparation and cooking. They almost certainly ate worse than did men who had formed or lived with families or in establishments where a female domestic was present. They did without washed or mended clothing and suffered through the inevitable bouts of sickness without skilled nursing. Bachelor freedmen sometimes set up households together for companionship and in order to share household duties. Such men lacked the time and had little incentive to improve their living arrangements, contributing to the sparse, crude domestic environments that long characterized the Tobacco Coast. Others boarded with married householders so that they could have access to women's domestic services.[54]

Free European women who chose to migrate to the Chesapeake hoped that the move would better the family's economic fortunes, while single servant women perhaps hoped for a chance to marry above their station. Many who survived long enough did realize these goals, but at a distinct price. Most lived isolated lives on scattered farmsteads, carved out of the ubiquitous forest, that were within convenient traveling distance of only about twenty other families. Familiar Old World gathering places—towns, marketplaces, and churches—were scarce or entirely absent. Shortages of manufactured goods and anything beyond the most rudimentary of shelters precluded compensating domestic comforts. Most servant women were not allowed to marry until they completed their terms, and they faced harsh penalties if a pregnancy resulted from premarital sex, either voluntary or coerced. At the same time they were inordinately pressured by fellow male servants, overseers, neighbors, and masters for sexual favors. European women likely also experienced greater risks in bearing children, as they were more susceptible to malaria during pregnancy.[55]

Stark material conditions, labor shortages, and the settlers' preoccupation with tobacco production made it impossible for many European women to resume Old World domestic routines. Although female servants in husbandry in England were not unaccustomed to spates of field labor, immigrants found the unremitting toil in tobacco fields that became the lot of many servant women distasteful and demeaning. Married women pursued a wider range of household work, including dairying, gardening, poultry raising, and sewing, but the wives of small planters continued to spend some time tending tobacco. Despite the difficulty of sustaining domestic ideals in early Chesapeake conditions, traditional assumptions about English women's proper role in the colonial economy went unrevised. The common practice of women servants "working in the ground," was glossed over as exceptional.[56] Eventually more balanced sex ratios, the growing availability of African labor, and depressed tobacco markets that encouraged crop diversification and import replacement activities enabled European and native-born women of middling means to return to more traditional housewifery and domestic production.[57] Initially few African women were assigned to the domestic tasks deemed appropriate for European women, although one can find exceptions on some very large and very small estates. It was primarily enslaved children who did domestic chores in white households.[58]

While English settlers were always ambivalent about whether regular field labor was appropriate work for European women, this ambivalence did not extend to African women. Until regular direct shipments from Africa began in the 1670s, sex ratios among blacks in the Chesapeake were evenly balanced, and although they were only a small percentage of the total labor force, enslaved women accounted for at least a quarter of bound female workers and in some localities as much as half. Perhaps influenced by accounts of women's arduous work in West Africa and by the example of their employment in heavy labor in the sugar islands, planters soon routinely assigned most African women and older girls solely to working in the ground. Unlike the English, most West African women would have considered field work appropriate labor, a perception that perhaps facilitated their exploitation by masters who viewed them as unskilled agricultural workers who could be employed interchangeably with men. But even if the labor itself was not considered demeaning, the lack of much gendered division of labor in the seasonal chores of clearing, planting, tending, and harvesting; the absence of separate women's and men's crops; and the periodic assignment of men to customary women's work like pounding grain must have been unsettling for both sexes. The plantation environment provided few opportunities for enslaved women to pursue domestic work outside agriculture—such as marketing, dairying, brewing, spinning, and dyeing—that were part of women's work in some of their home societies.[59]

Unbalanced sex ratios among Africans (as among European indentured servants) exacerbated the problems the Europeans faced in controlling these coerced workers. Larger slave owners encouraged the creation of family households as a strategy for reconciling enslaved men to bondage, discouraging running away, and motivating them to work harder. There were, however, decided limits to how far owners would go to accommodate families. Married couples were not infrequently assigned to different quarters. Cross-plantation unions were also relatively common, but more difficult to sustain, as such couples were usually allowed to be together at best only one day out of seven. For those women and men who did manage to form families, the threat of family break-up became a more potent means of control than was the threat of physical violence. Slave owners, however, denied unions between enslaved women and men any legal standing, retaining the right to permanently separate couples by sale, inheritance, or transfer to distant quarters.[60]

Because slaves, unlike European servants, served for life, the customary requirement of celibacy during service was neither appropriate nor enforceable. Enslaved women could not compensate their owners for labor time lost in pregnancy and childbirth, so the law compensated masters instead by making the offspring their property as well. So long as owners were unlikely to live long enough to profit from these children's eventual labor, they continued to value enslaved women primarily for their productive rather than their reproductive roles. They allowed mothers a bare minimum of time for nursing and child care during the working hours of sunup to sundown and no time during weekday daylight hours for domestic duties in their own households. Overworked mothers, often forced to live apart from their husbands, bore most of the responsibilities and burdens of child rearing either alone or with the assistance of other quarter residents.[61]

European immigrants found no reason to modify prevailing Old World conceptions of proper household and familial arrangements. Male heads of households were expected to provide for and govern dependent wives, children, and resident bound laborers. Where unusually high proportions of bound laborers posed a threat to this expected hierarchy, local and provincial courts and groups of neighbors formally or informally intervened to reinforce the authority and prerogatives of household heads.[62] Early death, coupled with somewhat higher ages at marriage for men than women and a frequent absence of any other kin, left many immigrant wives relatively young widows with sole responsibility for the estates of offspring, most well under the age of majority. Poor widows could seldom provide for children on their own. Some might be able to raise a bare sufficiency of food with the help of older children but had no means for replacing essential imported clothing and tools that could only be bought with more tobacco than such a truncated household was capable of producing. Finding a new husband or binding out some or all children to established householders were the only viable options, and the surplus of unattached men rendered the first course most common. More fortunate widows who inherited bound workers had the potential for managing on their own, and thus for preserving the assets that children of a first marriage might eventually inherit. However, absent the support of older children or other nearby kin, and given the hardships and isolation of frontier life, almost all immigrant widows opted to remarry. The risks later marriages posed for children of earlier unions were usually well understood, as was the general absence of other acceptable options.[63]

African women reared in societies in which polygamous marriages were common and where wives rather than husbands often had primary responsibility for providing for their children were perhaps able to contend with some of the difficulties posed by separate residences and cross-plantation marriages. However, neither immigrant nor creole-enslaved fathers could protect their wives and children from plantation discipline and sexual abuse, and slavery ensured that the owners assumed the role of primary provider. Little attention has been paid to the experiences of female African migrants. How these may have differed from or been similar to the experiences of transplanted African males is seldom considered, even in studies that directly address differences between migrant and creole generations. Given mothers' roles as primary transmitters of retained or recreated African cultures or of adopted European ways, African women's experiences in the colonies, as actors as well as victims, should have high priority in future research.

≺ V ≻

Community Formation

It is only at the level of localized neighborhoods that one can make meaningful comparisons of social organization and cultural developments among free and coerced migrants. The boundaries of Chesapeake neighborhoods were determined in part by geography and in part by patterns of repeated social interaction among residents; they corresponded roughly to the "limits," "precincts," or "hundreds" into which Virginia and Maryland courts subdivided counties. The numerous rivers, ridges, barrens, ravines, and swamps that impeded travel and discouraged dense settlement formed the exterior bounds of neighborhoods. Stretches of level, fertile riverside terraces that supported relatively closely-spaced farmsteads and afforded easy movement between adjoining households and quarters made up the cores. The better-established farms of wealthy planters (who were often also merchants and county officials) and parish churches, as well as the roads connecting them, served as focal points that further channeled most residents' ordinary social interactions, as did the stores, gristmills, artisans' shops, and tobacco warehouses that appeared in most tidewater Chesapeake neighborhoods by the early eighteenth century.[64]

Overlying the more clearly discernible European neighborhoods, enslaved Africans created neighborhoods of their own. Quarters on the larger plantations served as focal points, as did the homes of free blacks, and also more secluded places in woods and swamps where slaves could gather free from the prying eyes of owners or overseers. Other focal points—stores, mills, warehouses, and to some extent churches—were shared with whites. Although the presence of concurrent African neighborhoods is widely acknowledged, yet to be made are sustained attempts—even for those localities that have been the subject of intense "community studies"—to map patterns of interaction or to delineate neighborhoods from the perspective of the enslaved.

Dispersed settlement patterns meant that most individuals' interactions with other settlers were distinctly limited. Most repeated and ordinary contacts between free men and women involved other households lying within an approximate five-mile radius of one's dwelling, a journey on foot of an hour or two. The most frequent contacts involved even shorter distances, of between two and three miles. Around the middle of the seventeenth century, no more than fifteen households might commonly be found within that two and a half mile radius, and only about 25 within five miles. Later in the century, as population densities rose, the number of close-lying households rose to around 25 and those within five miles up to 60. The year-round labor that tobacco required kept farmers and farm laborers tied to the fields, while the need to care for small children made it difficult for women to travel far from their dwellings. Usually only officeholders, merchants, itinerant artisans, boatmen, and carters routinely traveled further distances.[65]

Initially neighborhoods were rudimentary associations of strangers, born of necessity and convenience, rapidly shifting in composition with the steady arrival of newcomers. Since most immigrants had no kin in the New World aside from—for some—members of their own household, they had to depend heavily on neighbors for companionship and aid. Friends and neighbors provided company and recreation, helped in times of crisis, witnessed vital events in individual lives, kept watch and ward, mediated local disputes, defined acceptable standards of behavior, exchanged produce, and occasionally organized communal celebrations. The assistance and companionship of neighbors was so vital that few European settlers were willing to risk the consequences of behaving unneighborly or of flagrantly violating neighborhood norms.[66]

Among forcibly-transported Africans, neighbors and neighborhoods probably did not function in quite the same way as they did for European settlers because of the multiplicity of cultures the Africans encountered. Disoriented, newly-arrived Africans must of necessity at first interacted primarily with other laborers on the same plantation. Until the mid-eighteenth century, however, most plantations had too few people living on them for individual estates to constitute a functional "community." Moreover, all the Africans living on home and adjacent plantations were unlikely to share a single common language and culture, and newcomers may initially have found little in common, aside from bondage, with native-born slaves. Once newcomers learned something of their surroundings, they interacted where possible with fellow countrymen on other plantations, and, more haphazardly, with others who were willing to offer companionship and aid despite greater difficulties in communicating. European servants or free householders living in the vicinity differed even more in language and culture and would have become more slowly incorporated into Africans' interactive networks; some whites welcomed interchange while others wanted nothing to do with "outlandish" people. Thus not all the individuals living in an immigrant African's neighborhood could be counted on to perform "neighborly" functions. Moreover slave owners' near absolute control over their enslaved workers made it difficult for neighbors to intervene in internal plantation affairs.

Bound workers' worlds were even more circumscribed than those of free householders. Servants were not supposed to absent themselves from the plantation during working hours without their master's or overseer's permission, and by law slaves were required to obtain permission to travel anywhere at any time. Moreover by the 1730s large gatherings of slaves came to be prohibited under any circumstances. Anxious whites feared the consequences of such meetings where plans for organized resistance might be laid. In practice, slave owners either condoned or were unable to prevent their slaves from visiting quarters on other plantations during the night and especially on Sundays and holidays. Only during brief periods when organized insurrections were suspected did owners and slave patrols attempt to strictly enforce the laws. Frequent social interactions were probably limited to nearby quarters, but some slaves were willing to forfeit rest to undertake much longer journeys to visit countrymen or more widely dispersed kin, and "large gatherings" of slaves did at times certainly occur. By the end of the seventeenth century it was common practice that "on Saturday nights, and Sundays, and on 2 or 3 days in Christmas, Easter, & Whitsontide, they goe and see one an other, tho at 30 or 40 miles distance."[67]

The great majority of emigrating servants shared the language, culture, and Old World regional origins of their masters and so had no reason for developing patterns of social interaction or for forming associations based on ethnic identifications that differed from those chosen by free residents. Tensions between Protestants and Catholics, for example, were a perennial, destabilizing factor in seventeenth-century Maryland. More committed practitioners, both Catholics and Protestants, did indeed develop senses of separate religious identity, so that when they had a choice, they did choose to form closer and more regular associations with fellow believers.

These choices, however, often crossed boundaries of both regional origin and economic and social status.[68] Straying servants were generally recorded as visiting neighboring farms or ship landings, frequenting horse races and taverns, and attending courthouse gatherings when county courts were in session—all in company with free men and women. Gatherings, clandestine or otherwise, composed only of "great numbers" of bound European workers are almost never mentioned in contemporary sources.

Captured Africans had no say whatever in their eventual destinations, and only a fortuitous combination of chances might result in their being sold into a locality where they were likely to encounter other Africans who shared even remotely similar cultures. What the new information on the slave trade demonstrates is that such combinations of chances did come together more often than usually supposed. Still there is abundant evidence to support Ira Berlin's contention that "a common desire for inclusion" was "the distinguishing mark of seventeenth-century black life." Slaves and white indentured servants lived, worked, socialized, ran away, and had sex together. Seventeenth- and early eighteenth-century court records, which often include depositions offered in evidence in cases brought before local courts, demonstrate that both enslaved and free Africans not only regularly traded with whites and formed patron-client relationships with elite European colonists, but sometimes also participated in convivial mixed race neighborhood social gatherings.[69]

Nevertheless, once numbers permitted, most Africans seem to have socialized primarily with other Africans and their descendants, as the preambles to governors' orders and laws enacted in the same period indicate. Only in the 1660s and 1670s did officials mention possible clandestine gatherings of some combination of European servants, "negroes," "molattoes," and Native American slaves or servants. By the 1680s, in neighborhoods where blacks were most numerous, it was they who were making use of "the great freedome and Liberty" that "many Masters" gave them "for Walking on broad on Saterdays and Sundays and permitting them to meete in great Numbers" to make feasts and to hold "funeralls for Dead Negroes."[70] Others got "Drunke on the Lords Day beating their Negro Drums by which they call considerable Numbers of Negroes together in some Certaine places."[71]

These gatherings, especially the "feasts and burialls," had spiritual as well as social aspects. It is likely that they involved groups of Africans who spoke mutually intelligible languages and who may have been re-creating African rituals commemorating the dead. This is suggested by the presence of traditional African grave goods in early eighteenth-century tidewater Chesapeake slave burials, and by the placement of some of the bodies in slave cemeteries on a north/south axis rather than in the east/west orientation employed by Europeans. The suspicion that gatherings, for the ostensible purpose of mourning the dead, of slaves who shared elements of language and culture could well lead to conspiracies for violent resistance is perhaps why masters were specifically ordered to prohibit slaves from "hold[ing] or mak[ing] any Solemnity or Funeralls for any deced Negros."[72] On the same plantation where non-European burials were found, artifacts linked to Ibo spiritual traditions have also been discovered in a root cellar into which libations of wine or brandy (evidenced by high concentrations of grape tannin) had apparently been poured. Spoon handles tentatively identified as inscribed with symbols used by Ibo diviners found at an adjoining quarter lend further credence to the notion that Africans in this neighborhood managed to re-create spiritual rituals associated with their particular African heritage.[73]

Whether there were enough individuals from related language groups living in most Chesapeake neighborhoods who had enough freedom of movement so that some newly developed sense of "national" identity might have become a locus for the maintenance of elements of African culture is at present unknown. Whether Africans in the Americas were aware of belonging to ethno-linguistic units encompassing geographic and cultural boundaries larger than small dialect or localized culture groups remains hotly contested.[74] African languages were clearly spoken in the Chesapeake, but surviving records are silent as to which ones. In some places there probably were sufficient concentrations of slaves from either Senegambia, the Bight of Biafra, or West Central Africa who spoke related dialects so that language might have formed a basis for cross-plantation collaborative groupings. Occasionally plans for organized revolt were discussed in gatherings in the slaves' "country language."[75] Evidence that might be interpreted as suggesting meetings that could have involved national groupings is limited to the period of the 1680s to mid-1730s when most new Africans were brought into the Chesapeake tidewater. The extant documentary record, however, seems too sparse to sustain much more than speculation, and archaeology alone may not contribute much to delineating the extent of transplanted or syncretic cultural practices.

While the presence of countrymen doubtless helped to mitigate some immigrants' sense of profound isolation, for both Africans and Europeans only closer relationships could meet individual emotional needs. The frequent absence of any biological kin in the colonies led many immigrants to create a variety of quasi and surrogate kin. In seventeenth-century England, geographic mobility more often than not effectively separated individuals from regular contacts with their communities of birth. Immediate friends and neighbors usually played a more important role in the daily lives of most people than did kinfolk.[76] Lineage, however, remained critical to identity and to economic and social status. For most British immigrants, transatlantic migration irrevocably severed ties to kin, who were sorely missed.

Suddenly isolated in ad hoc New World neighborhoods where almost all were total strangers, some European immigrants resurrected and tried to make use of the most tenuous of kin connections. For many, however, this was not an option. There is little direct evidence that European servants formed enduring bonds with their fellows who shared the transatlantic passage, but the fact that years later some servants brought former shipmates into court to testify in freedom suits suggests that shipboard friendships were at times maintained. Twenty to 30 percent of Chesapeake male testators died bachelors, and "emotions usually reserved for wives and children were either suppressed or invested in close friendships and relations with quasi kin." Among Anglicans and Roman Catholics, godparents not infrequently became surrogate parents when children whom they sponsored became orphaned.[77]

Kinship was a central organizing principle in African societies, although systems varied widely from one group to another. Moreover in those societies in which the institution of slavery was widespread, mechanisms had been developed for integrating unrelated enslaved peoples using the idiom of kinship. Enslaved Africans had both greater need and probably a greater predisposition to create surrogate kin in the New World. Ties to shipmates, who were usually from the same area and often from the same ethnic group, came first.

For the newly arrived, others of the same nation provided moral support and cultural reinforcement and also served as surrogates for families left behind in Africa. Individuals might subsequently also adopt a variety of fictive kinfolk.[78]

For enslaved people, whose movements were largely restricted to an area of roughly a five miles radius of their home quarters, it was within the local neighborhood that support networks were forged and shared strategies for survival and resistance developed. African languages and elements of culture were retained or re-created where possible, and a creole culture was formed from disparate elements of European and African ways. For the many slaves who lived on scattered small holdings with only a few other blacks, and to some degree slaves from large plantations as well since these were divided into several small work and residential units, the neighborhood rather than the estate constituted their community. Each such neighborhood was in many ways unique, with differing proportions of blacks and whites, differing combinations of ethnic and national groups, differing mixes of immigrants and creoles, differing mixes among the free population of rich and poor or among the enslaved of skilled and unskilled, and differing amounts of in- and out-migration. Across much of the eighteenth century cultural adaptations were inevitably highly localized and highly varied.

Among Europeans, by the early eighteenth century neighborhoods were becoming communities of people who knew each other intimately as a result of lifelong contact, with a sense of cohesiveness and solidarity, and acquiring new meaning and more familiar definition as they were built out of more longterm friendships and especially out of ever more elaborate kin ties.[79] By mid-century a similar transition was transforming black neighborhoods. Although slaves could not control where they lived and were ever at risk of forced moves occasioned by sale, estate divisions, or assignment to other quarters, before the 1760s most of this movement was confined to older areas and often to the same locality. Forced moves to distant destinations became commonplace only when substantial numbers of slave owners migrated west in the mid-1760s, either taking their workers with them or else sending them ahead to establish new farms. Thus there was a period of several decades around the middle of the eighteenth century, between the end of substantial in-migration and before the onset of substantial out-migration, during which tidewater slave communities could develop some small measure of rootedness and stability.

The time span during which regular influxes of new arrivals disrupted local neighborhoods was relatively brief, usually between 40 and 50 years. Thereafter, the numbers of creole children were more than sufficient to maintain plantation workforces, and planters abruptly ceased buying new African laborers. Among those Africans who succeeded in forming families, support networks were increasingly based on biological ties that frequently crossed estate boundaries. Men and women whose parents, and occasionally grandparents, had lived in the same neighborhood for up to a century came to have extended families living on the same quarter or on adjacent quarters located within a few miles of each other. The slaves cherished these extended connections, although they often found it difficult to maintain regular contacts beyond the home plantation. When faced with long-distance separations later in the century, some slaves were willing to risk harsh punishments in order to try to remain with their kin.[80]

By the middle of the eighteenth century, Chesapeake slave owners apparently thought that the character of most slave assemblies had altered to less threatening, primarily social, gatherings of friends and kin. From 1723, meetings of any number of slaves belonging to the same owner on any of that plantation's quarters were deemed "lawful meetings" so long as the owner or overseer gave permission, as were visits of up to five slaves owned by others. Gatherings of any number of slaves at church services, mills, and other places of business were also legally sanctioned. Despite frequently reenacted laws restricting their movement, slaves continued to visit neighboring plantations on Saturdays and Sundays and during the night, sometimes even appropriating plantation horses to speed their journeys. Whites were entirely unable to control slaves' movements under cover of darkness and were continually amazed, when they had occasion to go out after sundown, to meet "Negros both single, and six or 7 in Company" "at all Hours of the Night." Owners worried most about the effect of night time visiting on the slaves' work performance the following day, and secondarily about "night walking" being an occasion for "drinking and whoring" or petty theft. Local officials became more worried about "disorderly" assemblies than about "insurrections" and concentrated on keeping individual slaves from "strolling about from one plantation to another" without a pass. The dead continued to be buried with some sort of ceremony, but funerals ceased to be mentioned as threatening occasions. It seems likely that slave gatherings increasingly incorporated recreations and rituals that were, if not closely adopted European forms, at least less overtly African.[81]

A linguistic shift accompanied the shift from support networks based on co-resident strangers, quasi kin, and country men and women to networks rooted primarily in biological kin ties. As the number of Africans who could communicate fluently only in African languages declined, and the number of creoles who might well speak only English rose, English increasingly became the *lingua franca*. Children whose parents were of different nations were especially likely not to learn or at least to use any African language. The shift in language is indicative of other cultural changes, as more syncretic ways evolved. Long-resident Africans adapted more elements of European culture, and the proportion of creoles with no direct knowledge of Africa and greater familiarity with Anglo-European culture steadily rose. The transition to a fully articulated creole culture, however, seems to have been delayed for almost another 25 years, until the native-born became predominant, not just in the overall population, but among decision-making adults.[82]

The very young children who initially tipped the balance between an African and a creole majority between 1730 and 1750 were surely not making many important cultural choices, especially those choices most likely to be reflected in the surviving material record. Doubtless their very presence in enslaved communities led to some reorientation of individual and community activities and priorities. Still these children were seldom in a position to choose what sort of clothes they would wear (or whether they would wear any at all), to choose what foods would be raised, gathered, or caught to supplement owner-supplied rations (although they likely assisted in these endeavors), or to determine how available comestibles would be prepared. Instead, some combination of enslaved adults—the majority of them Africans—and their Anglo-Chesapeake owners made these decisions.

Similarly, it was adults who were crafting items for domestic use or trade, finding and administering remedies for common ailments, or acquiring European goods as allotments or castoffs from their owners or through trade or theft. Adults also determined, subject to whatever constraints their owners or local authorities were able to impose, how the dead would be mourned and buried, how more festive community gatherings would be conducted, and how spiritual entities, old or new, dealt with. Consequently the material record continues to reflect the outcome of exchanges and contests between forcibly-transplanted Africans and Anglo-Chesapeake whites for some years after an absolute creole majority emerged among the enslaved.

At the same time, however, these creole children were acquiring a greater fluency in the English language than most of their African-born parents had, an important cultural shift that was quickly noticed by their owners and other European observers. They were also learning about and often aspiring to more elements of the predominant European culture surrounding them, and selectively remembering and reinterpreting what African elders taught them about their ancestral heritage. Some disjuncture between the extent and timing of cultural changes noted in documentary records and in the material record is thus likely. The former includes changes in language and in modes of interaction among youths as well as adults; the latter reflects primarily standards and styles of living among adults. Consistent evidence for widespread cultural changes appears only in the last quarter of the century when some critical percentage of first- and second-generation creole children survived to become decision-making adults. Knowing when that actually occurred is crucial to understanding the processes of cultural change. As Jon Sensbach recently put it, "We generally have very little concept of the degree of lingering or redefined African consciousness that might have animated an enslaved Virginian in 1780 whose grandparents had been brought from different parts of Africa in the 1730s. The challenge remains to historians and cultural anthropologists to try to resolve the persistent vagueness about one of the momentous cultural shifts in American history."[83]

The story of the transit of Old World peoples to the New, and of the transformation of the cultures they carried with them, is usually told in terms of generations of experience. For Europeans, it is the experience of the immigrants, who freely chose to venture their lives across an ocean, who most command historians' attention and imagination. After surveying the motivations behind their momentous decision, and relating their encounters with and adaptation to a strange new environment, scholars get down to the business of deciding how successful the migrants were in transferring or adapting European and especially English culture and institutions. Although the general outcome is indisputable, scholars continue to debate the finer points, and indeed have yet to reach agreement even on such basic questions as whether colonial Chesapeake or New England society most resembled that of Old England.[84] Members of the first native-born generation in the Chesapeake appear in contrast less heroic and less interesting. Their goals and accomplishments seem all too prosaic. A reversion to a normal demographic balance, renewed reliance on kin connections, exceedingly modest economic and material advances, and the elaboration of a decidedly provincial regional culture render this transformation from immigrant to native something far short of high drama.

For peoples of African origin, the story is also told in terms of the contrasting experiences of immigrant and creole generations and of the transformation from African to African American. Because the immigrant generation made no free choice to migrate, they are portrayed in most accounts primarily as victims. The evidentiary record for coerced migrants in the Chesapeake is so sparse that most historians have tended to leave extended considerations of agency among immigrants to novelists and playwrights. And not surprisingly, issues of cultural formations and transformations so far remain little studied albeit strenuously debated. It is instead the better documented first and second native-born generations, who adopted the English language and more recognizable European ways, who occupy center stage. Closer comparisons of coerced and free migrations have the potential to afford a better balance to the histories of all migrants and their descendants.

Irish and German Migration to Eighteenth-Century North America

MARIANNE S. WOKECK

VOYAGERS LEAVING Irish ports and German-speaking lands for eighteenth-century North America made up relatively small currents in the massive stream that has carried European migrants across the Atlantic since the 1600s. Yet these flows were the precursors for the mass migrations from Europe to the Americas in the nineteenth century that many Americans now think of as "classic." The large absolute numbers of the later immigrant waves and the easy ethnic categorization of the newcomers according to national origin have obscured the importance of the eighteenth-century tides and their exemplary character. The early German and Irish flows represent a migratory regime that was basically voluntary in nature and that depended on sailing vessels for transportation across the Atlantic. Since the voyage was long, difficult, and expensive, relocation was expensive. The ocean and the high price of the fare for crossing it created obstacles for persons of limited means; contract labor offered ways for financing the move. Although this alternative was always restrictive and often coercive, indentured servitude was a common option of considerable impact. It broadened the pool of potential emigrants to include large numbers of ordinary people—single young men and families—eased the demand for labor in the American colonies, and made use of cargo space on vessels employed in transatlantic trade.

The eighteenth-century migrations from Ireland and German-speaking lands reveal the forces that created, shaped, and guided distinctly ethnic waves of voluntary migrants; and they show that the development of substantial migration currents depended on a self-generating effect to sustain free immigration over time and to determine cycles of ebb and flow. In efforts to generalize from observations about German and Irish immigration to colonial America it is important to examine comparatively first, the flow and composition of the two streams; second, the characteristics of the respective sending and receiving societies; third, the nature of the connections between the Old and New Worlds; and, finally, the impact this migration regime had on European areas of out-migration and on settlements in North America.

≺ I ≻

Common Characteristics of Irish and German Migration Flows

When comparing Irish and German migration to eighteenth-century North America, several features define the common outline.[1] The two immigrant flows were of roughly similar magnitude, originated in the preceding century, and extended, albeit unevenly in waves, throughout the 1700s. Irish and German voyagers to the West usually left from select localities and regions of their home countries and settled in distinct clusters along the eastern seaboard of North America. The particular details of these two migration currents played out within this framework—at times along similar lines, at other times charting different paths.

The flow and composition of the Irish transatlantic migration resembled that of German immigrants in several important respects. In the course of the eighteenth century until the American Revolution, about 127,000 Irish migrants made their way to mainland North America, and so did at least 111,000 German-speaking colonists (Figure 1).[2] Although all estimates about the sex ratio, age structure, and socioeconomic background among Irish and German immigrants are very rough because of the lack of good and consistent data, the fundamental characteristics are clear.

Both migration flows were made up of two distinct strands: single young people (predominantly boys and men) and groups of kin, including migrants bound by some commonality of background or beliefs.[3] The young men were often from among the "lower sort" and depended on indentured servitude as the means for financing their relocation to the American colonies. By contrast, the families among the immigrants tended to be relatively better off: especially

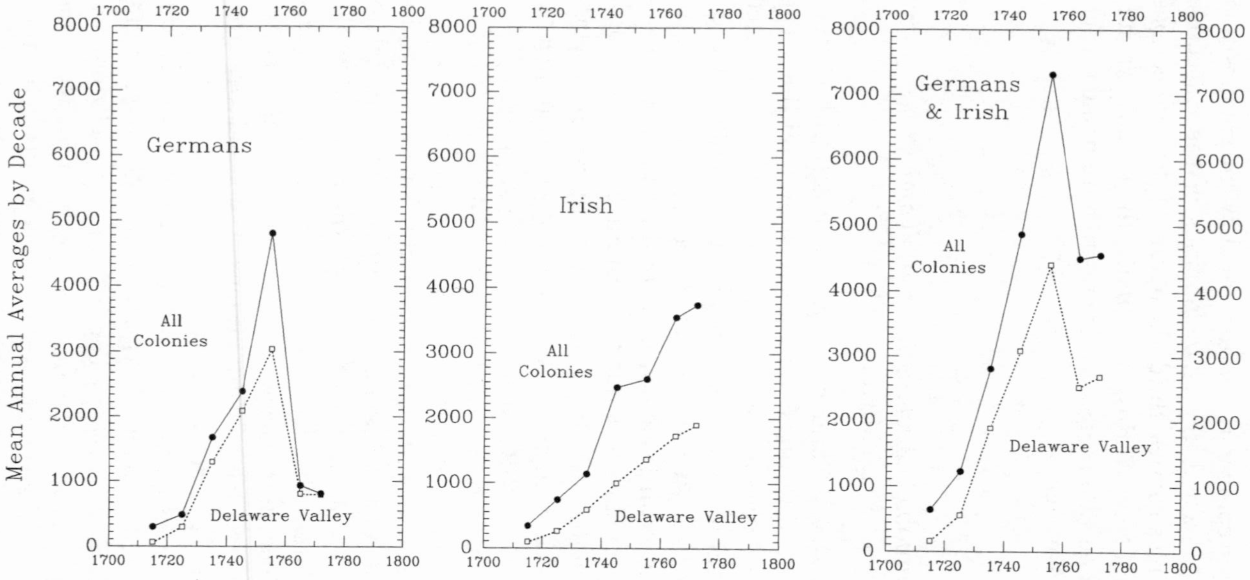

Fig. 1. Estimates of Irish and German Immigrants to North America, 1710–1775 (Decadal Means). Sources: Marianne S. Wokeck, *Trade in Strangers* (University Park, PA, 1999), tables 2 and 4; Audrey Lockhart, *Some Aspects of Emigration* (New York, 1976), appendix C; Robert J. Dickson, *Ulster Emigration* (1966; London, 1988), appendix E; P. M. G. Harris, *The History of Human Populations, vol. 2. Movements in Births, Deaths Migration* (New York, [2002]), chap. 4 (text to figure "Estimates of Irish and German Migration to the Thirteen Colonies"; Harris's estimate for the Irish migration differs from Aaron Fogelman, "Migrations to the Thirteen British North American Colonies: New Estimates," *Journal of Interdisciplinary History* 24, 4 [Spring 1992]: 704–7).

in the early stages of each swelling of the tide a significant portion of them belonged to the "middling sort." This characteristic was true for German-speaking families in the first decades of the eighteenth century, for whom relocation costs were particularly high. It was also true for families from Ulster who migrated in pursuit of better opportunities, not out of desperation.[4] Each of the migration surges had concentrations of voyagers from particular regions, predominantly the territories that bordered the Rhine and its tributaries in southwestern Germany and the hinterlands of the Ulster ports in Ireland.[5] In terms of religious make-up, the migration to the American colonies was largely Protestant, but it was composed of a variety of denominations (primarily Presbyterians among the emigrants from Ireland and mostly Reformed and Lutherans among the Germans and Swiss) and included a distinct minority of Catholics and a significant sectarian element such as Quakers, Mennonites, and Moravians.[6]

Similarities in the character of the migration flows also extend to a certain symmetry pertaining to the areas of out-migration. Both Ireland and Germany lacked clear national definition in the eighteenth century and regions that lost significant numbers of their populations to long-distance migration were unevenly distributed across the Irish isle and among the German-speaking territories of central Europe. As a result, any effects of emigration on the sending society varied considerably from place to place and the experience of emigrants in distant lands resonated differently in different parts of the country. Other features complicated—and emphasized—this regional aspect of migration from Ireland and Germany. One was the development of core districts that contributed to the transatlantic migration throughout the course of the century, helping to forge links between certain parts of the New and Old Worlds in the first place and then to maintain those connections over an extended period of time. The nature of overseas communication and travel in the eighteenth century meant that for ordinary settlers these connections were infrequent and unreliable in nature.

Yet letters, reports, and European visits by pioneering immigrants, "newlanders" (*Neuländer*) they were called in Germany, had powerful effects. Together they built the reputation of the American colonies; fueled further immigration; and directed where newcomers settled. In turn, the continued influx of immigrants maintained, extended, and strengthened informal ties of kinship and culture that spanned the Atlantic. As a result, this interchange between Europe and America was selective, favoring certain regions over others, such as Pennsylvania for most German immigrants.[7] Another symmetry was in the option to select their destinations. Most Irish and German emigrants had a choice, and even indentured servants had some say in choosing ships and masters. Turning west to settle in the American colonies and the new republic of the United States represented only one among possible directions and, in numerical terms, not the most popular one.[8]

Areas in Ireland and Germany with significant and recurring emigration were also alike in ways they experienced and responded to shifting pressure on existing resources. They were districts with a strong tradition of migration and with significant proportions of residents who had recently migrated into the region or knew kin or neighbors who had done so earlier. Both countries had long histories of considerable in-migration, repeatedly and over time. Ulster with its influx of Scottish settlers serves as an example for Ireland; the Rhine lands, which drew heavily on Swiss and other migrants in the aftermath of the Thirty Years' War, for Germany.[9] Tightly linked to local conventions that saw relocation as a reasonable answer to lessening prospects for a secure livelihood at home were modes of interaction among relatives, coreligionists, and neighbors that customarily provided those who considered leaving home with trustworthy news about opportunities elsewhere, with useful information about help along the way, and with support upon arrival in distant lands. Such association of communication and assistance among countrymen can be described as migration networks of "ethnic" character—a modern term that fits the distinctive and selective sets of connections among Irish and German emigrants in the eighteenth century.

The similarities between the German and Irish migrations extended also to the situation of newcomers in the American colonies. Irish and German immigrants settled in clusters that were unevenly distributed among the various regions along the eastern seaboard and in the backcountry. In each case, the manner of grouping was closely tied to particular ports of entry which channeled the incoming flow. Transatlantic trade connections had a critical impact on where people landed and first settled. Almost three-quarters of all

German voyagers came ashore in Philadelphia; about half of the migrants leaving Irish ports arrived in the Delaware Valley because sizable numbers disembarked in the Chesapeake and southern colonies and also Boston and New York[10] (Figure 1). Since opportunity for many Irish and German colonists depended on making a living off the land, immigrants typically moved on to places where available land was affordable, often areas of economic development in the borderlands that attracted newcomers of all kinds.

These types of locations shifted farther inland and southward over the course of the eighteenth century as settlements grew and filled up.[11] Irish and German immigrants played a significant role in this expansion because well-established resident Americans had little interest in restricting the flow of new colonists from Europe on whom they relied for the resources they brought with them—most importantly labor.[12] What had started out as useful policy grew into a tradition of tolerance of immigrants in most American colonies. While in practice tolerance was often limited and conditional, even then it contrasted sharply with laws and customs prevailing in most European countries. In the American colonies citizenship for alien settlers was usually tied to residency in a particular location and a declaration of loyalty to the Crown and its rightful representative in America such as William Penn and his heirs in Pennsylvania. In German territories, on the other hand, citizenship and residency were privileges that were tied to birth rights and the power to grant them was in the hands of the territorial lords. They could be obtained, but with considerable difficulty and at great expense.[13]

In important ways the connections that spanned the North Atlantic and that combined to hold migrants in complex webs of contacts on both sides of the ocean were similar, too, for Irish and German voyagers to the American colonies. In both cases, establishing reliable and lasting lines of communication and support depended heavily on bonds forged from kinship, shared beliefs, and compatriotism.[14] Evidence of group and chain migration among the flows from Ireland and Germany attests to the diverse ties that bound relatives, neighbors, and coreligionists among the many shiploads of Irish and German passengers.[15] Servants drawn from the hinterlands of southern Irish ports and Dublin represented a different strand than those indentured in Ulster ports; Quaker families from the southern counties in Ireland made use of connections on their way to North America different from those of Presbyterians from Ulster; sectarians, like the Mennonites and Moravians, differed in their experience of relocation from the majority of Lutheran and Reformed church people; migrants from Zurich relied more readily on other Swiss along the way while those whose origins were in Württemberg or the Palatinate thought their respective fellow countrymen to be most trustworthy; and members of households faced different challenges in coming to the New World than emigrants who made the move alone. Clearly, the flows from Ireland and Germany evolved variously to form stable links between particular points of contact in the Old and the New Worlds.

When enterprising, seasoned, and well-established immigrants became integral parts of the migration networks they played important roles in maintaining and expanding transatlantic connections. As cultural brokers they mediated between the Old World frames of reference of recent arrivals and the customary ways for making a living that had developed in their adopted land.[16] Under circumstances ideal for immigrants, former country men and women or coreligionists lent assistance, ranging from sound advice concerning preparations for the move across the Atlantic to easing the first steps after landing and helping in making informed decisions about work and acquiring land.[17] More often the situation did not favor the immigrants but rather the brokers who seized the opportunities for advancing their own interests. They made use of their special skills, knowledge, and experience in efforts to capitalize on the ignorance, unpreparedness, and helplessness of emigrants and greenhorn settlers. Some did so occasionally and on a small scale, such as those newlanders who recruited emigrants in German-speaking lands for shippers in Rotterdam in order to earn for themselves a place on board free of charge.[18] Others had vested professional interests in exploiting particular niches in the market, like tavern owners and boardinghouse keepers in the ports of embarkation and debarkation who targeted migrants for the sale of their services—at times ruthlessly at much inflated prices—and also merchants involved in the importation of passengers and the sale of servants. Still others sought to profit from ambitious recruitment schemes and speculative settlement ventures that depended on immigrant labor and capital.[19] As a result of all those interactions new connections formed, some of them fleetingly, others more lastingly, into new nodes from which yet other links could extend into different directions, thus constantly reshaping the networks that spanned the Atlantic.

≺ II ≻

Differences Between the Irish and German Migration Flows

Although the Irish and German migrations shared many fundamental characteristics, they also differed significantly in some ways. Common to both flows was a distinct wave-like pattern in the number of immigrants: rise, peak, and decline; yet the German tide crested before the Irish did. German immigration began to swell in the late 1720s, reached its maximum around mid-century (1749–54), and ebbed in the final decades of the century. In the case of the Irish, the extraordinary peak years in the late 1720s and early 1740s never fully developed into a wave that fit the modern type; but the later, larger surge did so when it reached high levels in the late 1760s and peaked in the final decades of the century before it subsided.[20]

There was also an important difference in the composition of the Irish and German migrations. Among German voyagers the proportion of families was relatively larger than among emigrants from Ireland, in part because more German-speaking boys traveled with their families. Young Irish males undertook the voyage more often on their own, neither acting as scouts for other family members to join them later nor to link up with relatives already settled in the colonies.[21] Moreover, a large proportion of single youths from Ireland came to the American colonies indentured to captains and ship owners who sold the indentures to the highest bidder upon arrival, which typically slowed or thwarted the immigrants' chances for success in the New World. German adolescents, too, were often bound out to serve, but usually their contracts were negotiated after their arrival in Philadelphia under circumstances that allowed parents some input in choosing American masters for their children.[22]

Closely related to the division among migrants according to whether they belonged to a family that relocated together or embarked on their voyage to North America independently was a striking geographical segregation among emigrants who left Irish ports. Most of the boys and young men boarded ships that sailed from Dublin and southern Irish ports, usually as servants bound to the merchants freighting the ships or the captains commanding them. Although their numbers fluctuated, the level of the migration made up of "parcels of servants" did not change dramatically overall.[23] Consequently, it was the families destined for the American colonies that determined the swelling and cresting of the tide from Ireland. The majority of these began their voyage in an Ulster port.[24] The differentiation of the Irish migration by geography also meant that the minority of Catholics among the mostly Presbyterian emigrants set out most often from the southern counties of Ireland to seek passage on ships stopping in Dublin and Cork.[25]

The make-up of the German migration did not reflect a comparable geographical segmentation, in part because the highly particularized political nature of the territories along the Rhine defies such regional analysis.[26] German areas of out-migration lost young men as well as families to the flow of migrants to North America. The observed shift from relatively more families in the early years of the German migration to fewer families during the peak period suggests that expansion beyond the core areas from which migrants were drawn attracted many of the young, single persons in search of opportunities wherever they opened up. As the tide receded in the decade before the American Revolution the relative proportion of families decreased even more.[27] Similarly, the denominational diversity found in the Rhine lands translated into a greater variety of religious beliefs and practices among German-speaking voyagers than was typical for Irish emigrants.

Most of the differences between the Irish and German migration flows, however, have their basis in the dissimilar order, laws, and culture of the two societies. Most fundamentally, because Ireland was part of Great Britain migrants were free to change their residence within its North Atlantic empire at will; and they could expect the norms of English law, language, and customs to extend to the colonies in which they settled. The right to move freely was much more restricted in German territories and set real limits for emigrants destined for North America. In theory everyone had a right to migrate, but in practice moving across territorial boundaries was a complicated bureaucratic process even for residents free from bondage. Bondspeople had to apply for manumission and subjects who were free needed passports and attestations that they were not bound to a "pursuing landlord."[28] Those restrictions increased not only the cost but also the risk of relocation and therefore raised the threshold for transforming potential migrants into actual emigrants.

For most Germans the decision to move across the Atlantic was final because, once released from obligations to their lords, they lost all rights and protection and had to start their lives in the American colonies as aliens unfamiliar with English ways and without the privileges English rule and law granted the country's natural-born citizens. Having experienced official dismissal, Germans bound for the American colonies became expatriates with a strong motivation to succeed in their lives overseas. They had used resources to pay for relocation in the first place, and those who tried to return faced high transportation costs and steep charges for re-admission as residents.[29]

Another critical difference between areas of out-migration in Ireland and Germany was determined by geographical characteristics. Southwestern Germany is landlocked despite the importance of the Rhine River as a major transportation and communication artery. Unlike their nineteenth-century counterparts who sailed from Hamburg and especially Bremen, German emigrants in the eighteenth century embarked in Rotterdam, which was a long way from where most voyagers started their journey. Traveling to Rotterdam added to the cost of relocation; and many emigrants were ill prepared to confront the hardships of the voyage across the Atlantic. In many instances the inland transportation to Rotterdam, especially when calculating expenses for food and hauling baggage, doubled the cost of the basic transatlantic fare of £5 sterling.[30] In contrast, life in Ireland has a distinct coastal orientation, with many residents living within walking distance of ports for ocean-going vessels. As a result, emigrants from there saved on the cost of the transatlantic move, the full fare of which from Irish ports to the American colonies fluctuated around £4 sterling, and they were more realistic about what to expect on board ocean-going ships, which was of help in planning for the venture.[31]

Also, some circumstances of settlement differed for Irish and German immigrants upon their arrival in the American colonies. The phases of ebb and flow were not synchronized between the Irish and German migration tides, and all immigrants who made their first steps toward building a new life in America at the same time were distributed across the colonies primarily according to the port of arrival and to where opportunities for work and for acquiring affordable land led after debarkation. Over the course of the century then, Irish and German servants had somewhat of a monopoly in the bound-labor market in some areas but had to compete in finding masters in other regions. In particular, the greater Delaware Valley was a market for German and Irish servants while the Chesapeake colonies imported many indentured Irishmen, including a sizable proportion of convicts, but relatively few Germans.[32]

Similarly, Irish and German settlers formed distinct clusters in backcountry regions that sometimes and in some areas seemed to hold promise mostly for Irish immigrants and at other times and in different locales mostly for German newcomers. In Pennsylvania, for example, German-speaking settlers were concentrated in parts of Lancaster, Berks, Northampton, and York counties while pockets of Irish settlement existed in Chester and Lancaster counties, the three lower counties that made up Delaware, and the western Pennsylvania counties that formed at the time of the Revolution. In the Shenandoah Valley and the Appalachian borderlands, settlement was more mixed but with distinctively Irish and German enclaves.[33] This ethnically differentiated clustering of colonists underscored perceptions of typically Irish or German ways of making a living and of building communities. The rise of ethnic stereotypes also led to competition—and tension—in areas where groups of Irish, Germans, and other immigrants and native-born Americans met and shaped regional cultures.[34]

Differences in the character of Irish and German migration networks were in large part reflections of the structure of transatlantic trade and communication. In the Irish case, commercial connections could develop without restrictions. By the beginning of the eighteenth century trade between Ireland and the American colonies was already fully integrated into the North Atlantic mercantile system, which provided merchants, captains, and migrants with reasonably reliable and fairly regular modes of communication and transportation. Trade in provisions and flaxseed and linen was central to this transatlantic exchange.[35] Under such circumstances migration networks were "human and prosaic" and could form and expand according to local practice along familiar and proven lines of special interests that linked people in Ireland and the American colonies, including partners in the business of supplying Irish servants to the American labor market, Quakers who followed through on William Penn's invitation to join in his holy experiment in Pennsylvania, and Irish investors in the American colonies who depended on their compatriots to settle and improve their lands.[36]

The situation was very different for the links that extended from the Rhine lands to North America. Without immediate and direct access to the British North Atlantic trade networks that provided for the transportation of goods and passengers from Europe to America, German emigrants had to rely on middlemen to offer and organize passage across the Atlantic, primarily merchants in Rotterdam and their partners in Philadelphia. The role of those agents varied significantly according to their own interests and also evolved over time in response to the changing nature of the German migration flow. The transformation of the occasional pursuit of transporting emigrants to America into a regular business in which profits depended on large numbers of passengers provided the organizational structure necessary for the trade in strangers to become firmly established and then to expand.[37]

Connections that were fashioned because of commercial interests and a desire for profit differed from those that were primarily personal in nature. The former were indispensable in providing the structural elements necessary for the transportation of emigrants across the Atlantic; the latter played a critical role in building the reputation of new settlements in the American colonies. The relationships that formed as migrants crossed the Atlantic were the basis for attachment between German expatriates in the colonies and their mother country, knitting strands of origin and destination together to create transatlantic networks. Such networks could spread the risks of long distance migration, assist new arrivals, provide labor and investment opportunities for established settlers, and cement ties between Old and New World localities.[38] In particular, language, local customs and tradition, and religion tied kin and former neighbors.

Among ordinary Germans, who viewed high German as the written language of the educated elite and authorities, the commonality of dialect probably was the most obvious bond among fellow countrymen. With the readily distinguishable idiom of regional tongues as foundation, shared local traditions and ideals about family, work, and inheritance could closely link groups of settlers according to geographical origin and distinguish them from others. Religion reinforced this regional, often local, diversity and fractured settlements within the colonies because German immigrants brought with them the experience of various Protestant churches and sects that played very different roles within the German territories. For example, the centripetal forces of regionalism affected the strength, if not the growth, of German Lutheranism in the American colonies.[39] In short, the informal ties that linked German settlements to their European origins depended on networks of communication and support and on cultural bonds that emphasized personal contacts and shared local or regional customs. Germantown and later also Philadelphia were particularly important nodes in the migration network because they provided a considerable number of German immigrants with their first way-station in the adjustment process of making their lives in colonial America.[40]

≺ III ≻

The Ebb and Flow of Irish and German Migration

Based on the comparison between the Irish and German migration flows in the eighteenth century it is clear that certain features characterized this kind of movement from Europe to America in more general terms. For an initial trickle of voluntary emigrants from a particular region or country to swell into a sizable stream that kept running over an extended period of time, a demographic profile that included families as well as single young people was required. In the seventeenth century, when the Chesapeake drew a disproportionate number of young men and the migration of mostly Puritan families to New England was cut off by civil war in England and its aftermath, this dynamic never fully developed.[41]

The mix of independent youths and groups of kith and kin was necessary to increase and sustain the migration flow. Young people alone could not draw large numbers of their countrymen to follow in their footsteps. They needed time to succeed in the New World before they could extend help to family members who had stayed behind or to unrelated newcomers whose labor offered attractive investment opportunities. Emigrating families, too, were restricted in whom they could entice to join them in the colonies. The high cost of relocation for families traveling together strained their resources, especially during the hard times that invariably accompanied their first years after landing. Such costs meant that families of some means could attract only the equally well-off among their relatives, coreligionists, and former neighbors; and that they had to wait before they could invite or employ those who needed assistance with relocation across the Atlantic. Once both kinds of immigrants were well established, however, the example of their success and their need for additional labor provided powerful incentives for a second wave of immigrants—single young men and women and families—to pursue opportunities overseas.[42]

For a tide of immigrants to gather depended also on the geographic and social composition of the migration flow. Significant movements across the Atlantic drew first and continuously on core regions with sufficiently deep and varied reservoirs of potential emigrants and then also periodically on other areas to augment the numbers of voyagers to the West. The major sea ports in Ireland and their hinterlands constituted cores whose boundaries extended farther inland at times of increased emigration; the counterparts in central Europe were the German-speaking territories along the Rhine. As a result, substantial segments among the migrants shared particular homeland origins but were reasonably diverse in their social and economic backgrounds. The pioneers from core emigration regions were usually relatively wealthy while many of those with limited resources could undertake the move only later, after the cost of relocation had dropped or when means for financing the voyage were available.

The timing of the flow, especially the beginning motions, was tied to circumstances in the area of out-migration. Among the many and wide-ranging conditions that contributed to the potential for substantial emigration, two characteristics were crucial. First was a tradition to migrate—not simply in reaction to adversity or in anticipation of difficulties at home but also as an enterprising strategy in pursuit of better opportunities far away. Second was access to trustworthy sources of pertinent information about work and settlement chances overseas.

For the transformation from potential emigration to actual relocation to occur, however, additional factors had to fall into place.

Foremost among them was the example of earlier emigrants who had made the move successfully and who presented demonstrable proof of their achievement—in letters, through reliable intermediaries, or in person.[43] Report of the accomplishments of those pioneers was most likely to trigger more emigration, especially when it was coupled with invitations or offers of assistance to those who had stayed behind. This "trigger mechanism" has been demonstrated often; the persuasiveness of letters, especially, can hardly be overemphasized—one of the reasons for governments intent on regulating migration to censor them and for merchants with interests in the transatlantic transportation of emigrants to use them as recruiting tools. Whenever persistent links between earlier migrants and potential emigrants were matched with affordable relocation costs, regular channels developed that drew increasing numbers from a broadening pool of emigrants. In turn, discouraging news from former neighbors not only curbed the expansion of the migration from the peripheral points of the networks but also slowed the flow in well-established channels. Reports about the difficulties the German-speaking settlers encountered in Nova Scotia and Kennebec, Maine, for instance, discouraged their friends from emigrating and forced recruiting agents for the settlement projects to cast a wider net in order to attract colonists.[44]

Particular circumstances on the American side of the Atlantic determined whether migration flows dwindled or surged. Most important for developing a persuasive reputation that endured was the fundamental legal and, eventually, social and cultural acceptance of immigrants as Americans. As critical as this assumption was for the integration of foreigners into American society, it was matched by the premise that foreigners abide by the laws and adjust to the ways of the country. Even on that foundation, the process of integration took time and did not come easily or cheaply. More immediate economic and social conditions also played significant roles. Peace times and economic growth generally encouraged immigration, especially when increasing development depended on additional labor. On the one hand, the many dangers of travel on the Continent and at sea during times of war are reflected in the small number of German-speaking immigrants listed in the Philadelphia shiplists in the 1740s, late 1750s, and early 1760s; on the other hand, the expansion of the economy in the greater Delaware Valley also shows in the increasing number of German newcomers during the first half of the eighteenth century.[45] Although such demand opened opportunities for immigrants, the prospect of social mobility—real or perceived—was critical in sustaining the influx of newcomers reacting to offers of work and land. With some promise that the risks and difficulties associated with moving, new beginnings, and hard work would pay off, prospects of land and labor not only served to mobilize emigrants with little choice but also attracted those who could afford to be more deliberate in pursuing chances far from home.

How migrants knew of and assessed opportunities for making a life in North America was closely tied to their access to pertinent information and to their skill in making use of it. Lines of communication usually paralleled networks of trade. For ordinary people, who made a living from pursuits in agriculture and as artisans, that meant news was most often filtered through people they knew locally, including officials, ministers, and innkeepers, who were likely to read newspapers, as well as journeymen, neighbors, and relatives who made use of traditional forms of oral communication.[46] Such diverse and multi-layered points of contact facilitated sorting and evaluating information, thereby allowing farmers and tradesmen and the various members of their households to judge what was true and important to them and also what kind of intelligence was reliable and which messengers were trustworthy. It is clear, however, that emigrants were extremely selective in their use of information and seem not to have calculated the odds for their survival and success realistically—or they would have stayed home.[47]

Whether and when local networks of personal interactions interlocked with existing channels in which migration flowed regionally depended on specific forms of recruiting. Successful recruitment to the American colonies not only made use of local connections in targeting and drawing emigrants but also relied on "ethnic" support in the relocation and settlement process. Long-term success of migration networks that spanned the Atlantic was built on establishing a positive reputation in the business of transporting and placing immigrants and on implementing feedback mechanisms that maintained significant links between areas of emigration in the Old World and areas of immigrant settlement in the New World. Recruitment played a critical role in transforming local networks through transatlantic extensions. Recruiting agents were an extraordinarily diverse group who differed in their goals as well as where and how they operated. Among them were competent and considerate leaders of particular parties of voyagers and also ruthless entrepreneurs who, in their quest for profit, exploited and defrauded migrants.[48] In any case, their numbers and schemes proliferated when migration peaked and competition for passengers and settlers was keen; they had considerable influence as cultural brokers and some impact on the timing and choice of destination of particular groups of immigrants.

≺ IV ≻

Effects on Areas of Out-Migration

For the voyagers caught in the migration flow across the Atlantic there was hardly any question that the move to the New World would fundamentally change their lives. For those who stayed behind in Europe the impact of emigration was more varied, as was the effect of immigrants upon those already settled in North America.

Overall, the short-term effects of emigration on areas that lost inhabitants were limited because the numbers of migrants to North America were relatively small. Even when the departure of emigrants was more concentrated in demographic terms, such losses were made up quickly, which meant regions that experienced pressures on their populations and resources gained only temporary relief. In social and economic terms, however, circumstances were different in localities that witnessed a major exodus at any one time or that underwent dislocation in the wake of repeated emigration.[49] Conditions changed, and most likely improved somewhat, for those who stayed home as they benefited from the redistribution of property the emigrants left behind and from the sale of goods and services to the colonists preparing for the move across the Atlantic.[50] Landlords and employers who had to adjust to the leaving of their tenants and laborers, respectively, complained vociferously about the disruption of their operations. Their rhetoric underlay the calls for restricting emigration in Ireland and Germany. They were silent about the chances such losses offered them to charge more for new leases and pay lower wages to newly-hired servants and workers.[51]

Territorial lords in central Europe and their officials viewed emigration in light of population policies deemed beneficial for their territories.[52] Consequently, they tried to control who of their subjects left or stayed put. Undesirable inhabitants were encouraged to relocate beyond the borders so that they ceased to be a burden to the state. For example, the Council of Bern actively backed the Carolina settlement venture of Georg Ritter and Christoph von Graffenried, in part to rid their territory of poor residents.[53] The authorities levied extra taxes and fees, however, in efforts to discourage productive and wealthy residents from moving away. Such measures were meant to prevent any losses of future capital, skilled manpower, and revenue. Nassau-Dillenburg raised the removal tax—just one example among many devised to restrict emigration.[54]

Ironically, the restrictive measures in German-speaking territories intended to curb emigration had also the unplanned effect of keeping connections between those who had left for America and those who had stayed behind open and active. The recovery of inheritances was especially important in this regard. Because emigrants who sought permission to leave had to pay taxes on their patrimony, settlement of estates with heirs in America required satisfaction of any claims overseas—making communication between descendants on both sides of the Atlantic imperative. What started out as an occasional private legal pursuit with few cases in the first several decades of the eighteenth century developed into a highly specialized, small-scale, speculative business that attracted casual as well as professional agents. After dismissal procedures in the Rhine lands tightened in reaction to increasing emigration, the number of newlanders who traveled to continental Europe to collect inheritances grew considerably around mid-century.[55] Their effect on triggering emigration did not escape official notice. As a consequence, territorial authorities tried to regulate, even ban, newlanders gathering legacies left to American colonists while enterprising businessmen made use of those brokers and their methods in devising their own schemes for recruiting and profiting from the transportation of passengers and their goods.[56]

In the American colonies the need for labor, tenants, and farmbuyers brought about ethnic diversity. The Irish and German migration regimes had significant impact on this development as newcomers from Ireland and Germany built ethnically distinct communities and developed diverse paths for integrating immigrants into

America. All immigrant settlements were part of the fabric of the receiving society and even the most homogeneously Irish or German clusters did not stay isolated and pure for long; thus dealing with neighbors who were different became a fact of American life. The creolization of cultures occurred especially in areas of expansion or growth such as the borderlands, where colonists displaced Native Americans from their ancestral lands, and also in the major seaports and their hinterlands, where immigrants first landed and which for many newcomers became temporary and even permanent stops on their way to becoming American.

In frontier as well as urban societies, immigrant success was determined and measured at the local level in comparison and competition with others who vied for prosperity and position. The yardstick for achievement and status varied from place to place and changed as the second generation replaced the pioneers and as other generations followed later. All such measures of accomplishment were always uniquely American; but some were cast in terms of Old World ways that had been successfully transplanted and adapted to New World circumstances—such as the Pennsylvania German barns that dot the landscape of the Delaware Valley.[57] Once immigrants, more often their children and grandchildren, had fulfilled the American dream and were assured of their acceptance as Americans, ethnicity could become a choice and ethnic identities and Old World links could be invented and reinvented in accordance with changes that transformed places over time. In the open-ended process of cultural construction, the exploration of immigrant cultures can go beyond the pioneering generation and delineate how the immigrants' descendants and their neighbors lent meaning to the particular ways and traditions of the communities into which they were born or had moved.[58]

Immigrants along paths to successful integration also held their good fortune in America up to European standards and used their accomplishments in the new land to draw others across the Atlantic. Irrespective of whether they did so to assist former countrymen or to profit from investment in the labor, skills, or goods of immigrants, the direct and personal links to Ireland and Germany helped trigger migration flows and build durable channels of communication. It mattered little if Irish and German settlers extended invitations to relatives, friends, and former neighbors implicitly or explicitly, if they did so occasionally or repeatedly, on a small or large scale—all such contacts had the combined effect of directing increasingly massive streams of German and Irish immigrants to the North American colonies and the early Republic. When German and Scots-Irish Americans were no longer able or willing to give preferential treatment to their respective compatriot newcomers, the flow ebbed.

≺ V ≻

Effects of Irish and German Immigration on Settlement in North America

The significance of the Irish and German immigrant flows to North America lies in the self-generating nature of the transatlantic migration that presaged the classic waves of the nineteenth century. Most importantly, the same migration regime fit eighteenth-century Irish and German immigrants. In both cases, the movement across the Atlantic started small; pioneering groups of reasonably prosperous colonists from the Rhine lands and Ulster transferred their households—family and servants—and succeeded in capitalizing on opportunities in American provinces with developing economies. Their success and the communities they built provided models for others, became pivotal nodes in ethnic networks that spanned the Atlantic, and drew others—single young people as well as families—to follow in the footsteps of the vanguard, thereby creating self-generating dynamics that shaped the character, intensity, and direction of subsequent immigrant flows.

Fuel for increases in migration remained scarce as long as relocation costs were prohibitive for most potential emigrants in southwestern Germany and Ulster. In an era of restrictively regulated trade and credit, mechanisms for financing the voyage were difficult and cumbersome even for passengers from Ireland but especially for those from the Rhine lands. Only when the redemptioner system was developed could German and Irish immigrants of limited means pursue opportunities in the American colonies. As a variant form of indentured servitude it allowed emigrants in effect to charge the price of the transatlantic fare until after their arrival in America—a financing strategy beneficial to single young men and especially families. Most often immigrants indebted for the voyage contracted with American masters for specified terms of labor in return for the redemption of their outstanding fares. This type of contract labor flourished primarily in the greater Delaware Valley and largely along ethnic lines; that is, German immigrants were bound mostly to German-American masters while migrants from Ulster usually became indentured to Scots-Irish settlers.[59]

The Pennsylvania model of modified indentured servitude was effective as a labor system, created intricate and far-flung networks of credit, and in its cultural—mostly ethnic—dimension shaped the character of families, households, and local communities. In the Delaware Valley bound servants competed successfully with family, wage, and slave labor. Consequently, the investment in contract labor for masters and servants alike had to be economically sound or provide other significant trade-offs for this type of servitude to remain a viable option throughout the century. The employment of contract labor was widespread among urban as well as rural residents of Pennsylvania and, conversely, a significant proportion of European immigrants—especially teenagers and young men and women—served some time as indentured servants. For masters as well as servants it was easy to calculate the respective economic returns from bound labor. Less obvious are how other considerations and circumstances made service in households, on farms, and in the trades sufficiently tolerable for contract laborers not to run away and how they proved satisfactory enough in terms of quality and performance for employers to choose servants from among other forms of labor. Extreme expectations, undue exploitation, and unjustifiable behavior by masters or servants strained the system. Yet as long as most participants gained from it, occasional difficulties and abuses had little lasting effect.

The modifications that made operation of the system of indentured servitude in Pennsylvania successful over a long period of time were founded in part on significant variability and flexibility in the supply of and demand for this particular kind of labor. Like other colonies that experienced labor scarcity, Pennsylvania started out satisfying its labor needs by first supplementing the servants whom the pioneers had brought when they made the move across the Atlantic as members of their households with slaves and also with indentured servants. The early settlers imported boys and single young men from England and Ireland whose labor contracts had been made in the ports of departure with the intent of selling those agreements at variable prices to interested American colonists. This source of labor continued in place throughout the colonial period, but it diminished in relative importance when increasing numbers of immigrants, especially German-speaking newcomers, became redemptioners. In Pennsylvania, there were no differences in legal terms between servants who were imported with binding contracts and those who negotiated their indentures in Philadelphia. However, the particular circumstances under which those agreements were made affected the specific terms and the customary features that shaped immigrant servitude and acted as selection criteria for prospective masters.

Conventional indentures covered the cost of the voyage for mostly boys and young men from England and Ireland who migrated to the colonies to serve for a set number of years—traditionally four or until reaching the age of maturity.[60] Servants were generally familiar with this kind of arrangement from practices common in their homelands; employers, too, acted according to their understanding of and experience with the system, which added freedom dues at the end of the servants' terms to their costs and which put a premium on matching immigrants' characteristics and skills with particular labor needs. Trained and competent artisans whose trades were in demand cost more than unskilled, ill-suited, or inept laborers. Making good choices was difficult for masters not only because they were constrained by what they required and how much they could spend. They also had to make their picks from a limited number of servants without benefit of reliable, independent information about them because the immigrants were strangers and usually came without recommendation and merchants and captains had vested interests of their own. Resales of indentures and running away can be viewed as reactions to bad matches between masters and servants.

What marked the basis of all indentures for service was a widespread belief in the usefulness, if not advantages, of investing in immigrant labor. Those who procured, traded, employed, and provided such labor did so primarily out of self-interest, but the economy of the province gained from the infusion of labor and capital, both important ingredients for expansion and development. In pursuing interest and profit individually, the various participants in the system clearly differed in how they defined their concerns and calculated their gains, although on balance their selfish motivation and behavior combined to attract immigrant labor over the long term. Much of the evidence about how well or poorly the system worked is indirect and sporadic, based on impersonal administrative records such as lists of indentures, advertisements for runaway servants, court proceedings concerning disputed terms of indentures, and merchants' accounts, rather than on personal tales. German-speaking immigrants complained about indentured servitude, but always about particular abuses or situations, not about the system as such. Henry Melchior Mühlenberg, a prominent German Lutheran pastor, condemned the circumstances that forced parents to bind out their children to strangers and that pressed German immigrants into service with Englishmen. Notwithstanding those concerns, he and many others like him made use of the system and employed indentured servants in their own households, thereby not only offering immigrants fare debt redemption but also modeling labor practices for their children and for newcomers in the greater Delaware Valley.[61]

Merchants with interests in developing the shipping of emigrants across the Atlantic into a profitable business introduced the innovative adaptation of indentured servitude—a strategy which depended in large part on the willingness of German settlers to invest in the future labor of kin and former neighbors. In effect, German colonists financed the surge of German immigration—families and single young men—that crested around mid-century. When German support for newcomers waned, emigration via Rotterdam declined, but the fundamental organization of the trade in emigrants remained in place until well after the turn to the nineteenth century. It provided the foundation on which other merchants based their operations on different routes, first in the case of migration from Ulster to the American colonies and new republic of the United States in the final decades of the eighteenth century. Colonists from Ireland established networks that attracted a significant portion of families from Ulster and that provided those newly-arrived countrymen with support in the relocation process.

After the turn to the nineteenth century shippers in other ports of departure in England and continental Europe modeled their operations on the earlier business in emigrants and adapted its basic features to the changed circumstances of their own time. In making profitable use of underutilized cargo space on westbound voyages they no longer had to rely on indentured servitude and the redemptioner system as financing mechanisms that allowed poor emigrants to relocate across the Atlantic. Instead merchants could improve the profitability of their operations by increasing the number of passengers they shipped because more emigrants took advantage of lower fares and easier forms of credit, mostly prepaid tickets. This payment option not only enabled already established immigrants to lend a helping hand to relatives and friends but also let American employers tap into a vast pool of labor.

What distinguishes the classic, nineteenth-century, migrations from the eighteenth-century German and Irish forerunners are differences in degree and certain particulars, not in the basic structure and dynamics. Most impressive to modern Americans is the difference in scale—in the nineteenth century populations in Europe and the United States were larger and the absolute numbers of immigrants were bigger. Other variances occurred because of developments in technology and international relations, especially trade, banking, and transportation. As the journey became shorter, relocation costs decreased and could be more easily financed. Those advances translated into operational features that made trade and investment in immigrants more widely profitable, for merchants on both sides of the Atlantic and for businessmen and employers in the United States. In turn, they had the effect of lowering the barriers for Europeans willing or pressed to move overseas, thus expanding the potential pool of emigrants significantly in social and geographical terms. The nineteenth century became the classic age of voluntary European mass migration to America. This migration was modeled on the tides of German and Irish immigrants in the eighteenth century—single young men as well as families—that swelled, crested, and waned as well-established German and Irish settlers in the American colonies and in the new republic found it advantageous to lend substantial support to their respective countrymen in relocating to the New World.

Migration and Collective Identities Among the Enslaved and Free Populations of North America

MECHAL SOBEL

CONCEPTIONS OF IDENTITY shaped the form and direction of migrant streams, as many of the chapters in this study illustrate.[1] This chapter will analyze transformations in identity that occurred as a result of migration, transformations that had enormous long-run implications for people in the Atlantic world. What follows are case studies of individuals who came to America between 1740 and 1810 and whose identity changes had a crucial impact on their own lives and often on the continuing streams of migration.

Sigmund Freud's use of the term identity is widely seen as seminal. In 1926, when speaking to his B'nai Brith group in Vienna, Freud told them he was a Jew not through "faith" or "national pride," but due to "many obscure emotional forces which were the more powerful the less they could be expressed in words, as well as a clear consciousness of inner identity, the safe privacy of a common mental construction."[2] Or so his German words have been translated. In the German original, the last phrase, Freud's explanatory words for identity, were "die Heimlichkeit der inneren Konstruktion," which alternatively might be translated as "the at-home-ness of a secret inner construction."[3] Whatever the best translation, it would appear that Freud saw his own identity as a constructed inner part of himself that he felt was "home," although we know that this was a conflict-ridden home for him.

To be at home with oneself as well as with a group identity can be seen as both very good and yet very dangerous. Leon Grinberg and Rebecca Grinberg have noted that "In children's games, zones of security are called home."[4] When playing hide-and-seek and baseball, home is a good place to return to, but in adult life those seen as "too" tied to home or too enmeshed in a collective identity are, in the contemporary West, generally regarded as immature or unhealthy personalities. (The Grinbergs note that such people find migration most difficult.[5])

Analysts of early modern Europe and of pre-Colonial Africa generally believe that most people on both these continents were deeply at home in their cultures. They also suggest that most people shared in collective identities that fostered we-selves: that their sense of self was so tied to that of others that they themselves were not conscious of where their selves ended and others began.[6] Although this may well have been the normative self for males and females in early modern Europe, change was soon underway both in Europe and in the colonies established by Europeans in North America. In America, over the course of the eighteenth century, and most markedly during and after the Revolution, people began to develop more individuated selves as they began to live lives that violated the previous norms and demands of their communities. Many began changing from a feeling of enmeshment to a sharply perceived individuation, from a sense of community to a sense of personal agency.[7]

The ideal and normative person in pre-modern societies, both in Europe and in Africa, looked to past generations for wisdom, accepted the authority of those in power, and did not establish firm personal boundaries but nevertheless hoped for a stable and unchanging identity. If these people narrated their lives they generally told of events they had lived through. They did not believe they had faced personal choices or could have become different people. In the late eighteenth century, when the number of personal narratives written by the poor and middling sort vastly increased, many individuals, often influenced by the self narratives of John Bunyan, began to narrate a different script involving painful changes in their selves.[8] They noted their rejection of old values (most often religious but increasingly political) and they recognized that they acted in new ways for which they took responsibility. They reframed their pasts as dramas in which they faced crises of choice and underwent new development.

One of the key ways in which such personal change was begun was through opposition to a selected enemy: one had to discover or invent an "alien, strange or hostile" other which then had to be "attacked and destroyed."[9] In view of this, it is likely that migration, both from Europe and Africa and within America, played a significant role in this process of change in identity, as during migration new enemy figures were readily "discovered." "Others" whom migrants actually met in their new situations were widely perceived as "alien, strange, or hostile." In turn, migrants became the alien others for earlier arrivals in their new communities. Africans came to play this role in the inner lives of Euro-Americans, and Euro-Americans played the same role for African Americans, while some ethnic groups, the Irish in particular, seemed to be the "butt" of all others. The classic alien figures of the opposite gender were often intertwined with the new enemies. Rejecting as well as introjecting aspects of these others led to radical changes in self.

The life narratives of migrants to America provide vivid evidence of this change in identity, and of the role played by alien others both in individual development and in shaping collective identities. This chapter considers the narratives of a small group of migrants who roughly represent the origins of the people who came to America by the end of the eighteenth century. By 1775 "almost half the colonists traced their ancestors back to countries other than England. About 30 percent of the settlers came from Scotland, Ireland, Germany, Holland, France and Portugal; one of every five American had African origins." By 1800 a significantly larger percentage of the settlers were from outside England.[10] The narratives chosen are those of thirteen migrants, four from England, four from Africa, two from Scotland, two from Ireland, and one from Germany. They include men and women; free people, indentured servants, and slaves; Anglicans, Animists, Catholics, Baptists, Methodists, and Moravians. In the cases where the greatest change in identity occurred, the individuals came to have an awareness of that which was other or alien that they did not want to be and actively opposed, as well as a commitment to something outside themselves, most often a new community with a collective identity that legitimated their change in the desired direction.[11]

≺ I ≻

Permeable Selves and Collective Identities

John Harrower did not write an autobiography, although perhaps he would have had he lived longer; but he did begin a diary when he began his journey from home on December 6, 1773. Home was at the northern tip of Great Britain, on the Orkney Islands. A tradesman who had fallen into serious debt, and may well have faced a prison term, Harrower virtually abandoned his wife and family and fled to London hoping to find employment there or in Holland. Down to his "last shilling" with no other choice at hand, he indentured himself to go to Virginia for four years and ended up as a tutor at Belvidera, the plantation of William Dangerfield outside of Fredericksberg. Harrower had come to America as an "accidental immigrant," as so many were.

Harrower's diary and his letters to his wife open a window on his identity and identity change over the next three and a half years. (He died in Virginia in July of 1776.) Harrower had clearly begun his journey with a strong need to maintain his Scottish identity and sought comfort in it. For his mess (or "Mace") on board ship he sought out Scotsmen, and he and the four who joined him were, as he notes, "always called the Scots Mace." Once in Virginia, he looked up others from Scotland and formed friendships with them, and he sought out the Scots among the British prisoners taken by the Patriots and befriended them.[12]

Although his attachment to home was very strong, only six months after he arrived in Virginia Harrower suggested that his wife join him there, and by December of that year (1774) he wrote her of his high hopes for a shared American life:

> I yet hope (please God) if I am spared, some time to make you a Virginian Lady among the woods of America which is by far more pleasant than the roaring seas around abo't Zetland. And yet to make you eat more wheat Bread in your old age than what you have done in your youth.

Two weeks after writing this letter a dream partially fulfilled his wishes. "Last night I dreamt that my wife came to me here," he wrote on December 20, 1774, but the dream left him very unhappy as in it his wife had left their sons in Scotland.[13] Harrower's dream probably expressed his longing not only for his wife and sons, but also for parts of himself that he had, as it were, left behind. A year later, feeling particularly depressed at the holiday season, he wrote a poem expressing this pain and longing:

> For in prison at large I'm plac't
> Boun'd to it, day and night . . .
> No freendly soul . . .
> My greiff to ease, or hear my moan.[14]

While Harrower probably began changing the day he left home, his pace of change accelerated in Virginia. At Belvidera he was adjured to "talk English" and to teach "English"—not Scottish—to his charges. Only six months after his arrival he wrote home that the teaching of English "was a little aquard to me at first but now quite easy." He found speaking "high English" more difficult but he noted that he did it "the best I can."[15]

Harrower, aware that he was changing in other ways as well, wrote his wife "I suppose you wou'd scarce know me now." He ostensibly was referring to his clothes, which in Virginia were all white cotton (and "I may put on clean linen," he noted, "every day if I please,") but it is clear that much else had changed as well. He presented himself to his wife as a new gentleman, eating his breakfast and a large mid-afternoon meal at the fancy table of Colonel Dangerfield and his wife, sitting together with their guests. While all the food was served in the "English taste," it was the fine wheat bread that he now ate (and told his wife of) that he regarded as the symbol of upper-class life. The company he now kept included not only many English people but many Africans as well and he found himself playing many new roles. While he continued to trade goods occasionally, he had become a successful teacher, instructing the Dangerfield children as well as those of neighbors, including a deaf and dumb child, and a group of the enslaved. He had briefly acted as an overseer, and he had even begun planting for himself. It is likely that he envisioned being a slaveowner and a landowner within a relatively short time.

Harrower's wife recognized that changes were occurring in her husband. We don't have her letters to him, but in one of his he responds to her "Jocks [jokes] upon me with respect to my getting a Virginian Lady." She clearly feared he wanted one, but he wrote he would let his sons marry Virginians, and that he hoped they would have her advice as to their choices.[16]

On many levels Harrower experienced an unusually comfortable period of indenture. He was treated with great respect by his master, and was allowed to earn money, by both teaching and trading. Although often very lonely and depressed, he made many new contacts. In this period he also adopted many new values into his world view. Symbolic of these is the term he used for the African woman who cleaned out his bedroom: he referred to her as "a bonny black bairn," and he hired her to do weaving for him after her work for Dangerfield was done. Harrower also taught a black catechism class without payment, and he temporarily took over as overseer when Dangerfield dismissed his manager. Contact with Africans was clearly an integral part of his New World experience. His diary records no negative comment on Africans, but neither does it reflect any negative feelings about the institution of slavery. He evidently had begun to envision that both he and his family would live out their lives in its midst. While he did not live long enough to fulfill this dream, his diary suggests that he was developing a new sense of himself.

Harrower died after an illness in July of 1776 when he had only six months left to serve as an indentured servant. During his three and a half years in Virginia, circumstances, American circumstances as it were, put Harrower in a position where he had to change. The act of enslaving himself for four years, followed by what was seen as responsible behavior on board ship as well as at the plantation, led him to a position that opened many new possibilities. With the aid of his master, Dangerfield, he was being groomed for introduction into a higher class than the one he had left in the Old World. Clean white clothes and fresh white bread symbolized the potential for a new identity that he did not live long enough to develop fully. While his diary provides strong evidence that he had begun to change, there is no suggestion of any inner dynamic, no inner conflict or outer problem that deeply engaged him. The war underway at his death might well have put him in a harder place had he lived longer. At war's outset he would not commit himself openly to the American side, but he seemed to take pride in patriot actions at the same time as he sympathized with the Scottish soldiers taken captive. The war, and a change in his status to freeman, might have forced him to commit himself, but until his death he avoided full commitment.

The next four people in this cohort, William Lee, John R. Shaw, Beulah Brockden/Magdalena, and Ofodobendo Wooma/Andrew, were migrants who lived in America for a far longer time than Harrower did, and whom we might expect to have changed more. Each of these four can be said to have arrived with a collective identity that limited his or her individuation. The first two seemed to maintain essential aspects of the sense of self that they came with, while the second two developed identities in America that seemed very different from their African identities but which may well have had deep parallels to those of their youth.

William Lee was a young English immigrant who arrived in America in 1768.[17] Born in Hadfield in 1744, he had completed an apprenticeship to a flax dresser before he left home. Ostensibly he set out to make more money than he could in England and was not on a voyage of discovery. However, he soon went out to the wilderness of western Pennsylvania where he went hunting with an Indian, a wild act for a young flax dresser seeking money. He did turn back to more routine employment when, like Harrower, he found that while not properly educated to be a teacher he could serve as one in the New World. He found a position as a tutor on a plantation near Lancaster; but hearing that wages were better in the South, he moved on and found employment on a Virginia plantation. A year later he chose to go north again and trekked across the Alleghenies and down the Ohio River, where he prepared to settle. When Indians attacked Lee moved once again. This time he held others responsible for his change in plans, maintaining that white land-grabbers had incited the Indians. In May of 1774 he reached New Orleans and began a career as a sailor, rapidly moving up the chain of command to become a captain. While in this position he proposed to a propertied widow, and after his marriage became a farmer on "his" new land. It turned out that "others" had stolen this land from Indians and Lee vented his anger at the white thieves when it had to be returned. He then became an overseer on a slave plantation; an owner of a trading vessel; and a commissary on an expedition to Mobile. In October of 1780 he moved on to Georgia, where he bought a plantation about 100 miles from Savannah.

In twelve years Lee had gone from a poor flax dresser to a slave and plantation owner. The relative independence from English class rigidity in America had played a role in his success, but the values he attributed to the Indians and adopted for himself had clearly been a repressed part of himself prior to his migration. He was attracted to what he saw as their freedom from moral restraints. His idealization of the Indians symbolized his separation from most Americans. After over a decade in America he felt no commitment to it. The Revolution, however, caught up with him, the "rebels" insisting that he fight with them or leave. He promised to join them, but hid out in the woods until his wife gave birth in August of 1781. "I left her the same evening," he was not ashamed to write, "and made my escape down to Savannah: for there was no safety in the country, as both loyalists and rebels went about plundering and killing all who joined the opposite parties!"[18] In mid-August Lee was on a ship heading for England when he was taken captive on a French privateer, but he was rescued by the crew of an English ship and returned to England in 1782. There he wrote the narrative of his adventures, emphasizing at length his interest in the Indians, but never suggesting that any interest or ties bound him to his American family. He signaled his pre-modern view of himself by counting up the miles he had traveled in thirteen years as though they were the sum of his life.

Lee was a traveler and a fair-weather migrant, who had succeeded in many enterprises but showed no sign of having significantly changed his identity in the process. His narrative is a record of the events that he witnessed but did not take responsibility for. His only duty seems to have been to save his body, without any concern for his soul. While he dreamed of living outside the confines of a white community, envying the Indians whom he saw as "a law unto themselves," he did not seem to crave a space for individuation. He simply wanted to be relieved of responsibility for others, and he achieved this by migrating once again. In his case, travel and change of society were not synonymous with inner change, as Lee did not create an alien other nor make any commitment beyond the one he had to his own needs.

John Robert Shaw, born in Yorkshire in 1761, also refused to accept responsibility for his own actions. His narrative describes a clearly permeable self: others led him to "vicious" and evil acts. "They" led him to run away from work as a stuff-weaver when he was sixteen. Believing that fate controlled his future, he went "to a magician, to have my fortune told."[19] Apparently fulfilling his fate, he went directly to join the army, where he soon found himself "tricked" into going to America. The Revolutionary War was apparently not what he expected, and a massacre at Tappan, New Jersey, that he witnessed and perhaps participated in, shook him deeply. Taken prisoner by the Americans, he was very harshly treated, but a drunken guard allowed him to escape. Claiming he had arrived in America as an indentured servant, he joined the American army; he also became an "accidental immigrant." Not having seen himself as very moral before he became a soldier, Shaw nevertheless blamed his companions in the army with breaking all his ties to Christian morality. He acknowledged that he had become a drinker and a gambler and an immoral man. He was legally married twice and was proud that his second wife, Mary O'Hara, who had come to America as a redemptioner, was a "pure" woman, while he acknowledged that he had established an additional "temporary marriage" and often spent time with prostitutes.

By the war's end Shaw was an alcoholic, and he turned to fortune telling to support his habit. His skills at magic, as well as his army training with explosives, led him to new work: he become known as a "water-witch"—a man who could use a divining rod to locate the proper place to dig or dynamite a well. He continued to drink and work, often injuring himself in the process. Blinded in one eye, he also lost one leg and was severely burned, but he went on digging wells.

Shaw had not chosen to come to America, and he did not consciously choose to become an American. He was not able to give up his excessive drinking, although he tried, and he also failed when he tried to become a Methodist. Shaw sought to change himself, but he made no outside commitment to aid him in this process nor is there any evidence that he developed an enemy other. Although he failed when he tried to adopt more middle class mores, the norms he conformed to were widely accepted by the poor.

The narratives of two African Americans, Beulah Brockden/Magdalena and Ofodobendo Wooma/Andrew, are very unusual in several respects: they are the narratives of a husband and wife, and they are from people enslaved in the first half of the eighteenth century.[20] Ofodobendo/Andrew, an Igbo who was enslaved at age eight, spent about a quarter of his short narrative reporting memories of Africa. He noted his circumcision, the fact that his people were forbidden to eat pork, his fear that some Africans were still cannibals (and might eat him), and his lack of knowledge that white people existed. He memorialized his enslavement in detail, holding his own poor brother responsible for pawning him in return for two goats. In his account he suggested that there was little he could have done to have changed his early life, although he still remembered that his first owner blamed him for damaging a tobacco pipe and sold him on this pretext. He recorded that on the slaver coming to America he felt totally isolated and came close to starving, which led him to eat pork for the first time. This change in diet was noted as a harbinger of the major external and internal changes he would continue to undergo.

By 1741 Ofodobendo/Andrew was the property of a man in New York City, whom he identified only as a Jew. He feared this man would sell him to traders he dealt with in the West Indies. At this point his narrative changed and his own actions began to take on new significance. The major portion of his narrative retells the story of the role he himself had played in getting a Mr. Thomas Noble to buy him. On the advice of neighbors, he prayed to the Christian God to help him. Taken on trial, he behaved in a way that led Noble to choose him over another candidate. He clearly had analyzed what it was that a very religious Christian would appreciate, and he did his best to fulfill Noble's image of an African anxious for the saving Grace of Christianity.

What began as self-serving behavior soon became a commitment to a wider goal. Moravian Brethren who held prayer meetings in Noble's home "often told me that our Savior had shed his blood for me and all black men and that He had as much love for me, and everyone, as for white people, which I did not believe." Ofodobendo/Andrew "resolved when possible to find out whether what I so often heard from the Brethren was true." Resolve became the key value in his narrative. He resolved to learn to read and did. He resolved to pray daily, which he generally did. In fact, he apparently came to a full plan of Christian behavior before he joined the Moravians. "I often undertook to do my work for the day joyfully, to deal in love with every man, and to pray continually." When he failed to live up to these undertakings, he feared that the devil was after him. He came close to committing suicide but found "it was as if someone pulled me back." He believed it was Jesus and fought to be baptized.[21]

At the close of 1745 Noble allowed Ofodobendo to go to the

Moravian community in Bethlehem, Pennsylvania, and by February of 1746 he was baptized and given the name Andrew. Named after another African convert, a man who had become a Christian in the West Indies and who had been a companion of Count Nikolaus Ludwig von Zinzendorf, the Moravians' patron and leader, Andrew viewed himself as "a genuine black offering to Jesus." While Andrew recounted little of his life subsequent to his conversion, the church official that recorded his narrative noted that his religious experience had been "a blessedly happy passage" and that "it was a true joy to him to be able to tell a poor black something of the Savior."[22]

Andrew's brief narrative of his early life in America indicates the development of a strong will to succeed, which was an important Igbo value as well. He did succeed in becoming a member of a very select and very strict communally-organized settlement. When he came to Bethlehem, men and women lived in separate "Choirs" that were dedicated to serving Christ. When Andrew joined the community the members were undergoing a period of intense religious introspection and communal change and turned to spend more of their time in prayer. Following Zinzendorf's direction, much more emphasis was put on each individual's relationship with Christ.[23] Andrew shared in this process, periodically talking over his spiritual development with leaders. The fact that he was once sent to a synod as a Choir representative attests to his personal development as well as the group's acceptance of him.

Notwithstanding this nominal acceptance, there is no doubt that both Andrew himself and his congregation saw him as a *black* Moravian. Both the white minister's comments that he was "happy"—a term not used in descriptions of whites—and that he "happily praised the Lord" when talking to the other blacks (not whites), as well as his own view of himself as a "black offering" suggest that in his years in the community, while he became a Moravian, he yet remained a "poor black" African.

In 1762 Andrew was married to Magdalena, another African in the Moravian church. The congregation had probably prepared a lot before this marriage, as they did prior to other marriages at that time. They believed that the lot was a way of ascertaining God's will. Usually the lot included the names of a number of eligible members. Was there a pool of names in the case of Andrew and Magdalena; or was it just a yes or no lot, without other possibilities? Other Africans did live in the community; there were some thirteen Africans later buried in the Bethlehem cemetery. It is unlikely that European migrants would have been considered appropriate, although in the 1730s a Moravian missionary, Matthias Freundlish, had married a free woman of mixed race, Rebekka, at the Moravian mission on St. Thomas. Both were arrested and sentenced to life terms, he in prison and she as a slave. A petition from the Moravians, and perhaps Zinzendorf's visit and his statements adjuring Moravians to adopt correct political behavior on the island led to their release.[24] When Andrew and Magdalena were married in 1762 in Pennsylvania it was long after this West Indian experience and long after many white Moravians had begun to adopt white Americans' views of slavery and Africans.[25]

Beulah/Magdalena, who was born in Little Popo on the Guinea Coast in 1731, did not report memories of Africa or her African name in her narration.[26] Perhaps she had been too young when taken into slavery to preserve many memories. Her narrative dealt with the period prior to her baptism into the Church, and in her memories her happiness also played an important role. Magdalena recounted that she had come to Bethlehem in 1743 under pressure from her "master"; she would have preferred to "enjoy" the "world fully." She well remembered that "My behavior in the beginning was so bad; I really tried to be sent away again, which did not happen." On the contrary, the members of the community enveloped her with their love no matter what she did. She was overwhelmed by their reaction. She became "content and Happy" in great part due to this "love of the Brethren," which led her to commit herself to the group and to Christ. She also remembered "How Happy I was for the words 'also for you did Jesus die.'" At her death on January 3, 1820, Magdalena was reported to have "happily departed."[27]

Both Magdalena and Andrew recalled willful events prior to their acceptance at Bethlehem: Andrew recalled his determination and fight to be accepted, Magdalena her fight against acceptance. They both became members of this community in which the only individuality approved of was a unique relationship with Christ. Both lived long lives within this community and left no hint that they did not fully share Moravian beliefs. Magdalena apparently accepted that she had been "deeply sunk in the slavery of sin" and that through Jesus she had received grace and "forgiveness for my sins." Given that they named her after a woman believed to be a reformed prostitute, Mary Magdalene, it is likely that the brethren also believed that her sins had been sexual. It would seem that Andrew was regarded differently: his narrative was recorded as that of "The Blessed Brother Andrew the Moor."

Both Andrew and Magdalena had found a new home and they shared in a new collective identity that apparently satisfied deep needs and longings and made them "happy" (meaning they had experienced religious ecstasy). They shared in a communal life of prayer, song, and work in which women and men were equally called upon to be simple and loving—a life of commitment but one without room for enemies or hated others, and with little room for individuality. Both Magdalena and Andrew did work they might well have done in the outside world: Magdalena as a washerwoman and Andrew as a farm and building laborer. They worked alongside others, white and black, and while the relationships of blacks and whites within the community changed over the years, they were still different from those in the world. While both Magdalena and Andrew seemed to treasure memories of the period in which they had been on their own, although not yet saved, they nevertheless had chosen to join and remain in an all-encompassing community where men and women lived apart, and prayed and sang apart, and in which they were expected to share in a communal we-self.[28] While they may have seen this as the best choice they could make, given their limited opportunities, it may well be that they felt particularly at home in this community in which Spirit, predetermination, collective identity, gender separation, secret societies, and music played central roles. In these important respects the Moravian community may well have been similar to their childhood homes in Africa.

≺ II ≻

Migrants Addressing Hatred of the Other

A second group of narrators, Venture Smith, William Otter, K. White, and Michael Martin, all developed hated alien others but accepted no outside authority to focus and legitimate their self-change through incorporation into a collective identity.

Broteer/Venture Smith, like Andrew, began his narrative with his memories of Africa; but unlike Andrew, he openly blamed white people for his enslavement at age six. He believed that the warfare that led to the end of his freedom was "instigated by some white nation who equipped and sent them [other Africans] to subdue and possess the country."[29] From that point on whites were his enemy. He saw almost all whites as brutal, dishonest, and unworthy of respect. His life was one of constant hard labor and debasement.

After having paid for himself several times over, he succeeded in buying himself. As a free man he continued his extraordinary labors in order to buy his children and his wife, as well as several unrelated Africans. He also purchased houses, land, and boats, but he had little joy from his accomplishments or his possessions. From his earliest days in America until his old age he found that whites did their utmost to exploit, cheat, and dishonor him, and he was filled with anger at white people. He recognized that the blacks he helped had also cheated him, but this cheating had little effect on his central rage. Only a brief listing on the last page of his narrative relieved his litany of anger. He was thankful for his wife, Meg, "whom I married for love and bought with my money," and for freedom, which "is a privilege which nothing else can equal." He did, however, take great pride in his own values: "It gives me joy to think that I *have* and that I *deserve* so good a character, especially for *truth* and *integrity*."[30] These, he maintained, were the ruling values of the African culture. Smith believed that whites valued lying and deception, the very opposite of his own values, and he hated them on these grounds.

Venture Smith's narrative reveals his deep longing for his lost African home and for the people and culture he remembered. While he had fought back when violated, and while he had gone to court to try to get justice, he had suffered again and again. He had apparently not found an adequate way to voice his anger until he wrote his narrative, nor had he found a spiritual home for himself. At his death in 1805 he was buried in the cemetery of the Congregational Church in East Haddam; however, there is no evidence of Christianity's influence on him aside from the closing phrase of his narrative, taken from Job: "Vanity of vanities, all is vanity."[31]

William Otter, a white immigrant who came to America just before Smith died, had a similar if less justified rage, which he vented against blacks.[32] Otter, born in 1787 into a poor family in Hull, England, had run away at age eleven after having been beaten by his father for not working hard enough. Pretending to be an orphan, he signed on a ship as cabin boy, and began a five-year adventure that took him to many distant places, including Greenland, and finally to New York City, to which his parents, who had assumed he was dead, had migrated. Although he sought them out, his narrative revealed that he was still angry with them; he violated his dying mother's wish by breaking his apprenticeship to a plasterer and fleeing to Philadelphia where he claimed that he was a free master craftsman. In Philadelphia he found work and good pay and found as well a set of new friends, a gang of young working men who went on sprees for fun, sprees that involved beating blacks, or Irishmen, or other outcasts.

Along the way Otter became a slave catcher, finding this a source of additional money but more importantly a source of pleasure that was endlessly renewable. He retold the tales of his slave-catching and the other tricks that he played on black and white women and black men again and again. They became the "Altogether Original" "Musical Incidents" (the subtitle of his autobiography) that filled every page of his life narrative and that pleased his audience of male drinking partners.

Otter, a very large man, developed an alien other, a negative reverse of himself, personified by a very large black woman selling blackberries in the market. He tricked and violated this woman by putting whitewash in the basket on her head, and then "saved" her by bringing water to wash her eyes and clean the berries. While Otter had an alien other, he did not have a commitment to a church, a charismatic leader, or a political movement, although he was elected "burgess" of the town of Emmetsburg, Maryland, in 1835. He was then 47 and felt "that time is making his inroads on me," but belief in God or any other outside force did not seem to play any role in his life. Otter, much like Shaw, conformed to a known disorderly type. He was the bullyboy who did not grow up, the gang member who participated in the growing disorders of the 1830s. His narrative reveals that his was a self with permeable boundaries, and he shared those boundaries with the white men who surrounded him.

K. White, a white woman, also developed a very strong rage against an enemy other, but her hated figure was not racial.[33] K. White came to hate all males. Born in Edinburgh in 1772, she was brought to America by her parents in 1775. By the time she was five her family was broken: the father, a Tory, in fear for his life, returned to England, while she was sent to a boarding school for girls in Stockbridge, Massachusetts. In a dream-like sequence in her narrative she related that while at this school she and three other children were captured by Indians who were fighting on the side of the British in the war. These Indians took them on a difficult trek, traveling four nights until they reached their camp, where she was poked and taunted until she fainted. Two of the four abducted children were killed, but she was rescued by an Indian family, as the mother "had taken a fancy to me." Several months later a young Indian man also took a fancy to her, and he fulfilled her wishes by taking her to a white man's house.[34]

Notwithstanding this description of her abduction, White seemed to find a safe haven in her memories of this three-month sojourn (or fantasy of migration) to the Indians. She remembered the Indians as having moral virtues, virtues she did not find among her family or other white people. She claimed that the Indians were humane and generous to friends; they kept their word; and they welcomed strangers. In contrast, White felt abandoned by her father and her mother did not seem to play any significant role in her life; she married but her husband abandoned her; and she was often suspected of being a spy (as well as a man) by both men and women. White became a conscious role player; she welcomed looking like a man, became independent and advertised her self-creation. She had reversed the alien Indian other into a role model, and she had also taken on attributes of her openly hated enemy—males. She had no community to support her, but claimed that she did not need one. She maintained that her girth and her abilities in running a business stood her in good stead. She presented herself as a role model of a new androgynous and independent individual and suggested that American society allowed room for her to be this new person.

Michael Martin is the last of this group who had an enemy other but no outside authority to legitimate and direct expression of that hatred.[35] He came close to having one but missed the opportunity. Born to a Catholic family in Ireland in 1792, he remembered himself as an ill-tempered and violent youth, whose father beat him severely. Indentured to his uncle, a brewer, when he was fourteen, he ran away when his uncle beat him as well. Martin wanted to change his life, and in order to do so he tried to make an ideological commitment. At the age of sixteen he joined the United Irishmen, to "redress grievances" that he and his people held against England. While the upper sort who joined this movement were assumed to have high motives, the lower sort were widely presumed to use their membership in the organization to cover up their stealing and violence. When Martin's father learned that he had joined he assumed that his son had the worst motives and once again beat him. Martin left home and was taken in by a cousin in Dublin. Here he fulfilled his father's expectations by stealing from his rescuer.

As Martin retold his life it was at this juncture that an older and experienced highwayman "lured" him into more serious crime; to escape punishment he fled to America. However, once in America he continued his criminal activities. Martin was captured and convicted of highway robbery in Cambridge, Massachusetts, in 1821, and was sentenced to be executed. While awaiting death he wrote a narrative of his life, in which it is clear that his father had been his enemy other. Without any commitment to channel his anger in a positive direction he had accepted the script written by his hated father. In this script he was slated to play the evil son, and he played it out to the end.

≺ III ≻

Immigrants Who Became Individuated Americans

Over the course of the eighteenth century an increasing number of migrants came to oppose an enemy other and to commit themselves to a legitimating institution which supported personal change.

When John Binns, who was born in Ireland in 1772, joined the United Irishmen, his well-off family and friends fully expected him to be an ideologically committed member. When he participated in radical activities in Ireland and England and was jailed for his activities, his family and friends were proud of him. When Binns migrated to the United States in 1801, he was supported by radical Americans and at their urging he chose to live in Philadelphia, where he immediately began publishing a newspaper in support of Jeffersonian democracy and immigrant rights. Unlike Martin, Binns lived a very long and productive life in America, one in which he can be said to have become a very committed American and a very innovative individual. Nevertheless, when he was writing his life narrative in 1854 he revealed his deep, unbroken, ties to Ireland and his Irish identity:

> Immigrants, even those who come to the United States from principle, and a warm attachment to its constitutional provisions, insuring to themselves the free exercise of their religious, civil, and political rights [as he had] must expect, for many years after their arrival here, to grieve for the loss of the friends, and the want of the companions of their youth, and the friends of their riper years. Much time must pass away, new friends, nay new relatives and kindred must gather round them before they can cease regretfully to think of the playmates and the playgrounds, associated with the remembrance of the firesides round which they knelt, and prayed, and sported, and of the graves over which they had often wept. When many of these recollections have faded, and those whom the immigrant loved, and left in health, have sunk into their silent graves, even then, the remembrance of the mother-country will cling to their hearts and they will continue to feel a warm interest in the welfare of the old country.

Binns was such a grieving and longing immigrant, as he acknowledged: "I feel it [my loss] now, after an absence of more than half a century."[36]

Ironically, migrants (as well as those born in America) who achieved a new sense of an individuated self most often found support for their self-growth in the collective identities fostered by demanding church communities. In order to change, to reframe the past and dream of and implement a new future, a radical change in values is necessary. This change in values apparently depends upon experiencing a major trauma, or accepting a new authority—or both.[37] Binns, an individualistic Jeffersonian, a political activist as well as a newspaper editor and owner, became a committed member of the Church of the Brethren. Virtually all of the immigrants in this group who seem to have achieved a modicum of individuation became committed church members who also had hated not-me figures.

The Grinbergs suggest that most migrants have to hide their longings for their first homes from themselves: their pain would be too destructive if they recognized it.[38] Indeed, few migrants in this cohort expressed their longing as openly as Binns did, but many seemed to reflect such a feeling in their ongoing search for a better place to be, a place that would feel like home. Sarah Beckhouse, born in Frankfurt, Germany, in 1745, was brought to Charleston, South Carolina, by her Catholic father in 1752.[39] As her mother was dead, it is likely that an enslaved African took care of her and became her fictive mother. Some eight years later, at the age of sixteen, Sarah Beckhouse married Alexander Hamilton, a wealthy Southern merchant, and became a slave mistress.

The Revolution was traumatic for Sarah Hamilton: her husband was killed in her presence and their property was burned. She was reduced to living on the charity of relatives. Some time later she accepted a proposal of marriage from a slave-owning Georgia planter and was about to marry him when a play about deaths during the Revolutionary War led her to have a very disturbing dream that changed her life. In this dream she saw herself as bound for hell. She saw the behavior of her betrothed and his companions, their card playing, drinking, and ostentatious dress, as evil, and recognized that she had been on her way to join them. Her dream led her to recognize her deep need for change and commitment. Hamilton dreamed that it was a black person who gave her the necessary push to make her begin her journey away from this evil life and toward salvation. While she did not yet understand how she should act, the next Sunday she chose to attend a black and white Baptismal service as she wanted to stop a slave "wench" owned by her fiancé from joining the Baptist Church, which she hated. She immediately recognized the white Baptist preacher as the man who had saved her from falling into the depths of hell in her dream, and she accepted the black woman being baptized as her spiritual model. This woman may have brought back memories of her fictive black mother and earlier attendance at black Baptist services. Hamilton herself was baptized on the following Sunday, and she then left Charleston to live with the mixed race congregation of this North Carolina preacher.

After three years in this community Hamilton was hounded out of the South by her father, who sought her return to his Catholic faith. Although she had become one of the persecuted, she chose to remain associated with the Baptists. It was in this community that she had expanded her inner self and her outward understanding of her role in life. Her black alien other had been transformed through introjection, and her hate had become love.

Elizabeth Ashbridge, who was born to an Anglican family in Cheshire, England, in 1713, was also in rebellion against communal values when she married a poor working man against her father's will at age fourteen.[40] When her husband died less than a year later, she had nowhere to turn until her mother's Quaker relatives in Ireland agreed to take her in. After a time with them, she sought to escape their influence as well. In order to do this she signed away her freedom, indenturing herself to come to America in 1731. She soon realized she had punished herself, as she faced harsh conditions and perhaps sexual harassment while a servant in New York City. Working as a seamstress after her assigned tasks were done, she was able to buy her freedom before the set time; but she quickly re-enslaved herself by marriage to a harsh man she did not respect. Again she left, this time traveling to Quaker relatives in Pennsylvania, where she began a personal journey to inner freedom that eventually led her to become a respected Quaker. She took on the role of Public Friend or minister, and returned to Ireland to preach. She encountered herself, as it were, through outer and inner journeys: migration became a metaphor for growth. She came to realize that she had always wanted to be a man, but had hated the males who had power over her. She empowered herself by introjecting part of the power she ascribed to her male enemy other.

Ashbridge was an unusually self-concerned Quaker. She recounted a crucial early dream or vision of a spirit-woman telling her that her light would not be put out. With self-awareness she set out to cultivate a strong persona, while becoming part of a communally oriented group. Although Quakers usually demanded self-effacement, the community did support her.

Olaudah Equiano/Gustavus Vassa is the last in this cohort of migrants to America, although his origins are now in some question. Equiano/Vassa was already known as an African abolitionist when he published his life narrative in 1794. The book was very rapidly regarded as a classic narration of enslavement and redemption, both physical and spiritual. In it Equiano/Vassa drew a picture of the world he claimed he had lost when he was kidnapped into slavery in 1756, and eventually sold to a Virginia slave owner. He wrote in detail of his African childhood, claiming "I was born in the year 1745

. . . in a charming fruitful vale, named Essaka." Equiano went on to provide a detailed description of his family home and of Igbo culture.[41] Notwithstanding this detail, after his narrative was published critics charged that he was not an African, but had been born in the West Indies. In the next edition of his narrative Equiano added his response to these charges, maintaining that he was an "Eboan African."[42] It is true that some of his description of Africa was taken from Anthony Benezet's volume, *Some Historical Account of Guinea* of 1771 (which he had cited), as well as from other published sources. This type of borrowing, however, was a common practice in the period and cannot be regarded as proof that he was not African himself.

Although Equiano strongly defended his claim to African birth, and historians as well as the public have widely accepted his claim, new evidence suggests that Equiano may well have been born in South Carolina and taken on the identity of one African born.[43] South Carolina was recorded as his place of birth at his baptism in St. Margaret's Church in London in 1759, but as he was then enslaved, his owner or his English godparents might well have supplied incorrect information. Thus this fact, which has been long known, was not seen as significant. Now, however, another document has been located, the muster records of the ship the *Racehorse*. Equiano/Vassa signed on for a voyage to the North Pole in 1773, and the muster book identifies him as "an able seamen, age 28, who had been born in South Carolina."

Vincent Carretta notes that as Equiano/Vassa was by then a free man, we can presume he was the source of this information.[44] Carretta suggests that Equiano's later claim that he was African may well have been a "rhetorical invention." I would maintain that if indeed Equiano adopted Africa as his homeland this was not an invention but rather the creation and assumption of an identity, and that it certainly was not rhetorical: it was not adopted for theatrical purposes. It was a most serious reframing of his past, one that might make a different future possible, both for himself and for myriad enslaved people in the Diaspora. It was possibly his most important act. He adopted a fictive homeland in order to help create a collective identity that could be realized by all those with African origins living in the Diaspora.[45]

The extensive research carried out by Carretta and many others has substantiated virtually all of Equiano's detailed narrative after his childhood.[46] Wherever he was born, Equiano certainly was a migrant, having traveled extensively between continents and cultures. He journeyed from America to England and back many times, and he lived in the West Indies and in England for long periods. His extensive travels brought him to Canada, Turkey, Portugal, the Arctic Pole, Central and South America, and even to John Harrower's homeland, the Orkneys, which he visited while Harrower was living there.[47] One continent he may not have visited is Africa, although he came close to doing so in 1787. Appointed "Commissary of Provisions and Stores for the Black Poor [sailing to] Sierra Leone," he was scheduled to accompany a group of Africans being repatriated. Although he may well have realized he was jeopardizing his position, he felt compelled to expose the "flagrant abuses committed by the agent" who was paid to supply the stores. After he accused this agent of wrongdoing he was dismissed from his post, and the poorly provisioned ship sailed for Africa without him.[48]

Clearly his birthplace is now in question. While he, much like Edward Said, may have chosen his homeland, the identity he created was most unquestionably African. Before the muster book evidence was known Paul Edwards and Rosalind Shaw made a very strong argument for the Igbo grounding of Equiano's worldview. They found that his narrative strongly reflected Igbo belief in *Chi*, "a spiritual entity which personifies the words spoken to the creator deity by the individual before birth when choosing his or her life-course."[49] Chinua Achebe suggests that "In a general way we may visualize a person's chi as his other identity in spiritland—his *spirit being* complementing his *human being*."[50] In Igbo culture having chosen a destiny, or having a *spirit being*, does not rule out individuality and achievement. On the contrary, an individual must work for and with this *Chi*. Achebe maintains that Igbo believe "in the fundamental worth and independence of every man."[51] This may be part of what Edwards and Shaw had in mind when they suggested that when Equiano became a Christian "he recognized . . . something he had always known, drawing . . . on the Igbo roots of his religious thinking and his moral principles."[52]

Equiano did indeed seem to find both a new home and yet a homecoming in the Calvinist faith he came to hold, which can be said to have reaffirmed the Igbo belief that a person's destiny is decided before birth, and also reasserted the need for each person to participate in the working out of that destiny. His new church helped him to develop an identity that seemed to have roots in the lost world of his idealized childhood and yet helped him to establish a new life as an African in the Diaspora.[53] If Equiano was born in South Carolina, he so valued the Igbo worldview that he could have learned of from others (perhaps from his mother as in his narrative he claimed to have been unusually close to her) that he constructed an identity that encompassed these values coherently. His mother may well have transferred enough of the values and myths of Igbo society to him that he grew up feeling that a country he had never seen was his true country.[54]

Equiano traveled on a very long journey in which he went from a (possibly fictive) free childhood to enslavement, witnessing and experiencing a vast range of "oppression, cruelty, and extortion," to become a self-emancipator in 1766. He was overjoyed with his freedom and increasingly appalled by the conditions of those still enslaved. Living in the midst of slavery, as he continued to do, he was always in danger of losing his freedom again.

In February of 1767, while serving on a vessel transporting goods and slaves to Georgia, Equiano repeatedly dreamed of himself as a savior. "I dreamt the ship was wrecked amidst the surfs and rocks, and that I was the means of saving everyone on board."[55] He reported having this dream three times, a number that was widely taken to mean that God had sent the dream. Equiano thought his dream was fulfilled literally when his ship was cast on rocks and his vigilance saved the drunken crew and the Africans imprisoned in the hold. However, it is likely that his repeated dream also expressed his deep need to become a savior of enslaved Africans wherever they were. He needed to find a way to dedicate his life to this purpose.

In 1774 Equiano experienced a devastating psychological blow when a black man who was kidnapped from a ship they were both on was re-enslaved. Equiano attempted to rescue this man but failed. When he learned that the man had died as a result of brutal punishment by his "owners" he went into a depression and contemplated suicide. He came out of this extraordinarily disturbed condition by means of a religious conversion. Only such a serious turn in his life could have rescued him from such a devastating blow to his sense of himself. He reported that in this deep consternation the Lord was pleased to break in upon my soul with his bright beams of heavenly light; and in an instant, as it were, removing the veil and letting light into a dark place. (Isa. 25:7) I saw clearly, with the eye of faith, the crucified Savior, bleeding on the cross on Mount Calvary. . . I was given to know what it was to be born again.[56]

Notwithstanding his depression over his failure to save this reenslaved man, as well as his conversion and the fuller freedom it promised, Equiano actually participated more fully with the slave system after these events. In 1775 he managed a slave plantation, first selecting enslaved Igbo to man it. It was only after he had done this, after he had played the white man and had been seen as one, that he came to recognize that he had to refuse to participate with the slave system in any way.[57] He actively sought an effective way to oppose slavery. He began to reframe his life, to see his *spirit being* and his *human being* as united in leading him to take on a powerful anti-slavery role. His reassessment of his identity reached its climax in his creation of the narrative of his life.

In writing his life narrative in 1777 Gustavus Vassa re-adopted or perhaps created an African name as his written persona. I think at that point Olaudah Equiano can be said to have had (with Freud) "a clear consciousness of an inner identity" and may have been at home with his inner self. But at the same time it is clear that he had been in a life-long state of crisis. He had experienced a burning need to free himself, both legally and spiritually. In the process of creating a free identity for himself, he had come to recognize that a sense of collective identity among Africans in the Diaspora was a necessary framework for self-development. Equiano realized the importance of a collective identity based on a shared myth of Africa as an Edenic home, and he played a crucial role in negotiating its early, limited, acceptance among the enslaved.[58]

≺ IV ≻

Migration and Collective Identity

While migration to America was, in part, fed by the will of free migrants drawn by dreams of more freedom than they had known—both economic and personal—above all it was brought about by enabling systems of migration that carried coerced peoples across the Atlantic.[59] Looked at from the vantage of these migratory systems, four of the thirteen people considered in this chapter, Magdalena, Andrew, Venture Smith, and Equiano or his mother, were forcibly brought from Africa to America to be sold as slaves. John Harrower and Elizabeth Ashbridge were brought from England and Ireland as indentured servants. John Shaw was sent as an English soldier. William Otter worked his way across the Atlantic from England as a sailor, while four migrants, William Lee, John Binns, and two children, K. White and Sarah Beckhouse, arrived from England, Ireland, Scotland, and Germany as passengers. (It seems unlikely that Michael Martin paid his way from Ireland—more likely that he stowed aboard.)

Thus, of these thirteen people seven came as unfree laborers, brought by organized migratory systems. The four who were enslaved were clearly forcibly brought to America. Of the two who were indentured, Ashbridge had hoped to come in as a free worker, while Harrower had hoped for a similar status in Holland. The one who came as a soldier was brought to America against his will; and there is little likelihood that the two children brought in by their parents were consulted.[60] Six did arrive as a result of their own decisions. However, of these Michael Martin was seeking asylum and not America, while William Otter, a teenager, came to America to look for his family and was forced to indenture himself after he arrived. Out of the thirteen migrants only three, William Lee, John Binns, and Elizabeth Ashbridge, had chosen America as their destination and one of these three (Lee) chose as well to return to his place of birth. The rest of this group can be viewed as forced or accidental migrants. Nevertheless, whatever their means of arrival or their own intentions, most lived out their lives in America. (Only Equiano made his life elsewhere, although Ashbridge died in Ireland while on a preaching tour there.) In America, as the analysis above indicates, the identity of most of the narrators changed, and willy-nilly they became Americans, many, like Equiano, sharing in the process of creating new personal and collective identities.[61]

The construction of a new collective identity was also consciously undertaken by those in power in post-Revolutionary America, who chose to consolidate and emphasize selected values that had brought about and were seen to support the Revolution's goals. This new identity was ostensibly to be shared by all settlers and most immigrants, but Africans, Indians, and others were nevertheless placed beyond the limits of this collectivity and were in fact viewed as enemy others against which values and the self were to be modeled. This new collective identity was based on the belief in the "metaphysical equality of all [white] individuals" as well as "the denial of the symbolic validity of hierarchy." This identity also fostered what might seem a value contradicting its collectivity—an "achievement-oriented individualism"—but this key value was well integrated within a collective value: while people were expected to establish personal boundaries and to achieve individually, these were intended to be shared collective goals.[62]

It was assumed that such an identity would prove very attractive to those coming from less individualistic, less achievement-oriented, and more hierarchical cultures, and this has certainly proven true over the generations. As the narratives in this cohort clearly show, many early migrants succeeded in negotiating such an achievement-oriented and individuated American identity for themselves. While some early migrants played an important role in the construction of this identity, many others, whites as well as blacks, found that the dominant groups in America regarded them as alien others and as such they were rejected and attacked. As a result these migrants developed a strong need to create different individual and collective identities that valued them and their pasts, yet projected an American future. Their success varied considerably, but when they succeeded their new collective identities—African American, Irish American, German American, or American Jewish—were in part based on fantasy. These were fantasies of home and self that could support very real individual and collective commitment and change.[63] The dangerous downside was that such identities were also dependent upon rejection and hatred of an enemy other. While creating a transitional home for the African, Irish, German, or Jewish migrants who were so often attacked as enemy aliens, these new collective identities also fostered the hatred of "others" by immigrants in order that they too might seek to be at home in America.[64]

In the contemporary West identity is widely viewed as "never being complete," but rather as "a circulation of meanings and values and positions" negotiated over the lifetime of a person in which both reality and fantasy play very important roles.[65] While in this cohort Equiano's narrative provides what seems to be a clear example of the need for a fantasy home as the basis for a new identity, the mix of "achievement-oriented individualism" with hatred of the other is particularly well illustrated in the narratives of the African man Venture Smith, the Scottish woman K. White, and the Englishman William Otter. All three became successful American entrepreneurs, all three developed a bound sense of self, and all three hated an alien other with a passion. Whites (for Venture Smith), men (for K. White), and blacks (for William Otter) played a key role in their development and remained "the projection of the not-me," a key guidepost for them as they became Americans.[66]

These migrants' changing identities clearly illustrate the circulation of meanings and values, and the roles of fantasy and reality, but above all they provide examples of the significance of the alien other in the creation of individual and collective identities in America. The weight of this powerful factor in identity creation—negative modeling as against an enemy other or not-me—has grown over time. However, it has generally remained a hidden or unacknowledged known in analysis of migration and identity formation. Toni Morrison is one of the few who have recognized it as the basis for American identity and locates its expression in key writings in the canon: "Black slavery enriched the country's creative possibilities. For in that construction of blackness *and* enslavement could be found not only the not-free but also, with the dramatic polarity created by skin color, the projection of the not-me."[67]

The discovery or creation of racial others was at the core of new American identities. White English men came to view their primary others as black African men, whom they posited as people they themselves should not be: brutal, uncivilized, and given to uncontrollable passions. However, to "control" such others whites quickly came to believe that they had to be brutal and give in to their worst passions. At the same time, however, they desired and often introjected other values and attributes that they saw as African, such as a freer emotional and religious life and fuller libidinal satisfaction.

In the wake of authoritarian and often brutal white men, black men and black and white women also came to posit themselves in opposition to those they would not be. Hatred of the other became the common basis for new identity development in virtually every American social and ethnic grouping. This is a heritage that we all share, and yet rarely take much note of. It is a legacy of the collective identities created by free and enslaved populations brought to North America, and an important reality in contemporary life.

7

Freedom and Indentured Labor in the French Caribbean, 1848–1900

DAVID NORTHRUP

As the campaigns to abolish slave trading and slavery achieved their goals in the Caribbean, two questions needed to be answered if plantation colonies were to continue prospering. Where could sufficient free labor be found to meet current and future needs? And what would "free" mean in this new context? This chapter traces the attempts to answer these two questions in the three French colonies of the Caribbean following the end of slavery in 1848: the islands of Martinique and Guadeloupe in the Lesser Antilles and the colony of French Guiana (Guyane) on the northern coast of South America. The problems the French encountered in this enterprise and the solutions they devised may serve as a case study of the larger situation of free labor and invite comparisons with the better-studied efforts of the British Caribbean colonies to contend with the same issues after they ended slavery and apprenticeship.

In a few Caribbean colonies, such as Barbados, the former slaves chose to continue their old plantation jobs under such new terms as emancipation brought them. But elsewhere in the Caribbean, where newly emancipated people had access to other types of employment or land for subsistence farming, large proportions of freed people refused to resume plantation labor. In order to replace these lost laborers and to provide sufficient hands for expansion, the colonies needed to resume some form of large-scale labor recruitment from overseas. A portion of the new laborers were recruited in Africa, a few from China; but most came from South Asia. Nearly all were recruited under contracts of indenture that bound them to work (for wages) for a period of years in return for their passage from overseas.

≺ I ≻

Slavery and Freedom

Arising in the shadow of the old slave trade, these new migrations have long raised troubling issues about freedom. Nineteenth-century opponents of slavery agonized and argued over what conditions of recruitment, transport, and employment would make these new indentured labor migrations a clear alternative to the old slave trade. Near the end of the century, changing conditions in the Caribbean colonies, nationalist opposition in India, and reformist governments in Europe combined to end indentured contracts as an acceptable form of free labor in the French colonies. Partly influenced by this change of perception and by the reform of labor contracts and conditions throughout the western world, one school of modern historians has sought to characterize these indentured laborers' working conditions and legal status as a continuation of slavery or at best a form of unfree labor.[1]

However, as Robert Steinfeld and Stanley Engerman warn, reading modern conceptions of freedom backward in time obfuscates understanding of the historical process by which ideas of free labor evolved. They point out that the line between "free" and "unfree" labor is not self-evident or natural but is a legal and cultural convention that has been repositioned several times during the last two centuries, and that it is difficult even today for the sharpest legal minds to agree where the line should be drawn. Rather than focusing on the artificial distinction between free and unfree, they "suggest historians of labor should focus on a more particularistic set of inquiries about the particular practices that different societies and polities permitted and prohibited, [and] the reasons for those decisions."[2]

In examining the new indentured migrations of the nineteenth century, then, one needs to pay attention to freedom's multiple meanings and the changing particular conditions that made labor acceptably "free." In addition to the recorded positions of western officials, one also needs to consider the perspectives of the laborers, however poorly articulated at the time. To these ends, this chapter considers three different views of freedom: first, the contested meanings of legal freedom in European eyes, especially as applied to African recruits recently released from slavery; second, the social meaning of "free" labor in non-capitalist African societies that largely lacked labor markets and the individual autonomy that made such markets possible; third, the growing freedom of movement for working people in Asia during this era as legal restrictions on leaving their community or state were being lifted and as transport by land and sea was becoming faster, safer, cheaper, and more readily available. In addition, the chapter examines the ways in which indentured laborers' recruitment, transport, and working conditions differed from those endured by slaves. Although a formal definition of slavery is not predicated on physical suffering, contemporaries were quick to evoke the specter of slavery when migrations were associated with high mortality, onerous working conditions, and rigid control mechanisms. Many modern historians have continued in that tradition.

On the whole, however, the particular circumstances of new indentured labor migrants had more in common with those of other "free" migrants in the nineteenth century than they did with those of slaves. Not only were conditions of transport and employment generally superior to those of slaves, but indentured laborers generally assented to emigration as the way to a better life. Even so, like other free overseas migrants, their dreams were often dashed. Paradise was not an ocean or two away. Despite revolutionary changes in ship design that made passenger vessels larger and faster, voyages from Asia to the Americas remained arduous and sometimes dangerous, especially for those already weakened by hardship and disease. Thanks to good food, detailed sanitation regulations, and the care of ships' doctors, many migrants arrived at their destinations in better health than when they boarded. Most others were no worse for the experience, but a minority (sometimes alarmingly large) either perished during the voyage of diseases that the medical knowledge of that age had not yet learned to control effectively or arrived in ill health. High mortality continued in the new tropical workplaces, at least until the survivors developed some resistance.[3]

In other ways in this age of growing freedoms, one kind of liberty came into conflict with another. Migrants exercising their freedom to emigrate risked finding themselves under the control of plantation operators who might feel free to treat them much as they had an older slave labor force. Growing free trade also put plantation owners at the mercies of a volatile global marketplace in which sugar prices

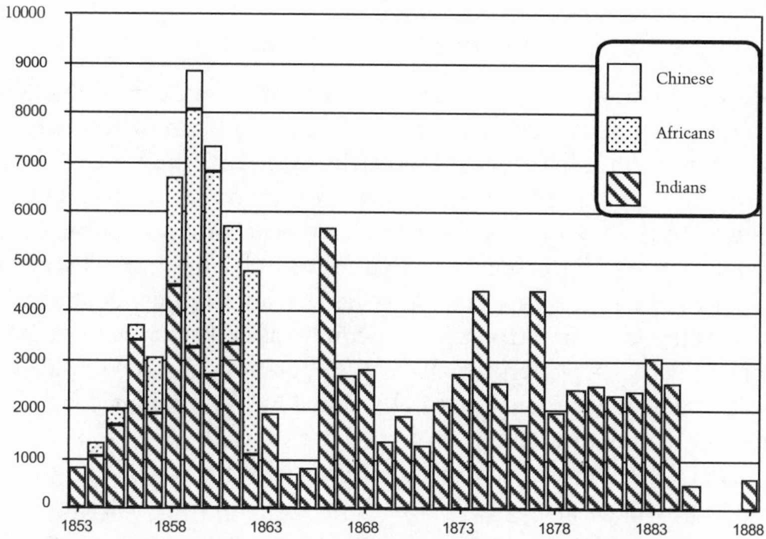

FIG. 1. Indentured Labor Migration to the French Caribbean, 1853–1888. (Source: Database from French Overseas, British Foreign Office, and British India Office archives.)

were generally declining. The mediating force in these conflicting freedoms was expanding government regulation. Colonial subsidies of labor migration helped ease the burden on planters. Metropolitan and colonial governments sought to balance the power of capital and the rights of indentured laborers. Indeed, the special circumstances of overseas indentured labor made it the most closely supervised of all free labor systems in this age of laissez-faire economics.

Historians have paid much less attention to the indentured labor trade to the French Caribbean colonies (Figure 1) than to the larger British trade, but both its unfamiliarity and special features make the French experience useful for studying freedom and migration. Most aspects of French and British recruitment were similar. Each nation's Caribbean colonies recruited similar proportions of their laborers from Africa and India. They employed the indentured laborers at similar tasks and under similar conditions. But in some ways the French system was more complex than the British. For one thing, the French methods of recruitment in Africa were more controversial at the time. For another, Indian laborers in French colonies were watched over by a dual system of French and British inspectors.

< II >

African Labor Recruitment

After the end of slavery in 1848, French planters considered additional Africans the obvious answer to the problem of replenishing the plantation labor force. New African recruits could be absorbed into the existing creole population that slave trade had created. However, the French had to resolve two issues involving freedom if supplies of African laborers were to be found. The first was the fact that free (that is, wage) labor was largely an alien concept in mid-nineteenth-century Africa. The second was to find a way to distinguish clearly their recruitment of Africans from the slave trade that the French government had finally ended in 1831 and had agreed not to resume under a convention signed with Britain in 1845.

As Igor Kopytoff and Suzanne Miers, the editors of the groundbreaking study *Slavery in Africa*, point out, "In most African societies, 'freedom' lay not in withdrawal into a meaningless and dangerous autonomy but in attachment to a kin group, to a patron, to power."[4] Thus most African individuals were not "free" to sell their labor in the Western sense because they "belonged" to a kinship-based community. Even if persons wished to leave, their kinsfolk or rulers were unlikely to feel their contributions could be dispensed with. Indeed, most coastal communities in the mid-nineteenth century found themselves short of the labor needed to supply rising overseas exports. To supplement their workforce, many purchased slaves, whose cost had fallen as the transatlantic demand ended. The one place in coastal West Africa where a labor market existed at this time was among the people known as the Kru in modern Liberia. For many decades Kru men had been recruited as laborers on passing European vessels that returned them to their homelands a few weeks later. However, the French had no more success in their efforts to recruit Kru on longterm contracts for the West Indies than did similar British efforts. Both nations did better in recruiting Africans they had newly freed from slavery.

The British secured African recruits for their West Indian colonies from the tens of thousands of individuals newly rescued from slave ships captured by the British navy's Antislavery Squadron. Beginning in 1808 Britain had conscripted some liberated Africans into military service in West Africa and the West Indies and apprenticed others to "respectable persons" under fourteen-year contracts. Between 1834 and 1867, the British diverted to their Caribbean colonies some 37,000 additional African "recaptives" newly liberated by Courts of Mixed Commission in the West African colony of Sierra Leone, the mid-Atlantic island of St. Helena, and some Latin American ports.[5]

The French lacked such convenient pools of Africans freed from the illegal Atlantic slave trade, but in the course of expanding their colonial presence in Senegal they had gained control over large populations held in slavery by African masters. French officials freed and apprenticed some of these to meet the labor needs of that West African colony.[6] This recruitment method was soon adapted to meet the growing labor needs in the French Caribbean. In 1839–40, 150 African "pioneers," who had been ransomed from Senegalese masters, were recruited for public works projects in Cayenne, the capital of French Guiana, on fourteen-year contracts (the same as military service contracts). Beginning in 1849, the French Ministry of Colonies tried without success to gain the approval of the Ministry of Foreign Affairs for broader emancipation schemes, cloaking pressing labor needs in language about extracting Africans "from the barbarity of their homelands" and putting them "in contact with civilization."[7] In October 1853, Emperor Napoleon III authorized the recruitment of free Africans for French Guiana and for the Indian Ocean colony of Réunion. In 1854, the *Cinq Frères* recruited Africans in small groups along the West African coast, including 37 from the British colony of Sierra Leone (some of whom were released from prison on condition that they emigrate to the French colony). Of the 244 recruits, six deserted in Africa and eight died en route to French Guiana. Though signed and certified to five-year contracts, many later claimed that they had been promised a shorter term of indenture and higher wages than they received.[8] Only about 1,100 Kru and other free persons were eventually recruited from Sierra Leone and the Liberian coast.

In 1856, when the 1845 anti-slave trading convention with Britain expired, French authorities felt free to change their methods to include the redemption of slaves in Africa (*rachat préalable*), so as to supply the pressing labor needs of their larger West Indian colonies of Guadeloupe and Martinique. Under government contract, French captains purchased slaves from local African authorities, declared

TABLE 1
Africans and Indians Recruited for the French Caribbean, 1853–1870, by Territory

	French Guiana		Guadeloupe		Martinique		Totals	
Year	Africans	Indians	Africans	Indians	Africans	Indians	Africans	Indians
1853						832		832
1854	251			314		759	251	1,073
1855	312			1,017		664	312	1,681
1856	321	822		528		2,050	321	3,400
1857	279	0	874	1,389	625	523	1,778	1,912
1858	210	0	755	2,448	1,231	2,051	2,196	4,499
1859	421	0	2,319	1,254	2,077	2,016	4,817	3,270
1860		550	1,818	1,625	2,303	538	4,121	2,713
1861		534	540	1,273	1,851	1,528	2,391	3,335
1862		0	466	1,089	3,257	0	3,723	1,089
1863		0		1,920		0		1,920
1864		277		430		0		707
1865		412		0		423		835
1866		395		1,260		1,293		2,948
1867		840		3,282		1,303		5,425
1868				1,418		953		2,371
1869				934		475		1,409
1870				893		949		1,842
TOTALS	1,794	3,830	6,772	21,074	11,344	16,357	19,910	41,261

SOURCE: Database from French Overseas, British Foreign Office, and British India Office archives.

them free, and signed them to indentured labor contracts. This method of recruitment yielded many more migrants for the French Caribbean colonies—by 1862 nearly 20,000 (see Table 1). To distinguish it from slave trading, every contract contained a clause giving potential recruits the right to refuse to sign the contract if they preferred to stay in Africa. Conditions of transport were precisely regulated with regard to provisioning, hygiene, medicines. About two-thirds of the 350 francs paid to the recruiter for each adult was eventually to be recovered through deductions from the recruits' wages in the colonies.[9]

Despite these differences, British authorities quickly and vigorously denounced this form of recruitment as a clandestine continuation of the illegal transatlantic slave trade. The British Foreign Secretary charged that "the Slave Trade is now practically carried on under the French flag" and asserted that "in reality these emigrants are slaves bought at so much per head, and brought by violence of every kind to the coast to be sold to the French purchaser," so that they could not be considered "free labourers in the just sense of that term."[10] Against these stinging charges, the French Minister of Foreign Affairs reaffirmed his government's commitment to the principles of the 1845 Franco-British convention ending the slave trade but defended the legality, morality, and utility of the ongoing labor recruitment in Africa. He argued that the French government felt, on the advice of its best legal minds, that such slave redemptions were fully legal as well as "an act of humanity," but gave assurances of his government's commitment to correcting any abuses in the system.[11]

However, the careful distinctions envisioned by superior legal minds in France proved difficult to execute flawlessly. For the French recruiters, the difference between redeeming and buying slaves was entirely theoretical (one recruiter even being convicted of slave trading), while obtaining Africans' consent in the presence of those who were selling them did not prove to be a meaningful exercise. To make matters worse, some captains ignored the carefully drawn up regulations for the care and feeding of the recruits. The consequently high mortality on many early voyages resurrected what had been one of the abolitionists' most persuasive arguments against the old slave trade. For various reasons, the most questionable methods and highest mortality occurred in the recruitment from East Africa for the French Indian Ocean colony of Réunion.[12] But mortality on voyages from Africa to the French Caribbean was still appallingly high, averaging 38 persons per thousand, about four times the rate on British voyages from Africa to the British West Indies in the same period. However, a fairer comparison might be with the first and busiest period of British voyages from Sierra Leone in 1846–50, when mortality averaged 44 per thousand.[13]

The French government was not slow in addressing the continuing problems in African recruiting. The emperor appointed his reform-minded brother, Jérôme Napoléon, to head the Ministry of Colonies. The new minister suspended all recruitment of Africans for Réunion in September 1858 but allowed recruitment for the Caribbean colonies to continue until the middle of 1862, in large part because of the cost of voiding existing contracts with private recruiters.[14] The recruitment of Africans to the Caribbean was terminated without the French ever conceding there had been anything fundamentally wrong with it, but charges of slave trading have continued to dominate the way this episode is interpreted. Virtually all modern historians echo the British criticisms. François Renault argues that in the effort to reconcile freedom and labor the former was the loser. David Eltis counts all of these recruits as slaves. W. G. Clarence-Smith identifies this episode as mostly "a thinly disguised slave trade," as does Paul Lovejoy. Monica Schuler argues that, while the Kru migration from Liberia was voluntary, the larger migration experience "smacked in many ways of the old slave trade."[15] In the end, the French have not overcome the view that their system either was a ruse to continue the banned Atlantic slave trade or at least promoted the continuation of the slave trade within Africa.

Despite this unanimity of opinion, drawing a sharp (and perhaps arbitrary) distinction between freedom and slavery may be less informative than examining the range of recruitment practices in Africa. One key issue is how different British recruitment of liberated Africans had been from the French practices they condemned. In addition, one can uncover deeper meanings by examining the ways freedom was perceived, not just by European officials, but also by African rulers and by the recruits themselves.

The status of the recruits as legally free persons was the primary issue for both the French and the British, even if officials disagreed over how to view the freedom of Africans newly emancipated from slavery. Most of the ambiguities resided in the unsettled nature of international standards, a problem with which the British abolitionist efforts had been wrestling for most of the century. David Eltis has pointed out that "almost half of all slave ships [the British] detained in the nineteenth century were adjudicated in British Vice Admiralty courts, and most of these were taken under the authority of . . . acts, which had no precedent in international relations," seizures that were in clear "disregard of international law."[16] Most of the vessels condemned on shaky legal grounds by such Vice Admiralty courts were not carrying slaves at the time of their seizure and thus accounted for the emancipation of only a small (but not insignificant) proportion of slaves liberated through British actions. From 1819, most African "recaptives" were emancipated by new international tribunals, known as Courts of Mixed Commission, made up of a British representative and a commissioner from the nation that had authorized the British navy to stop and search ships flying its flag that were suspected of dealing in slaves.

Although the French procedures for emancipation lacked the

sanction of another European power, as the Minister of Foreign Affairs indicated, they did have the approval of French legal experts. Moreover, purchasing the freedom of individual slaves had a long legal pedigree. French authorities in Senegal had been using such methods to recruit labor for colonial forces in prior decades. British individuals had redeemed slaves in the Americas by purchase from their owners in cases ranging from that of the eighteenth-century captive Job Solomon to the even better known Frederick Douglass. European missionaries in Africa redeemed slaves from African and Afro-Arab owners during the nineteenth century. Indeed, the practice is still in operation today in the southern Sudan and is still controversial.[17] Thus, the French practice of redeeming slaves from their African owners does not appear to have been exceptional on legal grounds.

To be sure, the ransomed slaves had little, if any, freedom of choice once they were emancipated by the French, but this too was not unusual by the standards of the day. Both British and French authorities had been redeeming slaves in Africa for military conscription and apprenticeship since early in the century. Nor was much freedom of choice offered to most Africans whom the British liberated from Atlantic slaving vessels. From 1844, British authorities in Sierra Leone refused to release newly liberated Africans from the liberation depot until they had exposed them to a hard-sell recruitment campaign for the British West Indies. No alternative to indentured emigration existed for the substantial numbers of Africans liberated on the island of St. Helena, which lacked the resources to support more than a small resident population. Thus, in offering freshly ransomed Africans no alternative to an indentured contract that would pay off the bond, French procedures departed little, if at all, from accepted British procedures. The British might argue, of course, that their methods were justified by the necessity of providing for the people that their great anti-slavery crusade had rescued from illegal slave traders. However, the fact that the African recruits also served to alleviate labor shortages in British Caribbean colonies made it hard for the French to see their efforts as any less a mixture of humanitarian and practical motives.

Moreover, the French handling of the African recruits after redemption gained favorable comment once the system was well established. Although a British naval officer reported that in July 1858 recruits freed by the French near the Congo River were kept in irons to prevent their escape and were guarded "in the same manner as slaves," two years later another British naval officer had no criticism of the "well-conducted" French depot at the port of Loango and, in a private journal, an American officer described recruits shipped from that depot on the *Splendid* as "well fed and contented" and "in every respect . . . better situated and cared for than the majority of passengers in emigrant ships from Europe to the United States."[18] These remarks support the view that, despite some early problems of implementation, French treatment of Africans bound for their Caribbean colonies was far removed from the horrors of the Atlantic slave trade.

≺ III ≻

African Perspectives on Recruitment

It is more difficult to challenge the British charge that French recruitment promoted the slave trade within Africa. Rather than liberating "surplus" slave populations, it seems clear that French actions encouraged African slavers to bring new captives to the coast for sale. One outraged British officer in 1858 declared that it was common to see Africans dragging their slaves to the Congo coast for sale to the French depot "in twos and threes, . . . secured by ropes to the forked end of a wooden pole encircling their necks, their hands strongly bound, . . . while a third negro hastens their movements by the lash."[19] This fact is confirmed by the testimony of African rulers who were active (or would-be) participants in French recruitment. Under close questioning by British officers, Thomas Cole, the African ruler of Manna Rock on the Liberian coast, conceded that he supplied recruits to the French exactly as he had once delivered slaves. Indeed, it later turned out, one of those Cole sold to a French recruiter was an apprentice stolen from the household of the Liberian Attorney General.[20]

African rulers usually found it hard to sell abroad their domestic slaves (or participate in European redemption schemes that would take them away) because such established servile populations had acquired partial rights in their masters' communities. Kosoko, a ruler who had set himself up farther west on the Slave Coast after the British exiled him from Lagos for persistent slave trading, was dissuaded from selling his servile dependants to French recruiters in 1859, less because of the treaty he had signed with the British agreeing to stop selling slaves abroad, than because of the argument of his advisors that his own slaves, "having for a few years past enjoyed a great amount of personal liberty, and having had, many of them the privilege of trading for themselves, would immediately desert when they perceived he was selling them."[21]

Additional testimony comes from an Old Calabar chief who had initially agreed to sell slaves for redemption to an abortive *British* effort to recruit West African labor in 1850. King Eyo Honesty II told a missionary: "It be all same as old slave-trade. I no have too many man for myself; I must send and buy people for them in all countries, and must charge them full price, for them man when he go away no will for come back." Through King Eyo did not say so, another reason for his not wishing to sell his own people was that Old Calabar's extensive slave population had also acquired a sense of belonging, as shown in the fact that slaves in another ward of the town arose in rebellion the next year in defense of their rights.[22]

With most of the "free" population in coastal Africa ill disposed to give up their membership in communal societies and many of the supposedly "unfree" likely to rebel if they were sold away, Africa was a frustrating place in which to recruit. However, it should not be assumed that all those whom Europeans redeemed from slavery were displeased at the prospect or devoid of their own perspectives on freedom. From the perspective of newly ransomed Africans, the key issue was not whether they had been freed in strict accordance to law nor whether they had the right to choose among different post-emancipation fates, but whether they saw in this act a step toward greater liberation and assented to it. The evidence for assessing their states of mind is limited. Both powers generated a paper trail of signed contracts, but neither British nor French recruitment of Africans was free of coercion and deception. African recruits have left no direct testimony about their willingness to emigrate, but there is circumstantial evidence that acquiescence was general in the case of both British and French recruitment of newly liberated Africans, namely, that it was normally unnecessary to employ the constraints long practiced on slave ships to prevent rebellions.

The French recruitment record contains some exceptions to this rule. A small number of disgruntled recruits deserted in Africa before captains learned to confine "troublemakers" below deck.[23] The one spectacular case of general discontent, the 1858 rebellion on the French vessel *Regina Coeli* off Liberia, occurred under unusual circumstances. The captain was not licensed by the French government to recruit laborers, the West African recruits were intended for service in distant Réunion, and the recruits were drawn largely from domestic slaves. The last point seems the most crucial in explaining why, after coming on board, the recruits rebelled, killing many French crew, and then escaped to the capital city Monrovia. It was not the conditions on the ship (nor perhaps the distant destination of the voyage) that drove them to rebel, but their perception that the French recruiter and their masters had conspired to sell them away from their homeland without their consent. The French suffered the effects of this action, but the rebels were equally angry at their African masters for this violation of their rights. Indeed, some expressed the wish that they had staged the revolt earlier, when their masters had been on board, so that they might have killed them too. By fleeing to Monrovia, the rebels sought to remain free of the control of their African masters.[24]

While the *Regina Coeli* rebellion reveals the complex perspectives of recruits in an extreme case, other evidence suggests that the more usual attitude of ransomed Africans was to accept the promise of something better in the French Caribbean as an improvement on their status as newly acquired slaves in Africa. The British Consul in Martinique, who investigated the shipment of 370 Africans to French Guiana on the *Orion* in 1857, was not about to accept the word of any French official on how freely the men and women had consented to emigrate and so put the question to that vessel's African interpreter. The interpreter assured him that the African recruits were glad (indeed, very glad) for an opportunity to gain release from the ill treatment of the African chiefs who owned them, not caring what was to come. In support of his claim that this migration was voluntary, the interpreter cited the fact that there had been no attempts at revolts on this ship as would have been the case on a slave ship. The comment of another British official that the recruits on one of the last French vessels from Africa appeared "cheerful," also supports this interpretation.[25]

The evidence just cited about African perspectives on recruitment is too limited to be conclusive, but it reinforces the view that drawing a sharp distinction between "free" and "unfree" migrations may obscure more than it reveals. Participants in these recruitment ventures interpreted the meaning of freedom according to their own self-interest without attempting to resolve all the inherent ambiguities. As the next section suggests, these ambiguities were instrumental in changing ideas of what constituted "free" migration.

≺ IV ≻

Indian Labor Recruitment

In replying to British charges that their African recruiting efforts were setting a bad example and encouraging slave raiding in Africa, the French Minister of Foreign Affairs observed that French colonies had to obtain plantation laborers from either Africa or India: "if the latter can be procured, the former will not be necessary."[26] The point was not lost on British officials. The British West Indies had been recruiting growing numbers of South Asians to meet their labor needs since the end of the apprenticeship program for freed slaves in 1838. By the 1850s Indian immigrants averaged over 4,000 per year. The French also began recruiting labor from their Indian enclaves of Pondichéry and Karikal in 1853. In the year 1858 the French shipped some 4,500 Indians to their Caribbean colonies, but the numbers fell by a quarter the next year and, for the first time, African recruitment surpassed Indian (see Table 1). The decrease in the number of Indian recruits was due to restrictions by Indian authorities on the departure for the small French enclaves of Indians from British Indian territories (or from Indian princely states allied to British India). Thus, the French Minister was arguing, if Britain wanted the French to cease recruiting in Africa, it would have to give them greater freedom to recruit British Indians. Anglo-French conventions in 1860 and 1861 granted the French the right to recruit British Indians on the same terms as British recruiters and allowed them to establish recruitment stations in British Indian ports. In return for these rights, French recruiters had to abide by the same regulations that applied to British recruitment, the chief of which restricted passen-

TABLE 2
Indian Arrivals in the French Caribbean by Ports of Origin, 1871–1888

Colony	French Ports	Calcutta	Total	% Calcutta
Guadeloupe	7,189	15,354	22,443	68
Martinique	9,521	1,463	10,984	13
French Guiana	3,067	1,386	4,453	31
TOTAL	19,777	18,203	37,880	48

SOURCE: Database from French Overseas, British Foreign Office, and British India Office archives.

NOTE: Arrival totals do not include children born during the voyage, who numbered 191 in the case of the French Ports and 177 in the case of Calcutta voyages.

ger density on ships to no more than 50 adults per 100 tons. In return for this greater access to Indians, France ended recruitment in Africa for the French Caribbean in 1862.

While the recruitment of South Indians from the French enclaves of Pondichéry and Karikal increased significantly from 1866 under the new agreements, the first voyages from Calcutta to the French Caribbean colonies did not begin until 1873. The French emigration agent in Calcutta cited three reasons for the long delay. In the first place, internal factors pushing Indians to migrate had temporarily eased, "the harvests having generally been very fine and having occupied more hands." Second, he believed some British officials were giving recruits a very unfavorable impression of conditions in the French Antilles generally on the basis of negative reports by the British consul about French Guiana. Third, and likely most significant, was his admission that the French Caribbean colonies were offering salaries that were only half those in British West Indian colonies.[27]

Despite these difficulties and a much higher mortality during the passage from India, Calcutta came to supply nearly half of the Indians arriving in the French Caribbean colonies during the 1870s and 1880s. As Table 2 shows, most of these went to Guadeloupe, making up more than two-thirds of its immigrants in those decades. French Guiana received about a little less than a third of its new laborers from North India in this period, while Martinique continued to rely predominantly on South Indians from the French ports. Higher mortality on the ships from Calcutta resulted primarily from the fact that cholera was endemic there and could not always be detected by

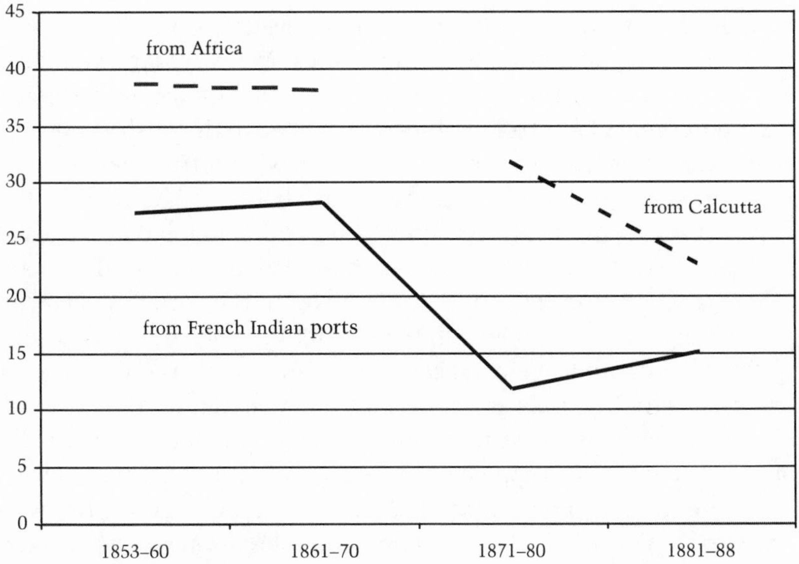

FIG. 2. Mortality on African and Indian Voyages to the French Caribbean, 1853–1888. (Source: Database from French Overseas, British Foreign Office, and British India Office archives. Mortality is per voyage (regardless of length) based on the average number at risk. Not included in the calculations of mortality are the 365 passengers on the *Souvenance,* which sailed for Martinique from the French ports in March 1871 and sank with no survivors.)

medical personnel before departure. However, screening and medical treatment during the voyages seem to have improved substantially as the trade went on. Mortality from the French ports fell steadily from 27 per thousand in the 1850s to under 12 per thousand in the 1870s, while mortality on ships from Calcutta also fell substantially, from 32 per thousand in the 1870s to 23 per thousand in the 1880s (Figure 2).

In response to the campaigns of British, French, and other European labor recruiters, hundreds of thousands of people streamed out of India to colonies in the Indian Ocean and Caribbean basins. Those who went to the French Caribbean were a cross section of Indian society—male and female, rural and urban, Hindu and Muslim, lowly and well born. Their motives were both deeply personal and reflective of the larger changes taking place in India. The peak in 1858 is partly reflective of the disruptions of the Indian Mutiny. As the French emigration agent quoted above suggests, other surges were products of regional droughts and famines. Many women were fleeing bad marriages, affairs that ended in their disgrace, and the general oppression of a patriarchal society. Added to the push of poverty, strife, and social misery was the pull of new opportunities overseas that Indian recruiters dangled before their eyes. Although Indian families and communities restricted individuals' freedom to leave, under British rule escape was safer than in Africa and railroads and other transport improvements made travel to the ports much speedier. Having reached the French recruitment depots and passed scrutiny for health and age, prospective migrants were asked for a positive assent to the terms of a contract to a particular destination. It is plausible that many first-time Indian emigrants had too little sense of world geography to appreciate how far away the Caribbean territories were. It is also plausible that their dreams of a better life were unrealistic, despite the French officials' explanations of the contract terms. Nevertheless, the new emigration routes overseas significantly increased Indians' freedom of choice in employment and the evidence is compelling that authorities took adequate steps to ensure that recruits' decisions to enlist were voluntary.[28]

≺ V ≻

Life in the Colonies

Ninety percent of the 100,000 African and Indian indentured laborers the French recruited were sent to the colonies of Guadeloupe and Martinique in the Lesser Antilles, where they were employed on sugar plantations. The rest went to the colony of French Guiana on the northern coast of South America. The early African laborers in French Guiana worked "on plantations, in logging camps, in the colonial Isle du Salut penal settlement, and in various colonial maritime services."[29] Because French Guiana's sugar economy never amounted to much, most Indian laborers were employed in the placer mines that sprang up during the colony's gold rush.

According to the British Consul in Martinique, regulations governing the first shipload of African laborers, who arrived there on the *Clara* in December 1857, were followed with "great strictness and care": new arrivals were examined by medical authorities (who transferred the ill to an infirmary), registered, and distributed in lots of ten to approved employers (with care taken not to separate relatives and friends), who had to pay 200 francs for each recruit plus 90 francs in other fees. The consul reported that Africans were "well treated" by employers eager to retain their services and were carefully supervised by French authorities.[30] The same official regularly reported that, despite sometimes serious losses of life due to cholera, measles, and other diseases, Indians arriving in the colony declared themselves entirely happy with their treatment during the voyage and were ready to begin work.[31]

The terms under which African and Indian indentured laborers served in the French colonies were similar, but there were some significant differences. Most Africans' contracts provided for a six-year term of indenture; most Indians for a five-year term. In both cases, the contract year was defined as 312 days (excluding Sundays and Christmas Day). Days missed due to illness or other reasons had to be made up, so it usually took longer to fulfill the contract than its nominal term. Initially most African men received wages of 12 francs a month; most Indian men received 12.50 francs. Indian women received 7.50 to 10 francs.[32] All employers were also required to provide free lodging, medical care, clothing allotments, and rations. Generally Africans were entitled to repatriation only if they paid for it through monthly deductions from their salaries; under the terms of the 1861 convention, Indians were entitled to free repatriation at the end of their first contract. In keeping with the labor practices of the period, the enforcement of the terms of the laborers' contracts was a matter of criminal rather than civil law.[33]

Although Africans and Indians received essentially similar treatment, employers' perceptions of their abilities changed over time. Many Indians newly arrived in 1859 were less prepared physically and mentally for the situations they faced than were the new African recruits. Indians' greater tendency to miss work due to illness, disinclination to accept unfamiliar medical treatments, and propensity to wander off reinforced the prejudices of employers for African laborers. Records from Guadeloupe show that, in the period 1860 to 1863, convictions of Indians for labor law violations averaged fifteen per thousand, three times the rate for Africans.[34] However, as the size of Indian immigration rose after 1865 under the Anglo-French convention of 1861, the character and health of Indian recruits improved, as did their eagerness to work. Gradually employers came to prefer Indians, regarding them as quicker to learn than Africans, more docile than Chinese recruits, and cheaper than either of the others.[35]

As their actions suggest, the early Indian immigrants may have been quite unsatisfied with the conditions of their employment. Gradually they learned how to lodge complaints with the two authorities charged with enforcing their legal and contract rights—French colonial officials and British consul authorities. During the course of the year 1877, for example, more Indians in French Guiana filed complaints against their employers than vice versa. Indians lodged 139 complaints with French authorities against their employers and 128 with the British Consul (which probably included many duplicates), compared with 113 complaints by employers against Indian laborers. However, the employers' advantage shows in the outcomes. Eighty-four percent of employers' charges led to convictions, resulting in fines or short prison terms, while most Indian complaints were dismissed or settled informally. In an earlier report, the consul in Guiana had categorized most Indian complaints as minor, trivial, or unfounded, but he investigated them all. He also praised the conscientiousness of the French authorities.[36]

The social and family life of indentured immigrants was affected by the composition of their community, particularly the proportion of women to men. Recruitment of women in Africa varied widely, apparently because of African supply conditions. Some ships brought only a handful of women; on two ships women were the majority of passengers. Overall, 39 percent of adult African recruits were women, a ratio of 64 women for every 100 men. The proportion of women among Indian immigrants had averaged only 24 per 100 men on voyages from 1858 to 1860, but the 1861 convention required that at least 40 women be recruited for every 100 men. Despite some difficulties in achieving that goal in the 1860s, the quota was met or exceeded on all voyages thereafter. Overall, women constituted about 27 percent of Indian adult immigrants to the French Caribbean.

The initial disproportion of three or four men for every woman among Indian immigrants narrowed very slowly as immigrant children and those born in the French colonies reached maturity.

Among Indians the proportion of adult men to women did not fall below 2:1 until about 1880 in Martinique and French Guiana, and not until twenty years later in Guadeloupe. Coupled with high mortality rates in the colonies, the sexual imbalance produced negative demographics among Indians throughout the century. The better balanced sex ratio among African immigrants and perhaps a greater resistance to local diseases, by contrast, resulted in population growth.

≺ VI ≻

Repatriation and Expatriation

The difficulty that many Indian men in the French colonies faced in establishing a family affected the exercise of one of their most important freedoms: the decision to return home or stay in the colony upon the completion of their initial contract. Relatively few Africans returned, even among the Kru, whose contracts provided them with that right. Of some 800 Africans who survived to the end of their contracts in French Guiana, 54 percent chose to stay in the colony, most entering into a new contract which came with a bonus of 200 francs (equal to over sixteen months pay), 29 percent deserted (some going to British Guiana), and just 17 percent were repatriated in 1860 and 1862. Nineteen out of the 74 who asked to be repatriated in 1860 changed their minds at the last minute.[37] There are some instances of Africans paying their own passage back to Africa, mostly among the Kru. However, nearly all of those who had been redeemed from slavery chose to remain in the Americas, if not in a French colony, a fact that is consistent with the hypothesis that they were glad to have escaped from servitude in Africa.

The proportion of Indians who were repatriated was higher, but many Indians also stayed on in the Caribbean colonies. As the first shiploads of Indians were nearing the end of their contracts, the French immigration commissioner in Guadeloupe expressed optimism that many would enter new contracts, but he acknowledged that the shortage of Indian women in the colony would drive many men back to India. Employers sought to retain these veteran workers through a system of bonuses of 100 to 150 francs paid to those who agreed to new longterm labor contracts. Many Indians who signed new contracts exercised their right to change employers, favoring those known for providing better treatment and living conditions. A few moved from plantation labor to domestic service. In Martinique, for example, 939 Indians signed new five- or seven-year contracts between mid-1858 and late 1862, compared to 376 adults who returned to India. Beginning in April 1861, a change in the law permitted contract renewals to be for as little as a year, but most Indians continued to sign new contracts for a term of five years.[38]

For some the decision to remain in the colonies reflected satisfaction with the life and work there; however, there were practical constraints as well. Many Indians found it necessary to sign new contracts in order to survive because no ships were available to carry them back to India. Opportunities for repatriation were particularly limited in Guadeloupe and French Guiana. Of the 21,000 Indians Guadeloupe had received between 1854 and 1870, only 2,034 had been repatriated by 1877. French Guiana had received some 8,200 Indian immigrants between 1856 and 1877 (of whom some 4,600 had died by 1883) but repatriated only 939 by 1883 and another 1,275 in 1884–87. Martinique received over 16,000 Indians between 1853 and 1870, repatriating just 3,054 between 1858 and 1878. British officials complained regularly about the low rates of repatriation and the high rates of mortality, both of which became more to their liking by the early 1880s. Even so, the government of India then suspended all emigration to French colonies, primarily because of far worse conditions in the much larger traffic in indentured laborers to the French colony of Réunion. The last ship left for French Guiana in 1876, for Martinique in 1883, and for Guadeloupe in 1885 (plus one shipload more in 1888–89).[39]

Because mortality was highest among newly arrived Indians, the end of immigration was a significant factor in improving Indian demographic performance. In Martinique the annual mortality among Indians fell from 50 per thousand in the 1850s and 1860s to 37 per thousand in 1871–80. In Guadeloupe, which had imported Indians at twice the rate of her sister colony from the early 1860s to the mid-1880s, Indian mortality dipped from about 75 per thousand in the 1850s and 1860s to about 30 per thousand in 1886–93. The ending of Indian immigration into the notoriously unhealthy French Guiana resulted in the most dramatic improvements in Indian demographics, deaths falling from 89 per thousand in 1877 to 26 per thousand in 1882.

The termination of new immigration also produced varied changes in the freedom and welfare of Indians in the different French colonies. In the view of a Government of India official in 1891, deprived of new recruits, officials in Guadeloupe "tried everything they could to keep Indians in perpetual servitude" through new contracts of indenture, while those in Martinique generally tried to persuade Indians to stay by easing the legal restrictions on them. In contrast to those in Guadeloupe, he reported, Indians in Martinique were "so happy and unmolested by the labour laws" and so "thoroughly acclimatized and accustomed to the ways of the place" that few wished to leave.[40]

The contrast between the two colonies may be a bit overdrawn. A few years earlier a French official had been scathing in his description of how employers in the commune of Basse Pointe, Martinique, were provoking justifiable discontent and desertion among the largest concentration of Indian laborers in the colony by their pitilessly excessive use of the courts, as well as by ceaseless harassment, abuse, and exploitation. He noted that convictions for failing to work, disorder and disrespect, drunkenness, and other matters in that district were more than twice as high as in the rest of the colony.[41] Perhaps because of such official criticism, the situation there began to correct itself, with convictions during the first half of 1885 falling below those of the previous year by more than 25 percent. Most employers seem to have realized that labor discontent was counterproductive, for some two years later the British consul on Martinique reported that, despite the existence of some unscrupulous employers of Indian labor, most did not make excessive demands on their immigrant employees.[42]

Improvements in freedom and welfare after the halt in new immigration were most dramatic in French Guiana, where the resulting labor shortage led to greatly improved wages and conditions in the mining camps; employers had to attract unindentured Indian and other labor instead of paying a fee to get new arrivals already bound to a five-year contract. Freed of labor contracts, some Indians formed successful gold working partnerships and two or three became "millionaires," no small accomplishment even when calculated in francs. In 1888 a British official praised the condition of 330 Indians returning from French Guiana to the French enclaves in southeastern India. Not only did they look younger and healthier than Indians returning from contract labor in Réunion at the same time, but many from French Guiana brought home large sums of cash and trunks full of possessions, while most of the Réunion veterans were penniless.[43] Finally, the colony stepped up its surveillance and enforcement procedures in hopes of persuading British India to rescind the suspension of Indian immigration to French Guiana, though the ban remained in force.

Despite these improvements, conditions for some Indian laborers in French Guiana remained very unsatisfactory. In 1882 there came to light the case of the Bar brothers, who, by dint of hard work and a tight-fisted money policy, had turned their small investment into a thriving plantation that annually exported £600 to £800 worth of annatto, seeds from a tropical shrub used for making a food dye. The 88 Indians on their model plantation "Ilet Portal" on an island in the Maroni River were exceptionally healthy and well fed, but they had been held by a variety of legal and illegal mechanisms in a state of virtual slavery, to which local officials had turned a blind eye. Once these conditions came to light, the French governor took firm action to correct the abuses, but many Indian laborers there ended up with no savings at the end of their contracts.[44]

≺ VII ≻

Conclusions

Because it has generally remained at the margins of prevailing scholarly debates, the French Caribbean can be a useful forum for examining the complex relationships between freedom and indentured migration. French recruitment of African labor was far from problem-free, but dismissing it as nothing more than a thinly disguised continuation of the trade in slaves unreasonably divorces it from quite similar but less often criticized French recruitment in India. More insight into the meaning of freedom can be gained by acknowledging the many similarities between French and British recruitment in Africa and between the recruitment of indentured Africans and indentured Indians. Despite their differences—real and imagined—French and British governments both cloaked their practical search for plantation labor in high-minded platitudes about freedom.

These European conceptions of legal freedom are only one aspect of the full story of the indentured African migrations and the Indian ones that replaced them. What is also needed is an appreciation of the perspectives of those who were recruited and of the communities they came from. The fundamental point is that most indentured migrants freely consented to their servitude. Their consent does not excuse the shortcomings and the mistreatment they had to endure, but it does make their experiences fundamentally different from those of slaves. From the migrants' perspective, migration offered an escape from the harshness of life and the many constraints on freedom in their homelands. For the Africans whom the French and the British liberated from slavery, signing an indentured labor contract may have been the only viable option, but it was one they assented to. Though far from perfect, the structure of Indian recruitment was better regulated and offered more choices.

How well did African and Indian immigrants to the French Caribbean fare? By today's standards their contracts were unconscionably long, their work hard, the risks to life and limb excessive, and their masters' powers of coercion draconian. No doubt, like many of the unindentured immigrants of their day, they were disappointed with their new lots. But, while indentured laborers' freedom was limited, it was not meaningless. Those who survived might accumulate modest savings from their hard-earned wages. They could make meaningful decisions to renew contracts, change employers, and be repatriated.

What did their choices gain them? There are many imponderables in the outcomes and the personal perspectives of the immigrants themselves are always muted. For many Africans overseas indenture was a phase on the road from enslavement to legal freedom. For all who survived, choices to stay or to return were constrained by personal, practical, and political circumstances, but the mere fact that such choices existed needs to be given careful consideration if the perspectives of immigrants are to be appreciated.

The records allow one to construct a profile of what may be regarded as typical in the case of Indian immigrants. Of a thousand Indian adults (725 males, 275 females) who emigrated from India to the

French Caribbean colonies in the 1870s, 17 did not survive the voyage and another 324 died during the first decade of their residence in the colony. Of the 659 survivors, nearly half chose to return to India, 22 dying on the way. Of those who made it back, between 74 and 100 of the original 1,000 returned with savings in cash, jewelry, and other possessions whose total worth was about 400 to 500 francs. Ten accumulated wealth in excess of 1,000 francs. Those who returned also took back 60 children, most born in the French colonies. Of the original 983 who survived the voyage to the French colonies, 349 adults (and their 82 children born in the colonies) would have chosen to remain.

To modern readers all the outcomes of this profile may seem grim and gruesome. Given the conditions that drove so many to leave India, however, the chance of one in ten who left returning with a modest nest egg and one in a hundred with more substantial wealth might have appeared acceptable, even appealing, to those who chose to migrate. Their perspectives deserve to be considered in any evaluation of the meaning of these migrations.

< 8 >

Asian Contract and Free Migrations to the Americas

WALTON LOOK LAI

ASIAN MIGRATIONS to the Americas in the nineteenth century intersect with a number of overlapping modern themes. These include the global immigration and redistribution of labor in the industrial age, in which Asians of all groups were a new and important element; the varieties of transition from slavery to free labor in the Americas, to some of which Asian indentured labor became relevant; the evolution of different kinds of coercive labor systems in the nineteenth century; the post-1840 expansion of Asian diasporal communities beyond traditional historical and geographical frameworks; and finally, the evolution of multicultural societies in the modern age, in the agrarian periphery as well as in the advanced industrial metropolis.[1]

Though overseas migration within the Southeast Asian region was centuries old for both China and India, it was the expansion of the global economy in the age of industrialization and imperialism which laid the foundation for the large migratory movements of labor from these countries to many labor-scarce regions in the colonial (and formerly colonial) periphery of the expanding Atlantic world system. The economist W. Arthur Lewis spoke of late nineteenth-century global development as being promoted by two vast streams of international migration, 50 million people leaving Europe for the temperate settlements, 13 million of whom went to the new countries of temperate settlement (Canada, Argentina, Chile, Australia, New Zealand, and South Africa), and another 50 million people leaving India and China to work in the tropics on plantations, in mines, and in construction projects.[2] The actual numbers involved in this second stream have always been a matter of ambiguity, as has indeed the regime under which they worked.[3] The reason for this ambiguity was the very large number involved in seasonal and return migration in South and Southeast Asia in the century between 1834 and 1937. It has been estimated that about 30 million Indians emigrated, and just under 24 million returned in this period, leaving a net migration of roughly 6.3 million Indians.[4] The Chinese migrations added another 7.5 million—6.5 million within Southeast Asia.[5] In addition, there were at least another million Indonesians, Japanese, and Pacific Islanders joining the migrant stream during this century of global labor mobility. Ongoing analyses of these various Asian migrations—region-specific, ethnic-specific, and comparative—have advanced our knowledge of the roles played by free and semi-free Asian labor in the growth of the far-flung sectors of the global economy in this period, as well as the degree to which the immigrants have adjusted to their new environments since then. Much, however, still remains to be understood about Asian migration. In particular, more comparative understanding of diasporal processes is needed even as we deepen our understanding of each of these migrations in their separate dimensions.[6]

I

Chinese and Indian Migrations Compared

Despite the overarching uniformity of the global economic processes propelling both Chinese and Indians into new territories of settlement, the most noticeable feature of the nineteenth-century migrations was the different orbits within which these two Asian groups largely traveled. The Indians went to Sri Lanka, Burma, Malaya in South and Southeast Asia; to Mauritius and Réunion in the western Indian Ocean; to Fiji in the Pacific; to Natal in South Africa, as well as to East Africa (Kenya, Uganda). Within the Americas, they went to the European colonies in the Caribbean, mainly British Guiana, Trinidad, and Dutch Surinam. They went also to Jamaica and the Windward Islands of Grenada, St. Lucia, and St. Vincent, as well as to French Martinique, Guadeloupe, and Cayenne.[7] Toward the turn of the century, there was also a trickle of free migration to the west coast of North America, under totally different push/pull circumstances.[8]

The Chinese also migrated mainly within Southeast Asia, but with the exception of British Malaya[9] they encountered small numbers of Indians where they went. They migrated mainly to older Chinese settlements in Thailand, the Philippines, and Indonesia. They also flocked in large numbers to new destinations: to Australia, New Zealand, and the Pacific islands (mainly Hawaii and Tahiti); to Mauritius and Réunion in the western Indian Ocean; to Transvaal in South Africa, and to the Americas. Unlike the Indians, their movements into the Americas were totally dispersed, covering North America (US and Canada), Spanish America (mainly Cuba and Peru, and later in the century, Mexico), in addition to the French, Dutch, and British Caribbean plantation societies.[10] The Indian migrations to the western hemisphere by contrast had remained largely concentrated on the Caribbean plantation societies, and only to the non-Latin ones at that. The Cubans made abortive attempts to acquire Indian labor in the 1880s, and there were significant post-indenture Indian migrations out of the West Indies to places like Venezuela, Cuba, and Central America,[11] but generally Indian migration was a non-Hispanic Caribbean phenomenon. Interestingly, the possibility of importing Indian labor into Louisiana in the 1860s was raised by planters with French West Indian connections, but this never materialized.[12]

Much of the discussion on the comparative fates of these two Asian migrant groups is shaped by the different labor traditions and labor cultures of the separate receiving areas. These had an impact on almost every aspect of the respective migrations, from the mechanisms and conditions of recruitment and transportation; to the ratio between voluntary and involuntary movements; to the nature of the migrants' reception, work experience, and adjustment to their respective new environments. There were destinations where their fates would overlap, mainly in the small European colonies of the Caribbean and western Indian Ocean, as well as in Malaya; but by and large most Chinese diasporas were formed in areas of the Americas, Southeast Asia, or the Pacific, to which very few Indians migrated. Broad comparative discussions about these two groups therefore primarily concern the differences between immigration and labor traditions of different groups of countries, even where the discussion may be on some overarching theme, such as the varieties of indentured or contract labor, the multiple transitions from slavery to free labor, or the nature of the work experience in the new environment.

Nowhere is the link between imperial connection and destination clearer than in India; there most migrants moved within the British Empire, or to destinations approved by British imperial authorities. Chinese imperial subjugation was more complex, and its migration traditions older. Indeed, outside of Malaya, the British component of Chinese multinational migration was never very significant, in spite of the role played by Hong Kong as a major nineteenth-century transit point for the Chinese to other destinations.[13] It is noticeable too how much of Indian indentured migration was connected to the global expansion of the British sugar industry, as it tried to transcend its seventeenth-century Caribbean origins (Jamaica, Barbados, and the Leewards) and reached out to new areas of cultivation in an age of slave emancipation and free trade (Mauritius, Guiana, Trinidad, Natal, Fiji). A significant portion of Chinese indentured migration to the tropical plantation complex was also tied to the fate of world sugar expansion, but that migration was mostly not British Empire-oriented, being destined mainly for Cuba and Peru, on the one end, and Hawaii on the other, countries with very different labor traditions.[14] The Chinese laborers destined for the sugar territories of the British, French, and Dutch colonies of the Caribbean and Indian Ocean numbered less than 27,000, whereas the numbers emigrating to Cuba, Peru, and Hawaii were in the region of 290,000. Smaller numbers entered other areas of the plantation world, such as the US South and Brazil, but public policy never crystallized in favor of Chinese immigration in either area—in the US South because of economic and legal factors, and in Brazil because of official ambivalence toward the Chinese as a race of potential immigrants.[15]

Both groups of Asians went to countries in which they formed part of a multiracial labor force—sometimes with each other, more often with others—as well as to countries in which they were the main element in the workforce. In Cuba, Chinese worked alongside African slaves; in the British West Indies, alongside Indian and Portuguese immigrants; in Hawaii alongside native Hawaiians; in Peru up to the 1880s as a majority workforce. Indians were generally part of a multiracial workforce in Trinidad and Guiana during the 1860s, but by the late 1870s and after they were the majority (and often the only) element on the plantations. By contrast, in the Windward Islands and Jamaica, as indeed the French West Indian islands of Martinique and Guadeloupe, they continued to remain a minority element in a workforce of African ex-slaves. In Mauritius, Natal, and post-1890s Fiji they were the majority element on the plantations. In Dutch Surinam from the 1890s, they shared the plantations with Indonesians from Java. In Fiji in the 1880s, they worked alongside Pacific Islanders. Both Chinese and Indians went to older colonies in transition where slavery had previously existed, as well as to newly formed colonies where slavery had never existed. Examples of the former were the Caribbean and Indian Ocean colonies and even post-Civil War Louisiana, Arkansas, and Mississippi.[16] Examples of the latter were Natal (Indians) and Transvaal (Chinese), Fiji (Indians) and Hawaii (Chinese), as well as Malaya (both groups). Indian migration orbited overwhelmingly within the tropical plantation (Afro-Asian) world, while a sizable segment of Chinese immigration also went to the temperate settlement zones, paralleling the European migratory movements of the time, attracted by the same pull factors if not necessarily destined for the same fates. In the white settlement destinations, the Chinese were miners, railway workers, agricultural workers, artisans, and merchants. In South and Southeast Asia, sugar was only a minority occupation for both groups, other plantation products taking priority.

Contrary to a commonly held perception, only a minority of both groups actually traveled and worked under the indenture system. Chinese migration to Southeast Asia, North America, and Australia was overwhelmingly (though not exclusively) non-contract migration. Four times as many Indian migrants (5.2 million vs. 1.3 million) went to Sri Lanka, Burma, and Malaya under labor arrangements quite different from the indentured contract migrations.[17] The question still needs to be asked, however, about the precise ratios of coercion to freedom under all the various labor arrangements under which they traveled and functioned. Apart from the large number who paid their own way to join family and village networks in Southeast Asia or elsewhere, Chinese labor migration arrangements are usually divided into the technically free credit ticket system which dominated in the Southeast Asian, Australian, and North American diaspora; and the indenture system practiced mainly in the Caribbean, Latin America, Indian Ocean, and more sporadically in other destinations (including Hawaii). The main differences between the credit ticket arrangements and the indenture arrangements lay firstly, in who controlled the operations (native Chinese intermediaries vs. Western recruiting agencies), and secondly, in the nature of the reciprocal obligations incurred on either side: free passage debt to be voluntarily repaid by laborer after arrival vs. free passage combined with often unstable promises of wage, housing, medical, and other benefits in exchange for *legally enforceable* bonds requiring specified field labor for a fixed term of years. There were often enough ambiguities on the ground to make the distinction between the two forms questionable,[18] but the technical distinctions were at least clear. In addition, there were important differences between the state-sponsored, state-regulated, and state-supervised system of indentured immigration typical of the British system, operating mainly out of Hong Kong and Canton, and the infamous private enterprise-operated Latin American indenture systems of Cuba and Peru, operating out of Portuguese Macao. A number of destinations, moreover, initially received indentured migrants not directly from China but via other regional or colonial connections, for example Malaya to Trinidad and Réunion, Java to Surinam, Panama to Jamaica, Cuba to Louisiana. Some laborer communities, for example Mauritius under the Dutch (1638–1710), actually originated in the seventeenth century, well before the mass migrations of the nineteenth.

Indian migrations are usually divided into the kangani[19] recruitment arrangements of South and Southeast Asia and the indenture systems of the sugar colonies and partially Malaya. Kanganis or labor headmen were influential immigrant workers sent by host country plantations back to their respective Indian villages to recruit new groups of workers on a seasonal or longterm basis. Unlike those under indenture, the immigrants were not bound by formal contracts or legal process, but there was an obligation owed to the kangani or recruiter-foreman who assumed responsibility for those recruited by him, many of them bound by extended family ties. The obligation here was more of a communal nature, as contrasted with the individualistic obligation of the indentured worker.[20] Unlike the Chinese credit ticket arrangements, the passage expenses were usually shouldered by the recruiting plantations themselves through the kanganis, and there were no third-party money brokers outside this arrangement. Recruitment to Mauritius during the high period of indenture also involved a hybrid arrangement between the forms. Here, the Indian laborers arrived as indentureds but their recruiters were mainly ex-indentureds acting as agents for the Mauritian plantations, similar to the kangani recruiters.

All of the previously mentioned forms of emigration are distinguished from late-century and turn-of-the-century voluntary migration of family, trader, and artisan elements. For the Chinese, this late voluntary migration generally went to most of the earlier destinations, and it often involved small-scale chain movements based on family, clan, and village networks. It might be enhanced in some destinations by special local factors, such as the increased Latin America/Caribbean inflow after the closure of destinations like the US following the Chinese Exclusion Act of 1882, or special welcoming policies organized by local governments like Porfirio Diaz's Mexico (1876–1911). In certain destinations, late free migration actually played a dominant role in the sense that more people arrived during this turn-of-the-century period than during the earlier indenture period. This was the case in destinations like Jamaica, Panama, and Mauritius, where very few indentured workers went in the initial immigration. It was also the case in Mexico, where there had been no indentured immigrants in the first period. For the Indians, free voluntary migration affected particular destinations such as East Africa, Natal, and the western Indian Ocean islands—physically close to India—and there was the special migration of Punjabi laborers to North America. Technically, it would also include a noticeable minority of formerly indentured Indians who had returned to India and who later came back voluntarily to their original plantation destinations (or often alternative destinations) under new circumstances. They were described in the immigration reports as "casuals" or "passengers."[21]

Free late-century or turn-of-the-century movements also involved a significant amount of relocating from one territory to another within a given regional nexus, for example among the different islands of the Caribbean and Indian Ocean regions. Chinese remigrated from Guiana to Surinam, Trinidad, Jamaica, and Central America; they moved between Réunion and Mauritius, Mauritius and Seychelles, and all of these and Madagascar. Indians relocated from the smaller West Indian islands (both British and French) to Trinidad and Guiana; they also migrated to Venezuela and Guiana from Trinidad; to Cuba, Costa Rica, and Panama from Jamaica; to Surinam and Trinidad from Guiana. It would seem too that a significant amount of early Chinese remigration in the Americas involved movements from the Caribbean and Latin America to the US, mainly the east coast. US immigration records would seem to suggest that a noticeable number of the early east coast (as opposed to west coast) Chinese originated in other areas of the Americas.[22] Several small communities of ex-Cuban Chinese were already living in the East and South before the Civil War.[23]

≺ II ≻

Push Factors and Regions of Origin

Both China and India had long histories of overseas migration within the South and Southeast Asian orbit which predated the arrival of the West in Asia. Many of these overseas communities proved transient, while many—especially among the Chinese—became stable immigrant enclaves. It is well known that when the Europeans arrived in Southeast Asia in the sixteenth century, they encountered sophisticated Chinese trade networks which had been formed in an earlier era.[24] While not always formally acknowledged or encouraged by the imperial authorities, coastal and maritime China had evolved a distinctive and vigorous tradition dating back as far as the seventh century A.D. (and possibly before). Out of these maritime traditions had arisen a number of early overseas Chinese settlements in Southeast Asia.[25] Moreover, China's own migratory cycle within Southeast Asia was quickened and stimulated after the 1560s by the early Western connection, so that by the time the modern migrations began in the nineteenth century, vastly expanded overseas enclaves existed in the Philippines, Java, Sumatra, West Borneo, Thailand, and the Malay peninsula. Indeed, some of the initial labor recruitment for the new destinations took place from these enclaves, rather than from the mainland proper.

Indian overseas settlements, in contrast, had not been permanent, although Indian traders and workers were a common sight in late eighteenth-century South and Southeast Asian port cities, and communities of South Indian slave, convict, and other migrant labor had arisen in the early nineteenth century in Mauritius, Sri Lanka, and British Southeast Asia.[26] Modern Indian emigration was a wholly British colonial creation, beginning after the abolition of slavery in the British Empire in 1834. However, there was a long tradition of domestic seasonal migration *within* India, which intensified with the British impact on the local economy, and it is this movement that eventually spilled over into the overseas emigration.[27]

British direct rule in India and the land, taxation, and trade policies introduced in its wake were largely responsible for generating disruptive push factors in the Indian countryside, which in turn created the large pool of floating labor directed toward domestic destinations like Bengal or Assam, or to foreign destinations like Sri Lanka or the sugar colonies. Natural and demographic factors were exacerbating causes, but the role of colonialism in disrupting the traditional economy while harnessing it to the needs of the distant British Industrial Revolution has been well documented.[28] Chinese push factors were more complex, a combination of domestically generated economic decline and political crisis (the Taiping and other rebellions), and Western-induced crisis (opium wars and unequal treaties). In both countries, however, it is noteworthy that both indentured and free migrations were confined to specific sending provinces and districts, and, however crucial in the formation of overseas communities, involved a very small percentage of the population of both countries.

The majority of China's migrants historically came from two southern coastal provinces, Fujian and Guangdong. This pattern applies to all three historic periods of Chinese migration (the traditional, early modern, and nineteenth century), and indeed even to a large extent to the twentieth-century period.[29] From as far back as the seventh century, port cities like Quanzhou (Chuanchow) in Fujian and Guangzhou (Canton) in southern Guangdong had seafaring and overseas connections long predating the arrival of the Western traders. Formosa (Taiwan) had been gradually colonized by overseas Fujianese and northeastern Guangdongese between the seventh and fifteenth centuries, seeking a base for trade with the mainland as well as Southeast Asia. Moreover, the Phillipines had direct and prolonged contacts with migrants from Fujian since the 1560s, stimu-

Map 1. Origins of Nineteenth-Century Chinese Contract Labor Going to the Americas.

lated by the newly established Manila-Acapulco connection. The Macao-Canton axis had also been an international enclave since the sixteenth century. The intensified intrusions of the nineteenth century in the aftermath of the two Opium Wars of the 1840s and 1860s only served to heighten the activities and migratory movements traditionally associated with these provinces. Within these broad regions, moreover, there were often several clearly identifiable micro-districts or counties which had long traditions of migratory dispersal at the center of their social and community life. Zhangzhou (Changchow), Quanzhou (Chuanchow), Jinjiang in south Fujian, Fuzhou (Foochow) in north Fujian, and Chaozhou (Chaochow) and Jieyang (Chia-ying) in northeast Guangdong had intimate links with the Southeast Asian nexus before the nineteenth-century migrations began.

Interestingly, the relative importance of these two sending regions was not the same to all destinations. Most Fujianese over time migrated mainly to Southeast Asia, whereas most American-bound nineteenth-century migrations originated from southeastern Guangdong. The Guangdongese are themselves subdivided into the northeastern Teochiu speakers emigrating from the port city of Shantou (Swatow) and surrounding districts, and the southeastern Cantonese emigrating from Guangzhou (Canton), Hong Kong, and Macao. Mingled among these groups were the Hakka dialect group, who lived dispersed in both provinces, but were especially concentrated in the border regions separating Fujian from northeast Guangdong. They emigrated out of all the sending ports.[30]

Some overseas destinations were closely linked to specific regional or dialect groups, for example Hokkien or south Fujianese merchants in Japan, the Phillipines and Java; the Hakkas in West Borneo; the Teochius in Thailand. Certain villages or districts became known as major suppliers of migrants: Zhangzhou, Quanzhou, Jinjiang in south Fujian (mentioned above); the Siyi (Four Districts), Sanyi (Three Districts),[31] and Zhongshan (Chungshan) in southeastern Guangdong. Some became closely (though not exclusively) linked to specific destinations: Jinjiang to the Phillipines; Taishan in the Siyi nexus to the US; Zhongshan to Hawaii; the Hakka-speaking eastern Pearl River Delta districts (Huiyang, Dongguan, and Baoan) to destinations like Surinam, Jamaica, and Tahiti; the northeast Guangdong Hakka district of Meixian to places like Mauritius. From some destinations, workers were returned to their homes of origin after their projects were completed, for example workers from the northern province of Shandong who were sent to Transvaal in South Africa in the 1900s and to Europe during World War I. Special traits applied to some migrations, such as displaced Christians (Hakka and non-Hakka) from southern Guangdong being relocated to British Guiana or Hawaii. By and large, the Fujianese tended to predominate up to the nineteenth century, while the south Guangdongese dominated the nineteenth, in the growth of the overseas communities. The same was true for the Chinese who went to the Americas, whether as indentureds or as technically free migrants. Cantonese-Fujian ratios were in the region of 86–14 for the British West Indies, 96–4 for Latin America as a whole, and probably 99–1 for North America.[32]

The links between sending and receiving regions forged by Indian migrants also exhibited systematic patterns.[33] South Indians, particularly Tamils, predominated in South and Southeast Asia and South Africa, North Indians in the West Indies, Punjabis and Gujaratis in Africa, Europe, and North America, though Indians from other regions were also present in all destinations. Two British Indian administrators, J. Geoghehan and George Grierson, wrote comprehensive accounts of the origins of the Indian indentured migrants in the 1870s and 1880s which appeared as official Indian government publications.[34] They noted that the Bhojpuri-dialect region in northern India, for example, which the British artificially divided in the late eighteenth century into Bihar (westernmost Bengal) on the one hand, and eastern Northwest Provinces on the other, was one major sending region.[35] Tamil and Telugu-speaking South India was another. Between 1842 and 1870, the sugar colonies of the Caribbean and Indian Ocean received just over 530,000 Indian migrants, 342,575 or 64.2 percent from the north emigrating through Calcutta, 159,259 or 29.8 percent from Madras and other South India ports like French Pondicherry and Karikal, and a small contingent of 31,761 or 5.95 percent from Bombay, who went exclusively to Mauritius. The main north Indian sending districts before and after 1870 were Bihar and the eastern Northwest Provinces (known later as United Provinces, and still later as Uttar Pradesh). These Bhojpuri-speaking districts, traditionally depressed regions with a long history of seasonal domestic migration predating the British arrival, were thrown into more acute depression as a result of British land and taxation policies, famine, and political unrest (the Indian Mutiny of 1857) in the mid-nineteenth century. Within these regions, specific districts provided most of the recruits for both domestic seasonal and overseas indentured migrations. By 1910 the Sanderson Commission of Enquiry into Indian Emigration was stating that most of the overseas-bound Indians were recruited in three districts in the eastern United Provinces—Fyzabad, Basti, and Gonda—and that 80 percent were born in 21 districts of Bengal and the United Provinces, with a combined total area of 55,000 square miles and a population of 34 million: north and south Bihar, the Benares, Gorakhpur, and Fyzabad divisions.[36]

A sizable minority of migrants came from Bengal proper, outlying western regions of the United Provinces, and smaller surrounding states. In the initial years of the overseas migrations (1840s and 1850s), most of the recruits were tribals from the Chota Nagpur district of southern Bihar. Between 1875 and 1917, of 92,243 migrants to Trinidad, 75 percent came from the United Provinces, 13 percent from Bihar, 4 percent from Central India, 3 percent from Nepal and the native states, 2 percent from the Punjab, 1 percent from Bengal, and another 1 percent from places like Orissa, Ajmere, and Bombay.[37] Between 1865 and 1917, the migrants to British Guiana were 70.3 percent from the United Provinces and 15.3 percent from Bihar; the rest were from neighboring regions and provinces.[38]

In summary, whereas Chinese migrations could be considered a nineteenth-century broadening—in the age of the Industrial Revolution—of an earlier regional overseas migratory cycle, overseas migrations of north Indians were more akin to an overflow from a well-established domestic seasonal migration of peoples which continued even during the nineteenth century to be much larger than the overseas flow. This internal migration went to the tea plantations of Assam, the textile industries of Bombay, the jute mills and coal mines of Bengal, government works and public construction, as well as into the colonial army. It has been estimated that about 20 million Indians were involved in this overall long-distance migration, only a small percentage of whom went overseas under any kind of labor arrangement.[39] South Indians, on the other hand, had a more established tradition of supplying both slave and semi-free labor for overseas employers in Southeast Asia and the Indian Ocean, and it

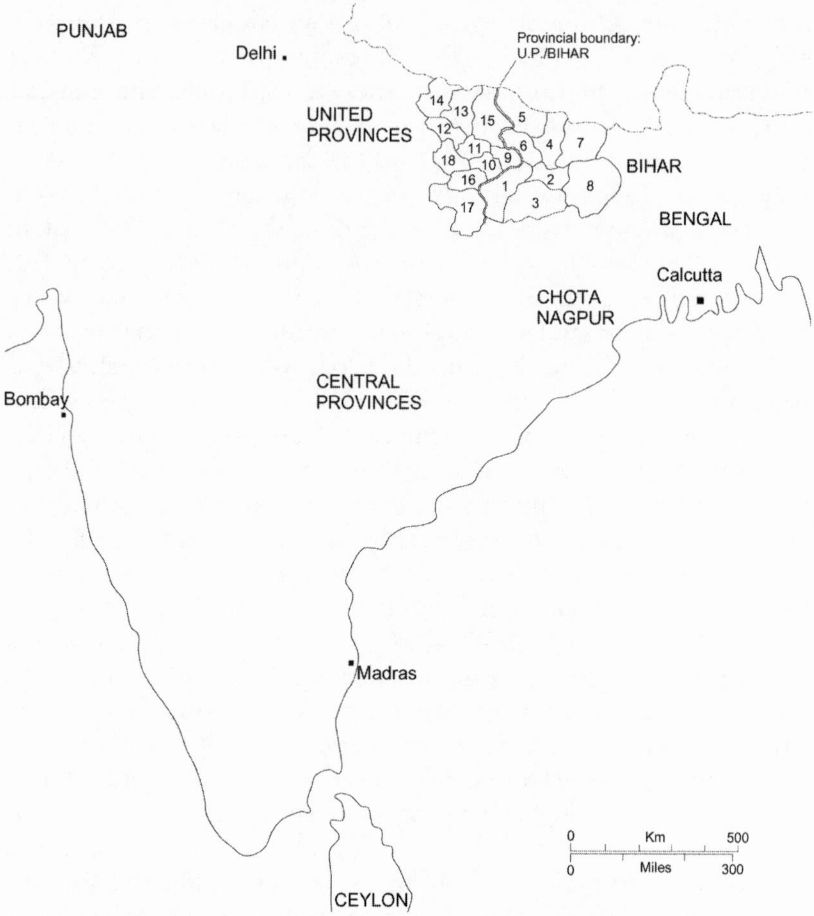

Map 2. Origins of Indian Contract Labor Going to the Americas.

Bihari Districts

1. Shahabad
2. Patna
3. Gaya
4. Muzaffarpur
5. Champaran
6. Saran
7. Darbhanga
8. Monghyr

Districts of the United Provinces

9. Ballia
10. Ghazipur
11. Azamghar
12. Fyzabad
13. Basti
14. Gonda
15. Gorakhpur
16. Banaras
17. Mirzapur
18. Jaunpur

was this tradition which was amplified by the Western recruiters. Within the Caribbean plantations, South Indians generally constituted a significant minority, perhaps just under 30 percent of all migrants; but in the French West Indian islands of Martinique and Guadeloupe, they formed a slight majority, originating largely in the French-held south Indian ports of Pondicherry and Karikal, despite a sizable post-1870 Calcutta contingent recruited under special arrangement with the British.[40]

≺ III ≻

Varieties of Caribbean Asian Migration

The most important issue from a comparative standpoint for the Caribbean Asian migrations is to determine the precise balance between coercion and freedom in the various arrangements at work during the century. Distinctions between coercion and freedom within any indenture arrangement involve not just the relation between official theory and actual practice over time, but also contradictions within the actual laws themselves, and the relation between these laws and those of technically unfree labor systems.

The following differentiations immediately suggest themselves. First, the distinction between the Chinese indenture systems of Cuba and of the rest of the Caribbean; second, the distinction between the Chinese and the Indian indenture experiences in the British West Indies; and third, the distinction between the indentured migrations and the free migrations at the end of the century and turn of the century.

The Cuban Chinese experiment began officially in 1847, with a shipment of 347 immigrants from Xiamen (Amoy). Between 1847 and 1874, 347 vessels brought 125,000 Chinese to Cuba, while 51 vessels brought around 18,000 to the British West Indies between 1853 and 1884: 39 to British Guiana (13,539), 8 to Trinidad (2,645), 2 to Jamaica (1,152), 1 to British Honduras (474), and 1 to Antigua (100). Most of the British West Indian vessels (all but 4) arrived before 1866. Surinam also received about 2,640 migrants in 20 large and small vessels between 1853 and 1874, and about 1,000 went to the French islands of Martinique and Guadeloupe in 3 vessels in the

1860s. With the exception of about 3 vessels, all the migrants came under some form of indenture contract.

A number of initial generalizations about the Cuban Asian migrations should be made. These migrations were exclusively Chinese. Attempts were made in the 1880s to acquire Indians from the British, but these efforts were rejected by the government of India and the British Colonial Office.[41] Cuba received the largest numbers of Chinese who came to the Caribbean and Latin American region, around 51 percent, while around 7 percent went to the West Indies and Guianas. In fact, in 1860 there were as many Chinese in Cuba as there were in the US—around 35,000. Moreover, the Cuban Chinese experiment (1847–74) took place, not during the transition from slavery to free labor, but during the height of slavery itself. The experiment even ended before slavery in Cuba was abolished (1886). The labor shortage to which it was a response was generated during slavery by an atmosphere of economic boom, as well as by the escalating costs of African slave labor in mid-century. It was not, as it was in the rest of the region during the 1840s and 1850s, a problematic post-emancipation development caused by ex-slave flight from the estates and escalating wage demands in an atmosphere of freedom.

After an initial trial period with migration from ports like Xiamen (Amoy) and Shantou (Swatow), Cuban operations came to be centered mainly in Portuguese Macao, where about 80 percent of the Latin America-bound Chinese embarked. West Indian operations by contrast were conducted by governmental agencies based in Hong Kong or Canton, even when on occasion migrants came from regions like Shantou and Xiamen.

All the Cuba-bound Chinese came under a version of the indenture system which was quite distinct from the one being used in the British West Indies. The main difference lay in its control by private entrepreneurs, from the ports of recruitment to the distribution and dispersal in Cuba, with marginal state involvement or supervision. Apart from having to obtain a license to import laborers from the China coast, Latin American importers (whether shipping firms operating the traffic as a speculative profiteering venture, or specific planter-employers chartering vessels to bring back specified amounts of laborers) were only minimally affected by the state and its agencies in their operations. By contrast, apart from a few early private enterprise efforts in British Guiana, the entire British operation was state-sponsored and state-controlled, just like the more large-scale operation in India. This involvement by the state had a marked impact on the levels of coercion, deception, and violence involved in recruitment, transportation, distribution, and work treatment.

The manner in which the Cubans and Peruvians arranged and sold labor contracts in the New World was often indistinguishable in practice from the slave trade proper. The reputation acquired by the Macao-based operators was nowhere duplicated in the British efforts, despite some glaring irregularities in the latter system. Cuban recruitment at the China end was entirely dependent on the payment of freelance recruiters or crimps, whose methods were officially condemned and often caused minor local riots. Precisely what the balance was between outright coercion on the one hand, and free choice by the migrant based on deception or false promises on the other, may never be determined, but the scale of the coercion/deception was clearly unique. The British recruitment, apart from being handled by state agencies, often depended on intermediaries like China-based European missionaries. On voyages to Cuba and Peru, passenger mortality as well as rebellion far exceeded levels experienced on movements to the non-Spanish West Indies between 1853 and 1884. Average mortality rates for the British West Indies-bound voyages were 4.5 to 6 percent, compared with 11 to 12 percent for the Cuba-bound. A British official who compiled a list of 34 mutinies and disturbances on board Caribbean-bound Chinese vessels between 1845 and 1872 listed only two of these as Demerara-bound, the rest being Cuba- and Peru-bound.[42]

The report of a Chinese government commission of enquiry, which visited Cuba in 1873 and interviewed hundreds of Chinese workers, remains the classic exposé of life on the Cuban plantations under the indenture system. So harsh were Cuban work conditions that many indentureds ran away from the estates, and, like the slaves, were hunted down and recaptured by "rancheadores" or professional slavecatchers. Many Chinese also joined the anti-Spanish Cuban rebel force in the first War of Independence (1868–78), in exchange for promises of freedom from bondage. Conditions on the British Guiana plantations were also investigated in 1869–70 by a commission of enquiry. This effort produced an official report published as a parliamentary paper in 1871,[43] as well as a dissenting independent publication by an ex-judge, Chief Justice Beaumont's *The New Slavery: an account of the Indian and Chinese immigrants in British Guiana*.[44] While the Cuban atrocities were not duplicated in the British territories, life was far from satisfactory for many of the Chinese who had migrated to the British colonies. Whereas in the Cuban case we have the formal testimonies of the Chinese laborers themselves, there are no such living testimonies from the Asian laborers on the West Indian plantations. Local newspapers like the Guiana *Royal Gazette* provided many details of specific incidents of dissatisfaction and harsh treatment involving the Chinese laborers,[45] but the most trenchant critics during the 1860s were people who came from the ranks of the elite, mainly judges and immigration agents.

The laws of Cuba often gave official sanction to some of the early cruelties of treatment, whereas in the West Indies the problems usually lay in the gap between the formal legal protections and some of the actual plantation practices. For example, the 1849 Cuban law on indenture included the following articles on appropriate punishments for worker indiscipline:

> *Article XI*. The colonist disobeying the voice of the superior, whether it be refusing to work, or any other obligation, may be corrected with 12 lashes; if he persists, with 18 more, and if even thus he should not enter on his course of duty, he may be put in irons, and made to sleep in the stocks. If after 2 months have passed . . . he should not give proof of amendment, in this case the whole shall be brought to the knowledge of the local authority, in order that it may come to that of the superior of the island.
>
> *Article XII*. If 2 or more should refuse to work, notwithstanding the orders or persuasions, there shall be given to them the punishment of 25 lashes, putting them in irons, and they shall also sleep in the stocks for 2 months.
>
> *Article XIV*. The colonist that runs away, besides being subject to Article VI (no salary, and expenses of recapture recoverable from later salary), shall be placed in irons for 2 months; for 4 in case of repeating it, and for 6 in the second, and during the punishment he shall also have to sleep in the stocks.

Subsequent protective laws were passed from time to time, and a formal mitigation of the above punishments pronounced, but they were always somewhat ineffective and secondary to the personalistic control over the laborers by the planters and their representatives allowed by the system, and to the general tendency of the authorities to look the other way whenever master/servant relations were an issue. Moreover, a Spanish Royal decree of 1860 reinforced this condition with the following stipulation:

Article VII. It is an essential condition and must be an express clause in every contract with Chinese . . . that the time of his engagement being completed, he cannot remain in the island of Cuba as a laborer without having made another contract of the same kind, as apprentice or workman under the responsibility of a master, or as being engaged in agriculture, or as a domestic servant guaranteed by his master, in every other case he will have to leave the island at his own expense, being obliged to do so 3 months after the termination of the contract.

The Chinese commission of enquiry concluded that

The distinction between a hired laborer and the slave can only exist when the former accepts, of his own free will, the conditions tendered, and performs in a like manner the work assigned to him; but the lawless method in which the Chinese were—in the great majority of cases—introduced into Cuba, the contempt there evinced for them, the disregard of contracts, the indifference as to the tasks enforced, and the unrestrained infliction of wrong, constitute a treatment which is that of "a slave, not of a man who has consented to be bound by a contract." Men who are disposed of in Havana, who are afterwards constantly, like merchandise, transferred from one establishment to another, and who, on the completion of their first agreements, are compelled to enter into fresh ones, who are detained in depots and delivered over to new masters, whose successive periods of toil are endless, and to whom are open no means of escape, cannot be regarded as occupying a position different from that of the negroes whose servitude has so long existed in the island, and who are liable to be hired out or sold at the will of their owner.[46]

The laws of British West Indian indenture, combined with the formal oversight of the immigration department and the judicial system, seemed to function with less imbalance and personal corruption than the Cuban system. The fact that abolitionist and antislavery lobbies were still active and alert in Britain no doubt played a role in creating this slightly less oppressive atmosphere. Nevertheless, there were still several layers of abuse in the British system, as pointed out by the Guiana critiques, and by Chief Justice Beaumont himself.[47] A few were actually sanctioned by the laws themselves, such as the pass system restricting the mobility of the indentured worker within a two-mile radius from his place of work; or the penal sanctions always attached to work offenses (fines and imprisonment), not as harsh as the Cuban sanctions to be sure, but still an anomaly considering that these arose out of violations of civil and contractual obligations.[48] But there were those that were not officially sanctioned but widely practiced. These included misrepresentation, by recruiters and even British officials at the China end, of the actual level of wages a prospective immigrant could hope to earn in the new environment, a complaint frequently made by the Chinese after arrival in Guiana, and which Chief Justice Beaumont mentioned in his critique. There were also chronic violations of health and housing regulations, bribes extracted from workers by plantation officials for all kinds of routine favors, arbitrary withholding of passes and wages, violations of minimum wage provisions especially in times of recession, physical violence against workers by managers and overseers, and excessive recourse to penal discipline sometimes for personal reasons. The result was that the jails were often full of immigrants imprisoned for minor and major offenses against the labor laws, living side by side with hardened criminals. There were also those abuses which were not adequately covered by the law, such as informal pressures to reindenture at the end of the five-year term of service. While not as blatant as the Cuban 1860 decree, they were often no less effective; for example, a whole list of potentially punishable work offenses might be piled up against an immigrant in his last year, which could be bargained off against his willingness to reindenture himself for another term. Finally, at the back of the entire system, there was the impersonal (and racist) indifference of the entire court system, which was designed to function as a neutral arbiter between management and labor but was more often than not another arm of the total disciplinary mechanism of indenture, given the background and predispositions of the majority of the judiciary.[49]

Chinese contract migration to Cuba finally terminated in 1874 under intense pressure from international actors, including the United States, Britain, and China. The 1873 Chinese Imperial investigative mission and its revelations played a crucial role in the final stages of the diplomatic pressure. Chinese indenture in the West Indies terminated because of estimated cost factors compared with the Indian indenture scheme, after a prolonged diplomatic wrangle in the 1860s over the costs of introducing a return passage clause in the Chinese contracts similar to the same provision in the Indian contracts. By the late 1860s it was effectively over, even though a few ships came in the 1870s and 1880s. Indian indenture continued until 1917, when it too was terminated under the combined pressures exerted by an aroused Indian nationalist movement on the one hand, and gradually changing politics (and colonial policies) in Britain, on the other.

Discussion of the British indenture system in the West Indies and Guiana centers on the comparison between the China- and India-based indenture arrangements. Chinese and Indian indenture shared four broadly common features under the British system. First, as previously mentioned, the state was actively involved in all aspects of recruitment and transportation in the East, as well as at points of arrival and distribution in the Caribbean, to the total exclusion of all privately sponsored indentured immigration schemes. Second, the state subsidized the financial expenses involved in operating the immigration experiment (recruiting and transportation, and maintaining the immigration establishment). Two-thirds of the financial costs were generally borne by the planters—through indenture fees for individual migrants, plus taxes on export produce or, in Guiana, property taxes on sugar plantations. The state paid the balance, mainly through taxes on consumer imports. Third, a five-year contract of indenture came to be standard. Laborers were bound to a specific plantation for that time period at a fixed rate of wages, with severely limited rights of physical mobility outside the workplace environment. A strict pass law system kept the worker within a two-mile radius around the plantation unless he or she had a formal pass permitting movement beyond this limit. This stringent pass law system was to be the major distinguishing mark of difference between an immigrant contract laborer and a free laborer. The laws gave the planter-employer a formal power over the immigrant laborer and his physical movements which clearly violated his theoretical status as a free agent and could be utilized either for the paternalistic protection of the immigrant in a new and strange environment or for the abuse of his labor power by unscrupulous plantation officials. Finally, an elaborate system of regulations in addition to the pass law system, contained in immigration ordinances passed by the local legislatures, outlined the reciprocal rights and obligations of planters and laborers and was backed by criminal sanctions (fines and imprisonment) in the event of contract violations, or violations of work-discipline regulations. These offenses included absenteeism, desertion, improper performance, habitual idling, various levels of insubordination, neglect of plantation property. The penalties could range from a simple fine to several months in prison, where work offenders and criminals of the more serious type were always thrown together in the same milieu, without regard to the nature of the offense.

The Chinese contract emigration nevertheless contained some unique characteristics. Mostly, these derived from the generally ambivalent circumstances surrounding the Chinese emigration, the competition from several nationalities involved in the recruitment exercise, and the fact that China was technically a sovereign country in its own right, making the decision-making process less clearcut than the colonial Indian case. There was, for example, no provision for a return passage to China at the end of the five-year term. Indeed, it was precisely the attempt to introduce such a provision in 1866 which led to the demise of the China emigration to the West Indies. Further, the wage clauses, as well as the commutation and redemption provisions in the Chinese contracts, were less standardized than the Indian contracts, and several types of arrangements coexisted with one another in the 1860s.[50] The contractual workday for the Chinese was generally seven and a half hours, while for the Indians it was nine hours for Trinidad and seven for the Guianese immigrants. In addition, the Chinese laborers might be given repayable loan advances as well as bounty payments for accompanying family members ranging from $10 to $20, whereas their Indian counterparts were not. The Chinese were also sometimes allowed free food rations as well as wages and other benefits for the five-year term, whereas the Indians were expected to pay for their own rations, delivered only for a short period ranging from three months to a year. Many Chinese contracts also mentioned free garden grounds, although it is not clear how many actually received such grants. Perhaps the most important distinction, however, was that Chinese women were not allowed to enter into contracts of indenture, but were offered instead what were called contracts of residence, which bound them to their designated plantations for the full term but did not oblige them to work.

The Chinese and Indian communities in the West Indies also responded differently to the end of contract migration. Many Chinese moved on. Several hundred ex-indentureds left Guiana and migrated to other colonies: Trinidad, Surinam, Cayenne, Jamaica, and Colon (Panama). In the sixteen-year period between 1872 and 1887 alone, about 3,000 remigrated out of British Guiana to various destinations, mainly within the Caribbean. More importantly, toward the end of the century, there was also the beginning of a low-level small trader migration common to most branches of the Chinese diaspora. Some of it was family- and village-related, some of it was part of a larger deflection of migration flows toward Latin America in the period after the ban on Chinese immigration to the US in 1882. The early years of the twentieth century also saw a new wave of migrants entering the Caribbean region. These were mainly voluntary artisan and small trader elements responding to internal domestic turmoil in China just before and after the fall of the Ch'ing dynasty in 1911. Chinese migrated to the British and Dutch Caribbean as well as to Mexico and Panama. By the mid-1920s, there were over 24,000 Chinese in Mexico, a destination which had assumed significance only in the 1880s, and which had never gone through a period of indenture. Between 1900 and 1940, over 7,000 arrived in the European colonies. The Chinese in Surinam increased from 784 in 1920 to 2,293 in 1941; those in Jamaica from 2,111 in 1911 to 6,879 in 1943. The foreign-born Chinese alone of Trinidad rose from 832 in 1901 to 2,366 in 1946. The Chinese of British Guiana rose from 2,622 in 1911 to 3,567 in 1946. Noticeable in the new migration was the importance of new destinations like Jamaica, which had played a minor role in the indenture period. Barely 6 percent of the nineteenth-century migrants had gone to Jamaica, although a number of Guiana-based ex-indentureds had remigrated to that island in the 1880s. Many of the new migrants actually arrived by a circuitous route, often residing in one or another American destination (including western Canada and Latin America) before eventually settling in their final island destination. Eventually the demographic distribution of Chinese between the islands came to be altered, and by the late 1930s Jamaica's had become the second largest of the Chinese communities in the Caribbean, after Cuba.[51]

Originating in the nineteenth-century global labor dispersals, the turn-of-the-century migration flows built on those connections but were motivated more by domestic push factors than by diasporal pull factors. With their small-trader and family orientation, they were also closer in essence to the classic patterns of Chinese diasporal formation elsewhere. By the 1940s, the descendants of the original indentured laborers were significantly replenished by this new community, but thereafter the migration flows declined for the same reasons that migration flows from mainland China declined generally in the 1950s.[52]

With the end of Indian indenture in 1917, different communities of overseas Indians exhibited markedly divergent patterns of behavior. Unlike the generality of Chinese overseas settlements,[53] only some Indian communities—those in Africa and the western Indian Ocean—were replenished by voluntary migration of trader elements from India, usually from regions and social groups different from those of the indentureds. Many communities in the Caribbean region, however, received no new inflows from India of any kind.[54] The primary issue in the Caribbean region revolved around how many ex-indentureds chose to return to India, rather than remain permanently in the Caribbean, whether in their original island/mainland destination or in another, freely chosen. The available statistics up to the 1930s tell us that about 29 percent chose to exercise their right of return, while about 71 percent opted to remain in their new homes.[55]

≺ IV ≻

Adjustment and Assimilation across Diasporas

Any assessment of assimilation should first acknowledge that Chinese and Indians evolved diverse (and divergent) models of adapting to their new environments. The foremost issue for Chinese diaspora minorities was the nature of the formal restraints against mobility in the new societies, the range of options allowable in any given society. The levels and expressions of welcome for the Chinese migrant varied from society to society, and indeed from period to period within any given society. These manifested themselves in the form of laws passed by the local legislatures, laws which might be inspired either by elite policymaking imperatives (ranging from racism to legitimate or illegitimate elite power concerns) or by pressures emanating from below, from constituency sentiment. Local sentiment itself may be influenced by quite different factors in different environments. The immigration exclusion laws of the US in

1882 were concessions to the fears of white trade union elements, resentful of job competition from the Chinese in a period of economic contraction, as much as they were reflective of an overall racism in the society toward non-white immigration. Laws passed in northern Mexico expelling the Chinese in the early twentieth century were designed to address popular resentment against a successful entrepreneurial and trader class perceived to be inimical to the interests of an incipient left nationalism.[56] Restraints existed not only in the laws, but also in the form of informal pressures to confine the Chinese immigrant to certain levels of advancement, certain physical and social spaces acceptable to the local power elites and local public opinion. For example, Cuban post-indenture restrictions on mobility were not necessarily duplicated in Peru or the British West Indies.

Other factors influencing assimilation include the range of concrete options open to the migrant in any given environment, the migrants' own attitudes to these options, and also the nature of the difficulties (financial, competitive, or otherwise) faced in making the transition from laborer to trader, in some societies. There were marked differences in levels of wealth acquisition, social status, and acceptance for the middlemen minorities of Southeast Asia and Mauritius, Cuba, and Trinidad. There were also marked differences between the middleman minority experiences of these countries and what has been called a ghetto-like minority experience in white majority societies like the US, Canada, Australia, or Europe. As Edgar Wickberg and others like Lynn Pan have pointed out, up to the 1960s at least, the Chinese in Southeast Asia might feel culturally vulnerable, but they could take pride in a history of economic success and local preeminence. North American and other metropolitan-society Chinese were conscious of being marginal both culturally and economically.[57] The tasks faced, and the options open to, these groups in overcoming their unique local restraints were thus quite specific. In the metropolitan white majority societies, the struggle to change official national self-definitions from a Eurocentric model to a multicultural model constituted the basis of one kind of challenge. In Southeast Asia and the rest of the Third World, the need to effect some form of modus vivendi, first with the specific European colonizers, and later with the forces of anti-colonial nationalism and independence, constituted another. Responses to the latter challenge have varied. Some communities have chosen assimilation, some a form of plural integration into the local elite; many have remained on the respectable outer fringes of the local social hierarchy, while many have chosen flight and remigration to more receptive environments.

Indian assimilation to new host societies over time has taken on three basic models of multicultural adjustment: where the community is numerically large enough to create a competitive pluralism not only in the culture but also in the politics of the host country; where Indians have remained a culturally and politically marginal minority; and where the evolution is within a multicultural metropolitan environment with steadily evolving policies toward racial minorities. Mauritius, Guiana, Trinidad, Surinam, and Fiji—all with sugar-based immigrant communities formed in the nineteenth century—are examples of the first type. In all of these societies Indians form close to or more than 40 percent of the new society, and their numbers have given them constituency strength and aspirations to state power on a scale achieved by no area of the Chinese diaspora.[58] The second model is divided between those societies where Indian numerical marginality is accompanied by economic underachievement (low status agricultural workers and peasants), and those where migrant economic achievement has corresponded to the middleman minority status achieved by most Chinese overseas communities in the non-Western or Third World. Jamaica and the French and British West Indian islands of Martinique, Guadeloupe, Grenada, St. Lucia, St. Vincent, are examples of the former type of marginality. East Africa represents the latter type, with South Africa representing a blend of the two. The third model, a metropolitan one, is a mid- to late twentieth-century development, because Indian migration to the Western countries—barring the small Punjabi migration to North America mentioned before—basically started after World War II, with the migrations to Britain and later North America.

With the exception of the third model, which falls outside the scope of our discussion, and the East African model, all the areas of the Indian diaspora mentioned differ from the Chinese diaspora in the sense that the majority of their communities have continued to remain largely agricultural communities, often—though not everywhere—still tied to sugar. Their economic and professional middle classes, when not comprising distinct immigrant trader groups, are made up of upwardly mobile sectors of a larger community still tied to agriculture in some form. Processes of autonomous development and assimilationist challenges have not been experienced or posed in quite the same fashion, even where both groups (Indians and Chinese) have formed part of a vigorous expanded pluralistic entity (Guiana, Trinidad, Surinam). Group cultural attitudes, as well as host society attitudes to both groups, have also played a role in this differentiation. It should be noted too that, as in the Chinese case mentioned above, the challenges of multiculturalism in a formerly colonial new nation-state entity are quite different from the challenges of multiculturalism in a metropolitan white-majority society. Fledgling nations evolving out of colonialism often have no patience with recognizing the complexities of multiculturalism, especially where there is disagreement on whether such recognition would erode the economic or political aspirations of the dominant majority.

V

Conclusion

A number of conclusions about Asian migrations in the nineteenth century follow from the above review. First, in the massive migration movements of the nineteenth century, Asians, who were a new element in the global distribution of labor, continued to migrate primarily within Southeast Asia, rather than to the Western nexus of the expanding Atlantic system, periphery or metropolis. This migration was directly stimulated by the intensified impact of the industrializing West on the Asian region, to be sure, but the majority of the migration continued to remain more regional than global, as it had for centuries. Second, most global Asian labor (Chinese, Indian, or other) was absorbed by the agricultural periphery of the expanding world system, rather than within its growing industrial sectors. Some Chinese migration did find itself on the metropolitan frontiers, as part of the mining boom in the US, but except for west coast and southern railway construction, none of it could be said to be integral to the industrial expansion of the period, which was dominated by European migrant labor. Third, Indian migrations were mainly (if not exclusively) extensions of British Empire globalization, even in Southeast Asia, whereas Chinese migrations were generally multinational, even within Southeast Asia. Fourth, for both groups the relation between free and coerced labor migration was more complex than at first appears.

If the emphasis is placed on the voluntary will of the migrant, it is clear that, unlike the African slave trade of the previous (and even nineteenth) centuries, the majority of Asian migrants voluntarily opted to migrate to their various host societies, regardless of the legal arrangements under which they eventually did migrate. This voluntary migration applied to contract indenture, to credit ticket indebtedness, and to kangani/maistry recruitment alike, as well as to demonstrably free migrations like that of the Chinese to much of Southeast Asia. There were, however, many startling exceptions to this pattern, where slavery-like forms of capture, recruitment, and transportation clearly demonstrated the continuities with older traditions of labor coercion. Such was the case with much of the Latin America-bound Chinese coolie trade, with early Indian indenture recruitment schemes in the 1840s and 1850s, and with a great deal of labor recruitment among Pacific Islanders. Coercion may even be said to have been the experience of many Chinese credit ticket passengers in Southeast Asia, who often found themselves shunted off to destinations within the region different from the ones they had chosen.[59]

When the nature of the labor regime itself is examined, the picture is far more complex. Contract indenture arrangements were all similar in the sense that employers and employees were explicitly bound by the terms of the signed contracts, and the legal and immigration systems of the host countries were technically empowered to ensure that these terms were strictly enforced. But not all contracts were the same. Some (like the early Cuban contracts) contained explicit references to the possibility of employer-determined punishments no different from slavery. None mentioned the existence of automatic penal sanctions (fines and imprisonment) for contractual violations, yet under all the host jurisdictions such sanctions were embedded in the labor legislation governing indenture. While this anomalous feature could still be found in some master-servant ordinances in Britain itself as late as 1875, it is noteworthy that, by the early nineteenth century, US courts were largely opposed to the notion of applying penal sanctions to labor contracts.[60] Moreover, legal enforcement of obligations and protections contained within the host country laws were dependent not only on the letter of the law, but also on the cultural and labor traditions of the host country and its authorities. While British Indian indenture arrangements—after some early hiccups in the 1840s to 1860s—came to be more standardized globally, the Chinese versions were always open to the vicissitudes of local labor traditions, whether in the US South, Cuba and Peru, the British, French, or Dutch West Indies, the Indian Ocean, or Malaya. Informal traditions of compelling enforcement, the cultural and political relation between the legal system and the plantocracy in observing the local laws, made for widely divergent indenture experiences. This divergence was especially the case in host countries with a prior tradition of slavery. The determining factor was often not the legal form, but the historical labor tradition and the relationship between the letter of the law and its practice.

The same ambivalence surrounds the credit ticket (or even kangani) arrangements, which were technically free in the sense that the immigrant's movements were not coercively circumscribed after arrival in the host country, his only obligation being the repayment of the passage money to the original lenders within an agreed period of time. But that ideal did not apply to all credit ticket arrangements. In Southeast Asia, brokers sold the passengers (and their financial obligations) to employers (Chinese and Western) for a profit, in ways that were not far removed from the Latin American indenture traditions. The difference here was basically the difference between an informal non-contractual arrangement and a formal contract arrangement (however flawed in practice). Indeed, the British authorities in Malaya tried to impose contractual indenture arrangements on this traffic in order to correct the abuses involved in the informal arrangements.[61] While this practice did not generally apply to North American credit ticket indebtedness, transfer of debtors (and their debts) to specific employers in the US and Canada was not unknown, despite the opposition of the law to such practices. Moreover, there still remains the nebulous question of how precisely repayment of debts was enforced, in the absence of formal legal intervention. Where formal criminal or civil sanctions were not recognized and enforced by the state, informal community sanctions, indirect compulsion laws (wage holdbacks, pressure on guarantors, mutual supervision arrangements between creditors and shipping companies, even criminal violence) were all ways of compelling performance, beyond the pale of the law. The dividing line between freedom and coercion under such practices was clearly complex and difficult to draw.[62]

Finally, wherever indenture succeeded slavery in the Americas, there was enormous variety.[63] In many islands where there was no labor scarcity or major labor problem, such as Antigua in the Leeward Islands, Barbados, and Spanish-speaking Puerto Rico, the transition to free labor was made without recourse to the indenture option. Wherever indentured labor was introduced, in no host country did it exist as the sole labor arrangement. It invariably co-existed with some form of free wage labor in what became a hybrid labor tradition through much of the century. Such was the case in Guiana, Trinidad, and Dutch Surinam, where Indian indentured immigration played a major role in reviving a crisis-ridden sugar industry. African labor, even when it was utilized within the sugar industry, was generally free-wage labor. In Cuba, slavery, Chinese indenture, and free-wage labor coexisted from the 1850s to the 1880s, often on the same plantations. In Jamaica, the Windward Islands, and the French West Indies, Indian (and other) indenture was a halfhearted and ultimately ineffective minority alternative to the spread of free-wage labor. The overall relationship between free and coerced labor tended in the final analysis to be defined by local circumstances, even where it appeared to be clear-cut in theory and legislation.

Convicts: Unwilling Migrants from Britain and France

COLIN FORSTER

Britain and then France, systematically and on a large scale, scattered their convicts to their colonies around the world for over two hundred years. The number of convicts so dispatched totaled some 340,000. In broad outline, there were three principal episodes: Britain sent about 50,000 convicts to its American mainland colonies chiefly between 1718 and 1775, and 160,000 to its Australian colonies between 1787 and 1868; France sent 103,000 to French Guiana and New Caledonia between 1852 and 1938.[1] Some other Western countries transported their convicts to their colonies, but none approached anything like this scale. What stands out is the long period and sequential nature of the three ventures. That it was sequential indicates the relationship among the three. Britain began transporting convicts to Australia only when access to America was closed, and France began transportation only after a long and careful study of the results obtained from sending convicts to Australia.

The long time span meant that the transporting authorities could learn from previous practice and adjust the conditions under which transportation took place. However, it also meant that the historical circumstances under which transportation took place changed markedly and both permitted and required significant changes in the convict regimes. Perhaps the most significant aspect of transportation to affect the role of the convicts in their place of exile was the extent to which they were placed in a settled society or were used as a pioneering labor force to open up the colonies for European settlement. And although there were numerous and changing motives behind this convict migration, one remained constant and important—the desire of the mother country to rid itself of criminals. This is the main feature that distinguishes transportation from other forms of migration. Over the whole period it is also the case that the circumstances of transported convicts had some common characteristics which differentiated them from free migrants: they had been convicted of a criminal offense and were forced to leave their homeland; their destination was chosen by their government; they arrived in the colonies bearing the stain of their criminal conviction; their freedom and activities after arrival were severely circumscribed by law for the period of their sentence; and their ability to return home was often restricted. These characteristics overlapped in some ways those of two other migrant groups, the slaves and the indentured servants of eighteenth-century America.

≺ I ≻

Transportation to America

In 1718 the British Parliament passed the Transportation Act, which began the systematic and regular shipping of convicts to its American mainland colonies as a punishment for a range of criminal offenses. Transportation across the Atlantic had already existed for more than one hundred years, but it had been intermittent and unmethodical. Moreover, the numbers had been small. Fogleman estimates that between 1607 and 1699 2,300 convicts and military prisoners were sent to the American mainland colonies. This estimate may well be too low, but the numbers appear to be of this order of magnitude. They are dwarfed in comparison with the immigration in this period of 33,200 slaves and 96,600 indentured servants, two other groups with restrictions on their freedom.[2] Almost all this small number of convicts appear to have come from England,[3] and their transportation was the outcome of an evolving English legal system, which ultimately led to transportation becoming a major avenue of penal punishment. These convicts had been found guilty of capital crimes but obtained a pardon on the condition of their transportation. John Beattie suggests that most were transported in the 1660s, after the Restoration, when, in the light of the unsatisfactory range of punishments available to them, courts began to consider more closely the option of transportation.[4]

Death was the accepted penalty for a number of crimes, especially those involving extreme personal violence such as murder and rape, but there were considerable difficulties in finding an appropriate penalty for lesser offenses, especially those against property. When the property involved was above a certain value the penalty was the extreme one: death. However, the property owner, deterred by the severity of the penalty or the cost of a legal case, was often reluctant to press formal charges. If the case proceeded, then the court might undervalue the property—again, in response to the severity of the punishment. More important was the avoidance of death through "benefit of clergy." The ability to read, historically associated with the clergy, converted the death penalty to a simple branding on the thumb. This test was not as discriminatory in favor of the literate as it appears, because judges had the power, which they often exercised, to deem a non-reader to have read from a selected book. Commonly, the text was the opening verse of the 51st Psalm, which the illiterate could learn beforehand.[5] A number of offenses involving property were regarded as so serious as to be "non-clergyable"; these included robbery (personal confrontation, commonly with violence), burglary (house-breaking at night), and horse theft. Even taking into account these exclusions, it was felt strongly that there remained a range of property offenses which required a penalty significantly more severe than branding of the thumb, but less severe than death.

The transportation of pardoned capital offenders declined markedly after the decade of the 1660s because of difficulties both in England and in the colonies. In England merchants bought convicts, transported them to Virginia, Maryland, and the West Indies (the principal destinations), and resold them for the term of their sentences. This method of disposal worked well enough for the fit and the skilled, but the others were left on the hands of the authorities in England. On the colonial side, in 1670 Virginia prohibited the landing of convicts on the grounds that "the great numbers of felons and other desperate villains" presented a "danger to the colony."[6] Maryland followed suit in 1676, and neither colony received any convicts between their prohibitions and 1718.

In response to these restraints on its ability to transport, a variety of actions was taken in England. To reduce the rising jail population of those awaiting transportation, more pardons were granted—some absolute, others conditional on joining the army or navy. Additionally, stronger non-capital penalties were applied: clergyable charges of grand larceny were often reduced to petty larceny, for which there was the stronger punishment of whipping. There was some branding on the cheek rather than on the thumb. An act of 1706 which removed the literacy test for benefit of clergy at the same time increased the penalty: now judges could commit clergied felons to up to two years in a house of correction or workhouse.[7] In other words, the discipline and work imposed on the poverty-stricken were now applied to certain types of prisoners both as a punishment and as an attempt at reform. One alternative to transportation, long terms of imprisonment with hard labor, was not adopted until the nineteenth century. Not only would it have been more costly, but convicts laboring in chains and the development of a coercive bureaucracy their doing so would entail were seen as conflicting with the English view of their country as a land of liberty.

No satisfactory solution to the problem of an appropriate secondary punishment was found until transportation was established by law in 1718. The timing of the Transportation Act appears to have been influenced by rising crime in London and the emergence of a politically strong and confident British government.[8] The main purpose of the act was stated in the first lines of its formal title: "an act for the further preventing robbery, burglary, and other felonies, and for the more effectual transportation of felons."[9] The act overruled the colonial laws which prohibited the landing of convicts. Transportation was made a more general sentence by making it a punishment imposed by the courts (not only as the result of a royal pardon for a capital offense), and it could be applied to crimes of a petty nature as well as to clergyable grand larceny—although in fact most petty larcenists continued to be whipped. The standard sentence was for seven years, fourteen for pardoned capital offenders. Return to Britain before completion of the sentence was a capital offense. Almost simultaneously a change in policy ensured the actual transportation of all those so sentenced. Now the British authorities made per capita payments to shippers who were required to take all transportees. The sum was sufficient to make the trade profitable, sometimes very profitable.[10]

The effect of the act on sentencing was dramatic. In Surrey between 1663 and 1715, 57.8 percent of males sentenced to non-capital punishments for property offenses obtained clergy and were branded and discharged, and 4.5 percent were sentenced to transportation;

between 1722 and 1749 the position reversed: 8.7 percent obtained clergy and 59.6 percent were transported. A similar shift took place with convicted women.[11]

Beattie argues that "at mid-century it [transportation] had been a striking success for thirty years" by increasing the range of options available for punishment,[12] and in fact numbers transported remained high into the 1770s. But doubts as to its effectiveness as a deterrent emerged. Increased crime, particularly in London, was seen as resulting in part from returned transportees, especially those who had bought their freedom and returned well before their sentence expired. Some, indeed, had served no time in America at all. Moreover, it was claimed, transportation had lost some of its terrors as the ocean crossing became safer and conditions in America had improved. Perhaps concerns of the time about depopulation were also relevant: why not again put male capital offenders into the army or navy? As a result, it appears that there was some decline by the 1770s in the proportion of those sentenced being transported, before the American Revolution put a stop to the process. Increasingly, for less serious offenders, the courts had begun to turn to the alternatives of shortish sentences in jails and houses of correction, often with a whipping.

The Act of 1718 applied in England and Wales, but Scotland, with its own legal system, did not follow suit. In Ireland, on the other hand, acts similar to the English one were passed in 1719 and 1722, and from 1726 a subsidy was paid to the transporting merchants. It is possible to make only rough estimates of the numbers transported from these countries, but it seems that something like two-thirds came from England and Wales and one-third from Ireland. One or two thousand transportees came from Scotland. In total, convicts and military prisoners (there were a few in the latter category from the rebellions of 1715 and 1745) now made up a more significant proportion of immigrants. Fogleman estimates that whereas they were 1 percent of immigrants between 1600 and 1699, they increased to 9 percent between 1700 and 1775. However, in the second period the two other unfree groups remained numerically larger: slaves were 47 percent of immigrants and indentured servants 18 percent.[13]

To what extent could the convict immigrants be regarded as committed, even dangerous, criminals? Clearly there was a broad spectrum of crimes, but in Beattie's view the transportees do not appear to have sprung from a criminal class. They were not raised to a life of crime, although some would be professional criminals and some members of organized gangs. Property theft was the most common reason for transportation; sometimes a significant degree of violence was involved, but more often it was simple, if recurrent, theft, carried out by those who were normally in non-criminal occupations,[14] and whom before 1718 the courts returned to society with a branding on the thumb. Although this penalty was thought too light, it was nevertheless a big step to a sentence of seven years' transportation. Attempting to generalize, Ekirch sees the majority of persons transported as "reasonably serious malefactors," those who were the less serious capital offenders who had been pardoned, or the more serious non-capital offenders; in general, those who could be regarded as a threat to social peace "reasonably threatening criminals."[15] This still leaves what would appear to be a sizable minority, for whom transportation was a very severe penalty.

Convicts could wait in English jails for up to a year for their transport to America and were then embarked on a voyage lasting six to eight weeks. Conditions in both jails and ships were commonly dreadful, disease prevalent, and the death rate high. Mortality on the voyage is estimated to have averaged as high as 10 percent in the first half of the period, but later improved to about 3 percent.[16] The convicts' destination in America was overwhelmingly the three colonies of Virginia, Maryland, and Pennsylvania, with the first two (the Chesapeake colonies) taking about 80 percent of the total number transported. Governments of both these colonies continued to oppose the import of convicts, but the transports went there because of the colonies' demand for convict servants, and because of their ability to provide cargo for backloading to Britain.

On arrival convicts were sold for the term of their sentence. Some 80 percent of them were male, predominantly young and low skilled, and in the labor market they competed particularly with slaves and indentured servants. Their price was significantly affected by the length of their sentence. On average they appear to have brought about one-third of the price of slaves who, of course, were held in perpetuity. Indentured servants normally had a four- or five-year term and often commanded a termination payment, so they usually brought a lower price than convicts. There was of course great variation in the prices of individual convicts, depending on such factors as skill and fitness. One contractor claimed that he had to give a premium with the old and infirm.[17] Convicts were commonly sold off in small lots, often one per buyer. They were employed in a variety of occupations—mainly as field hands in rural work, tobacco cultivation mostly, with some in wheat and corn. Being less suited for heavy labor and with the risk of pregnancy, women convicts brought a lower price than men. The fact that buyers could inspect convicts before purchase suggests a reasonably efficient allocation of labor.

Because they were confined largely to the Chesapeake, convict density was quite high in some local areas. In 1755, for example, they made up 10 percent of all adult white males in four of Maryland's most populous counties.[18] Historians disagree about the conditions under which convicts worked. Smith, rather casually, refers to "a life of physical labor in the open air, with adequate food and careful supervision," and then largely concentrates on indentured servants.[19] Ekirch acknowledges Smith's views, but argues that their material conditions were not so different from those of black slaves. "Whippings were commonplace, especially for unruly servants, as were collars and chains"; they were regarded as outcasts in society, and while recourse to the courts for abuse by their masters was possible, the odds were against them.[20] Bailyn takes the contrary view: "As for their lives in America, far from suffering degradation, savage punishments or life-long stigmatization, they seem to have found, even in their bondage, release and a measure of freedom." Further, in contrast to Australia, "America proved from the beginning to be a bountiful not a fatal shore."[21] He argues that to obtain work from the convicts, their masters realized that the carrot was more productive than the stick.

These divergent views can be reconciled, to some degree, by recognizing that the convicts would not have had a common experience. Their treatment and behavior would depend heavily both on their own attitudes and those of their masters, and on the extent to which they had useful skills. Where a convict was viewed as recalcitrant, it is obvious that some form of physical coercion would be used. Whipping of Englishmen, for example, was not unusual: it was carried out in England and in the American colonies both officially as a punishment for crime and privately in a disciplinary context.

For most convicts, those who worked in the fields, their lot of hard labor, to which they were often unaccustomed, would be difficult to accept, though it would be typical for their small-scale farmer-owner.

Escape was a possible option for the convicts and it was "very common," although the penalties if captured were severe. Ekirch estimates that perhaps 9 percent of Maryland's convicts appeared in runaway advertisements, and since capture was often difficult and costly, some owners would not bother to advertise; "great numbers" fled to the frontier, to the larger urban areas, or to the preferred destination, Britain.[22] Whether crime increased in the Chesapeake with the arrival of the convicts is doubtful. Contemporaries, with their highly critical view of British convicts, thought that it did,[23] but detailed examination of court records by Ekirch leads him to the opposite conclusion, and he argues in part that the rural environment in which most convicts worked made crime less likely.

Taking an overall view of transportation to America, it should be emphasized that the convicts' departure from Britain was involuntary. The American colonies were not attractive to them and, overwhelmingly, they did not wish to leave Britain. The conditions which led to their expulsion are summed up officially in the preamble to the 1718 act:

> Whereas it is found by experience, That the punishments inflicted by the laws now in force against the offenses of robbery, larceny and other felonious taking and stealing of money and goods, have not proved effectual to deter wicked and evil-disposed persons from being guilty of the said crimes . . . and whereas in many of his Majesty's colonies and plantations in America, there is great want of servants, who by their labour and industry might be the means of improving and making the said colonies and plantations more useful to this nation; be it enacted . . .[24]

In the broadest sense it can be seen that the impetus to use transportation arose out of the culture of England that had created a legal system in which there was no severe punishment other than death. Transportation appeared to offer an appropriate punishment, an intermediate punishment for a range of crimes, sufficiently feared to act as a deterrent, while at the same time possibly offering the opportunity to reform. One of its most attractive features was that it removed undesirables from the British Isles. There were strong economic aspects to their forced migration: what made transportation possible and cheap was the existence of British colonies where there was a demand for convict labor. Their economic circumstances may have turned many of the convicts to crime and the value of their labor permitted their movement to America, but the compelling motive behind their migration stemmed from a particular culture and legal system. Arriving in America as bonded workers, they formed part of the great flow of unfree immigrants to that country in the eighteenth century.

The treatment of most of the convicts in America appears to have been somewhat akin to that of the lowest level of indentured servants: unskilled workers who had arrived penniless owing their fare, and so with little bargaining power. These servants, though, had some legal rights denied the convicts; where no previous contract existed, they were commonly indentured according to the "customs of the country." The main economic impact of the convicts was that they made a useful addition to the labor force in localized areas. It might be thought that the general social impact of bonded felons would have been large, but in the Chesapeake where such a significant proportion of the population was bonded in one form or another, their impact on society was limited. Regarded as criminals outside decent society, they, like the slaves, only partially mixed with the white community. At any one time the number of British convicts in America probably did not exceed 7,000, while the population of the Chesapeake was 225,000 in 1730 and 650,000 (39 percent black) in 1770. Death rates of convicts were high in their early period of servitude when they were first exposed to local diseases, and of those who escaped or served out their sentence a sizable proportion returned to Britain. Actual numbers are unknown, but since convicts had been compelled to migrate, it would be reasonable to assume that the proportion returning home would be larger than that of other migrants from Britain. Certainly there were numerous complaints in London concerning the criminal activities of returned convicts.

Those who did stay were simply absorbed into the population, but again their impact may have been limited by their circumstances. Seven to fourteen years had been removed from their childbearing life, and in any case it is possible that within the Chesapeake their convict stigma would have made them less attractive as marriage partners. Almost no record remains of their fate, but the generalization that very few rose to prominence is probably true. Those with low-level skills would have found it difficult in the eighteenth century to accumulate enough capital to become farmers. Most would become laborers, though with incomes perhaps higher than those of laborers in England.[25] In terms of their overall impact, it is worth bearing in mind that the total population of the thirteen American colonies in 1776 was about two and a quarter million.

≺ II ≻

Transportation to Australia

Transportation to America was sustained until the Revolutionary War, but we have seen that in Britain there was increasing dissatisfaction with this punishment. As early as 1752, for example, possibly influenced by the example of France, a parliamentary committee had recommended the alternative of "Confinement, and hard Labour, in His Majesty's Dock-Yards."[26] Increasingly other punishments were used. But convicts were still departing for America at a sufficiently high rate for the cessation of transportation in 1775 to bring on an immediate crisis of crowding in the jails. Initially it was thought that there would be only a short-term interruption to the flow to America, but in 1776 the British government felt compelled to find some alternative. It introduced an act "to authorise for a limited time, the punishment of hard labour to offenders who, are or shall become liable to be transported to any of his Majesty's colonies and plantations." The preamble noted that transportation had been "found to be attended with various inconveniences, particularly by depriving this kingdom of many subjects whose labour might be useful to the community, and who, by proper care and correction, might be reclaimed from their evil courses." It was accordingly recommended that fit male convicts be employed "in raising sand, soil and gravel from, and cleaning the river Thames." These convicts were to be housed on old ships, the hulks, moored on the Thames.[27] This punishment constituted a radical change in penal policy. Previously, free-born Englishmen working in chains in England had been regarded as cutting across fundamental English liberties. Females and unfit males were now to be sentenced to hard labor in houses of correction.

As more convicts were sentenced to the hulks the number of these was increased, with some being positioned at Plymouth and Portsmouth. But the hulks had been viewed as a temporary response, and it soon became clear that they could not meet longterm needs. It was not just the pressure of convict numbers in the prisons as well as in the hulks, though these built up to extreme levels, nor the problem of the high death rate of prisoners, on which criticism of the existing arrangements was based. It was also felt that confining criminals together made them more evil; that ex-convicts, with the stain of their conviction, found the obtaining of employment difficult, and so were pressured back into crime; and that with the hulks being close to urban centers, escapes and riots were particularly dangerous. These criminals were better out of the country.[28]

A return to transportation seemed both desirable and inevitable. In 1783 the courts again began passing sentences of transportation, and in 1784 the government legislated formally to reintroduce this sentence and to permit those so sentenced to be held in the hulks until a place for transportation could be found.[29] The government still had in mind a continuation of the American system, as the act provided for private contractors to dispose of the convicts overseas.

Finding a transportation site that would accommodate large numbers of convicts proved difficult. Various places in Africa, Canada, the West Indies, even the United States, were all closely considered, and some were tried, but none was found to meet the purpose. Sir Joseph Banks, the distinguished naturalist, who had examined Botany Bay in 1770 when exploring with Cook, was one of those who pressed the case for that site, and in 1786 the decision was made to use it. Some Australian historians have found evidence that the British government was influenced in this choice by considerations of trade routes, strategic concerns, and the search for naval stores,[30] but there seems little doubt that the overriding motive was a penal one. Certainly in its formal announcement to the House of Commons in January 1787 the government stated: "A plan has been formed . . . for transporting a number of convicts, in order to remove the inconvenience which arose from the crouded state of the jails in different parts of the kingdom."[31] The choice of such a little-known and distant place symbolizes both the desperation of the British government and its determination to expel criminals from the country. Botany Bay had the advantages of reported fertility and of being temperate, so that the government was encouraged to believe that costs could be contained by the colony becoming quickly self-sufficient. Distance from England added to the cost but, in contrast to the American experience, it had the very great advantage of discouraging the return of time-expired convicts. It was also believed that some accommodation could be reached with the local inhabitants who in any case, according to reports, would not be able to resist successfully. There were strong criticisms of the scheme, but in 1787 the government dispatched a thousand people, three-quarters of them convicts, in a fleet of eleven ships half-way around the world to establish a penal colony in a virtually unknown land. The voyage took eight months.

If the Revolutionary War had not occurred, it seems likely that Britain would have persisted with transportation to America. Its great attraction was that the government had no responsibility or expense once convicts were handed over to the private shipper. The only cost was that of a subsidy for the voyage, and even that was stopped in 1772. The immediate contrast with the Australian venture is sharp. The government now had to take full responsibility for a penal establishment in a distant, unsettled location, and for the conduct and supervision of the convicts involved. Nothing like this had been done before, and it was indeed a daring and risky venture. In its early years the settlement struggled to survive.

In all some 160,000 convicts arrived in Australia between 1788 and 1868. The timing and destination of this flow is set out in Table 1. Overwhelmingly convicts were sent to New South Wales and Van Diemen's Land (Tasmania), where transportation ended in 1841 and 1853 respectively. The last consignments of convicts, about 10,000, went to Western Australia in the 1850s and 1860s. In the period to 1830 some small convict settlements were established around the coast of Australia (and Norfolk Island), partly, with the French in mind, to extend British sovereignty. For the first quarter century numbers transported were low because of the war with France—crime decreased during the war and convicts were used in the dockyards and in the armed forces. In the 32 years to 1820 28,000 convicts arrived, and in the succeeding 30 years 116,000. The highest decade was the 1830s with 51,000 transportees, roughly the same number as was ever transported to America.

TABLE 1

Convict Immigration to Australia, 1788–1868

Year	NSW	VDL	WA	Australia
1788–1800	6650	—	—	6650
1801–1810	4300	290	—	4590
1811–1820	15030	2140	—	17170
1821–1830	21830	10570	—	32390
1831–1840	31200	19490	—	50690
1841–1850	3340	29810	175	33325
1851–1860	—	6190	5270	11460
1861–1868	—	—	4198	4198
TOTAL	82340	68490	9643	160473

SOURCE: Charles Price, "Immigration and Ethnic Origin," chap. 1 in Wray Vamplew, ed., *Australians: Historical Statistics* (Sydney, 1987), 4. Reprinted from *Australians: Historical Statistics* by kind permission of the Macquarie Library Pty Ltd, Sydney.

TABLE 2

Projection of European Population Composition, NSW and VDL, 1790–1850

	Convicts and ex-convicts		Free immigrants		Colonial born	
Year	no.	%	no.	%	no.	%
1790	2000	87.1	260	11.3	35	1.5
1800	5330	86.7	365	5.9	454	7.4
1810	8671	76.9	634	5.6	1971	17.5
1820	24244	75.6	2100	6.5	5746	17.9
1830	48214	71.0	7998	11.8	11724	17.3
1840	83963	46.3	55060	30.4	42236	23.3
1850	95391	28.9	119760	36.3	114472	34.7

SOURCE: N. G. Butlin, *Forming a Colonial Economy, Australia 1810–1850* (Cambridge, 1994), 37. Reprinted with the permission of Cambridge University Press.

How important were these convicts in the growth of the non-indigenous population? In the period to 1850 they made up 43 percent of immigrants. It is interesting that this figure is very close to the proportion of slaves in eighteenth-century American immigration, but in Australia's early years convicts made up a much higher proportion of the population. Accurate census figures are not available, but Butlin attempts a "broad picture" of the civil composition of the population of New South Wales and Van Diemen's Land. These were the first two colonies settled, and in 1850 they still contained about 85 percent of Australia's white population. The broad picture is set out in Table 2. Butlin's estimates indicate that convicts and ex-convicts absolutely dominated population numbers in the early years, and that they did not fall below half the total until the late 1830s—half a century after original settlement.

In 1850, just before the massive free migration resulting from the gold discoveries, they were still 29 percent of the population in these two colonies, and about one-quarter of the total non-indigenous Australian population. Some convicts and ex-convicts also had children, and in 1850 perhaps about 50,000 of those born in the colonies had at least one convict antecedent.[32] Demographically convicts contributed to a male-biased society; females made up only one-sixth of those transported to the eastern colonies, and the final consignment of convicts sent to Western Australia was all male.

Overwhelmingly, only young and reasonably healthy convicts were selected for transportation. For this reason and because of health controls on the transport ships, the mortality rate on the long voyage was, after some early disasters, at the very low rate of about 2.4 per thousand per month.[33] No new disease awaited the transportees, as it had in America, and conditions in Australia promoted a significantly longer life than was the case in urban Britain. The convicts were mainly juveniles or young adults, and about 90 percent were aged between 15 and 35.[34] Youth and health are part of the explanation for the large numbers of ex-convicts in the colonies, but there was another reason, and it was one that had encouraged Britain to begin transportation to Australia in the first place: of all the convicts sent to Australia, it is thought that only about 5 percent ever returned to their homeland.

Initially, the convicts were from the accumulated stock that would otherwise have gone to America. The first fleets of convicts were made up of those who had already served significant terms of imprisonment while a transportation site was being sought. Some indeed had only a year or two of their sentence to serve. Presumably most were degraded and brutalized by their experiences. It was not until the mid-1830s, when transportation was at its height, that Britain committed itself to building the prisons which would provide the large-scale alternative to transportation. Until then about one-third of all those convicted in the higher courts in England were transported, but thereafter the proportion declined. It was 14 percent in 1847–48. At its peak in the 1830s and early 1840s only about 70 percent of those so sentenced were actually transported, but again the number fell, reaching 40 percent in 1847–48. As to the crimes committed, Shaw argues that up to 1835 court records do not give a complete picture, but after that date as imprisonment became a more viable option, only those guilty of the more serious crimes were transported. Overall about four-fifths of those transported from Britain and Ireland are recorded as having been involved in some form of theft. "Considerably fewer" than 1,000 from England and Scotland could be considered political prisoners, and of the 39,000 directly transported from Ireland, Shaw concludes that only about 5,000 had committed political or politically related offenses.[35]

How, then, should the criminal record of the vast majority of the convicts be judged? There are two difficulties here. The first relates to the long period over which transportation took place and the changes in British legal policy and practice. The marked decline in the proportions sentenced to transportation and in the sentences actually effected are testimony to these changes. Nothing so radical occurred during the American period. The second difficulty relates to the evidence concerning the convicts' criminality, which permits important differences of emphasis in interpretation. The view which emerged in the 1950s and 1960s saw the convicts, especially the English urban convicts who made up over half the English total, as products of a criminal subculture.[36] Historians making this claim were influenced in part by nineteenth-century studies of English society. Mainly on the basis of their court records, the convicts were regarded as largely professional and habitual criminals. Clark writes that "a very high proportion of the men and women transported . . . were dependent on crime for a living."[37] Shaw considers that most were not "atrocious villains," but were "ne'er do wells": "all in all they were a disreputable lot."[38] In Ireland, although there was more politically-driven crime and more desperate want, he argues that the general picture of the convicts was similar, although offenses were not as serious. There may be some broad support for this view of the convicts in the records of Robson's random sample of about one in twenty of those transported to eastern Australia; he found that only about 40 percent of the males had no previous convictions. The length of the sentences of all the male convicts transported also suggests a serious aspect: while about a half got the minimum of seven years, a quarter received a life sentence.[39]

There is support, however, for an alternative view of the convicts. In its extreme form it has recently been advanced by Nicholas and Shergold. They argue that "the convicts transplanted to Australia were ordinary British and Irish working class men and women. They were not professional and habitual criminals, recruited from a distinct class and trained to crime from the cradle." They continue: "most were first offenders found guilty of petty theft. Most had been employed as free workers in the British or Irish labour markets prior to their conviction."[40] This description of the convicts is very similar to Beattie's conclusions concerning the eighteenth-century convicts transported to America. However, the assessment by Nicholas and Shergold, which is based on a large sample of convicts transported to New South Wales between 1817 and 1840, relates to that colony only; and since the more serious offenders were sent to Van Diemen's Land, it cannot with confidence be applied to all convicts. Thus the difference between their figure of 61 percent for convicts deported for their first offense and Robson's 40 percent could result entirely from his inclusion of Van Diemen's Land.[41] In any case, there remains the problem that then, as now, a recorded first offense is an ambiguous measure of criminality.

Justice cannot be done here to the evidence presented in support of these two contrasting views of convict criminality, but their broad thrust is clear. They would agree that the convicts' crimes ranged over a wide spectrum. But one view argues that "most" convicts came from a criminal environment, committed fairly serious crimes, and were to a degree habitual criminals; the other, that the crimes were petty and commonly first offenses, and were committed by workers in non-criminal occupations. What all convicts had in common was that they were found guilty of breaking the law and were transported. But the degree of their criminality, from the point of view of their impact in Australia, is important only to the extent that it affected the skills, character traits, and attitudes which they brought with them and which influenced their behavior in this new environment. This aspect will now be examined within the broader context of the convicts' role, first in the workforce and then in society as a whole.

Numerically, convicts largely were the workforce in Australia for the first half-century. It has been noted that convicts contributed to a youthful and male population, and these attributes stand out even more strongly in relation to the workforce. Butlin has estimated that in New South Wales and Van Diemen's Land males aged between 12.5 and 59 years made up three-quarters of the total population in 1800, were still 70 percent in 1830, and then were reduced to 45 percent in 1850. Especially up to the 1840s these are extraordinarily high figures. Male convicts and ex-convicts dominated this age group at between 80 percent and 90 percent to the mid-1830s. Their importance then began to decline, but they still made up about a half in 1850. From the population composition it is obvious that females were a much smaller proportion of the potential workforce and, conventionally measured in terms of their contribution to marketable output, their share of the actual workforce would have been even smaller. Female convicts and ex-convicts still made up over half of this female potential workforce in 1830.[42]

Because they provided the numbers, the convicts also provided the skills of the workforce. At a basic and important level it would seem that the convicts' literacy, in terms of their ability to read or to read and write, was at least equal to that of the English and Irish populations from which they came.[43] As to their specific skills, the evidence available relates to the occupations the convicts declared themselves as having when they appeared in court. There are, of course, reasons why a convict would have given himself a respectable occupation (none declared a criminal occupation), and in any case questions remain as to degree of skill and length of experience. It is therefore difficult to know how much reliance should be placed on their own classification. For a number of reasons—work-related crime, the detail of much of the self-ascribed occupational description, convict origin and location of industry in Britain—Nicholas and Shergold argue that the occupations given by the convicts in their New South Wales sample are substantially accurate. If this is so, the convicts' skills were, by and large, representative of the working class in their homeland. They do show the urban English as more skilled than the predominantly rural Irish.[44] Their skills were very important, but so was adaptablity; given the nature of the economy convicts were required to turn their hands to a variety of occupations.

What were the labor market conditions for the convicts serving their sentences? Their number was constantly being swelled by arrivals and reduced in the main by discharge. Their actual number was greatest after the high level of arrivals in the 1830s; in 1840 there were 56,000 convicts in New South Wales and Van Diemen's Land, the males making up about half the male workforce in those colonies. The convicts had been sent to Australia to work and as far as possible reduce their cost to the British tax payer, and put to work they were. Probably the most striking features of the convicts' experience in the work place were the degree of their freedom and the extent to which they were privately employed. As long as they were publicly employed they remained a cost to the government, and dissatisfaction with the extent of this employment led to the policy from the beginning of the 1820s of removing as many as possible from public support. Between 1810 and 1840 some 15 percent to 20 percent were employed by the government mainly on public works, on creating an infrastructure for the colonies; but increasingly after the late 1820s there was a punishment aspect to this work. The remainder were "assigned" to private employers, who obtained them free but were required to maintain them at a level of rations and clothing prescribed by government.

The number of convicts assigned by the government to an individual employer depended formally on the employer's perceived need for labor, and from about 1821 it was felt that the convicts' good behavior and reform would be encouraged by sending them to country districts. The extent to which convicts were allocated according to the demand for their reputed skill is uncertain,[45] but where there was large-scale employment of convicts, public or private, there would be a greater opportunity to apply skills. To obtain a satisfactory amount of work from the convicts, employers had various sanctions available. Obviously they could bully and harass convicts in various ways, and they could also withdraw any privileges that had been granted. A more formal sanction was to have convicts charged for an offense before a magistrate, and it seems that in the mid-1830s such a charge occurred annually to between a half and two-thirds of them.[46] The magistrate could take action between the extremes of dismissal of the charge or admonition and sentence to a period working in chain gangs for the government. A more common punishment was a flogging and return to the employer, a penalty favored by employers since they would not lose the convicts' labor. Flogging of convicts could be done only by an authorized flogger on the order of a magistrate, and the type and distribution of the main offenses that incurred this punishment in New South Wales in 1835 is interesting.[47] Absconding made up 12 percent of the total, absenting (less than 24 hours) 15 percent, disobedience 11 percent, drunkenness 9 percent, neglect or idleness 22 percent, disorderly conduct 12 percent, and insolence 7 percent.

There is obviously a good deal of overlap in these offenses, but their general nature suggests a coerced workforce in which members had the ability to express their discontent in overt conduct. The actual number of floggings each year was large: in New South Wales in the early 1830s, they amounted to about 15 percent of the total number of male convicts.

The proportion rose to about 25 percent in the mid-1830s and then began to decline. The number of lashes per flogging averaged about 45.[48] Convicts therefore worked with the threat and actuality of flogging, but how likely was an average convict to be flogged? Using the high mid-1830s figure, it has been calculated that if floggings were distributed among the convicts in random fashion over a five-year sentence about one-quarter of the convicts would not be flogged at all and two-fifths would receive one flogging.[49] Of course floggings were not random. A common contemporary estimate was that 10 percent of the convicts were incorrigible, and as a result they received a grossly disproportionate share of this punishment. Reasonably good behavior was common, partly because employers offered inducements such as better conditions, better rations, and payment for longer hours. But the greatest incentive for good behavior was the possibility of remittance of sentence by the government. Sentences of seven years, fourteen years, or life could be reduced to four, six, or eight years respectively by the granting of a "ticket of leave" or a conditional pardon. This concession permitted the convict, subject to continued good behavior, to participate fully in the free labor market. Of those convicts who had qualified for tickets in 1839 by serving the minimum time, about a quarter had received them in New South Wales and a third in Van Diemen's Land.[50] For the first 35 years of settlement, even while serving his sentence, a convict had formal access to the free labor market outside quite restricted bonded hours. Thereafter bonded work was limited to 56 hours over a five-and-a-half day week, and outside that period a convict could be self-employed.[51] It is clear that the government attempted to supervise the assignment system closely. It could withdraw convicts from unsatisfactory masters, and equally masters could return unsatisfactory convicts.

The system of assignment came under sustained attack in Britain in the 1830s. It had always been regarded as an unsatisfactory punishment because of its lottery aspect: would the convict get a harsh or a benevolent master? But in the 1830s criticism intensified around two conflicting arguments. Assignment was regarded on the one hand as a system of slavery, degrading to convict, employer, and society; and on the other as providing convicts with such a good life that transportation was no longer a deterrent. As a result, the British government decided in 1838 to abandon assignment. It actually stopped in Van Diemen's Land in 1839 and in New South Wales in 1841.

Transportation itself was concentrated in Van Diemen's Land between 1841 and 1853, during which period some 36,000 convicts arrived there. This was a very large number for a small economy to absorb; arriving convicts in the 1840s were about six times the number of free immigrants, and at times the number of convicts was more than the government or the economy could contend with. Convicts were now placed in camps away from settlements and worked in large gangs on public works—preliminary to what could be early release on probation and supervised work for wages. The new arrangements did not work well, and the British government reacted in various ways, but always with economy in mind. From the middle of the 1840s transportees had to spend an initial period in a penitentiary in Britain, and then, being regarded as partly-reformed characters, they were given passes to work in the private economy on arrival. No longer "convicts," they were termed "exiles." But mounting opposition to transportation in both Britain and eastern Australia meant that the last shipment of convicts reached Van Diemen's Land in 1853.[52]

From the first settlement to the beginning of the 1850s convicts were the source of the greater part of the workforce. They were young, possibly adequately skilled, and predominantly male, and they exercised a degree of freedom not usually associated with a penal sentence. For private employers they provided a cheap supply of labor, and those employed by the government helped build the infrastructure of the economy. Their term as convicts was often significantly shorter than their original sentence. Their attributes and their circumstances contributed in a positive way to a high level of output per head of population, and soon after the first settlement they were a major component of what was emerging as a successful capitalist economy.

Nothing like this could have occurred without capital. Like their American counterparts, the Australian convicts had almost no capital, but they brought with them funding by the British government. Involved in this funding was not simply the maintenance of convicts; there was also the upkeep of the civil and military establishments and the provision of the stores and equipment necessary for the establishment and support of the new colonies. Some of this funding was involuntary, as colonial officials used a variety of means to draw on public funds in London. For the first 30 years the colonies were almost totally dependent on this capital inflow, after which the colonies gradually turned to local funding for public activities and to private capital arriving with free immigrants.[53]

The integration of convicts into society was assisted by their having a range of political and legal rights—much greater than had convicts confined in England. Indeed such a range was essential, given the convicts' involvement in the affairs of the colony. In the first 30 or so years of settlement, the free side of the society would have found it difficult to function at all without the active participation of convicts. What can be seen in marked fashion is the adaptation of the law of England to a very different society, a penal colony. It began immediately after the arrival of the First Fleet, with the first civil case to be heard in Australia. In July 1788 a convict couple, Henry and Susannah Kable, originally sentenced to go to America, sued the captain of an accompanying transport ship for damages for the loss of their property (donated in unusual circumstances in England and brought out in the care of a clergyman). Such action would have been impossible in England, where they could neither have owned property nor sued. They won their case. On the court writ where "occupation" should have been recorded, "New Settlers of this place" was crossed out and the space left unfilled. Possibly the entry "convict" would have made too obvious the flagrant breach of law. (Kable became a constable in 1790 and chief constable in 1794.)

Other adaptations of the law followed, and although there was some restriction of convict rights from about 1820, convicts could bear witness in courts, own property, sue and be sued over debts and property matters. Convicts on tickets of leave were in the same legal position.[54] At the end of the 1820s, well-behaved convicts were still being recruited to the police force, and in New South Wales most of the clerks in government offices, including those holding convict records, were convicts.[55] In the early years no record existed in the colonies of the original crime of a convict; more important than the crime were the convict's attitude, skill, and application.

To what extent did convicts persist with criminal behavior while under sentence? As ever, it is not easy to interpret the figures. Shaw points out that from 1831 to 1835, 2,087 persons were convicted in the higher courts of New South Wales, and that even if all of them were convicts this would amount to only 3 percent of the convict population in this period.[56] Of course they were not all convicts, and in 1841 the proportion of those tried in these courts who were convicts was very close to the proportion of convicts in the population. As has been mentioned, convicts were also sentenced by magistrates, and those guilty of what were regarded as serious offenses against convict discipline or offenses of a criminal nature not worthy of a higher court were usually sent to penal settlements or chain gangs. Penal settlements were set up in both New South Wales and Van Dieman's Land as places of severe punishment. In chain gangs men worked in irons, mainly on road construction. In New South Wales in 1836, although only 8 percent of all male convicts were actually in one or the other, Shaw estimates that over the previous ten years between one-fifth and one-quarter had spent some time in them, if only for a brief period.[57]

Permanent escape was not feasible on the scale practiced in America. The bush was inhospitable, and it was not possible for escaped convicts in any significant numbers to leave the country by sea or be absorbed into the free population. One famous form that escape took was to join organized criminal gangs in rural areas—the bushrangers. Their life expectancy was low.

Nearly all convicts eventually became ex-convicts—"emancipists." What was their situation in society? They appeared before the courts in numbers disproportionate to their share of population, but possibly not disproportionate to the young adult male population of which they were a substantial part. To a significant degree this was a frontier society, and two governors of New South Wales went out of their way to emphasize how law-abiding the ex-convicts were. Sir Richard Bourke, for example, stated that the crime rate in New South Wales in the 1830s was no higher than that in other new settlements where there were no convicts.[58] Sydney, it was often claimed, was a safer place than London.

Emancipists' legal status was that of other free citizens, except that they could not practice as lawyers or be magistrates, and it was not until 1831 that they could act as jurors. They did add to the existence of a status-conscious, stratified society. The "exclusives"—those free migrants, army officers, and officials who were in the uppermost echelons of society—firmly distinguished themselves from the emancipists, but probably only to a degree more than from the lower orders in general. Nevertheless, strong feelings and resentments for this reason were a feature of societal relationships. Obviously the great majority of ex-convicts were wage earners, tradesmen, or petty traders; but some were landowners. On gaining their freedom the better behaved convicts were assisted by small land grants until 1828. Especially in the period up to the 1820s, when there was such a pronounced shortage of skills, the way was open to ex-convicts to reach positions of importance and wealth in commerce and in the professions. Indeed, in 1819 it was reported that ex-convicts "held well over half the wealth of the colony and were masters of the same proportion of assigned convicts."[59]

Two general aspects of convict influence on society are worth mentioning. One is that, although any pioneering settlement in Australia at that time would probably have required some degree of authoritarian rule, the penal element both increased and prolonged the power of the governors. At the same time the involvement of the British government with the convicts meant that it kept a close check on the activities of the governors and was also an avenue of appeal for the colonists. The other aspect is that the male dominance of convict numbers contributed to a malfunctioning society, in that for a considerable period the creation of family structures was restricted. Governors encouraged convicts to marry by giving them favorable treatment; indeed such was the concern over the gender imbalance that the British government took the unusual step of giving free passage to a large number of wives and children of well-behaved convicts—nearly 200 a year in the 1830s.[60] By 1850 colonial-born made up about one-third of the white population, and it was commonly held that in general they were healthy, industrious, and law-abiding.

The Australian economy and society were shaped by the penal character of the settlement. They developed in a way that was different from a colony founded on free migration, yet also different from a colony run as a giant prison. It was on the largely successful intermingling of these two aspects that Australia's first half century was based. Overall, the penal influence began to decline from the beginning of the 1840s, and with the cessation of transportation to eastern Australia and the large influx of gold-seeking immigrants in the 1850s, any direct effects soon became negligible.

≺ III ≻

France and Transportation

In 1852, the year Britain ceased sending convicts to eastern Australia, France began to transport its own convicts. The French action was taken only after very close examination of the Australian experience, and after a long debate in France as to whether this was an appropriate treatment for criminals. From the middle of the eighteenth century prisoners sentenced to hard labor, who formerly had been made oarsmen in the galleys of the French navy, were sent to work in the *bagnes*, the naval dockyards. With the Revolution, prisons were also established for less serious offenders. Neither institution was thought to work well. The structure and organization of the prisons were unsatisfactory, and their purpose ill-defined. There was also a general conviction that the prisoners in the *bagnes*—regarded as the most dangerous criminals—came out even more villainous than they went in, and that recidivists were the main source of serious crime.

The supporters of a comprehensive and reformed prison system in France found strong backing in the report in 1832 by Gustave de Beaumont and Alexis de Tocqueville on innovatory developments in the American prison system.[61] The authors strongly opposed transportation and used the Australian experience to argue that such a penal colony would be very difficult for France to establish and that, in any case, Australian transportation had failed dismally to secure its penal objectives. Nevertheless, there was strong support for transportation which also relied on the Australian experience: it seized upon the most favorable aspects of convict behavior and on the changes made by Britain to improve the system. And, of course, it was emphasized that transportation was a solution to recidivism in France.

The navy also backed transportation. Not only did the navy wish to rid itself of the task of supervising convicts in its dockyards; it also saw, in a phrase of the time, that "colonies required a navy and a navy required colonies." In the years following the Restoration (1814) French naval authorities searched the world for a site for a penal colony that would rival Botany Bay. No satisfactory location was found, and no decisive action was taken until 1852, when the emperor, Louis-Napoleon, who had just seized power, announced that the old French colony of Guiana, a tropical enclave in South America, would be the site of a penal settlement. It was not seen as an alternative to prisons, since only those formerly sentenced to the *bagnes* would be sent there. Louis-Napoleon, then the president of France, had foreshadowed this decision in 1850 and set out its aims: "Six thousand convicts, imprisoned in our *bagnes* at Toulon, Brest and Rochefort burden our budget with their great cost, become more and more corrupted and ceaselessly threaten our society. It seems possible to make the punishment of hard labor more effective, more morally-improving, less expensive, and, at the same time, more humane by using it in the development of French colonisation."[62] The decision to begin transportation was a popular one, and although there were strong doubts about the suitability of French Guiana, Louis-Napoleon may have been influenced by the labor situation there. Slaves, on being freed in 1848, had deserted the plantations and it was said that the jungle was reclaiming the cultivated land.

Louis-Napoleon wanted immediate action, and because it would take some time to pass the appropriate law, volunteers were called for in the *bagnes*. Prison authorities painted such a rosy picture of conditions in Guiana to the convicts that response was enthusiastic, and 2,000 were dispatched in 1852.[63] The law of 1854, modeled on the British system, set out the conditions of transportation. The main formal change was the introduction of the principle of *doublage*: when freed, those sentenced for seven years or less had to spend an equal period in the colony before they could leave. If sentenced for eight years or more, convicts had to stay for life.[64]

Guiana had long had a sinister reputation in France—and with good reason. In the eighteenth century a colonizing settlement of 11,000 people there had been almost wiped out by disease, and the survivors were repatriated to France. A similar fate had befallen the small number of political deportees sent there during the Revolution. However, the convicts' hopes on their arrival may still have been high when they were welcomed by the governor, who addressed them as follows: "My friends, there is not under the sun any more beautiful, any richer country than this. It is yours. Prince Louis-Napoleon has sent me to ensure you share it. You are going to go ashore, work, prepare the ground, erect huts. During that time, I shall survey the colony. I shall select the most charming sites, the most fertile districts; then these lands cultivated in common will be shared among the most worthy."[65] Such was not their future, and the 18,000 convicts transported in this period were not spared the fate of previous migrants. In 1855 and 1856 mortality was 24 percent and 26 percent respectively, and between 1852 and 1866 7,035 of the convicts died, 39 percent of the total.[66] Finally it was accepted in France that the death rate was too high, and in 1867 it was decided that henceforth the Pacific island of New Caledonia should be the sole destination for transportees from France; convicts from other French colonies would still be sent to Guiana because, it was argued, they were inured to the tropics. Another motive has been suggested for the change in destination for French convicts. France saw in New Caledonia, with its more benign environment, the place where convicts could establish a settlement, reform, and mix with a flow of free French migrants to create a white colony in the Pacific: a French Botany Bay.[67]

The French had taken possession of New Caledonia in 1853, giving as the official reason their intention to establish a penal colony there. The first convicts arrived in 1864 after a journey of four months, and, as in Guiana, they were welcomed by the governor. He held out the hope that they would become free settlers and concluded reassuringly: "Your rehabilitation will be the constant object of my care; resolutely help me to lead you there; this will be my sweetest reward both as man and as governor."[68] Over the whole period of transportation, 1864–97, the convicts numbered about

31,000, but were of different backgrounds and had different fates. Considering men first, there were more than 21,700 transportees, including 1,500 North Africans.[69] There were also 3,350 *relégués*; they were mainly petty thieves and vagrants, but by the law of 1885 persistent offenders, after serving a prison sentence, were sent into exile for life. It has been remarked that this permanent exile "made more than one magistrate . . . hesitate before using the terrible sentence."[70] Finally there were 4,250 political deportees, communards from the Paris uprising of 1871. Women convicts were sent overseas only if they agreed, and few did: 200 transportees, 450 *reléguées*, 24 deportees, and 335 volunteers from jail. The promise of marriage was an inducement.

Men sentenced to transportation were given the work of establishing and maintaining the penal establishment and of engaging generally in public works. Some were assigned to private employment on farms, but increasingly they were sent to privately-owned nickel mines. Discipline and punishment were severe. Particularly recalcitrant convicts were sent to an establishment nicknamed *"le camp de l'horreur."* A very few *relégués*, able to support themselves, had virtual freedom; the remainder were given similar work to the transportees and were supported by the government. The treatment of the communards depended on how seriously the authorities regarded their offense: 3,000 were given their freedom on the nearby Isle of Pines; 900 were placed under military surveillance and 323 were treated in the same manner as the transportees. All surviving communards (400 died) were granted amnesty in 1879–80, and almost all returned to France. A group of about 100 deported Algerians also arrived in 1872 but did not obtain amnesty until 1891.[71]

Given the nature of the figures, comparison of the characteristics of New Caledonian with Australian transportees should not be pressed too closely. But more French appear to have committed serious offenses, their sentences were longer, and they were significantly older. The *relégués*, like some Australian convicts, were persistent trivial offenders, but they were much older, older even than the French transportees, and were thought of as broken-down. It seems possible that on the whole French convicts offered less promise as adaptable workers and as settlers. Another difference lay in mortality: 31 percent of the French died during their sentence, half that number during the first five years.[72] In spite of the environment being healthier than Guiana's, diseases such as dysentery, scurvy, typhoid, and tuberculosis were prevalent. In 1896 lepers were isolated on a small island. One group with a high early mortality was the 1,500 North African transportees; some obtained agricultural concessions, but at a place known as the "*vallée du malheur*."[73]

Well-behaved convicts could have their sentences reduced and obtain concessions especially in the form of land grants. In total about 10 percent became peasant farmers, but with indifferent success, and for most the occupation was short term.[74] In a critical vein it was said of the ex-convicts generally that "they refuse the peasant's life for one, less monotonous, of vagrancy, of theft, of life in gangs."[75] It does seem that they did nothing much at all, and remained an unsettled and troubling group. On the other hand opportunities for them were very limited. On completion of their sentence, convicts were given some clothing, and then embarked on "the desperate search for the means of subsistence."[76] In 1883 the Governor wrote in desperation to his Minister in France that the problem of the ex-convicts was "fundamental"; there was no work to give to "these unhappy ones who ask for it . . . we have not found the solution to this terrible dilemma."[77] The French authorities tried to encourage the development of a more normally structured society; some 800 marriages which were at least partly penal took place up to 1895, and 258 wives from France were able to join their husbands. A small flow of free migrants was assisted to settle on the land, and it was particularly the expansion of occupied land that brought about a Kanak uprising in 1878.

There were several reasons for the ending of transportation to New Caledonia in 1897. Cost was relevant, but more importantly there appears to have been the belief in France that transportation there did not inspire sufficient dread.[78] The authorities now had Guiana in operation again as a fearsome alternative. The governor of New Caledonia in the 1890s also saw a different future for his island: he tried to promote free, assisted migration and lobbied to turn off "the tap of dirty water."

Half a century after New Caledonia was claimed by France and 40 years after the first convicts arrived, the achievements there were modest. Some infrastructure had been created, but the population remained small. In 1901 there was a European population of about 23,000, of whom one-quarter was female and about one-half under the direct control of the penal administration. There had been some free migration, but there had also been an exodus of disheartened settlers. Mining appeared to offer the best economic prospects, and there was an imported, tractable workforce of 4,600 from Asia and the Pacific Islands. By 1921 the European population had fallen to 17,000.[79] As for the penal establishment, it increasingly became a "vast old people's home."[80]

In 1887 Guiana was re-opened for transportees and *relégués* from France. The flow continued until 1938. During the whole period from 1852 about 73,000 convicts were sent there. Of these about 55,000 were transportees, 18,000 were *relégués*, and several hundred were political deportees. Included in this total were about one thousand women.[81] Racially they were a mixed lot: between 1886 and 1938, 63 percent were Europeans, 25 percent Arabs, 7 percent Africans and 5 percent Asians.[82] Guiana continued to be a human disaster for these convicts. Mortality, which had been extremely high during the 1850s, remained high. There were peaks of 16 percent in 1902 and 10 percent in 1909.[83] Illness was universal, with disease, inadequate diet, and maltreatment being the main causes. Such was the death rate among the women—three to six years being their average time of survival in Guiana—that their transportation was ended in 1906. Any thought of a convict-based population was thus abandoned; and "reform" of the convicts was no longer a goal.[84]

Work was of all sorts: road building, forestry, agriculture; and there was some assignment to private employers; and as in New Caledonia many were employed in keeping the penal establishment running. Treatment was brutal. The most terrible of the roadworks was that of Route No. 1, along the coast of Guiana; it was said that each meter cost the life of a convict.[85] One of the more extraordinary ventures was the attempt to develop the interior of the colony by dumping about 500 Indo-Chinese convicts (including about 100 political deportees) there in 1931; nothing had been prepared for their arrival, and their work was supervised by a troop of Senegalese *tirailleurs*.[86] There were some concessions of land for well-behaved convicts, but their number was small and the results disappointing. Of the 1,659 men and women given concessions between 1852 and 1900 only about 12 percent were still working the land in 1900.[87]

What with sentences requiring exile for life and *doublage*, there were always several thousand freed convicts (*libérés*). There was little for them to do, and they were mainly reduced to odd jobs and begging. Local pressure kept them out of a number of occupations and out of some urban areas. Escape—*"la belle"*—was of course always a possibility, and in spite of the difficult environment, the sea and the surrounding countries made this a tempting option. Figures are available for some years, and are startling: in 1906, 879 attempts to escape were recorded, of which 250 were successful. They were successful only in the sense that the escapees were not recovered by the authorities, and the number who died in the attempt must have been large. Over the whole period to 1938 it is thought that about 9,000 of the convicts disappeared.[88]

There was never any suggestion in France that the life of the convicts in Guiana was too easy and that crime in France was thereby encouraged. The convicts' view of their lot is indicated by the names they gave to Guiana: *"la guillotine sèche," "les portes de l'enfer," "la mort au ralenti."* Increasingly after World War I, criticism was directed at the penal colony. Partly there was the question of high costs with little accomplished, but, more importantly, the penal colony had become a scandal both in France and internationally. The French were particularly sensitive to the strength of American criticism. Transportation to Guiana was stopped in 1938, but the *bagne* there was not officially closed until 1947. A new commandant from Indochina enforced the rules so ferociously between 1940 and 1943 that the convict population was halved in that short period.[89] In 1945–46 the French Assembly decided on the progressive repatriation of the aging survivors—2,020 *libérés*, 837 transportees, and 290 *relégués*. This was not finally completed until 1953. Several hundred chose to stay in Guiana. Some had settled successfully, but the greater number "descended into alcoholism and vagabondage."[90]

≺ IV ≻

Conclusion

Convicts from Britain and France were part of a great intercontinental flow of migrants taking place over several centuries. They were migrants of a special type: products of country- and time-specific cultures and legal systems that viewed transportation of criminals as an appropriate response to crime. The primary motive behind transportation was the desire to remove criminals permanently from metropolitan society, but there were a number of other penal objectives which varied in importance. It was felt that transportation should involve conditions for the convict sufficiently severe to be a punishment for crime and a deterrent for prospective criminals. At the same time, and rather paradoxically, it was also felt that transportation should offer conditions and prospects that would encourage these criminals to lead a reformed life. Considerations of economy influenced the penal decisions: governments either handed the convicts over to private employers or, if they retained control, attempted to use the convicts productively. Not only were convicts unwilling migrants, they had no choice over their destination. There they were sometimes used as a colonizing force associated with their country's imperial ambitions.

For the receiving country the immigration of convicts had very different implications as compared with that of free migrants. As coerced migrants, given whatever tasks authority chose, immigrants would have low motivation for work; the response by their employers was a mixture of force, often very harsh, and incentives. Demographically, young males dominated to an extent unusual even among normal migrant flows; the growth of the workforce was thus accelerated, but the small proportion of females meant a low base for population growth. Both during and after their sentence the convicts inevitably had some adverse effects on the society around them: the greater number had a background of persistent offense, serious crime, or both.

While it is possible to generalize about aspects of transportation, this study has emphasized how the actual outcome of this form of immigration depended very much on the conditions attaching to the convicts' sentences, on their personal qualities, and on the circumstances of the receiving country. In America transported convicts were a local phenomenon, largely confined to the Chesapeake. They went to a settled society and were sold in small lots to private employers for the term of their sentence. To a significant degree the employer "owned" the convict during this period, so that a convict's treatment depended on the personal behavior of both parties. Most convicts were put to hard laboring work in agriculture, where they made a useful addition to the labor force. Recidivism may well have been at a low rate, but perhaps this was because the surrounding environment made crime, particularly theft, difficult. The general impact on society of the introduction of bonded convicts was reduced by the large numbers of other types of bonded people. This was not a free society. Unknown but significant numbers escaped, often back to Britain. Ex-convicts had no noticeable impact; in the main they simply disappeared into an expanding American economy. For this receiving country as a whole during this period, the immigration of convicts was marginal to its development.

Convicts played a much more vital role in Australia: they were Australia's Pilgrim Fathers. The establishment of a penal colony was the primary reason for British settlement. Without this penal aspect, the timing, rate, and nationality of the European occupation of Australia would have been quite different. Responsibility for the convicts remained with the British government. The penal aspect almost totally dominated the settlements for the first 30 or so years, and although this gradually diminished, for the next 30 years the convicts and ex-convicts constituted the principal workforce. Some convicts were kept on public works, but the great majority was assigned to private employment, with ultimate supervision retained by the government. In general, some combination of convict bargaining power and good behavior brought opportunities for payment for work, private enterprise, and greatly reduced sentences. Recalcitrant behavior could result in the lash, consignment to road gangs, and confinement in penal establishments. Like the Chesapeake, this was not a free society. In the early years the Australian penal colonies were totally reliant on British public capital, and this dependence was only gradually reduced as free migrants arrived. The availability of cheap convict labor and the infrastructure they had built were substantial inducements to free migrants with capital. After about 1820 ex-convicts contributed substantially to an expanding market economy and helped to create a society in which they could lead normal lives. Few freed convicts ever returned to Britain.

French transportation was modeled on the Australian experience, but it did not lead to anything like similar results. Two French colonies were chosen as destinations for the convicts—Guiana, where French colonization was struggling, and New Caledonia, which was basically unsettled. In neither case did transportation lead on to significant free migration and the development of an expanding and viable economy. Most convicts remained under direct government control and were used on public works. Ex-convicts languished with little demand for their labor. Especially in Guiana, miserable living conditions and early death through disease and maltreatment were the fate of the majority. Little permanent settlement resulted in either place.

Britain and France succeeded in their intention of ridding themselves of some criminals. Transportation was a punishment for crime, but there were always doubts as to whether it had any particular success as a deterrent. Many advocates of transportation hoped that the experience would reform convicts, that they would emerge from their penal experience to lead productive lives, lives akin to those of free migrants. In this regard even the best result could only be partial. But some features of the transportation system in Australia—particularly the placement of convicts with private employers under conditions controlled by government, and with the possibility of remitted sentences—contributed to this desired outcome. As Robert Hughes has written: "For all its flaws . . . the assignment system in Australia was by far the most successful form of penal rehabilitation that had ever been tried in English, American or European history."[91] Today, a similar claim cannot be made for "three strikes and you're out."

Migration in Early Modern Russia, 1480s–1780s

RICHARD HELLIE

FROM THE DAWN of Russian history down to the present day, migration has been a constant feature of the Eastern European Plain. Prior to, say, 500 A.D. almost all of what has been called "Rus'/Russia" was inhabited by non-Slavs. In the south, in what is now Ukraine and Central Asia, the basic population was Iranian, which, thanks to the Great Migration of Peoples, in the first half of the first millennium A.D. was complemented by Huns and Turkic peoples from the east and Goths from the west. In the north, in what is now Russia, the indigenous peoples were Finns and Balts (the ancestors of today's Latvians and Lithuanians).

Russian history was adumbrated by the migration of Slavs from the west into Ukraine around 700 A.D. and to Novgorod and the Gulf of Finland around 800. Slavic migration apparently was triggered by the Goths, who began to move south from the southern shore of the Baltic around 200, splitting the Slavs into Western Slavs (who moved as far west as Hanover), Southern Slavs (who at one time occupied much of what is today Greece as well as the Balkans), and Eastern Slavs (who began Russian, Ukrainian, and Belorussian history). Another migration of Slavs, from the region of Bohemia, commenced around 1000 and began to penetrate the Volga-Oka mesopotamia. Mixing with the primarily native Finnic peoples, they reached the confluence of the Oka with the Volga around 1300 and served as the basis of the Great Russian people.[1] The heirs of these people continued to expand as "colonists" throughout the existence of the Russian/Soviet Empire, and especially the USSR, until 1991, when a retreat back to Russia commenced; it is still under way. In the year 2000 about 23 million "Russians" were in the "near-abroad," outside the Russian Federation, but their numbers diminish every year.

This chapter will concentrate on the migration processes occurring between the 1480s and the end of the eighteenth century, when Moscow secured political hegemony over all the Eastern Slavs, commenced the formation of an empire with the lightning acquisition of the Middle and Lower Volga (Kazan' in 1552 and Astrakhan' in 1556), and then extended its sway over the Urals and Siberia to the Pacific Coast. Perhaps it may be said that this "period" ended with the suppression of the Pugachëv revolt by Catherine II in September 1774 (which "closed the frontier") and the liquidation and annexation by her in 1783 of the Crimean Khanate (which put an end to the forced migration of hundreds of thousands of Russians and Ukrainians into slave markets throughout Eurasia, the Middle East, and North Africa). This was also the time of expansion of the Russian Empire westward with the three "partitions" of Poland in 1772, 1793, and 1795. Although those annexations proved to be extraordinarily deleterious to Poland and also to Russia, it is not clear that Catherine's moves had much demographic impact—other than allowing Jews to move into the Russian Empire. By the end of this period, the Russian Empire came into direct contact with other major empires (German, Austrian, Ottoman, Persian, and Chinese), which inhibited further imperial expansion and the East Slavic migration which typically accompanied it.

≺ I ≻

The Expansion and Growth of Muscovy and the Russian Empire

Muscovy expanded enormously between 1480 and the end of Catherine II's reign. Around 1470 Muscovy was about 430,000 square kilometers, by 1533 it was 2,800,000 square kilometers, by the end of the sixteenth century 5,400,000, and by the end of the seventeenth century 15,280,000. At the end of the eighteenth century the Russian Empire encompassed about 16,298,000 square kilometers, and at the end of the nineteenth century, 22,430,000. The population of Muscovy was perhaps 5 or 6 million in 1500, 9 or 10 million in

TABLE 1

Size and Population Density of the Russian Empire in 1678, 1719, and 1795

Region	Area (1000 sq. km.)	1678	1719	1795
Central-industrial region	611	4.0	9.5	14.1
Central-agricultural region (1)	692	2.3	5.9	13.1
Agricultural borderlands (2)	1,335	–	–	1.7
Northern Urals	485	0.3	0.8	3.7
The North (3)	1,290	0.2	0.4	0.7
Baltic region	92	–	–	12.6
Lithuania and Belorussia	190	–	–	21.2
Right-bank Ukraine	165	–	–	21.0
Siberia	11,438	0.003	0.02	0.1

SOURCE: Ia. E. Vodarskii, *Naselenie Rossii za 400 let (XVI–nachalo XX vv.)* (Moscow, 1973), 152. (1) Without Left-bank Ukraine in 1678; (2) Including Sub-Caucasia; (3) Without Novaia Zemlia.

1700, and around 28.5 million in the census of 1782, so the density per square kilometer fell dramatically between, say, 1550 and the first partition of Poland in 1772. This is considering all of the territory of the Russian Empire—much distorted by Siberia. Table 1 presents Ia. E. Vodarskii's density calculations for various parts of the Russian Empire per square kilometer.[2]

Migration was stimulated by the formation of empire, as Moscow sent out governors and troops to garrison the territorial acquisitions. The population typically followed the making of territory safe (or safer) against slave raids; but occasionally the population went in advance of the governors, evoking an enraged reaction from the government, which tried to force the population back northward into areas under its control. These repeated, well-documented efforts by the government are prime evidence that it did not want any population to escape its clutches.[3]

In 1480 the Great Russians were largely confined to the Volga-Oka mesopotamia. In the Northwest Great Russians from Moscow annexed Novgorod beginning in 1471, and by the mid-1480s many of the "native" Novgorodians had been deported (a few were also executed) and replaced by colonists dispatched from Moscow. Then in 1510 Pskov was annexed in a manner similar to Novgorod. The western boundary of Muscovy was rounded off in 1514, when Smolensk was retaken from Lithuania, which had seized it in 1404.

Members of the Great Russian elite were sent from Moscow to command both Pskov and Smolensk while the basic urban and rural population throughout this period remained East Slavic.

Although the western frontier was in theory defined and closed in this period with only elite Muscovite merchants being allowed to cross the frontier, in practice treaties and instructions to Moscow governors in the region regularly mention the fact that the frontier was porous with the local Russians, Finns, Lithuanians, and Poles crossing at will and without causing excessive consternation to anyone most of the time until the end of our period.[4] Apparently depending on the economic, climatic, and military conditions of the day, the local rural and urban population moved east or west across the frontier without much concern for the political formalities of interest to the politicians.

More interesting between 1480 and 1783 was migration north of the Volga (north of a line running between today's St. Petersburg and Kazan'), south of the Oka into the steppe and to the shores of the Black Sea, and east of the Volga into the Urals and Siberia. Much of this migration to the south and east superficially resembled American migration to the west. One must not become overly enthused about parallels with the American experience, however, for there were enormous differences as well. In both cases the pull of free, untilled, often richer/better agricultural land was a powerful magnet. The Russian government was highly conscious of the fact that its hold on the new lands in the south (the steppe) and east (the Urals and Siberia) was extraordinarily tenuous if they were not settled, and part of the government actively worked to settle those areas. Such activities conflicted with other governmental interests, which demanded that the population be prevented from leaving the Volga-Oka triangle for reasons that will be discussed below. In Muscovy labor was the scarce economic factor (along with capital; land was abundant), and no one in government wanted any of the population to be beyond the reach of the garrison state.

A major precursor event in the expansion of Russia into the southern steppe and Siberia was the annexation of Kazan' in 1552 and Astrakhan' in 1556. The rest of the Volga in between Kazan' and Astrakhan' came under Muscovite control in those years and was crucial for the migration history of Russia. The conquest of Kazan' opened the road to the Urals and then Siberia. After 1552, Ermak, a cossack freebooter acting with Moscow's consent, warred against the Siberian Khanate, which suffered a major defeat in 1582, and towns were built in 1586 in Tiumen' (near the ruins of the Tatar town of Chingi-Tur) and in 1587 in Tobol'sk (which was moved to its current location in 1610) and others. Elsewhere east of the Volga Moscow built forts in 1584 on the Viatka River. In 1586 a fort was built at Ufa on the Balaia River, in the heartland of the Bashkirs, a Turkish people who are now trying to assert some independence from Moscow in their republic of Bashkortistan. By the end of the seventeenth century Russian conquest and settlement had reached the Pacific.[5] Russian civilian migration flowed to those secure locales, but very slowly because not many people were willing or legally able to settle there.

The conquest of the Volga cut the Turkish world in two, weakening it substantially.[6] The conquest of the lower Volga and Astrakhan' had a downside for Moscow for two reasons. One, the Astrakhan' Khanate and Crimean Khanate were frequently at war, and Moscow's destruction of the former freed the latter from a major enemy. Two, the Russian conquest of the Volga region raised a barrier between the Crimean Khanate and the Nogais, who previously had been battling one another regularly.[7] The Crimean-Nogai rivalry was so intense that throughout much of the period 1475–1556 the Crimeans were allied with Moscow against the Nogais. After 1556, when the Volga barrier "protected" the Crimeans from the Nogais, however, the Crimeans felt at liberty full time to raid the Russians because they did not have to keep their eyes all the time on their eastern flank. In turn, the Crimean attacks on Muscovy led the Russians to focus on their southern frontier to the point that they took effective measures to defend it (see below), which opened up more and more of the area south of the Oka to Russian migration and colonization while pushing the Crimeans back into their peninsula.[8]

≺ II ≻

The Legal Stratification of Muscovite Society: Enserfment

Russia almost constantly experienced events/phenomena which tended to push population out of the Volga-Oka homeland. Regularly-increasing taxation and occasionally labor obligations to support the Muscovite service-state pushed many Great Russians out of the Volga-Oka triangle. Serfdom developed in this period; it was completed by 1649 and began to take on hues of slavery, which triumphed after 1762. For those unacquainted with the evolution of serfdom, the following is a brief summary of certainly the major determinant of the migration story in early modern Russia. A rough analogy might be the following imaginary exercise: assume that the United States had been started by those Europeans who settled Montana and the Dakotas and then the US out from there. Had it not been for serfdom and the binding of the townsmen to their urban areas, I suspect that the Volga-Oka mesopotamia today well might have the same population density and global importance that Montana and the Dakotas do.[9]

Serfdom began as a result of a civil war in Moscow between 1425 and 1453 which caused chaos as marauding rival armies plundered the land and caused the peasantry to move more frequently than usual in a search for security. As a result, selected monasteries got the "government" to issue them charters forbidding their debtor peasants to move at any time of year except around St. George's Day in the autumn (November 26). This was that "thin edge of the wedge" that one must always be on the lookout for because, while the numbers of monasteries and peasant debtors were few, the precedent that the government had the right to control peasant labor mobility was being set in the third quarter of the fifteenth century. For reasons that are still not clear (perhaps because other political jurisdictions nearby were enacting similar measures), the government in 1497 forbade all peasants to move except during the week before and the week after St. George's Day. Except for the precedent, however, the introduction of the St. George's Day limitation on peasant mobility made little difference because St. George's Day coincided with the pagan East Slavic end of the agricultural year (like our Thanksgiving) when peasants tended to move anyway. Moreover, competition for labor between 1497 and 1558 was probably less than at almost any other time in Russian history because population density was increasing thanks at least partially to the fact that domestic turmoil was at a minimum, the three-field system of agriculture was being introduced to replace the traditional slash/burn methods, and areas into which Russian population subsequently migrated (north of the Volga, south of the Oka, and into the Urals and Siberia) had not yet had any perceptible attractive impact.

The situation was radically changed by the 25-year Livonian War (1558–83) with its ruinous taxation and especially Ivan the Terrible's mad debauch, the Oprichnina (1565–72), which ruined the Great Russian homeland and the Novgorod region to the extent that census takers often found 85 percent of the land uninhabited.[10] As a result of the First Service Class Revolution, commencing after the annexation of Novgorod in the 1480s, a new form of cavalry army was introduced which maximized the military forces the Russians could put into the field while simultaneously maximizing pressure on the peasantry. Moscow assigned possession of the agricultural land confiscated during the annexation of Novgorod to its cavalrymen, who were also called service landholders (*pomeshchiki*) after the service landholdings (*pomest'ia*) assigned to them. These cavalrymen had a dual role: to fight the light cavalry steppe predators who annually raided Muscovy in search of slaves and other booty and to fight the Poles and Swedes on the western frontier interested in annexing Muscovite territory. Without peasants farming their service landholdings, the cavalrymen were without income and could not render military service. The turmoil resulting from the Oprichnina meant that many of the cavalrymen had no income and could not serve. (Lest anyone think that this was some kind of a joke for the Russians, please recall that the Crimean Tatars burned Moscow in 1571[11] and its suburbs in 1591, and "harvested" tens of thousands of slaves in the process.) In the 1580s some of those cavalrymen asked the government to forbid their peasants to move, which was done. This anticipated the 1592 measure which established the "Forbidden Years" (years in which peasants were forbidden to move from their villages, vitiating St. George's Day). The provision was proclaimed to be a temporary one, and certainly in 1592 no one envisaged that it would not be repealed until 1906.

By 1592 peasants were migrating in all directions into the newly annexed territories as well as internally, to the estates of lay and clerical owners. These estate-owners were the people who traditionally ran the government, and they found peasant mobility to be to their advantage in the scramble for scarce labor. These "powerful/contumacious people" (*sil'nye liudi*) basically attached a rider to the Forbidden Years decree: a statute of limitations specified that claimants of fugitive peasants had to find them and file suit for their return within five years after the peasants had fled. For the provincial cavalrymen, the statute of limitations provided an insurmountable obstacle to the recovery of their fugitive peasants. These provincial cavalrymen expressed their frustrations in a concerted petition campaign of 1637, 1641, 1645, and 1648 in which they asked for the repeal of the statute of limitations on the recovery of fugitive peasants.[12] The government (whose ruling elements were still benefiting from whatever peasant mobility remained, both as owners of large estates and as directors of an expanding empire that needed to be populated by Russians) was resistant, so rather than repeal, the statute of limitations was extended from five years to nine in 1637 and then to fifteen in 1641. In 1645 the government promised that, once a census had been taken, the statute of limitations would be repealed. In 1646–47 the census was taken, but the statute of limitations remained.

The corruption of young Tsar Aleksei's administration (headed by the grasping, avaricious genius Boris Ivanovich Morozov) provoked popular uprisings in June of 1648 in Moscow and a dozen other towns. One of the rioters' demands was a codification of the law, so the government appointed the famous five-man Odoevskii Commission to prepare a draft. This was submitted to a popularly elected proto-parliament, the Assembly of the Land (*Zemskii Sobor*), which met from October 1, 1648, until January 29, 1649, to debate the Odoevskii Commission draft and to consider petitions from the delegates to the Assembly of the Land. One of the demands at the Assembly of the Land was the repeal of the statute of limitations on the recovery of fugitive peasants. The product of the Assembly of the Land was known as the *Sobornoe ulozhenie* (or *Ulozhenie* for short) of 1649.[13] Chapter 11, Articles 1 and 2 completed the enserfment of the peasantry by repealing the statute of limitations on the recovery of fugitive serfs. After this time, any serf who had run away at any time in the past could be claimed by his possessor (the person who possessed the service landholding or owned the estate) if he could find him. Moreover, the state got into the business of fugitive serf- and slave-hunting, so recovery no longer depended solely on the resources of the serfholder.[14] This argument it should be noted was unlike the rule for fugitive townsmen, who also were forbidden to move, but could be recovered only if they fled in the future, after January 29, 1649.[15]

All peasants were bound to the land wherever they happened to be registered. Article 1 applied to peasants living on palace court land or without a lord (in the future, state peasants/serfs); Article 2 applied to peasants living on seignorial land, either service landholdings or hereditary estates. In the *Ulozhenie* there was no distinction among peasants: none of them could legally move of their own volition; all were legally bound to the land. This, I would maintain, is what preserved the high density of population in the Volga-Oka mesopotamia (especially in the central-industrial region) shown in Table 1.

Distinctions in the real-life conditions between seignorial and non-seignorial peasants appeared already in the first half of the sixteenth century, when landholding cavalrymen were permitted to collect the traditional rents on their service landholdings (*pomest'ia*) in person. The personal subjection of seignorial peasants took a decided turn for the worse when during the Oprichnina Ivan IV issued decrees ordering such peasants to "obey their lords in everything" (the "obedience formula" which replaced the previous words requiring only the payment of traditional rent). The position of the seignorial peasant further deteriorated in the seventeenth century. One landmark was the *Ulozhenie* decree permitting estate owners to move their peasants from one estate to another without consulting the peasants.[16] There is considerable debate in the literature about whether lords could sell peasants without land after 1649 and whether unequal exchanges of land (the actual market for land seems to have been almost non-existent) were actually disguised sales of peasants. I am not convinced that there were significant numbers of such transactions, although one cannot deny the decree of March 30, 1688, on registering purchase documents on seignorial peasants in the Service Land Chancellery and the requirement that a 6 percent tax on the sum listed be paid when peasants were "ceded" (a disguised form of sale) by one lord to another.[17]

In the eighteenth century the position of the seignorial peasant decidedly took an even greater turn for the worse. No doubt this was pushed along by the abolition of the service landholding and its conversion into hereditary property in a decree of March 23, 1714.[18] Also degrading was the tax system, which made lords responsible for their peasants' taxes, with all of its second-order consequences. The result was that by 1720 the seignorial peasant's status was close to that of a slave. He or she legally had not been able to move on his or her own volition since 1592, but the worsening enserfment measures since that time increased the lord's personal interest in his serf's immobility.

The condition of the seignorial peasant was worsened further by the infamous decree of February 18, 1762, by Peter III freeing what had been the service class but was now a gentry from service obligations.[19] Theretofore gentry had been compelled to render 25 years of military service in exchange for their estates, but after 1762 service became optional. The general pattern was for gentry youth to attend military schools and serve in the armed forces until they married. After marriage, those who could afford it retired from service and lived in the capitals, in small provincial towns, or on their estates. Gentry living on their estates sometimes took to supervising their serfs in person, replacing the bailiff or wife who had done the supervising prior to 1762. In turn serfs occasionally were removed from what had been "their" land and the usurped property added to the lord's demesne. The peasants were forced to work on the demesne with the distinction between such peasants and slaves more of terminology than anything else. Rent was calculated in two ways, in cash or in kind paid by the peasant to his lord (*obrok*) and labor rent, corvee (*barshchina*), in which the serf labored much like a slave on his owner's estate. This system progressed to the point that it appeared as though the entire seignorial peasantry might be converted into slaves. Emperor Paul on April 5, 1797, put a limit on this system by his "three-day *barshchina* decree" which said that lords could force their serfs to work for them no more than three days a week. Sunday labor was also prohibited.[20] Thus 1796 is widely regarded as the apogee, the crescendo of Russian serfdom. After that, more and more people regarded serfdom as an institution akin to slavery and therefore immoral. This led to the 1861 emancipation of seignorial serfs from dependence on their lords and finally in 1906 to laws freeing serfs from their binding to the land initiated by the Forbidden Years and the *Ulozhenie* of 1649.

≺ III ≻

Serf, Slave, and Townsmen Migration

Serfs who did not find such increasingly slave-like lord-peasant relations to their liking were tempted to flee their masters. Considerable study has been done of this peasant migration, and the major conclusion has been that the peasants, burdened with their livestock and inventories of grain and tools, moved not much more than the equivalent in distance of one province at a time. Such migrations were in family or larger groups and hardly secret as they headed off with all their movable possessions—typically when the lord was absent.[21] Single peasants, as well as many slaves, on the other hand could move almost any distance, from the center of the Muscovite state to the realms of the cossacks on the southern frontier or even greater distances into Siberia. Their only restraint was their own physical strength.

Until the middle of the seventeenth century the government made no attempt whatsoever to recover fugitive peasants in Siberia. In 1669, however, the government began to prohibit slaves and peasants from moving into Siberia to settle on others' estates, but those who settled on state lands were permitted to stay there, provided that they registered with the Siberian Chancellery (in Moscow). After 1669 the government made rather feeble efforts to search for fugitive seignorial serfs in Siberia and return them, but the results were trivial. The fact was that only the Moscow-area serfowners were interested in the serfs' return to the center and the governmental personnel had no spirit for such activity; the outcome was correspondingly insignificant. Nevertheless, decrees to Siberian governors in the future continued to insist that fugitives be returned, and the governors refused to do it lest their domains be depopulated.

A remarkable story is still extant about peasant migration to Siberia in 1673. A relatively large group headed off in that direction and finally hired local cossacks as guides. The group came to a sentry station which was unaware of any government interest in populating Siberia and forced the group to turn back. Thereupon the guides robbed their convoy, whose members lodged charges against the cossacks—which resulted in the existence of the document.[22]

One point must be made about peasant migration that is not necessarily obvious to people of the early twenty-first century. Prior to the end of the fifteenth century, the Russian peasantry engaged almost exclusively in extensive farming. The podzolic soil of the Volga-Oka mesopotamia was only a few inches thick and easily exhausted, typically in three years. It took 40 years for such farmed land to recover its fertility. The result was that the Russian peasant was typically on the move, at least to his place of employment. His house need not have moved, of course, but every three years his labor focus was typically somewhere else. (One might envisage the peasant successively farming wedges of a pie, while all the time living in the center of the pie.) Landownership under such conditions was defined by the phrase "wherever the axe [to cut down the forest] and the plow have gone."

At the beginning of our period, however, at the end of the fifteenth century to be precise, conditions began to change ever so slightly; population growth forced peasants to shift from extensive farming to a three-field system of crop rotation. The three-field system, which caused peasants to have greater interest in a specific plot of land and probably less willingness to move the entire household, was mentioned in the Court Handbook (*Sudebnik*) of 1550 (Article 88), whereas it had not been in the 1497 *Sudebnik*. The three-field system expanded until the chaos of Ivan IV's reign in the 1560s initiated the depopulation of much of the heartland of the Muscovite state and agriculture reverted to the older extensive type. The extent to which the three-field system recovered in the later 1620s and on is debated, but it is likely that extensive agriculture was practiced in much of Muscovy down to 1750. The relevance of this to the issue of peasant migration should be obvious. If the peasant had to break in new land anyway, it made comparatively little difference whether that land was "across the road" or across the province. Moreover, Russian log cabins could be constructed in very little time—even some churches were built in a day. Given those conditions, peasant migration was hardly the hardship that it might seem to Americans centuries later. (This is not to say that V. O. Kliuchevskii was correct in making peasant migration provoked by the nature of Old Russian agriculture one of the major engines of Russian history.)

An important piece in the Russian migration puzzle was the issue of land, its ownership or possession and distribution. Although the leaders of Muscovy might not have been able to pass a modern economics course, they fully comprehended the importance of two of the major factors of any economy, land and labor, while they could do little about the third, capital. Much of this chapter is devoted to the government's efforts to control labor, but here a few words are in order about land. In the area north of a line running from St. Petersburg to Kazan', the government did little to control land and allowed it to be cultivated by the non-seignorial peasants who lived there. Monasteries were active in the Russian North, but agriculture and the relatively few agriculturalists in the area were not their prime concern. This area was settled by Russians primarily after the 1560s, when the chaos in the Volga-Oka mesopotamia generated by Ivan IV's Oprichnina forced the population to scatter in all directions, but the Russian migrants seem to have had few disputes with the native Finnic peoples and Moscow made no attempt to award their lands to military servicemen—probably because the population was too sparse and the distances to the military fronts too great.

In the rest of Muscovy, however, the state was concerned about the possession, control, and allocation of nearly every square inch of land from the time of the annexation of Novgorod onward. Beginning in the 1480s cadastres were compiled listing who had owned the Novgorodian lands, who possessed them at the time the cadastres were compiled, and what the resources on those lands were.[23] These records were kept in the Service Land Chancellery (*Pomestnyi prikaz*), and as soon as was possible, similar records were compiled for the rest of the country. When new areas were annexed, cadastres were compiled as soon as possible. This compilation was a central element in the First Service Class Revolution, for the cavalry was supported by grants of those lands (*pomest'e* lands), and in theory the servicemen could claim them and collect rents from the peasants farming those lands only so long as they continued to render military service. Allegedly desire by the cavalrymen for such lands was one of the engines for Muscovite expansionism, but evidence to support such an hypothesis is hard to come by: the "voice" of any segment of the population in Muscovite foreign policy issues is rarely extant. What is unquestionable is the fact that whenever Muscovy added populated land to the inventory recorded in the Service Land Chancellery, cavalrymen were soon asking that the new acquisitions be added to their income properties. They also insisted that the peasants on the lands not be allowed to move, be enserfed.

The cavalry servicemen were dissatisfied with the *pomest'e* system of land tenure because it was a possession, a holding, not something which was theirs that legally could be passed to heirs or otherwise alienated. They wanted to convert *pomest'e* land into hereditary estate property, the Russian *votchina*.[24] The government resisted, but once it lost in 1649 the struggle to keep the peasants from being completely enserfed, it seems to have given up. In the second half of the seventeenth century this struggle was being lost, and in the March 23, 1714, decree it surrendered and decreed that all service landholdings were hereditary estates, which hereditary estates all (as in 1556) had to render military service. After that, the action changed to granting to lords lands that belonged to the sovereign (as court lands) or to the state (inhabited by formerly "free" peasants who had been enserfed by Article 1 of Chapter 11 of the *Ulozhenie* of 1649). Until 1762, all the owners of landed estates had to render military service, and the peasants living on them had to support their lords. Those who did not like this status had the option of fleeing to the towns or to the frontiers.

Muscovy also knew a rather large, primarily household slave population which, although psychologically highly dependent on their owners, tended to flee if conditions were not to their liking. They typically were individuals who had little if any property, and when they fled it typically was with objects their owners claimed had been stolen from them.[25] It would probably be fair to say that their condition of psychological dependence limited their mobility and the distance of their flight. Marginal nutrition and lack of property (even changes of clothing to cope with the changing seasons) also limited the radii of their flight. There were other categories of slaves to whom these generalizations probably did not apply. There were elite slaves of two types. The first were estate managers who had a normal demographic profile (married, equal numbers of male and female children) and probably rarely fled at all. Then there were military slaves whose price was five times that of ordinary slaves. They were probably adequately fed and typically had little incentive to flee—unless driven out by their owners who could not feed them for one reason or another. Not accidentally, Khlopko and Bolotnikov, leaders of the 1603 and 1606 uprisings of fugitive or abandoned slaves on the southern frontier during the Time of Troubles (the period of invasion and civil war between 1589 and 1618), had been military slaves. Many of them were energetic, leadership types, the sole limits of whose mobility were those they imposed on themselves.

Between 1592 and 1649 taxpaying townsmen were bound to their towns at the same time as the serfs were bound to the land. Townsmen fled if conditions elsewhere looked better. Taxes were assessed collectively and if some in the collective fled, those remaining were prone to flee also because they could not pay the burden which had been assessed on everyone.[26] In "ordinary times" they probably migrated to a neighboring, more populated locale, but they had the capacity to leave the Volga-Oka triangle for any points north, east, or south—or probably even west. With the townsmen the distinction between migration and flight was probably the least clear of all the social categories of Muscovy. I would be inclined to equate any flight with migration when there was no intention of returning, as was certainly the case of peasants who moved with their inventory the distance of a province or to the frontier. When townsmen, on the other hand, fled simply with the goal of escaping the tax collector and hoped to return, that certainly was not migration.

≺ IV ≻

Causes of Migration

Warfare on Muscovite soil tended to depopulate the region of conflict and thus provoked migration. On the western frontier conflict typically was over territory. Enslavement by captors was the fate of "enemy" civilians, who were part of the incentive booty that motivated the opposing armies to fight. Those captured on the western frontier remained the military captives of their enslavers until a peace treaty was signed requiring the manumission and return of all enslaved captives. As far as I know, the dimensions of this traffic (Russians being carried westward; Poles, Lithuanians, Latvians, and Swedes being carried eastward) have never been quantified. In this period there were several major invasions of Muscovy that must have caused major demographic losses, such as the Polish invasion and capture of Moscow in 1610 and the Swedish invasion and capture of Novgorod about the same time.[27] Conversely, the Muscovite conquests during the Thirteen Years War (1654–67) of much of Ukraine as well as lands west of Muscovy unquestionably produced major harvests of military captive slaves for the Muscovite troops. Such captives were a major component of the total western frontier migration picture. The Russians had one "advantage" in this competition for labor which their enemies did not: they could and did (until the later 1940s) dispatch their harvests to Siberia, whence retrieval and return to homelands in the Rzeczpospolita, Sweden, and Germany were almost impossible.[28] This was somewhat analogous to Russians who fell victims to Tatar slave raiders, who then sold their booty into distant slave markets whence they could not be ransomed or otherwise recovered.

On the southern frontier, the opposing war aims were varied. The Crimean Tatars were primarily interested in seizing sedentary Poles, Ukrainians, and Russians as booty for the Crimean slave market in Kefe. This area was one of the two major "slave basins" or "reservoirs" of the world—the other was Africa. The slave traffic to Kefe has been calculated as numbering about 10,000 persons a year (not all of them were Russians, of course).[29] The number of casualties was far higher, for perhaps as few as one-tenth of those apprehended by the Crimean Tatar raiders actually made it to the slave sale blocks in the Crimea. Old people, the very young, and obstreperous males were likely to be slaughtered upon capture, although some adult males were enslaved for possible ransom or sale into immediate labor service such as on Turkish galleys in the Mediterranean.[30] More died from hunger, thirst, and maltreatment on the way into captivity. Crimean raids were annual events, with a defenseless Moscow the ultimate goal of the Crimean predators. In 1571 the Crimeans captured, sacked, and set fire to Moscow, and in 1591 they reached the outskirts of Moscow. These raids continued into the 1630s, when the Belgorod fortified line put a stop to them.

The Crimean Tatars were not, however, the sole enslavers of Russians in this period. The Nogais also took tens of thousands of Russians into the slave markets, and they were joined by the Kalmyks and Kazakhs in harvesting the sedentary Slavs as well as other nomads for sale in the Central Asian slave markets of Bukhara, Samarkand, Khiva, and elsewhere.

For comparative purposes, a crucial point that the reader must realize is that none of these Turkic peoples was indigenous to the Black Sea steppe or even Central Asia. Just like the Slavs, the Turks had been part of the Great Migration of Peoples. In Central Asia they conquered the indigenous Iranian people, and then one another, as the Turkic Bulgars were followed by the Khazars, who were followed by the Pechenegs, the Polovtsy, and then the Mongols who conquered Rus' and the steppe in 1236–40. The Crimean Tatars politically were offspring of the Mongols, and ethnically included Pechenegs, Polovtsy, and others who had been conquered by the Mongols and gradually Turkicized, the Mongol Golden Horde (the Mongol grouping that collected tribute from Russia). Others in the Crimean region conquered by the Mongols included indigenous Iranian Alans, Armenians, Greeks who had been living there for centuries, Goths who had settled there in the fourth century, Slavs who had migrated there in the ninth and tenth centuries, and others. Only between 1426 and 1443 did the Crimean Khanate emerge as an independent, autonomous political entity.

The Kalmyks—the Western Mongolian Oirats—migrated into the Russian sphere of interest only at the end of the sixteenth century.[31] In the 1660s there may have been as many as 270,000 Kalmyks following their herds along the southern Muscovite frontier from the Volga eastward into Siberia.[32] The Nogais, primarily a Turkic people, evolved from the Golden Horde and formed their own Horde in the second half of the fifteenth century. Their base varied over the course of time but usually was in the Kuban steppe, until 1783, when, right after the conquest of Crimea, the Russian regular army forced nomadic Nogais to flee to the Urals, the Crimea, and Turkey. The Kazakhs were also primarily Turkic in ethnicity and formed the Kazakh Horde in the second half of the fifteenth century in much of what is today Kazakhstan. In summary, most of the Turkic peoples at whose expense Russian migratory colonization southward occurred were of no greater antiquity in their locales than were the Slavs, while their political formations typically were more recent than was that of Great Russia.

The fortified lines were a central element in the Russian migration story, for in general sedentary agriculturalists could only farm behind (on the Russian side) the frontier defense system. The construction of the 800-kilometer-long Belgorod fortified line, between the Vorskla and Chelnovaia rivers, in the years 1636–53, after Muscovy's recovery from the Time of Troubles and the Smolensk War, put an end to the annual Crimean and Nogai Tatar depredations into central Muscovy.[33] Later, lines were built further south, hemming in the Crimeans further southward toward their peninsula. One such line was the Izium fortified line, built in 1679–80 for 530 kilometers to protect the region between Belgorod and Khar'kov.[34] This was Muscovy's "frontier" until the 1730s, when a "Ukrainian line" was built between the Dnepr and the Northern Donets. Elsewhere the system of fortified lines was extended eastward (most notably the Simbirsk line, 1648–54) and prevented the nomadic Nogais, Kalmyks, and Kazakhs from raiding westward and northward into Russia proper and into Siberia. Another major fortified line was the trans-Kama line (1652–56) between the Bashkirs and Kazan', which was strengthened by the addition of new forts in the early 1730s. The Syzran' line was constructed in 1684 and the Iset' in 1685. The major fort of Orenburg was built in 1735 at the mouth of the Or' River; it was moved along the Iaik (Ural) River first in 1740 and then finally in 1743, separating the Bashkirs from the Kazakhs and securing the southern Urals for St. Petersburg. The culmination of the Russian campaign against the Turkic enslavers was the conquest of the Crimean Khanate in 1783, which forever put an end to Crimean slave raids that for centuries had populated Eurasia with Russian slaves.[35]

Behind the fortified lines and around the forts available migrants—often peasants previously living on other state lands—could settle wherever they desired.[36] The outcome of the nomads' predations was what one would expect: the more the steppe peoples looted and kidnapped, the harder the Russians tried to keep them out. Moscow and St. Petersburg had the will and the resources to do this. The Russians' efforts led inevitably to the extermination of the nomadic way of life and the settlement of the steppes and other formerly migratory herding grounds by Russian colonists, some of whom were voluntary/fugitive peasants/serfs and townsmen, others involuntary seignorial and state serfs resettled on their owners' orders.

The Muscovites had other war aims than did the Turkic slave raiders. Stopping the annual Crimean slave raids was the first goal. The second was making the area south of the Oka safe for Muscovite agriculturalists as the blacksoil (*chernozëm*) region was gradually annexed by the Russians. The third was enslaving Tatars, something not typically discussed in Russian historiography, although it is mentioned in the Law Code (*Sobornoe Ulozhenie*) of 1649.[37] The numbers of Tatars enslaved by the Muscovites are unknown, although they must have been trivial by comparison with the Russian losses to the Crimeans. Later, in the eighteenth century, as the Russian Empire began to incorporate steppe territories herded by Tatars, Nogais, Kalmyks, and Kazakhs, the Russians worked to bring other members of those peoples who were outside the empire into the region controlled by the Russians. As Empress Catherine the Great noted in her famous Instructions (*Nakaz*) of 1767 to the Legislative Commission that was intended to update the *Ulozhenie* of 1649, the name of the game was population, the goal of the Russian Empire was to get more people.[38]

Although the new formation regiments, introduced for the Smolensk War (1632–34), ultimately drafted rank and file peasants into the infantry, such recruiting (to my knowledge) was not a major precipitator of peasant and townsman flight prior to 1700 as actual combat remained primarily the domain of the professionals, either the life-long members of the Muscovite service classes or the imported hireling mercenaries of the new formation regiments. Serfs and townsmen had been drafted in the seventeenth century, but it was Peter the Great's Second Service Class Revolution (launched in 1700) that initiated the practice of routinely drafting a certain percentage of all male peasants and townsmen every year to fill the ranks of the new standing army. Between 1719 and 1744, for example, 513,000 were drafted, 6.6 percent of the entire male population.[39] Being drafted was considered the equivalent of a death sentence, for service was for life and if someone was discharged he was not permitted to return to the place whence he had been drafted. When a male was drafted, a formal lament (*plach*) was launched much like that for a person who had died; should he have been married, his wife was declared a "widow." As a result, the draft from 1700 on was something that males did not anticipate with pleasure and were inclined to flee if they had the opportunity. Escape was not easy, for the government sent each locale a quota, and it was the locale's duty to meet the quota. Consequently the local landlord or peasant collective had an incentive to inhibit flights by those it had chosen to fill the quota, for each successful fugitive had to be replaced by another member of the same collective. Not accidentally, when a male was drafted, his head was shaved and he was shackled so that he could not flee during transport to the induction center. I have no information about how many males fled to the frontiers and into Siberia as a result of the draft, but the numbers must have been substantial.

Muscovy was a violent place and the violence caused enormous population dislocation.[40] In addition to drunkenness and incredible brutality, there were urban revolts, peasant and frontier uprisings, and all-out civil wars. Although walled towns tended to attract population from the countryside, as was the case everywhere else in the world, there can be no doubt that people fled the cities and returned to the countryside at times of domestic disorders. These disorders occurred with regularity, such as in 1547, in 1584, in 1612, in 1648–49, and in 1682, and almost certainly each one of them pushed people out of the towns. We know that this deurbanization happened during the Soviet civil war of 1918–21, and there is no reason to assume that earlier urban disorders did not produce the same results.[41]

Bizarre events such as the Oprichnina also contributed mightily to population movement. Ivan gave his Oprichniki license "to collect as much from their peasants in one year as they traditionally had paid in rent in ten years."[42] Peasants tended to flee from the Novgorod and Moscow regions especially to the newly annexed middle and southern Volga regions (1552, 1556), to the area north of the Volga previously inhabited largely by Finns, and to the area south of the Oka rather than yield to such exactions. As noted above, combining the Oprichnina and the very successful Crimean Tatar invasions with an epidemic or two and excessive taxation to pay for the Livonian War (1558–83) resulted in locales with 15 percent or less of the population which census takers had discovered the previous time they surveyed the same places.

There were also grandiose civil wars during the late Muscovite period, such as during the Time of Troubles (1598–1618) and later during the Church Schism, which split the Old Believers from the state church (*Raskol*, 1654–75).[43] They caused people to scurry around seeking safety inside the Muscovite state, leaving some areas depopulated, as well as to flee to the frontiers in the North, to Siberia, and south of the Oka.

On balance, migration was townward. Fugitive serfs often ended up in towns in the second half of the seventeenth century. The government had an interest in at least minimal urbanization, probably because towns paid cash taxes whereas the major contribution of the serf-farmers was to the direct support of the army. In consequence, the government decreed amnesties for serfs in town, who did not have to be returned to their lawful possessors. A decree of September 8, 1665, specified that any slave or serf who had fled into the court settlements of Moscow prior to September 1 should not be returned to any lords. This was subsequently extended to March 14, 1666. A decree of December 17, 1684, included in the Moscow tax rolls fugitive serfs who were employed in the capital. A decree of August 7, 1685, bound to the towns all serfs who had fled there after 1649. This was repeated for all towns on July 6, 1686.[44] Hundreds of years after the West, in Muscovy town air sometimes made a fugitive serf or slave free. That this was not always so was evident in a 1686 measure in which wanderers (*guliashchie liudi*—people not yet bound to any estate as a result of the *Ulozhenie* of 1649) who were illegally living in Moscow were beaten with the knout and exiled to towns on the southern frontier and Lower Volga, and in Siberia. Thus there were struggles for peasant migrants between middle service class cavalrymen, service landholders, large estate owners, towns, and the frontiers.

The Muscovites knew a "pull" phenomenon unknown in North America, the cossacks. Since the first millennium of the new era the steppe areas in what is now Ukraine were inhabited primarily by nomads, but the river basins were inhabited by semi-settled peoples who made their living by engaging in agriculture, fishing, and piracy. In the Muscovite period, these peoples were the cossacks, runaways from primarily Muscovy who often lived a predatory life. The cossacks were important both in Russian history in general and in the history of migration. The more of them there were, the more they attracted others because of the security of their numbers. The sums dispersed when cossacks were on the Muscovite government payroll give us some idea of how many there were.[45] The cossacks came to number in the tens of thousands, as during the Thirteen Years War, when some battles in Ukraine involved 50,000 Muscovite troops, 50,000 Polish-Lithuanian troops, 50,000 Crimean Tatars, and 50,000 cossacks. The last would fight for that "side" which would pay the most.

The cossack concentrations ("hosts") moved eastward from one river basin to the next: first the Dnepr, then the Don, then the Volga, and lastly the Iaik (Ural). When Catherine suppressed the Pugachëv uprising, that brought the rebellious Iaik cossacks under control and essentially closed the frontier. As a result, rebellious youth could no longer flee to the frontier and instead began to rebel against their lords. After 1775 serf uprisings regularly increased in number until 1861 and have been claimed by some (Tsar Aleksandr II said "better from above than from below") to be the cause of the "Emancipation" of the serfs (the freeing of them from their lords' personal control; they were then bound to their communes and not permitted to move freely until 1906). The cossacks had been one of the few exceptions to the rule that migration did little to enhance freedom in early modern Russia. Although it is true that fugitives to the frontier escaped serfdom and the increasing personal tyranny of a landlord, only the most enthusiastic romantic would imagine that being a cossack under the tyranny of the elders and the "host" was in any way equivalent to freedom on the American frontier.

Another major "pull" phenomenon was the nature of the expanding frontiers themselves. Most obviously, the chernozëm soil south of the Oka and along the Middle and Lower Volga was more favorable to agriculture than was the podzolic soil of the heartland, and peasants willingly moved there in search of the higher yields obtainable there. As the frontier moved south (see below), government agents tried to recruit settlers with talk of the better conditions and tax exemptions for a number of years. Although I know of no way to measure it, almost certainly this "pull" was as important as the "push" of enserfment and poorer natural conditions north of the Oka. Similar factors pulled Russians east of the Volga to the Urals, and on into Siberia.

The major "pull" of Siberia was furs, and trappers were the first migrants into the area east of the Urals, just as trappers often were the first Europeans in the westward movement across North America. It probably would be at least semi-spurious to term the typical trapper a "migrant," but the consequences of their actions, and especially the organized Stroganov extraction of furs and salt, was a form of migration as those who set up the trading stations remained there. Anika Stroganov got into the salt-boiling business in Sol'vychegodsk in 1515. After the annexation of Kazan' in 1552, in 1558 Tsar Ivan IV granted the Stroganovs huge tracts in Perm' Land along the Kama and Chusovaia rivers. They attracted Russian peasants to their lands, who engaged in farming, fishing, trapping and other hunting, salt boiling, and mineral extraction. They built forts and towns and used their private armies to suppress natives who objected to their usurpations. They helped organize Ermak's 1581 campaign into Siberia, for which they were further rewarded with new properties in the Urals and Siberia. In the eighteenth century they organized iron and copper extraction industries in the Urals. They utilized their close connections with the government to gain and keep the migrant laborers they required to man their enterprises.[46]

≺ V ≻

Causes of Involuntary Migration

The forces motivating migration which have been discussed so far resulted in "voluntary" movement, with the degree of "volition" open to interpretation in many cases. (Military captivity and kidnapping for sale in the Crimean slave markets are excluded from the "voluntary" migration categories, of course.) This must be contrasted with completely involuntary motivations for migration, which definitely existed in Muscovy as well. These forms of involuntary migration were two, two and one-half, or three in number, depending on how one regards military service, which will be discussed first.

As we have seen, Muscovy was the scene of the first service class revolution and the result was the garrison state. The major frontier we are talking about here is the southern frontier, and to a lesser extent, Siberia. In 1500 Muscovy considered the Oka to be its southern boundary. The conquest of the Volga in the 1550s left the "wild steppe" virgin lands between it and the Severskaia Zemlia (Putivl', Novgorod Severskii, Chernigov, Ryl'sk, and Starodub), annexed by Moscow in 1500, as both an avenue for constant Crimean Tatar raids and a prime economic target (the extent to which the Russians considered the latter is unknown). In the 1570s Moscow was building forts south of the Oka on the Donets which later became towns.[47] This process was accelerated in the 1590s, when Muscovy under the direction of Boris Godunov was more prosperous and had more surplus for such activities than it did either earlier or in the immediately following decades.[48] The construction of the Belgorod and other fortified lines sometimes resulted in the forced migration of the builders, although perhaps typically they could return home after completion of their corvee labor if they desired. The government, or rather that part of the government concerned with fortifying the frontier, of course hoped that the builders of the forts would stay and settle in the area, either as townsmen or as agriculturalists.

The expanding southern frontier forts had to be garrisoned by military personnel, typically members of the lower service class. Those servicemen had lifetime service obligations and once dispatched (typically involuntarily) to the frontier, they were not expected to be returning at any time soon to their places of origin north of the Oka. A number of them complained that they were forced to farm in order to live. How women were provided to the southern frontier military colonists is not known to me, although the *Ulozhenie* of 1649 permitted southern frontiersmen to "buy" women who fled there, presumably looking for husbands.[49] (The somewhat analogous problem in Alaska comes to mind.) A quarter century later, in 1676, the government repealed that provision and decreed that a free man who married a fugitive serf or slave woman could not be claimed as a serf or slave by his wife's owner and, furthermore, he did not have to pay for her, either. The lower service class military personnel were paid both badly and irregularly, and consequently sooner or later were forced to settle down as townsmen or farmers in order to survive.[50]

The area protected by the Belgorod line was under the jurisdiction of the military chancellery (*Razriadnyi prikaz*), and only later, in the 1670s, did the area become of interest to the service land chancellery (*Pomestnyi prikaz*), as upper service class members from the center began to lay claim to and even move into the area in search of lands which, they hoped, would be inhabited by serfs. As had typically been the case when members of the middle service class moved into the area earlier and discovered that they themselves had to farm in order to survive, so the members of the elite were often disappointed as the area remained settled by colonists who had no serfs. Upper service class claims to lands south of the Oka were ignored by Moscow if these lands had been settled earlier by members of the middle service class, even when the latter had not completed all the required "legal formalities."[51] Military servicemen also played a major role in the conquest of Siberia.[52]

Slaves and peasant serfs were transported on their owners' volition from an old estate to a new one. Boris Ivanovich Morozov already in the 1640s was moving his peasants to his Volga estates, along with others' fugitive serfs so that their lords could not find them.[53] One can assume that the practice became more common in the 1670s when the trans-Oka region became more the center of the government's legislative attention (as the magnates became interested in the region) and, with the ending of the Thirteen Years War in 1667, a flood of colonization poured in from right-bank Ukraine. The frequency of resettlement by landlords of their own serfs and slaves cannot be determined, although it is well described by Sergei Aksakov in his *Family Chronicle* for the 1770s. One can well imagine, however, that something similar happened whenever magnates obtained new lands in the Middle Volga region, south of the Oka, or in places such as Aksakov's Bashkiriia. The only way to turn those new estates into productive assets was to move the scarce factor, labor, from an old estate to a new one. One can surmise that the serfs were on balance happy about the move because the new chernozëm lands were so much more fertile than the old podzolic soils north of the Oka. On the other hand, at least until the completion of the Belgorod abatis line, the issue of security (because of the risk of being enslaved by the Crimean Tatars) made the desirability of such involuntary migrations a toss-up. In the eighteenth century, the state moved some of its "state peasants" to areas around the bastion of Orenburg to populate the region with some Russians. Involuntary movement of these peasants never converted them into freed men.

The final source of migrants to the frontiers was felons and others being sent into exile. The Russian government has used exile as a dual-duty device—to rid the center of undesirable elements while populating the frontiers—for hundreds of years. Russian etymological dictionaries do not discuss the origins of exile (*ssylka*), but other sources inform us that it was first mentioned in legal documents in 1582. It was practiced considerably earlier, at the beginning of our period, during the reigns of Ivan III and then Ivan IV. The *Ulozhenie* of 1649 mentions exile in ten articles. In 1680 the government became more serious about the institution of exile when it replaced many of the mutilation penalties that the *Ulozhenie* had prescribed for felons with permanent exile. Other legislation of the time revealed a preference for exile rather than incarceration or corporal punishment. Footloose elements who resisted being bound to the towns or enserfed in the 1680s and 1690s were subject to being beaten with the knout and then exiled to areas in Ukraine, the Lower Volga, or Siberia.[54]

Exile as a means of social control made a great leap forward in the 1760s at the expense of the peasantry. A law of December 13, 1760, permitted serf owners (lay landowners, the imperial court, the Holy Synod [the church], high church officials, monasteries, merchants, and the state itself) to exile to Siberia peasant malcontents, who were counted as part of their quotas of army recruits.[55] Such malcontents almost universally are males aged 15 to 35, and often the most energetic (if rambunctious and obnoxious) individuals in a population. Be that as it may, the 1760 decree did not instill the discipline and quietude lords desired among their chattel, so a measure of January 8, 1765, permitted masters not only to exile their serfs, but to request that the exiles be sentenced to forced labor as well.[56] The 1765 decree reflected the fact that at least some serfs were enraged by the fact that their masters had been freed from compulsory service by Peter III in 1762; they believed that they also were going to be freed and then rebelled when they were not. The institution of exile probably made the homeland safer[57] and unquestionably helped to populate both the southern frontier and Siberia. In late Soviet times Siberians wondered why their land was used as the disposal bin for criminals, and perhaps Muscovites/Russians of the seventeenth and eighteenth centuries wondered the same. It probably made settling in those regions less desirable for law-abiding types and aggravated the level of violence often associated with frontier regions.

To round out the story, a few words must be said about immigrants into the Russian Empire. Aside from the steppe peoples already discussed, the Germans were certainly the major settlers. The Germanies in the second half of the eighteenth century were perceptibly poorer than other lands and also suffered from religious persecution, with the result that an explosion of German migrants throughout the world occurred. Catherine II lamented her empire's low population density and took whatever measures she could to remedy the situation. One of her remedies for the population deficit was to encourage the immigration of German settlers (recall that she herself was a German) into the Russian Empire. Between 1764 and 1774 over one hundred German colonies were founded in the Middle to Lower Volga Region, between Saratov and Kamyshin. In 1774 the region which came to be known as "New Russia" was seized from the Crimean Tatars. Twenty thousand state peasants were settled in Tavridiia in 1781 as Catherine hastened to populate the area. They were supplemented by Russian religious dissidents. (Recall that the Crimean Khanate still existed, and St. Petersburg was concerned that the Crimeans might try to recover their lost territory.) These Russian groups proved inadequate, so Germans were invited as well and they became prosperous farmers.[58] These Germans were in addition to the approximately 100,000 Germans who had lived in the Russian Empire by the middle of the eighteenth century, some of whom had come to work in the Academy of Sciences founded in 1724, most of whom lived in Baltic regions annexed by Peter.

≺ VI ≻

Summary

Slavs, and especially the Great Russians, have been among the "winners" in the global "demographic sweepstakes" in the past 1,500 years. Modern scholars have been hard put to find any trace of Slavs in 500 A.D., or Great Russians in 1000 A.D., but by 1991 they had populated a fair portion of Eurasia. The Slavs (and Great Russians) have not been the sole "winners," it must be stressed, in these global sweepstakes. Black Africans also were hard to find in 500 A.D. or even in 1000 A.D. Germanic and Turkic peoples also occupied much less global territory in 500 A.D. than they do now. On the other hand, Chinese and Indians occupied large territories already in 500 A.D., and have continued to migrate outward ever since. Romance-language peoples also expanded outside of their core areas in 500 A.D. If there were "winners," so were there "losers." The Celts, who once occupied much of Europe, were pushed to its western edges. Finnic peoples were relegated primarily to the northeastern fringes of Europe. Iranian/Persian peoples are certainly linguistically dominant in considerably less of Eurasia now than they were in 500 A.D. Other "losers" have been the aboriginal peoples of the Americas and Australia.

Much of what has caused these great migrations of peoples, the enormous expansion of some and the contraction of others, is not known. It is known, of course, that climatic changes, diseases, advantages conferred by inventions, and "culture" all played a role.

This chapter has concentrated on the East Slavic Great Russians since 500 A.D. The practice of sedentary agriculture in a region where it was little practiced before 500 A.D. must account for much of the advantage in multiplying the Russians had over the previous inhabitants, especially those in the Neolithic Volga-Oka mesopotamia region. Rye, introduced prior to the time covered by this chapter, was the crop which sustained the Russian population growth; during the period of the 1480s to the 1780s no new crops which would have facilitated population growth were introduced.[59] Crop yields did not increase and in general incomes did not rise in this period. Technological (especially military) advantage and administrative prowess (the capacity to control and keep whatever was annexed and gradually colonized) account for much of the rest of the Great Russian expansion.

It is doubtful that epidemiologically the Russians had an "advantage" over other peoples. Diseases they carried did not cause mass exterminations in the areas they moved into outside their Volga-Oka mesopotamian homeland, while the Russians themselves suffered greatly from epidemics such as the Black Death in the mid-fourteenth century and plagues such as those of 1570–72, 1652–53, and 1771 which wiped out as much as a third of the populations of the afflicted areas. Moreover, early on, such as in 1570 and 1601–3, Russia suffered from horrible famines which recurred on a lesser scale every four to seven years.[60] The Russians also suffered other demographic losses as hundreds of thousands were captured and sold into the international slave markets in Central Asia, the Crimea, the Mediterranean world (both Islamic and Christian), and Western Europe. In spite of these losses from Russia itself as well as the continuous flow of migrants into the borderlands of the Russian Empire, until 1914 the Russian population always had the resilience to bounce back, to the point that in the 1880s–90s considerable portions of Russia proper were definitely considered to be "overpopulated." Diminution of civil wars and wars fought on Russian territory no doubt also contributed to the demographic success of the Russians.

Muscovy expanded enormously between 1480 and the end of Catherine II's reign, about 38-fold geographically and 5.7-fold demographically. The density per square mile fell dramatically. In 1480 Muscovy's population was concentrated in the Volga-Oka triangle, but by 1785 Russians were inhabiting a much larger fraction of Eurasia all the way to the Black Sea and to the Pacific. The government wanted to populate the expanding area—without losing control of its population for taxation and service obligations. Between 1480 and 1556 the government launched the first service class revolution whose backbone was a provincial cavalry supported by conditional land grants (*pomest'ia*). The land grants were worthless without peasants tilling the land. The expansion of Muscovy gave the peasants many alternative places to do their farming; but every time one of them left the Volga-Oka mesopotamia, it cost a provincial cavalryman (who on average lived off and provided service from the rent provided by 5.6 peasant households) part of his livelihood. By 1648–49, the provincial cavalrymen forced the government to enserf the peasants. The movement of the peasants north of the Volga after the 1560s; east of the Volga after the annexation of Kazan'; into Siberia after the defeat of the Siberian Khanate; and south of the Oka beginning in the 1570s and especially after the 1630s caused the rigid legal stratification of Muscovite society while populating the new lands. Peasants, pulled by opportunity and pushed by serfdom and oppression (taxes, rent obligations, and violence), were joined in the migration to the frontiers by military servicemen, fugitive slaves, and townsmen. Freebooting trappers and cossacks were other agents of expansion who prepared the way for more permanent migrants. The consequence was that most of Russian society in 1785 was unfree while at the same time Russia controlled much of Eurasia.

Certain events were major preconditions for and precipitants of migration in these centuries. The annexation of the Middle and Lower Volga in 1552 and 1556 was the first. It permitted Russians to move not only into those Volga regions, but beyond, into the Urals and then into Siberia. Immediately following were the horrors of Ivan IV's reign, the 25-year Livonian War (with its oppressive taxation) and the Oprichnina (with its general oppression of most in its path). The civil wars of the Time of Troubles were next and resulted particularly in the deurbanization of Muscovy. Probably the third major event or process was the completion of the enserfment and the general formal legal stratification of society in 1649, which in the second half of the century provoked the migration of hundreds of thousands of people, most of them fugitive peasants. The government was of two minds about this migration. On the one hand, it deprived the increasingly obsolescent middle service class provincial cavalry of its basic financial support as well as made the collection of taxes more difficult, but on the other hand it permitted Moscow to control vast territories which it would have found impossible to do were it not for the new settlers.

Regrettably, no internal governmental debates on the pros and cons of migration are available. The unwillingness of the government to finalize the enserfment process until forced to do so by the civil disorders of 1648 indicates where the real sentiments of those in power lay. Although government agents returned thousands of fugitives after 1649, enthusiasm soon waned. Amnesties were declared for those who fled to towns. Local officials on the frontiers and in Siberia sometimes did as little as possible to return fugitives to the Volga-Oka mesopotamia, a phenomenon repeated during the 1930s when provincial officials to enhance local labor supplies tried to avoid turning over those sought by the NKVD. The end result was a rather rapid diffusion of the Russian population throughout the area controlled by Moscow. Throughout the eighteenth century at least 1,700,000 people settled on the frontiers of the Russian Empire, most of them migrants from the old heartland of Russia.[61] I would speculate that the legal stratification of society significantly curtailed the out-migration from the center to the periphery which would have resulted in the drastic depopulation of the podzolic Volga-Oka mesopotamia; but this remains a counterfactual which cannot be proved.[62]

Never can it be said that migration enhanced general freedom in Russia. Keeping the Russian population from being enslaved by others was the major project of the first service class revolution, which resulted in the oppressive garrison state. Serfdom's primary task was binding the peasantry to the land, to prevent peasants from moving where desire and opportunity beckoned. I would argue (and doubt that many would disagree with me) that the major impetus of Muscovy's state expansion southward was almost exclusively defensive in intent. Russia had so much land that it did not need any more. What it explicitly did not need was depletion of its population by predatory kidnapping and that is what it tried to protect itself from. That this resulted in the annexation of millions of acres which then "had" to be populated was almost incidental.

I cannot see that Moscow and then St. Petersburg had any alternative. The steppe people had no system of morality that any sedentary people who worked for a living could recognize. Their very existence was predatory, and it made no difference to them whom they preyed upon. Russians, any of the other steppe peoples, their own with whom they were currently engaged in a civil war—practically anyone in sight was a proper subject for kidnapping, murder, ransom, or extortion. There was no such thing as a respite, for freelancers were always willing to step into any official breathing spell resulting from a treaty or other agreement. Peace with Russia's southern steppe neighbors was absolutely impossible because their societies were based on the booty and prestige they gained from constant combat with the Russians. Moreover, no payment of extortion ("gifts," "tribute") was ever enough (even the million rubles paid to the Crimeans in the years 1613–50) because the predators always wanted more and were willing to do whatever they could to collect it. The only way to deal with such predators was to put them out of business, either by defensive measures (putting everyone in service, building fortified lines that put a higher price on the predators' extortion than they were willing to pay) or offensive measures (going into their camps and destroying them or cutting off their herding routes). Coexistence between sedentary and nomadic peoples was impossible. In the long run, the sedentaries won and migrated into and settled the areas formerly used as herding grounds by the nomads.

At one time it was fashionable to allege that the Mongol conquest and rule of Russia (1236–1480) was responsible for the absence of freedom: for the autocracy, which lasted from the early sixteenth century until 1991, and for serfdom, which commenced in the 1450s and lasted until 1906, and then was renewed by Soviet collectivization. For decades scholars have realized that this was much too simplistic. The Mongols had nothing to do with the ideology of autocracy, which began at the beginning of the sixteenth century with the borrowing by Hegumen Joseph of the formula of the seventh-century Byzantine monk Agapetos that the ruler was God's viceregent on earth. Serfdom is recognized as a device to contend with a perceived population shortage, which had several causes. First, internal chaos dispersed debtors and rent payers. Second, the steppe heirs of the Mongols had a predatory lifestyle which made coexistence with the sedentary Russians impossible. Third, Russian governmental efforts to curtail steppe predation combined with the internal chaos and other pressures plus the attractiveness of the lands outside of Muscovy proper to launch enormous pressures for migration.

Significant segments of the Russian military and social elite constantly pressured the government to curtail the migration. The solution would have been two-fold: liquidate the steppe predation, which was done (unless one wants to consider contemporary Chechnia a continuation of the old pattern); and move the capital from Moscow or St. Petersburg to some place like Khar'kov, which was not done. Had the capital been moved to Khar'kov after the steppe menace had been liquidated, peasants could have freely abandoned the infertile *podzol* region for the better *chernozëm* areas. From Khar'kov a less autocratic government might have been able to mobilize the resources from a free population to keep the Swedes, Poles, Ottoman Turks, Persians, and Chinese at bay. This counterfactual was not in the cards. Russia mobilized the necessary resources, but at the cost of nearly everyone's freedom. Migration was destined to play a central role in Russian history from the 1480s to the 1780s no matter which option was chosen.

Peasant Migration, the Abolition of Serfdom, and the Internal Passport System in the Russian Empire

c. 1800–1914

DAVID MOON

THERE WAS A substantial increase in peasant migration in the Russian Empire over the nineteenth and early twentieth centuries. Growing numbers of peasants left their home villages to work temporarily as migrant laborers. In addition, ever larger numbers settled permanently in the empire's industrializing cities and the relatively sparsely populated regions on the southern and eastern peripheries of the empire. This period also saw the abolition of serfdom, which had bound peasants to the estates of nobles, in 1861, and major reform of the internal passport system, which had restricted peasants' geographical mobility, from the 1890s. The aim of this chapter is to consider the relationship between the abolition of serfdom, the reform of the passport system, and the growth in peasant migration.

Before more detailed discussion, a few points need to be noted. Before 1861, the serfs of noble estate owners (*pomeshchiki*)—or seigniorial peasants (*pomeshchich'i krest'yane*)—were only part of the Russian peasantry. They were about half the total in the 1850s. The other large category, also around half in the 1850s, was the "state peasantry," who lived on state land. There was also a small category of "appanage peasants," who lived on the estates of the imperial family. The mobility of all peasants was restricted by law as part of a wider policy of state regulation of population movement.[1]

Although peasants were banned from moving on their own initiative without authorization, they were liable to be moved under coercion. Large numbers of male peasants were drafted into the armed forces for long terms of service in most years after Tsar Peter the Great (1682–1725) introduced regular levies of recruits in 1705. Recruits were forcibly taken from their families and, until the 1830s, had little prospect of ever returning home.[2] Another example of coerced movement was judicial exile to Siberia for serious offenses. The most famous exiles were revolutionaries, but most were peasants.[3] Coerced movement of peasants through conscription (which was reformed in 1874) and exile continued into the twentieth century. Seigniorial peasants were also liable to be moved by their owners. Nobles moved their peasants from one estate to another and bought peasants from other nobles and moved them to their domains. Until 1858, nobles could convert their peasants to household serfs, taking them off the land to work as servants or in other capacities in their town and country houses. Nobles also hired out their peasants as laborers. From 1760, moreover, they could banish them to Siberia without trial.[4] State peasants were also liable to be moved under coercion. They were assigned to work on construction projects and in mines and factories, especially in the Urals, which were rich in minerals but short of labor. In the early nineteenth century, some state peasants were sent to the new military colonies. From 1760, state peasants could be exiled to Siberia by their communities. On occasions, moreover, the authorities resettled state peasants in frontier regions.[5] In addition, countless peasants moved as unauthorized, or "free," migrants.[6]

I

Legislation on Peasant Movement

Over the period from 1592–93 to 1649 the Russian state imposed a general ban on peasant movement in Russia. As a result of provisions of the Law Code of 1649, peasants who had left their villages were liable to be caught and returned without time limit. In other words, they were bound to the land in perpetuity. The places peasants were bound to were recorded in the census of 1646–47. The ban on movement applied to all peasants, regardless of whether the land they lived on was the property of the state, the church, the court, or private estate owners. The ban on movement enabled estate owners to increase their power over the peasants on their land and to demand higher obligations from them in forced labor (*barshchina*) or in dues (*obrok*) in cash and kind. The Law Code of 1649 thus marked the legal consolidation of serfdom.[7]

The Law Code of 1649 also, however, permitted peasants to seek wage labor. In the seventeenth century, peasants leaving their homes to work were given papers by their owners or local officials. Peter the Great regularized the practice by introducing a system of internal passports for the entire population. In a decree of October 30, 1719, he required people moving around to have passports or other documents. The requirement was tacked on to a decree on catching deserters, suggesting that Peter's main aim was to keep track of recruits, and potential recruits, for his armed forces. Further decrees in 1722 and 1724 laid down precise procedures. Peasants moving to work within their home districts (*uezdy*) or less than 30 *versty* (about 20 miles) needed a written pass (*pis'mennyi otpusk*) signed by their owners, estate stewards, or parish priests. If peasants wished to travel to other districts or more than 30 *versty*, their owners (or stewards or priests) were to submit their passes to the local authorities, who were to record the details and issue the peasants signed and sealed permits (a *propusknoe pis'mo*) valid for up to three years. These decrees were connected with the census Peter ordered in 1719 to compile a register of men, mostly peasants, who were liable to pay the new poll tax. The tax census was periodically revised until 1857–58. The introduction of internal passports was accompanied by new punishments for "harboring" fugitives, and by the providing of search parties to find them.[8]

The internal passport system was part of Peter's constant struggle against fugitives, vagrants, deserters, and anyone he felt was escaping his demands for men to serve in his armed forces, for laborers for his construction projects, and for taxes for his treasury. By the end of Peter's reign in 1725, all peasants were bound to the land twice over: by the Law Code of 1649 and by the internal passport system of 1719–24.

Peasant movement was also restricted by a custom that long predated the poll tax, internal passports, and serfdom: collective responsibility (*krugovaya poruka*) of communities for the payment of taxes and other obligations. If one member defaulted on his share of the community's obligations—for example because he had left his village illegally—then his neighbors were obliged to pay his share as well as their own. Many noble estate owners enforced the same custom for the obligations they demanded. It was therefore in peasants' own interests to try to ensure that other members of their communities did not leave and that they paid their dues and taxes. Peasants who were away with authorization were required to remit their shares back to their communities.[9]

In the 1830s, all legislation regulating population movement was summarized in the *Digest of Regulations concerning Passports and Fugitives* in volume 14 of the new *Digest of Laws of the Russian Empire*.[10] It was regularly updated to incorporate new laws. What follows is a summary of the regulations, in particular those affecting seigniorial peasants, in the 1857 edition.[11] The fundamental principle, which had been laid down in 1719, was: "No one may leave their place of permanent residence without a legitimate permit or passport" (art. 1). The "permanent residence" of all peasants was the place where they were registered in the most recent revision of the tax census (art. 10). Seigniorial peasants, moreover, were not allowed to move against the will of their owners.[12] Authorization for peasants of all categories to leave their places of residence came in three types: a permit (*pis'mennyi vid*); a pass (*bilet*) on official stamped paper; and a printed passport (*pechatnyi plakatnyi pasport*). The type peasants needed depended on how far they would be traveling and how long they would be away (art. 111).

A written permit (*vid*) was sufficient for peasants traveling inside their own districts or less than 30 *versty*. It was also adequate for seigniorial peasants who were taking their owners' produce to market, or were away on other business for their owners, even if this entailed traveling further than 30 *versty* (art. 112).[13] Written permits could be given out to seigniorial peasants by their owners, stewards, and village elders, and to state and appanage peasants by their village and township officials (art. 114).[14] The permits were to include the peasants' names, description, where they were going, and for how long (art. 117).

Peasants traveling further than 30 *versty* but for less than six months needed a pass (*bilet*) written on official stamped paper (art. 118). Passes were introduced as a cheaper and simpler variant of passports in 1827 (see below). They could be issued by estate owners, their managers, or local state authorities (arts. 118–19). Passes were required to have similar information to permits, but more detail about their holders, their places of residence, and the issuing authorities (appendix to art. 130). Peasants were allowed one month's grace after their passes expired to renew them. Moreover, the issuing authorities could add notes that they could be renewed without the holder having to return home (arts. 125–26). Stamped paper for a one-month pass cost 15 copecks, for a two-month pass, 30 copecks, and for a three-month pass, 60 copecks (art. 130).

Finally, passports were required if peasants were traveling further than 30 *versty* and would be away for more than six months, up to a maximum of three years (arts. 141–42). Passports were issued by the district offices of the state treasury, which were to keep a record of them (arts. 141, 153, appendix to art. 153). However, estate owners and managers on seigniorial estates, as well as village and township officials on state and appanage lands, could keep supplies of blank passports to issue to peasants (arts. 145–47, 151, 154–56). Passports required more detailed information than passes and, as a further protection against forgery, they had to be printed (art. 214, appendix to art. 214). Under certain conditions, peasants could renew their passports at government offices without returning home (arts. 194–208). Passports were more expensive than passes. A six-month passport cost 85 copecks; a passport valid for a year, 1 rouble 45 copecks; and a full three-year passport, 4 roubles 35 copecks (art. 187).

To give an indication of the relative cost of passports and passes: the annual poll tax payment for a male peasant in 1840–61 was 95 copecks;[15] the average level of dues (*obrok*) demanded by nobles per male peasant each year in the 1850s was 8–10 roubles.[16] Thus, the cost of passes and passports was quite high relative to other taxes. On the other hand, some migrant laborers earned fairly high wages. In 1858, the average earnings of all laborers involved in non-agricultural work in Vladimir province in the Central Non-Black Earth region varied from 25 to 97 roubles a year. However, this was less than was needed to support the average family. In addition, middle men and contractors as well as nobles took their cuts. Agricultural laborers fared worse. In southern Tambov province in 1856, they earned, on average, 18 roubles for a summer's work.[17] These comparisons suggest that the cost of passes and passports was a constraint on authorized peasant movement. The authorities recognized this constraint; and when harvests failed, they occasionally issued passports free of charge to allow peasants to leave the affected areas legally to seek work.[18]

Peasant migrant laborers were obliged to present their documents to the police when arrived at their destinations (art. 327). People apprehended without valid documents were considered vagrants (*brodyagi*) or fugitives (*beglye*). The authorities were so concerned about unauthorized movement that everyone was obliged to try to catch anyone without a passport. There was also a general obligation to assist the police in seizing such people. Financial rewards were laid down for those who succeeded (arts. 582–613).

When suspects were apprehended by the police, if there was evidence of who they were and where they came from they were to be punished and sent home (arts. 614–15). If there was no evidence, then they were to be questioned, inquiries made to verify their statements, and their descriptions sent to the official press. While awaiting responses, the police were to dispatch men aged 17–60 who were fit for work to penal labor companies. Others, including women, were to be held and put to work. If the inquiries revealed that suspects' statements were true, or if an estate owner or village community claimed them, they were to be sent home (arts. 617, 620–23, 638). If suspects' statements proved to be false, if they claimed to have forgotten their names and origins (*nazvat' sebya nepomnyashchim rodstva*),[19] or if they refused to divulge any information, they were to be tried and punished. Adult males were to be branded on their lower right arms with the letter "B" (the initial letter of "vagrant" and "fugitive" in Russian). Those deemed fit were to be sent to the army. Others were to be sent—depending on their fitness, gender, and age—to penal labor companies, work houses, or local welfare institutions, or to Siberia for settlement (arts. 617–19, 625–35). If estate owners and communities could prove they owned vagrants or fugitives who had not divulged their correct names and origins, then they could reclaim them. If the culprit had been sent to the army, however, he could not be returned, and in his place the authorities sent his owner or community a certificate of exemption from supplying a recruit at the next regular levy (arts. 637–56).[20]

Further evidence for the importance the state attached to unregulated movement can be inferred from the detailed regulations on the procedures for dealing with, and punishing, people who hid or harbored vagrants, fugitives, and deserters (arts. 584, 588–89, 591, 698–729).

Peasants' right to move was affected only slightly by the Statutes of February 19, 1861 that abolished serfdom. Full discussion of the terms of the statutes ratified by Tsar Alexander II (1855–81) is beyond the scope of this chapter; what follows is a brief summary. All seigniorial peasants received personal freedom at once. They could no longer be bought and sold or moved by their former owners, and they could enter legally binding contracts. For two more years, however, they remained under seigniorial authority and continued to serve the same obligations for their estate owners in return for their land allotments. The Statutes contained provisions enabling peasants who performed labor services for their owners to have them commuted to monetary dues. Much of the authority that estate owners had wielded under serfdom was transferred to reconstituted village community and township (*volost'*) organizations that were run by peasants but were subordinate to local officials.

In 1863, the freed serfs entered a transitional stage of "temporary obligation" to their estate owners. During this stage, peasants' allotments and the obligations they paid estate owners for them were regulated in charters according to principles laid down in the Statutes. The final stage of the reform was the "redemption operation": peasants purchased ("redeemed") their allotments from estate owners through the intermediary of the government. The government paid compensation to the estate owners for the loss of part of their land, and the peasants repaid the government in "redemption payments" over 49 years. In the Russian provinces of the empire, as had been the practice before 1861, land was usually allotted to village communities, not individual peasant households, and communities paid their obligations and redemption payments jointly.[21]

The Statutes of 1861 made little change to the regulations concerning temporary absences. Responsibility for issuing permits, passes, and passports was transferred from estate owners and their appointees to the new institutions of peasant self-government. The new township elders (the *volostnoi starshina*) were to issue documents to peasants on the authorization of the elder (*starosta*) of their village community (General Statute, art. 58, clause 10, and art. 84, clause 8). During temporary obligation, rural authorities were not permitted to issue passports to peasants whose communities were in arrears with their obligations to their estate owners without the written agreement of the latter (Local Statute for Great Russia, art. 262). Once the redemption operation was under way, peasants whose communities were behind with their redemption payments could receive passports only with the written agreement of the local peace mediator (the official who supervised the implementation of the reform) (Statute on Redemption, art. 129).

In addition, and this was a right that had not been enjoyed by seigniorial peasants under serfdom, the Statutes of 1861 permitted peasants to leave their villages and move permanently to other locations. They could do so, however, only in very limited circumstances.[22] The main procedures were laid down in articles 130–40 of the General Statute. In order to be released by their communities, peasants had to renounce forever their claims to shares of the communal land, return their allotments to the community, pay their tax liabilities in full up to January 1 of the following year, and have their parents' permission to leave and written agreement from another village or urban community that it was prepared to admit them. Peasants could not be released, moreover, if they had any arrears in their state, local, and village taxes, or in their obligations to the estate owner; or if they were subject to any court proceedings.

On top of these provisions, for the first nine years after 1861 further conditions were laid down by the Local Statutes. According to the Local Statute for "Great Russia," the peasant wishing to leave his village community also needed the agreement of the estate owner and village community unless he paid in full the redemption sum for his land allotment (the sum was calculated by capitalizing the annual dues peasants paid the estate owner for the allotment at 6 percent, that is, by multiplying by 16.667), or the estate owner agreed to take the peasant's allotment back and remove it from the community's land, or the community agreed to pay the peasant's dues (arts. 139–45).

The legal situation regarding peasants leaving their village communities changed during the redemption operation. In villages redeeming their land jointly, a peasant wishing to leave had to pay half the redemption sum for his allotment and get the agreement of the community to take responsibility for the other half. Peasants were permitted to leave communities that were in arrears with their redemption payments or taxes only with the agreement of the provincial Bureau for Peasant Affairs. These restrictions referred only to heads of households. Other household members, including most women, were subject only to the provisions in the General Statute; in particular, they needed their parents' permission (Statute on Redemption, arts. 172–79). Thus, the Statues of 1861 maintained the custom of collective responsibility in the Russian provinces in order to ensure that peasants paid in full their obligation to estate owners and their redemption payments to the government (General Statute, arts. 187–91; Statute on Redemption, arts. 34 and 127).[23] The reform settlement was also intended to discourage the former serfs from leaving their villages so that they would continue to work for their former owners, albeit now in return for wages, cultivating the parts of estates retained by nobles.[24] There are interesting parallels here to the attempts in the Caribbean to restrict the movement of ex-slaves off the sugar estates in the aftermath of abolition.

It was slightly easier for peasants in most of Ukraine and elsewhere in the non-Russian western parts of the empire to leave their communities. In most of these areas, after 1861, peasants continued to hold their land in individual household tenure and were held individually responsible for obligations and payments.[25] Thus, in contrast to the Russian provinces, collective responsibility did not pose a barrier to peasants leaving their communities. Moreover, peasants who were redeeming their land individually, rather than jointly, had only to sell their allotments and responsibility for the outstanding payments to someone else if they wished to move (Statute on Redemption, arts. 169, 175).

In addition to the abolition of serfdom, the other main categories of peasants (state and appanage) were the subjects of reform. These reforms came in three stages: in the 1820s–40s, the late 1850s–60s, and the 1880s. By the late nineteenth century, virtually all peasants in the Russian Empire had been granted personal freedom and the right to purchase allotments of land under redemption operations administered by the government.[26] Furthermore, as a result of the reforms, all peasants, regardless of their former categories, were subject to similar restrictions on their movement.[27]

The Statutes of 1861 that formally abolished serfdom put an end to one of the main reasons why the state had restricted and regulated the movement of a large part of the peasant population (the serfs of the nobility) since the late sixteenth century.[28] The main other reasons why the state put constraints on the mobility of the rural population between the late sixteenth and the late nineteenth centuries, however, were remarkably constant, and endured after the reforms of the 1850s–60s.

In 1859, a special commission in the Ministry of Internal Affairs concluded that it would be impossible to reform the internal passport system because of the existing systems of taxation and conscription.[29] Controlling peasant movement facilitated the assessment and collection of the main direct taxes: the land tax until mid-seventeenth century, then the household tax and, after 1724, the poll tax.[30] Tying peasants to the land also meant that they were guaranteed access to land and thus had the wherewithal to support themselves and meet their taxes.[31] Indeed, partly for this reason, the Statutes of 1861 granted peasants permanent use-rights of land allotments, albeit reduced in size, during temporary obligation, and the opportunity to buy their allotments under the redemption operation. Moreover, as we have seen, the Statutes seriously limited peasants' freedom of movement, in part to ensure they fulfilled their obligations, taxes, and redemption payments. For the same reasons, the restrictions on the mobility of former appanage and state peasants continued after the reforms. Moreover, passports had been a major source of revenue since payment was introduced in 1763. Receipts from the sale of passports increased by a third over the second quarter of the nineteenth century, reaching an average of 1.6 million roubles a year in the 1850s. This had risen to 3.5 million roubles by the 1880s.[32]

The state also regulated, and continued to regulate, peasant mobility in order to control the movement of men eligible for military conscription. On top of the standard restrictions, peasants who were liable to serve and were away from home had to return when levies of recruits were due.[33] Under the terms of the Statutes of 1861, peasants in line for military service could be released from their village communities only if the release would not prevent their serving.[34] Moreover, strict regulations were laid down for catching and punishing fugitive recruits and deserters.[35]

A more general, but strong, motive for restricting peasant mobility was a concern among many officials and nobles that allowing greater freedom of movement would upset the social order. The big fear was that peasants would lose their ties to the land and become "proletarianized" and prone to take part in revolutions similar to those that had occurred in western Europe since 1789. This was an important factor behind the government's decision to make sure the former seigniorial peasants had land after 1861 and to retain the peasants' communal institutions and collective responsibility.[36] The officials who prepared the Statutes abolishing serfdom were strongly influenced in their decision to create a landed peasantry by serious peasant disorders in 1858 in Estonia, where in 1816 serfdom had been abolished without granting land to the peasants.[37] Moreover, the internal passport system facilitated police surveillance over the population.[38]

There were also reasons why restricting peasant movement was detrimental to state interests. It limited the mobility of the labor force and thus inhibited economic development. It also limited peasants' ability to leave their homes to earn the money they needed to pay their taxes. Forcibly assigning state peasants to factories and mines and permitting peasants to leave their homes for work with written authorization facilitated only limited labor mobility. In spite of the concerns about the possible implications for social stability of a more mobile labor force, there was a growing awareness of the economic arguments for reform among more enlightened bureaucrats in the first half of the nineteenth century.[39] In the eighteenth century, the authorities had responded to the need for more labor in the Urals by permitting fugitive seigniorial peasants to remain if they had become skilled workers.[40] The government took some limited steps toward allowing greater labor mobility from 1826. It was made easier for peasants to obtain written authorization for short-term absences: for example passes (*bilety*) were introduced, the cost of documents was reduced, and peasants were permitted to renew their documents without returning home (see above).[41] From the 1880s, the government consciously promoted economic and industrial development so that the Russian Empire could compete economically, and militarily, with the more developed states of northwestern Europe. A mobile labor force was a prerequisite for such development. The man behind many of the economic policies of this period, and who favored liberalizing the internal passport system, was Sergei Witte, the minister of finance from 1892 to 1903.[42]

A further problem created by restricting peasant mobility was that it inhibited a long-standing objective of the Russian state, that dated back at least to the seventeenth century, of settling the borderlands of the expanding Russian Empire with an agricultural, tax-paying, and preferably Slavonic, population.[43] The government tried to overcome this dilemma in several ways. There was some forced relocation of state peasants and others to frontier regions. More regularly and successfully, the government promoted the settlement of particular regions by offering "privileges," for example tax exemptions, loans, and land grants, to attract state peasants and others, including foreigners, to settle there of their own accord.[44] Resettlement of peasants who were short of land was part of the reforms of the state peasantry enacted by P. D. Kiselev in the 1830s and 1840s.[45] On a few occasions, the central government, and more frequently local authorities in frontier areas, turned a blind eye to the illegal status of fugitives, including fugitive seigniorial peasants, and permitted them to settle. This policy was applied, for example, on the steppe frontier in the Central Black Earth region in the seventeenth century, in southern Ukraine ("New Russia") in the late eighteenth century, and in the North Caucasus in the early nineteenth century.[46] Periodically, the government issued decrees recognizing the *fait accompli* of illegal migration and formally registered peasants in some border regions.[47] These did not, however, deal adequately with the state's desire to settle the borderlands.

From the 1880s, the government began actively to encourage the settlement of outlying regions, in particular Siberia. The government wanted to promote the economic development of these regions, and it saw migration as a solution to economic distress among some peasants in overcrowded provinces in the European part of the empire. In July 1881, temporary rules on migration suspended some of the restrictions in the Statutes of 1861. Peasants seeking to leave their communities no longer needed written agreement from other communities that they would accept them. And, peasant-migrants could postpone paying their taxes to their old communities until January 1 of the following year.

A new, general law on migration was issued on July 13, 1889.[48] Peasants wishing to migrate had to seek permission from the Ministry of Internal Affairs and that of State Domains. If permission was granted, migrants were allotted state land in the regions they were moving to and were given loans and temporary exemptions from state obligations. Authorized migrants did not need to seek formal discharge from their existing communities. In addition, they did not have to pay any arrears in their taxes and redemption payments to their former communities. In return, however, these communities received the land allotments formerly held by the migrants. Peasants who had settled in Siberia without authorization were permitted to remain, but they had to pay the arrears in their obligations to their previous communities. Further changes in the law to facilitate legal migration were enacted in 1896–97. A law of 1904 decentralized the authorization of migration to district committees, and peasants were granted greater freedom to migrate by a law of March 10, 1906. Peter Stolypin, the prime minister from 1906 to 1911, promoted peasant resettlement in Siberia as part of his wider package of agrarian reform.[49]

For both these reasons—economic development and internal migration—in the 1890s, the government finally moved toward relaxing the overall restrictions on peasant mobility. The way was cleared by the fall, one-by-one, of the main institutional and fiscal barriers to reform. The abolition of serfdom of 1861 was followed by the military service reform of 1874, which made all young men (not just peasants and townsmen) liable to serve, and the term of service was greatly reduced.[50] The poll tax was abolished in the European provinces with effect from January 1, 1887, and in Siberia in 1899. It was replaced mainly by indirect taxes that did not require strict regulation of population movement.[51] Collective responsibility for redemption payments was finally ended in 1903.[52] The redemption payments themselves were cancelled in November 1905, effective from January 1, 1907.[53] And, in 1906, Stolypin enacted a law permitting peasants to leave their village communities and separate their allotments from the communal land and convert them to individual property.[54]

After several years of government prevarication, Finance Minister Witte and Minister of Internal Affairs I. N. Durnovo proposed a reform of the internal passport system. This led to the "Statute on Residence Permits" of June 3, 1894. The new law contained several significant innovations for the rural population. All peasants were entitled to receive the new "residence permits" (*vidy na zhitel'stvo*), which served both as proof of identity and as internal passports valid for up to five years. Peasants, but not factory workers, could be absent from their places of residence inside their home districts or within 50 *versty* (around 33 miles) for up to six months without further written authorization. Peasants who traveled further or were away for longer had to pay one rouble a year for the privilege. (The fee was ended in 1897.) Peasants who were in arrears with their shares of the obligations for which village communities were collectively responsible (for example redemption payments) could leave their villages only with the permission of their communities. Communities could withdraw permission from peasants on the request of their heads of household, or if their families were unable to support themselves in their absence. Young men liable to military service were given residence permits on colored paper.[55]

Thus, the law of 1894 greatly eased authorized movement by peasants. A more radical reform was prevented by the continued existence of collective responsibility and the authority of village communities and household heads. All but the last of these had been abolished or undermined by 1906–7. Moreover, in 1905–7 the tsarist government faced revolution. One of the reasons it survived was that it made concessions. The most famous was the October Proclamation of 1905, in which Tsar Nicholas II (1894–1917) announced elections for a legislative assembly (the Duma). The end of the redemption payments, announced in November 1905, was a concession directed at the peasants. A further concession to peasants came in a decree of October 5, 1906. The preamble stated that the abolition of serfdom had laid the basis for the gradual equalization of the peasants' rights with those of the rest of the population. Among the rights now granted to peasants was that of freedom of movement on the same terms as "privileged" members of the population.[56] The last edition of the "Fundamental Laws of the Russian Empire" before 1917 included the clause: "Every Russian subject has the right freely to choose [his or her] place of residence and occupation."[57] Thus, half a century after 1861, Russia's peasants finally regained the right of freedom of movement that their ancestors had lost in the late sixteenth century.

Map 1. Regions of the Russian Empire in Europe, 1850.

≺ II ≻

Peasant Migration

Most peasant migration in the Russian Empire can be divided into two main types: temporary migration by wage laborers and permanent migration to resettle in urban or rural areas. All peasant movement can also be divided into coerced, regulated (that is, authorized), and free (that is, unauthorized). Unfortunately for the historian, full data do not exist to examine all these types in great detail. Much free migration, in particular, escaped the record precisely because it was unauthorized. Nevertheless, the main trends can be traced.[58]

Temporary migrant laborers (*otkhodniki*) worked in a wide range of occupations. To some extent, these reflected the geographical variations in the economy, which, in part, were a result of the environmental division of much of the Russian Empire. There was the forested northern half, with relatively infertile soils, long winters, and a damp climate; and the much more fertile, warmer, but drier steppes to the south. The border between the two, the northern limit of the fertile black earth, lay to the south of Moscow. Also important in influencing regional variations in the economy and employment were the location of the two main cities, St. Petersburg and Moscow, in the northwest and center, and the transport networks, which were based largely on the rivers before large-scale railroad construction began in the 1860s. As a result of the opportunities afforded by the environment and the location and accessibility of markets, the economy was largely agricultural to the south and more diverse to the north. Indeed, the two main economic zones in the heart of Russia are referred to as the Central Agricultural or Black Earth and the Central Industrial or Non-Black Earth regions. Regional specialization in the Russian economy became more developed from the mid-eighteenth century, creating greater opportunities for wage labor in production for the market in the main regions, and in trade between them.[59] (See Map 1.)

Non-agricultural employment was more prevalent in the northern half of Russia. Temporary migrant laborers in these regions worked in industry, mining, forestry, construction, transport, trade, and domestic service. Only to a small extent did they work in agriculture. The main hubs of employment for migrant laborers were St. Petersburg and Moscow, which were growing centers of industry that needed workers and of a population that demanded goods and services. The mill towns of Vladimir province also attracted many peasants seeking work. The mines and foundries of the Urals were the destinations of thousands of migrant workers, who augmented the assigned peasants sent there in the eighteenth century. Many migrant laborers found work as lumberjacks in the forests of the north.[60]

Opportunities for migrant agricultural labor were most widespread in southern Ukraine and southeastern European Russia, along the lower reaches of the Dnepr, Don, and Volga rivers, and in the North Caucasus, as a consequence of the fertile black earth, access to ports on the rivers and the Black Sea, and the relatively sparse local populations. The migrant agricultural laborers in these regions came mostly from the Central Black Earth and Volga regions of Russia and from Ukraine. In addition, the river Volga, the main transport artery between the agricultural south and the industrial center before the advent of railroads, provided labor for thousands of peasants.[61] The regional patterns of employment remained broadly similar throughout the period under consideration, but one major change was the emergence of a new industrial area in the Donbas region of southeastern Ukraine in the late nineteenth century. Thousands of peasants from other parts of Ukraine and adjoining regions of Russia moved to the Donbas to seek work in mining and industry. The migrants included the family of future Soviet leader Nikita Khrushchev.[62]

Some migrant laborers left home to seek work without authorization, or stayed on after their documents had expired. They were among the thousands of "fugitives" and "vagrants" apprehended every year.[63] The cossack communities of the south and southeast had long employed unauthorized migrants, including fugitives from serfdom.[64] There were examples of mass illegal migration by persons in search of work. In 1847, as many as 10,000 seigniorial peasants left their homes in famine-struck Belorussia without permission to work on the construction of the St. Petersburg-Moscow railroad. They were rounded up and returned.[65]

Not all migrant laborers left their villages by choice. Under serfdom, some nobles hired out their peasants and took a cut of their earnings. Of a sample of around 6,000 seigniorial peasants working in Moscow in 1738–79, 61 percent had been sent by their owners. In the 1840s, to take another example, Count Sheremetev hired out thousands of peasants from his estate in Tver' province to work on the construction of the railroad between St. Petersburg and Moscow that passed through the province. Some magnates, for example Sheremetev and Gagarin, sent with migrant laborers estate officials to supervise them and collect part of their wages.[66] After 1861, some young men were sent to work by their parents against their will. But, over the late nineteenth century, the younger generation willingly sought the greater freedom of working and living away from their parents and village elders.[67]

After 1861, heads of peasant households and elders of village communities took over from nobles in seeking to control migrant laborers and ensure they remitted part of their earnings back to them. Some households and communities depended on money sent home by migrant workers to cover their obligations. Jeffrey Burds has explored the efforts at control by village communities in the Central Non-Black Earth region between 1861 and 1905. Communities used their authority over the issue of passports to their members to ensure compliance; they worked with the local police to threaten migrant laborers who defaulted on their obligations with the forced sale of their property; they tied migrant laborers to their home villages by ensuring they married before they left; they made agreements with employers to send part of migrants' wages directly to their communities; and they relied on the importance peasants attached to their reputations, which could be lost if their conduct undermined the well-being of their communities.[68]

Migrant laborers did not conform to the wishes of their communities only under duress. Many deliberately remained members of their communities and thus kept the right to land allotments as security for the future. Some migrant workers returned to their villages if they were laid off during recessions.[69] Many migrants, moreover, intended to return home after earning some money. The wives and children of many male migrants stayed in the villages, living with their parents-in-law and grandparents. Migrant workers regularly went back to their home villages for holidays and to help with haymaking and the harvest. These "peasant-workers" occupied a netherworld "between the fields and the city": they were rural peasants in the city, but urban workers in the village.[70]

An indication of the scale of authorized labor migration can be gained from the numbers of passports and passes issued. It was most widespread, and developed earliest, in the Central Non-Black Earth region. Migrant labor, especially in non-agricultural occupations, became common in the late eighteenth century and continued to increase over the following decades. At the start of the nineteenth century, in most provinces of the region, the number of passports issued was the equivalent of around 10 percent of the male peasant population. By the end of the 1850s, estimates suggest that over a quarter of the male population of the region, nearly 900,000, had passes or passports. The proportion was highest in Moscow province, where the numbers were 35 percent of the male population. In some areas, for example the district in Yaroslavl' province containing the Volga port of Rybinsk, most adult male peasants were migrant laborers. Moreover, in the 1850s, 34 percent of state revenue from selling passports came from this region, which contained 13 percent of the population.[71]

Although less detailed data are readily available for other regions before 1861, it is clear that authorized migrant labor was far less widespread in the largely agricultural regions to the south. In the eight largely agricultural districts of southern Tambov province in the Central Black Earth region, passports and passes were issued to only 5.7 percent of male peasants in 1856. Many worked as agricultural laborers in the Don Cossack territory, or as carters and boatmen transporting agricultural produce. The numbers of migrant laborers from the southern districts of Tambov province in 1856 may have been higher than usual as that year's harvest was "unsatisfactory," compelling peasants to seek other sources of income. On the other hand, in the same year, passports and passes were issued to almost a quarter of the male peasant population of the four northern districts of Tambov province. Most worked in non-agricultural activities. The economies of these districts were similar to the economy of the Central Non-Black region they adjoined to the north.[72]

In all regions combined, the number of passports issued to both seigniorial and state peasants almost doubled, from 574,000 to 1,084,000, between 1826 and 1857.[73] The actual number of authorized migrant laborers was much greater, however, since passports were needed only by those traveling more than 30 *versty* and remaining at the destination for more than six months. Passes were given

TABLE 1
Average Number of Passports Issued, 1860–1910

Years	*Ave. no. of passports issued p.a. (millions)*	*Index*
1860–70	1.29	100
1871–80	3.69	286
1881–90	4.94	383
1891–1900	6.95	539
1901–10	8.87	688

SOURCE: P. Gatrell, *The Tsarist Economy, 1850–1917* (London, 1986), 89.

out in similar or larger numbers.[74] No data are available on the number of permits allowing peasants to move shorter distances.

More detailed data are readily available about the scale of peasant migrant labor in the decades after the end of serfdom than before. The main trend was the marked growth in the numbers and proportion of peasants involved in authorized migrant labor. The average number of passports issued each year grew nearly seven-fold between the 1860s and 1901–10 (Table 1). This was well over twice the rate of natural population growth in the same period. The proportion of the total rural population (men and women) issued passports increased from 2.1 percent in the late 1850s to 8.4 percent by 1910.[75]

One of the problems in using the numbers of passports and other permits to gauge the scale of migrant labor is that these documents were valid for periods ranging from one month to three years. Boris Mironov overcame this problem by converting the crude figures on all documents into the equivalent of one-year passports (Table 2). Most passports were issued for less than one year, and his adjustment therefore gives a low figure for the proportion of time spent by the labor force in authorized migrant labor. Mironov also sought to differentiate between industrial and agricultural migrant labor by dividing his data into northern "industrial" regions and southern "agricultural" regions (including the Donbas industrial region). Migrant labor remained far more widespread in the northern regions than in the southern. Furthermore, because passports were issued in disproportionate numbers to the urban population, the figures for all passports overstate the scale of migrant labor among peasants. Mironov calculated that in 1900, in the European part of the empire,

TABLE 2
The Average Numbers of Passports (1-year) for Every 100 Members of the Population (both sexes) of the European Part of the Russian Empire, 1861–1910

Region	1861–70	1871–80	1881–90	1891–1900	1906–10
Industrial	2.5	4.5	4.7	8.1	9.5
St Petersburg & Moscow provs	4.0	5.7	6.1	9.6	9.4
Central Non-Black Earth	3.9	7.2	7.7	11.1	14.6
Northwestern	1.7	3.5	3.4	6.5	7.7
Northeastern	0.6	1.6	1.9	4.4	5.4
Baltic	1.0	1.4	1.6	5.1	5.8
Agricultural	0.9	1.9	2.3	4.2	4.4
Central Black Earth	1.4	2.8	3.3	6.0	7.0
Mid-Volga	1.1	2.7	3.0	5.4	6.4
Eastern (Urals)	0.3	0.8	0.7	1.6	2.1
Southeastern	0.2	0.7	1.1	2.5	1.3
Belorussia	0.9	1.7	2.3	4.0	4.0
Ukraine	0.5	1.4	2.0	3.7	3.7
'New Russia' (southern Ukraine)	0.6	1.4	1.7	2.6	2.5
TOTAL	1.4	2.7	3.0	5.3	6.0

SOURCE: B. N. Mironov, *Sotsial'naya istoriya Rossii perioda imperii (XVIII-nachalo XX v.)*, 2 vols. (St. Petersburg, 1999), 1:247.

only 3.8 million peasants, 4.7 percent of the rural population, were involved in migrant labor. His main conclusion was that, in spite of the increase in authorized labor migration, even by the early twentieth century the scale was "insignificant" outside the Central Non-Black region and Moscow and St. Petersburg provinces.[76]

One change that *was* significant was the increasing involvement of women in migrant labor. The numbers of women issued passports and passes in the first half of the nineteenth century were very small. In Yaroslavl' province in 1842–52, only 2.6 percent of all passports issued to peasants were for women. In the southern districts of Tambov province in 1856, only 7.3 percent of all passports and passes went to women.[77] The numbers remained low in some provinces, especially in the Central Black Earth region, but grew substantially in more industrialized provinces, in particular Moscow, Vladimir, and St. Petersburg, and also in southern Ukraine. By 1880–1913, around 20 to 30 percent of passports issued in some of these provinces went to women.[78] The growth of migrant labor among

TABLE 3
Urban Population Growth, 1811–1914
(Cities with over 200,000 Inhabitants in 1914)

City (region)	Population (000s) 1811	1863	1897	1914	Increase 1811–1914
St Petersburg (Northwest)	335.6	539.5	1264.9	2118.5	631%
Moscow (Cent. Non-Black Earth)	270.2	462.5	1038.6	1762.7	652%
Riga (Baltic)	32.0	60.0	282.2	558.0	1743%
Kiev (Ukraine)	23.3	68.4	247.7	520.5	2234%
Odessa (S. Ukraine)	11.0	119.0	403.8	499.5	4540%
Saratov(L. Volga)	26.7	84.4	137.1	235.3	881%
Ekaterinoslav (S. Ukraine)	8.6	19.9	112.8	211.1	2455%
Vil'no (Lithuania)	56.3	69.5	154.5	203.8	362%

SOURCE: A. G. Rashin, *Naselenie Rossii za 100 let: Statisticheskie ocherki* (Moscow, 1956), 89–91.

NOTE: Table excludes Russian Poland.

peasant women had a profound impact on their lives, making them more independent and better able to challenge the patriarchal village order. The women left behind in villages by male migrants experienced similar changes in their lives.[79]

Over the nineteenth and early twentieth centuries, growing numbers of migrant workers settled more or less permanently in the cities.[80] The urban population (including temporary migrants from the villages) of the Russian Empire grew rapidly in this period, roughly doubling in size over the first half of the nineteenth century.[81] In the 1850s, the number of urban inhabitants in the empire was around 9 million, 10 percent of the total population. By 1913, the number had almost tripled to 25 million, while the proportion had nearly doubled to 18 percent.[82] The populations of St. Petersburg and Moscow increased over sixfold from 1811 to 1914. Some smaller cities grew even more rapidly. Most dramatic was Odessa, which grew in population from 11,000 in 1811 to just under half a million by 1914.[83] (See Table 3.)

Most of the increases were due to migration from the villages, rather than natural increase.[84] It is difficult to gauge the numbers of peasants who abandoned their villages altogether, because the urban population of late imperial Russia was in constant flux. Streams of peasants were arriving while others were leaving.[85] Between 1858 and 1897, the numbers of peasants (defined by legal social estate [*soslovie*]) who lived in cities increased almost fivefold. Nearly half the urban population in 1897 were peasants. The proportion of peasant migrants was highest in the biggest cities. Over two-thirds of the inhabitants of Moscow and St. Petersburg in 1897 were incomers from the villages. At no point between 1881 and 1910, moreover, did people born in St. Petersburg total more than 32 percent of its population.[86] Studies of data from the 1897 general census and city censuses have shown that most migrants to St. Petersburg and Moscow came from the Northwest, Central Non-Black Earth, and the north of the Central Black Earth regions, where non-agricultural activities played an important part in the peasant economies, thus preparing them for some of the types of work they found in the capitals.[87]

At least as important as peasants who moved to towns and cities were the peasant migrants who settled permanently in outlying regions of the Russian Empire, in particular southern Ukraine, southeastern Russia, northern Kazakhstan, Siberia, and the Far East. In contrast to peasants who settled in cities, most migrants to the borderlands came from agricultural areas, especially the relatively densely populated Central Black Earth and Volga regions of Russia and Ukraine.[88] They sought more land in less heavily settled regions further afield in order to continue relying largely on agriculture. In some regions, for example the arid steppes in the southeast, migrants adapted or changed their agricultural practices. Migrants used different implements and sowed new crops, or raised livestock rather than growing cereals. Many migrants, however, chose to settle in regions with environmental conditions similar to those they had left. Peasants from the steppes of southern Ukraine and the lower Volga moved to similar steppe regions east of the Urals. Peasant migrants also encountered and interacted with various ethnic groups, with cultures and ways of life different from their own.[89]

Russian and Ukrainian peasant settlement of the southeastern steppes and Siberia can be traced back to the sixteenth century. It continued at a growing rate, with migrants traveling ever further from the heartlands of Russian and Ukrainian peasant residence, over the nineteenth and early twentieth centuries. The main trends in the scale and direction of migration by Russian peasants over the period under consideration can be shown by comparing the regional distribution of the peasant population of Russia over the nineteenth

TABLE 4

Male Peasant Settlement by Region in Russia, 1811–1897*

Zones/regions	Peasant population (thousands)		
	1811	1857	1897
Forest Zone			
Central Non-Black Earth	3,513	3,839	5,097
Northwest	808	888	1,897
North	484	626	910
N Urals	1,009	1,717	2,757
TOTAL	5,814	7,070	10,662
Steppe Zone			
Central Black Earth	3,304	4,160	5,778
Mid-Volga	1,315	1,802	2,626
Lower Volga and Don	602	1,183	2,751
S Urals	334	662	2,100
TOTAL	5,554	7,808	13,255
Siberia	600	1,114	1,949
TOTAL (RUSSIA)	11,968	15,991	25,866

SOURCE: Moon, "Peasant Migration," 863.

*Territory covered by 1st revision of poll tax census, 1719–21 and Don Cossack Territory. See D. Moon, "Peasant Migration and the Settlement of Russia's Frontiers 1550–1897," *HJ* 30 (1997): 865 n.8.

TABLE 5

Male Peasant Settlement by Region in Russia, 1811–1897*

Zones/regions	Percentage of peasant population		
	1811	1857	1897
Forest Zone			
Central Non-Black Earth	29.35	24.01	19.71
Northwest	6.75	5.55	7.34
North	4.04	3.91	3.52
N Urals	8.43	10.74	10.66
TOTAL	48.58	44.21	41.22
Steppe Zone			
Central Black Earth	27.60	26.01	22.34
Mid-Volga	10.98	11.27	10.15
Lower Volga and Don	5.03	7.40	10.64
S Urals	2.79	4.14	8.12
TOTAL	46.41	48.82	51.24
Siberia	5.02	6.97	7.54
TOTAL (RUSSIA)	100.00	100.00	100.00

SOURCE: Moon, "Peasant Migration," 864.

*Territory covered by first revision of poll tax census, 1719–21 and Don Cossack Territory. See Moon, "Peasant Migration," 865 n.8.

century on the basis of data from the revisions of the poll tax census in 1811 and 1857–58 and the general census of 1897. (See Tables 4 and 5.) There were substantial declines in the proportions of the total Russian peasant population of the Central Non-Black Earth and Black Earth regions, and significant increases in the proportions in the outlying steppe regions of the Lower Volga and Don, the North Caucasus and Southern Urals, and also in Siberia. Southern Ukraine experienced a large growth in its population as a result of migration from the more traditional areas of Ukrainian settlement to the north as well as Russia.[90]

The legal status of migrants varied. Throughout the servile period, official records contained countless cases of unauthorized migration, or "flight," by peasants, some of whom left for the borderlands.[91] The forebears of the last Soviet president, Mikhail Gorbachev, were peasants from Voronezh province in the Central Black Earth region who fled to the North Caucasus in the early nineteenth century.[92] Two examples illustrate the scale of peasant "flight." In 1838–46 officials recorded that 7,876 peasants had left Tambov province in the Central Black Earth region illegally. In Poltava province in Ukraine between 1840 and 1847, over 2,000 peasants were recorded as "fugitives." Unauthorized migration continued at an increased pace after 1861; in the early 1880s, officials estimated that 40,000 peasants a year were moving without authorization to outlying regions.[93]

Unauthorized migrants resorted to various expedients to get around the law. There was a healthy trade in forged passports, with which fugitive seigniorial peasants claimed they were state peasants or others who had permission to resettle. Fugitives exploited loopholes in the law, including the fact that if they concealed their names and origins they could not be sent home. On occasions, for example in the North Caucasus in the 1830s, the government allowed fugitives who claimed to have forgotten who they were and where they came from to settle. The ensuing flood of migrants prompted the swift reinstatement of severe punishments for fugitives who made such claims.[94] Even after the government began to promote migration to Siberia in the 1880s, many migrants moved without authorization. For example, following a temporary halt to government-authorized resettlement in western Siberia in 1892, large numbers of peasants simply crossed the Urals without authorization.[95]

On the other hand, considerable numbers of peasants migrated with official authorization. For this very reason, their numbers are easier to gauge. Between 1831 and 1866, around 320,000 state peasants took advantage of government-sponsored opportunities to move from areas where land was in relatively short supply to more outlying regions where there was less pressure on the land.[96] Detailed data are readily available for the scale of authorized peasant migration to Siberia in the late nineteenth and early twentieth centuries and for estimates of the numbers of unauthorized migrants and of the significant minority of migrants who returned home. The figures show both the growing pace of peasant migration in late imperial Russia and the importance of Siberia as a destination where land was still plentiful.[97]

In the late nineteenth century, in contrast to village communities in northern regions, most of which tried to prevent members leaving permanently for the cities, many communities in agricultural regions were prepared to allow some members to depart for outlying areas. In agricultural regions, the land that communities gained after the exodus of some members was more valuable than the contributions the migrants had made to their burdens of taxes, obligations, and redemption payments. Villages that had lost land as a result of the land settlement of 1861, but had experienced large (natural) increases in their population, were especially keen to encourage some members to leave.[98]

The reason for the population growth in the borderlands was only partly migration from central Russia and Ukraine. The available data do not permit exact figures, but it has been estimated that immigration accounted for around a third of the total population growth in the southern and eastern regions, while the rest was due to natural increase. Figures that are available on migration suggest that in the almost two centuries from the 1670s to 1860s, around six million people migrated to frontier regions throughout the empire. The pace of migration increased sharply from the 1870s. Between 1871 and 1897, 3.8 million people migrated to outlying regions, and between 1897 and 1916 a further 5 million.[99]

III

Interpretation

In order to reach general conclusions on the relationship between the abolition of serfdom in 1861, the subsequent reforms of the internal passport system, and the growth in peasant migration over the nineteenth and early twentieth centuries, it is necessary to consider general reasons behind migration and particular reasons related to the government's measures. In general, peasants migrated because of factors prompting them to leave their homes and factors attracting them to other places. Among the former were infertile land or shortages of good land relative to the population, high demands for taxes and obligations, harvest failures and other natural disasters. Some of these factors were present, to varying degrees and at particular times, in much of the central regions of Russia and Ukraine. The factors attracting peasants to other places included information about available fertile land and greater opportunities for wage labor. It has been claimed that peasants were susceptible to rumors about better conditions in "promised lands" on the frontiers.[100] However, such rumors were often based on fact. There was more, and more fertile, land in the southern and southeastern regions of the empire, and there were more opportunities for wage labor in the empire's peripheral agricultural regions and growing cities. Moreover, prior to 1861, serfdom was absent from many outlying regions, including Siberia, and throughout the period the government did periodically offer privileges, including tax exemptions, loans, and land, to migrants in certain borderlands. Additionally, peasants often sent out "scouts" to investigate conditions before setting off.[101]

Were there any changes in the degrees to which peasants experienced these general factors over the nineteenth and early twentieth centuries? The geographical distribution of soil fertility, with more fertile black earth in the steppe regions to the south and east, has already been described. There were some changes in soil fertility in parts of the Central Black Earth and Volga regions in the late nineteenth and early twentieth centuries: over-intensive and careless cultivation and over-grazing of land led to widespread soil erosion.[102] Peasants in some areas resorted to using the land in ways that damaged it because of "land hunger." Rapid population growth was

TABLE 6

The Population of the Russian Empire (Inside the Borders of the Late Nineteenth Century), 1795–1916/17

Census and Year	*Population (000s)*	*Ave. growth p.a. (%)*
5th revision* 1795	46,587	0.93
8th revision* 1834	66,731	0.79
10th revision* 1857/8	80,499	1.20
General census 1897	128,203	1.47
General census 1916/17	171,750	

SOURCE: S. I. Bruk and V. M. Kabuzan, "Dinamika chislennosti i rasselenie Russkogo etnosa (1678–1917 gg.)," *Sovetskaya etnografiya* no. 4 (1982), 14.

NOTE: Figures include all ethnic groups.

* of poll tax census

partly to blame. Taking the territory inside the borders of the late nineteenth century (that is, discounting territorial expansion), the total population of the empire grew from 46.6 million in 1795 to 171.8 million by 1916–17. The largest part of the increase occurred after 1858, and the rate accelerated again after 1897. (See Table 6.) Around 85 percent of the population were peasants.[103] By the early twentieth century, the most densely populated areas included the Central Black Earth and Mid-Volga regions of Russia, Ukraine, and Belorussia, in all of which agriculture was the main occupation. In almost all these areas, the number of people per square mile had at least doubled over the previous century, and in some cases it grew more quickly.[104]

While there is some correlation between the provinces with the highest population densities and those that were the main sources of migrants, migration was not the only response to population increase. Some peasants diversified their economies by engaging in non-agricultural activities without leaving their homes. In 1900, nearly three-quarters of all peasants involved in activities other than agriculture were involved locally.[105] Peasants also rented or bought more land.[106] Some peasants, moreover, made more intensive use of the land without causing excessive harm, for example, by growing potatoes and adopting more productive crop rotations.[107]

The connection between population densities and migration is further complicated by the fact that peasants also left less populated regions. There was migration from the Lower-Volga and Southern

Urals regions of southeastern Russia, which were experiencing population growth but were still sparsely inhabited compared with the central regions. Contemporary specialists argued that the important point was the farming systems peasants employed. While some peasants were prepared to change to more intensive systems, others were not. Some peasants in the southeastern regions, where extensive, long-fallow systems of cultivation were common, preferred to move to Siberia, where they could continue with their customary methods, rather than change to the more intensive systems used in the central regions.[108]

Many historians have argued that one of the reasons for the increase in peasant migration in the late nineteenth century was a "crisis" in peasant living standards, especially in the central regions, caused in part by population growth, "land hunger," and high taxes and obligations.[109] There are two problems with this argument. First, recent scholarship has greatly revised the notion that there was such a "crisis." Stephen Wheatcroft has argued that "crises" were limited to particular regions at certain times. Other historians have gone further in their re-interpretations.[110] Second, it is not sufficient to assert that poverty drove peasants to migrate. Poverty could be a barrier to migration as migrants required resources to transport their families and belongings as well as to set themselves up in their new homes. Migrants could not rely on the assistance that was sometimes available from the government. The question of whether "poor" or "middle" peasants predominated among migrants has been the subject of much debate. It seems that in the late nineteenth century, the majority of migrants were of middling prosperity, while in the early twentieth century, poor peasants began to prevail.[111]

Peasants also migrated from particular areas to escape harvest failures or other natural disasters.[112] Large parts of Russia, especially the Volga regions, were hit by famine and cholera in 1891–92.[113] The scale of the disasters caused a big increase in migration from the stricken areas.[114] Overall, however, famines and epidemics cannot be considered a cause of increased migration in the late nineteenth and early twentieth centuries, because the incidence of such disasters was declining, especially compared with the first half of the nineteenth century.[115]

An important factor attracting migrants to other places was growing opportunities for wage labor in the cities and peripheral agricultural regions. These opportunities grew further in the late nineteenth and early twentieth centuries as a result of the development of the economy and growing regional specialization. The availability of land in outlying regions was a further spur to migration. After the mid-nineteenth century, migration was greatly facilitated by the construction of a nationwide network of railroads. The total mileage of railroads in the Russian Empire increased from only 850 in 1855 to 48,000 by 1914.[116] One of the major achievements was the Trans-Siberian railroad, built between 1892 and 1904. Indeed, one of the motives for the construction of the railroad across the Urals was to assist the colonization of Siberia by peasants from the European part of the empire.[117] The advent of railroads made traveling, especially long distances, much easier and cheaper. For example, in 1890, it cost roughly 57 roubles for a family to travel from the Central Black Earth region to Tomsk in western Siberia. In 1900, a family of authorized migrants could make the same journey by train for a subsidized fare of only 14 roubles 70 copecks. There is little doubt that railroads contributed to the rapid growth in the numbers of migrants to Siberia from the mid-1890s. (See Table 6.)[118]

Did the abolition of serfdom of 1861 also play a role in the increase in peasant migration? The granting of personal freedom to almost half the peasant population in 1861 meant, at least in theory, that the former seigniorial peasants were no longer subject to the arbitrary whims of nobles. Moreover, the dues and obligations they owed for the use of their land were now set by law. As peasants gradually became aware of the new order, they gained confidence that they really were permitted to take more actions on their own initiative (subject to the control of their households and village communities). Very importantly, peasants realized that any extra income they earned was not liable to be taken away by the nobles. As a result, peasants were more prepared to seek additional earnings to spend on consumer goods. One of their main sources of income to spend on such goods was working as migrant laborers.[119]

The land settlement of 1861 also had an effect on migration. Many peasants lost part—around 20 percent in the Central Black Earth region—of the allotments that they had worked for themselves under serfdom. In addition, many nobles allocated poor land to the peasants in exchange for more fertile allotments. Many nobles, moreover, retained much of the meadow, pasture, and woodland on their estates so that they could charge the peasants for access.[120] Thus, the terms of the land reform of 1861 were one of the causes of the "land hunger" that was a factor behind migration.

Moreover, the dues the freed peasants had to pay for the use of their allotments during "temporary obligation" were higher per acre than they had been under serfdom. In the Northwestern region, the increase was around 16 percent, and in the Central Non-Black Earth region, over 10 percent.[121] A study carried out in the late 1870s demonstrated that peasants' incomes from their allotments in heavily populated regions were not adequate to meet the dues.[122] Thus, peasants needed to earn extra income. It was no accident that the reform increased peasants' dues substantially precisely in those more economically developed northern regions where peasants were able to earn more money, in particular as migrant laborers.[123]

A further way in which the abolition of serfdom served as an impetus to migrant wage labor involved the provisions to commute labor services to cash dues. Thus, many peasants who had worked on nobles' land under serfdom found themselves owing dues in cash. By 1881, only 15 percent of former seigniorial peasants who had worked for their owners under serfdom in the Central Black Earth region continued to do so.[124] Many peasants in this region had lost significant parts of their land after 1861, and opportunities to produce more crops for sale were reduced. Thus, one of the best ways for the peasants to earn the cash they now needed in greater quantities was to leave in search of wage labor. Many of those in the north of the region went to Moscow, and in the south they headed to the commercial grain-growing regions on the periphery.

Once peasants began to buy their land under the "redemption operation," however, the level of their dues fell by around 20 percent in the Central Black Earth region, though less elsewhere.[125] At around the same time, the abolition of the poll tax, which was paid mostly by peasants, and the switch to indirect taxes, to which the entire population was liable, seem to have reduced the burden of taxation on peasants who remained in the villages.[126] Nevertheless, the level of peasant migration, both temporary labor migration and permanent resettlement, was increasing at this very time, suggesting that levels of exploitation were not a major cause of the growth in migration.

The regional variations in the terms of the abolition of serfdom affected migration differently in different parts of the empire. Levels of migration were higher in parts of Ukraine than in neighboring Russian regions. One of the reasons for the difference may have been the preservation of communal land tenure and communal responsibility for taxes and dues in Russia, while in the Ukrainian provinces the reform maintained individual household tenure and individual responsibility for taxes and dues. (See section I.) Thus, Ukrainian peasants were subject to less pressure from their neighbors and communities to remain in their villages rather than seek work or more land elsewhere.[127]

Former state peasants were also more likely to migrate than former Russian seigniorial peasants. It has been argued that this tendency was due to the greater freedom of movement state peasants enjoyed.[128] However, all peasants were subject to similar legal restrictions on their movement after the reforms of the 1860s. (See above.) It is more likely that two other factors influenced state peasants' decisions. First, former state peasants were better off than peasants on nobles' land as a result of the reforms, which allotted them more land and required them to pay lower dues.[129] Thus the former state peasants had the resources to migrate successfully.[130] Moreover, state peasants might have sought to move because they feared that their economic position would be adversely affected by rapid population increase. In the Central Black Earth region in the 1860s–70s, the number of former state peasants grew twice as fast as the number of peasants on noble land.[131]

Finally, what impact did the changes in the law on internal passports and resettlement have on peasant migration? Peasants, of course, did not leave their homes only if they had authorization. Some idea of the scale of unauthorized migration can be gained from the figures on the regional distribution of the population in Table 5. The growth of the population in outlying regions, for example the Lower Volga and Don, Southern Urals, and Siberia, exceeded that due to natural increase and authorized migration and can be explained only by illegal migration. Substantial percentages of migrants to Siberia were not authorized. Several historians have argued that the numbers of migrants who did not have authorization exceeded those who did.[132]

In the case of both temporary labor migration and permanent migration for settlement, the data presented in this chapter suggest that the numbers were growing prior to changes in the law, for example the legislation of 1827 introducing passes and lowering the prices for documents, the changes that were part of the reforms of the 1860s, the new state settlement policy that began in the 1880s, the substantial reform of internal passports in 1894, and the law of 1906 granting peasants freedom of movement. The available data also suggest that the numbers of authorized migrants increased after all these measures. It could be argued that it was the changes in law that caused the increased migration. It could also be argued that the changes in the law were designed to regain control over existing increasing numbers of unauthorized migrants.

To take an example, the temporary rules on migration of 1881 followed a big increase in the numbers of unauthorized migrants over the preceding two decades. This increase had prompted the authorities to issue retrospective authorization to illegal settlers in the Southern Urals region in 1876. Growing numbers of peasants, moreover, sent petitions requesting permission to move. Around a thousand were received by the authorities between 1876 and 1881 alone.[133] It is possible that the increasing numbers of authorized migrants after 1881 and later laws were a result of more peasants seeking official permission to move, but who would have migrated anyway. This notion can be detected by reading between the lines of the memorandum presented by Witte and Durnovo to the State Council in 1893, arguing for the change in the internal passport law that was enacted the following year. The two ministers wrote: "Our passport legislation . . . in principle *does not conform to the actual conditions and needs of life* and . . . is in direct opposition to the good actions of the government, which at various times have been undertaken with the aim of freeing the labor of the people from unnecessary restrictions and to increase its productivity."[134] A much less veiled statement was made in 1914 by a specialist on migration, who argued that "the first legislative acts which permitted migration beyond the Urals in actual fact constituted merely a recognition of the existing phenomenon," and, in general, that "the history of migration legislation is the history of the development of irregular migration."[135]

The legislation on peasant movement and the abolition of serfdom was one factor among several that lay behind the considerable increase in free movement by members of the Russian Empire's rural population over the late nineteenth and early twentieth centuries. To some extent, the other causes of increased peasant migration considered earlier were sufficient to explain part or even all of the increase in the late nineteenth century. But it is perhaps most appropriate to see the growth in peasant migration over the whole period considered in this chapter as the result of the interaction between government attempts to regulate and direct peasant migration and the decisions and actions of millions of peasants.

REFERENCE MATTER

Abbreviations

AHR	*American Historical Review*
AMG	*Akty moskovskogo gosudarstva* (3 vols; St. Petersburg, 1890–1901)
ANSOM	Archives Nationals, Section Outre-Mer, Aix-en-Provence, France
FO	Great Britain, Foreign Office; archives in the Public Record Office, Kew, UK
HJ	*Historical Journal*
IO	India Office Archives, British Library, London
JAH	*Journal of American History*
JEH	*Journal of Economic History*
PP	Great Britain, Parliamentary Papers
PRP	*Pamiatniki russkogo prava* (8 vols., Moscow, 1952–61)
PSZ	*Polnoe sobranie zakonov Rossiiskoi imperii*, first series (45 vols; St. Petersburg, 1830); third series (33 vols. St. Petersburg, 1885–1916)
RZ	*Rossiiskoe zakonodatel'stvo X–XX vekov* (9 vols., Moscow, 1984–94)
SUPB	*Svod Ustavov Blagochiniya: Svod ustavov o pasportakh i beglykh*
SZ	*Svod zakonov Rossiiskoi Imperii* (15 vols., St. Petersburg, 1835–36)
WMQ	*William and Mary Quarterly*
ZhMVD	*Zhurnal Ministerstva Vnutrennikh Del*

Notes

INTRODUCTION

I thank William H. McNeill, Philip Morgan, Richard Davis, and all the contributors to this volume for comments on earlier versions of this introduction.

1. Heather Pringle, "Hints of Frequent Pre-Columbian Contacts," *Science* 288 (2000): 783–84. The earliest sea-borne contacts with China appear to have been by Arab, Persian, and Indian navigators and did not result in settlement. The first overseas Chinese settlements involving ocean voyages—in the Malay Peninsula and Sumatra—date from the early fourteenth century, though intermittent trading contacts go back to BCE. See Victor Purcell, *The Chinese in Southeast Asia* (London, 1965), 11–16; Wang Gungwu, "Merchants Without Empire: the Hokkinen Sojourning Communities," in James D. Tracy, ed., *The Rise of Merchant Empires: Long-Distance Trade in the Early Modern World, 1350–1750* (Cambridge, 1990), 400–421.

2. Cherchen man provides evidence of exchange between China and western Europe BCE (see Elizabeth Wayland Barber, *The Mummies of Urumchi* [London, 1999]). The plaid textiles on the mummies, interred in north-western China about 1000 BC, could only have been woven on European-style looms; the mummies themselves have large noses, fair hair, and round eyes, and some are six feet tall. These findings suggest that Chinese and European civilizations did not develop in isolation from each other. Yet it is a large jump to the argument that cultural contact and integration of the type made possible by ocean-borne trade existed in these early days.

3. Robin Law, "Ethnicity and the Slave Trade: 'Lucumi' and 'Nago' as ethonyms in West Africa," *History in Africa* 23 (1997): 1–16.

4. See chap. 5 below.

5. See <http://www.cilt.org.uk/commlangs/intro.htm>.

6. Peter Linebaugh and Marcus Rediker argue that a "multiethnic class . . . was essential to the rise of capitalism and the modern global economy" (*The Many-Headed Hydra: The Hidden History of the Revolutionary Atlantic* [London, 2000], 6–7).

7. Space constraints mean that Eastern Europe here is taken as Russia,

though it is clear that many other areas underwent a second serfdom. The classic article remains Jerome Blum, "The Rise of Serfdom in Eastern Europe," *AHR* 62 (1957): 807–36.

8. Philip D. Curtin, *Why People Move: Migration in African History* (Waco, TX, 1995), 42–44; and chap. 10 below.

9. For the dramatic impact of overseas migration on life expectancies, see chap. 3 below; for the east, see David Moon, "Peasant Migration and the Settlement of Russia's Frontiers 1550–1897," *HJ* 30 (1997): 859–93. One of the best larger views is still William H. McNeill, *Plagues and Peoples* (New York, 1976).

10. Theodore W. Schultz, "Migration: An Economist's Viewpoint," in William H. McNeill and Ruth S. Adams, eds., *Human Migrations: Patterns and Policies* (Bloomington, 1978), 377–86.

11. Kevin Bales, *Disposable People: New Slavery in the Global Economy* (Berkeley, 1999).

12. It might be argued that a third form of coercion was the raising of barriers against the entry of unwanted migrants—a form of control that re-emerged in the twentieth century as the main method that societies have of controlling migration (chap. 2 below). The Great Wall of China and Hadrian's Wall testify to the earlier prevalence of this method. A general relationship is suggested between, on the one hand, barriers to entry or barriers to departure, and on the other, the dominant migratory regime (slave trade or free migration) prevalent in the wider world.

13. Eric Jones, *The European Miracle*, 2d ed. (Cambridge, 1987), 70–84, referred to lands brought suddenly within European control as the ghost acreage.

14. There was no counterpart to this in the Americas despite a minor literature on whites captured and enslaved by aboriginals. However, it seems clear that Spanish conquest ended a significant traffic in slaves into the Aztec empire that drew on subject peoples in what is now northern Mexico.

15. Donald W. Treadgold, *The Great Siberian Migration: Government and Peasant in Resettlement from Emancipation to the First World War* (Princeton, NJ, 1957), 33, estimates 250,000 to Siberia between 1801 and 1850 alone. French and British governments transported 150,000 convicts out of Europe between 1607 and 1938. It is unlikely that the Spanish and Portuguese governments sent any more than this in the same period. Timothy J. Coates, in "Exiles and Orphans: Forced and State-Sponsored Colonizers in the Portuguese Empire, 1550–1720" (PhD diss., Univ. of Minnesota, 1993), 33, estimates a maximum of 28,000 degredados exiled between 1580 and 1720.

16. Calculated from Treadgold, *Siberian Migration*, 3, and David Eltis, "The Volume and Structure of the Transatlantic Slave Trade: A Reassessment," *WMQ* 58 (2001): 17–47.

17. Marianne S. Wokeck, *Trade in Strangers: The Beginnings of Mass Migration to North America* (University Park, PA, 1999), 86 has a low of

five pounds for the mid-eighteenth century. Steerage fares by the 1850s were three pounds. Farley Grubb, "The Long-Run Trend in the Value of European Immigrant Servants, 1654–1831: New Measurements and Interpretations," *Research in Economic History* 14 (1992): 184, argues for increasing fares between 1750 and 1825.

18. Alfred W. Crosby, *Ecological Imperialism: The Biological Expansion of Europe, 900–1900* (Cambridge, 1986), 2–3.

19. See chap. 9 below and John J. McCusker, *The Economy of British America, 1607–1789* (Chapel Hill, NC, 1985), 136, 172.

20. Thus children of convicts in New South Wales were born free, unlike the children of slaves. See David Neal, *Rule of Law in a Penal Colony: Law and Power in Early New South Wales* (Cambridge, 1991), 15, and for other comparisons of slave and convict status, see 34–41.

21. See chap. 6 below.

22. For the emergence of the rules of war in northwestern Europe—one manifestation of a growing sense of "Europeanness"—see Matthew Strickland, *War and Chivalry: The Conduct and Perception of War in England and Normandy, 1066–1217* (Cambridge, 1996), esp. 183–203 and 291–340.

23. For West Indian slaves sent to New South Wales as convicts see Barry W. Higman, *Slave Populations of the British Caribbean, 1807–1834* (Baltimore, 1984), 392; British Public Record Office, PC1/76, Pirie and Sons to Capper, Mar. 21, 1828 (enc.).

24. Roger P. Bartlett, *Human Capital: The Settlement of Foreigners in Russia, 1762–1804* (Cambridge, 1979), 15–56.

25. James Forsyth, *A History of the Peoples of Siberia* (Cambridge, 1992), 140–51, 185–89, 216–19.

26. See chap. 8 below.

27. See chap. 7 below.

28. Herbert S. Klein et al, "Transoceanic Mortality: The Slave Trade in Comparative Perspective," *WMQ* 58 (2001): 93–118, esp. 98–102, which shows there were parallel improvements in ocean-borne passenger traffic.

29. Robert Steinfeld, *The Invention of Free Labor: The Employment Relation in English and American Law and Culture, 1350–1870* (Chapel Hill, NC, 1991), 163–72.

30. Evsey D. Domar and Mark J. Machina, "On the Profitability of Russian Serfdom," *JEH* 44 (1984): 919–55.

31. Peter Kolchin, *Unfree Labor: American Slavery and Russian Serfdom* (Cambridge, MA, 1987), 368.

32. Paul R. Gregory, *Before Command: An Economic History of Russia From Emancipation to the First Five-Year Plan* (Princeton, NJ, 1994), 50–52.

33. See chap. 11 below.

34. See the literature on the spread southward of rice cultivation technology reviewed in Jones, *European Miracle*, 213–18.

35. Peter Clark and David Souden, "Introduction," in Clark and and Souden, eds. *Migration and Society in Early Modern England* (Totowa, NJ,

1988), 22. See also the essays by John Patten, Paul Slack, and Roger S. Schofield in that volume. For estimates of the sources of urban growth, see Jeffrey G. Williamson, *Coping with City Growth During the British Industrial Revolution* (Cambridge, 1990).

36. P. E. H. Hair, "Ethnolinguistic Continuity on the Guinea Coast," *Journal of African History* 8 (1967): 247–68. For African states in 1625 see John Thornton, *Africa and Africans in the Making of the Atlantic World* (Cambridge, 1998), x–xxxi.

37. Calculated from E. A. Wrigley and R. S. Schofield, *Population History of England, 1541–1871: A Reconstruction* (Cambridge, MA, 1981), 227, 574; S. L. Engerman and J. C. Das Neves, "The Bricks of an Empire: 585 Years of Portuguese Emigration," *Journal of European Economic History* 26 (1997): 478, 485.

38. For conflicting positions on the size of sub-Saharan populations and the impact of the slave trade on their rates of growth, see Patrick Manning, *Slavery and African Life: Occidental, Oriental and African Slave Trades* (Cambridge, 1990), 27–85; Joseph C. Miller, *Way of Death: Merchant Capitalism and the Angolan Slave Trade* (Madison, WI, 1988), 140–41; Joseph E. Inikori, "Introduction," in Joseph Inikori, ed., *Forced Migration: The Impact of the Export Slave Trade on African Export Societies* (New York, 1982), 19–38; and David Eltis, *Economic Growth and the Ending of the Transatlantic Slave Trade* (New York, 1987), 64–71. Slave departures from Africa, 1750–1850, are estimated at 7.1 million (Eltis, "Volume and Structure"), and an allowance of 1 million is made for all other slave departures—via the Indian Ocean and Sahara.

39. Hans Fenske, "International Migration: Germany in the Eighteenth Century," *Central European History* 13 (1980): 332–47; Georg Fertig, "Transatlantic Migration from the German Speaking Parts of Central Europe, 1600–1800: Proportions, Structures, Explanations," in Nicholas Canny, ed., *Europeans on the Move: Studies on European Migration, 1500–1800* (Oxford, 1994), 192–235.

40. See most recently, Anthony J. Barker, *Slavery and Antislavery in Mauritius, 1810–33* (Basingstoke, 1996) and Deryck Scarr, *Slaving and Slavery in the Indian Ocean* (New York, 1998).

41. Manning, *Slavery and African Life*, 79–85; Ralph A. Austen, "The Trans-Saharan Slave Trade: A Tentative Census," in Henry A. Gemery and Jan S. Hogendorn, eds., *The Uncommon Market: Essays in the Economic History of the Atlantic Slave Trade* (New York, 1979), 23–76; id., "The 19th Century Slave Trade from East Africa (Swahili and Red Sea Coasts): A Tentative Census," in W. G. Clarence-Smith, ed. *The Economics of the Indian Ocean Slave Trade in the Nineteenth Century* (London, 1989), 21–44.

42. Wokeck, *Trade in Strangers*, 42–47.

43. P. E. H. Hair, "The Enslavement of Koelle's Informants," *Journal of African History* 6 (1965): 193–203.

44. See chap. 4 below.

45. Isaiah Berlin, *The Proper Study of Mankind: An Anthology of Essays*, ed. Henry Hardy and Roger Hausheer (London, 1997), 191–242, but especially 239–40; Robert W. Fogel, *Without Consent or Contract: The Rise and Fall of American Slavery* (New York, 1989), 388–417.

46. Marianne Wokeck has found that for a short period in the mid-eighteenth century German migrants experienced person per ton ratios similar to that on slave vessels (Wokeck, *Trade in Strangers*, 79). On the other hand,even a century later a naval officer could describe a slave ship that he had just captured with 126 slave children on board in terms that no one could ever use for immigrant vessels: "this vessel measured as follows, Extreme length 36′ 6″, Extreme breadth 10′ 4″, Extreme depth of hold, 5′ 7″, and that . . . the height of the space . . . for the stowage of slaves was only one foot 2 inches, that one half were obliged always to lie on deck, where they were so confined that every foot of the deck was occupied, while the remainder below were squeezed to excess all the slaves being obliged to lay flat down, that there was no room whatever for the master and the crew who were obliged to live entirely on deck." (John Barrow to Foreign Office, sub enc. "Proceedings of Trial of 'Minerva'," British Public Record Office, FO84/441).

47. It would, of course, have been even more efficient (and the repeopling faster again) if the slave vessels had obtained their slaves in Europe rather than Africa, but given the cultural constraints that made this impossible, a slave trade from Africa was the next "best" possibility, and certainly brought over more labor than would have been available from Europe under an indentured/free migratory regime.

48. Gregory, *Before Command*, 37–52, 83; Treadgold, *Siberian Migration*, 239–40.

CHAPTER I

1. For a recent survey of the African context of migration see Philip D. Curtin, *Why People Move: Migration in African History* (Waco, TX, 1995), 42–44.

2. Large-scale military movements under the leadership of Genghis Khan or the attacks of the Huns on the Roman Empire provide the closest parallels.

3. Calculated from tables in the appendix. The African-European ratio is a revision of the figure that appears in David Eltis, "Free and Coerced Migrations," *AHR* 88 (1983): 251–80.

4. Robert J. Steinfeld, *The Invention of Free Labor: The Employment Relation in the English and American Law and Culture, 1350–1870* (Chapel Hill, NC, 1991) and "Changing Legal Conceptions of Free Labor," in Stanley L. Engerman, ed., *Terms of Labor* (Stanford, 1999), 137–67.

5. For this argument see David Eltis, *The Rise of African Slavery in the Americas* (Cambridge, 2000), 137–92.

6. B. H. Slicher van Bath, "The Absence of White Contract Labour in

Spanish America during the Colonial Period," in Pieter C. Emmer, ed., *Colonialism and Migration: Indentured Labour Before and After Slavery* (Dordrecht, 1986), 19–32. Ida Altman points to heavy representation of hidalgos, artisans, and professionals from two cities in southwestern Spain (Ida Altman, "A New World in the Old: Local Society and Spanish Emigration to the Indies," in Ida Altman and James Horn, eds., *'To Make America': European Emigration in the Early Modern Period* (Berkeley, 1991), 39–40, 43–47). For the volume and geography see Magnus Morner, "Immigration into Latin America, Especially Argentina and Chile," in P. C. Emmer and M. Mörner, eds., *European Expansion and Migration: Essays on the Intercontinental Migration from Africa, Asia, and Europe* (New York, 1992), 211–43; Peter Boyd-Bowman, *Patterns of Spanish Emigration to the New World (1493–1580)* (Buffalo, NY, 1973); S. L. Engerman and J. C. Das Neves, "The Bricks of an Empire: 585 Years of Portuguese Emigration," *Journal of European Economic History* 26 (1997): 471–510.

7. Nicolás Sanchez-Albornoz, *The Population of Latin America*, trans. W. A. R. Richardson (Berkeley, 1974), 86–112. The Brazilian population, however, has yet to reverse this decline. See John Hemming, *Red Gold: The Conquest of Brazilian Indians* (London, 1978), 487–501.

8. Stuart Schwartz, *Sugar Plantations in the Formation of Brazilian Society* (Cambridge, 1985); Eltis, *Rise of African Slavery*, 193–223.

9. David Eltis, "The Slave Economies of the Caribbean: Structure, Performance, Evolution and Significance," in Franklin W. Knight, ed., *The UNESCO General History of the Caribbean* 3 (Kingston, Jamaica, 1997): 114.

10. Douglass North's explanation for falling transatlantic freights prior to the mid-nineteenth century—the fall in the incidence of piracy and the attendant drop in crew-per ton ratios—has been questioned. But perhaps there is a case to be made for applying it to sixteenth- and seventeenth-century transatlantic commerce. Piracy was certainly a key cost-raising factor before 1750, but at some point in the mid-seventeenth century it became feasible to set off for the Americas (and Africa) in a single vessel (albeit heavily armed) as opposed to a flotilla. Convoys became a strategy reserved for wars long before 1700, whereas before say 1630 they were the normal way of organizing transatlantic shipping in both peace and war time.

11. Ian K. Steele, *The English Atlantic, 1675–1740: An Exploration of Communication and Community* (Oxford, 1986); and Kenneth J. Banks, *Communications and Imperial Absolutism in the French Atlantic, 1713–1763* (Montreal, forthcoming). For interpretations of the African contribution see Eltis, *Rise of African Slavery*, 137–92; and for the rapidly increasing literature on the black Atlantic see Ira Berlin, *Many Thousands Gone: The First Two Centuries of Slavery in North America* (Cambridge, MA, 1998), esp. 29–63.

12. Mary Stoughton Locke, *Anti-Slavery in America* (Boston, 1901, repr. 1968), 9–12 and more recently Betty Wood, *Slavery in Colonial*

Georgia, 1730–1775 (Athens, GA, 1984), 1–73. In the sixteenth century, the Spanish and later the Portuguese restricted the enslavement of Indians, but this was not the same as a prohibition against all slavery.

13. For a fuller elaboration of these points see Seymour Drescher, "White Atlantic? The Choice for African Slave Labor in the Plantation Americas," in David Eltis et al., *Slavery in the Americas: Reinterpretations* (Cambridge, forthcoming). The inference that Drescher draws is, however, the opposite to the one drawn here.

14. For the African situation see Paul Hair, "Ethnolinguistic Continuity on the Guinea Coast," *Journal of African History* 8 (1967): 247–68. For the English case see Peter Linebaugh, *The London Hanged: Crime and Civil Society in the Eighteenth Century* (London, 1991).

15. For long-run trends in slave prices, see David Eltis and David Richardson, "Markets for Slaves Newly Arrived in the Americas: Price Patterns, 1673–1865," in Eltis et al., eds., *Slavery in the Americas*.

16. Personal communication from Timothy Coates, June 10, 2001.

17. The best discussion of the origins of the system is David Galenson, *White Servitude in Colonial America: An Economic Analysis* (Cambridge, 1981), 3–15.

18. Russell R. Menard, "From Servants to Slaves: The Transformation of the Chesapeake Labor System," *Southern Studies* 16 (Winter 1977): 355–90; David Galenson, "The Rise and Fall of Indentured Servitude in the Americas: An Economic Analysis," *JEH* 44 (1984): 1–26.

19. Charlotte Erickson, "Why did Contract Labour Not Work in the Nineteenth Century United States," in Shula Marks and Peter Richardson, eds., *International Labour Migrations: Historical Perspectives* (Hounslow, 1984), 34–56; Farley Grubb, "The End of European Immigrant Servitude in the United States: An Economic Analysis of Market Collapse, 1775–1835," *JEH* 54 (1994): 794–825; Steinfeld, *Invention of Free Labor*, 163–72.

20. This paragraph is based on Eltis, *Rise of African Slavery*, 85–113, and C. R. Boxer, *Women in Iberian Expansion Overseas, 1415–1815* (New York, 1975).

21. This and the following paragraphs are based on David Eltis et al., *The Transatlantic Slave Trade: A Database on CD-ROM* (Cambridge, 1999). See in particular the introduction.

22. See R. A. Easterlin, "Influences in European Overseas Emigration Before World War I," *Economic Development and Cultural Change* 9 (1961): 331–51; and J. D. Gould, "European Inter-Continental Migration: The Role of 'Diffusion' and 'Feedback'," *Journal of European Economic History* 9 (1980): 267–315, for a description of this process.

23. For a fuller discussion of this see David Eltis, "The Volume and Structure of the Transatlantic Slave Trade: A Reassessment," *WMQ* 58 (2001): 17–47.

24. Stephen D. Behrendt and David Eltis, "Competition, Market Power, and the Impact of Abolition on the Transatlantic Slave Trade: Connec-

tions between Africa and the Americas," unpublished paper presented at the American Historical Association, annual conference (New York, 1997).

25. S. D. Behrendt et al., "The Costs of Coercion: African Agency in the History of the Atlantic World," *Economic History Review* 54 (2001).

26. Herbert S. Klein et al., "Transoceanic Mortality: The Slave Trade in Comparative Perspective," *WMQ* 58 (2001): 93–118.

27. Marianne S. Wokeck, *Trade in Strangers: The Beginnings of Mass Migration to North America* (University Park, PA, 1999), 55–56, 214–15.

28. See the literature summarized in John J. McCusker and Russell R. Menard, *The Economy of British America, 1607–1789* (Chapel Hill, NC, 1985), 227–35, and since then, Trevor Burnard, "European Migration to Jamaica, 1655–1780," *WMQ* 53 (1996): 769–98, and "A Failed Settler Society: Marriage and Demographic Failure in Early Jamaica," *Journal of Social History* 28 (1996): 63–82; B. W. Higman, *Slave Populations of the British Caribbean, 1807–1834* (Baltimore, 1984), 377–78.

29. Robert W. Fogel, *Without Consent or Contract: The Rise and Fall of American Slavery* (New York, 1989), 114–53.

30. Ibid., 138–42; Higman, *Slave Populations*, 280–89; David Eltis, "Nutritional Trends in Africa and the Americas, 1819–1839," *Journal of Interdisciplinary History* 12 (1982): 453–75.

31. This paragraph is based on Eltis, *Rise of African Slavery*, 224–44.

32. Michael Gomez, *Exchanging Our Country Marks: The Transformation of African Identities in the Colonial and Antebellum South* (Chapel Hill, NC, 1998).

33. "The laws of migration," *Journal of the Statistical Society* 48 (1885): 167–227; and 52 (1889): 214–391. See, inter alia, Everett S. Lee's evaluation of these in "A Theory of Migration," *Demography* 3 (1966): 47–57.

34. For a convenient summary see William H. McNeill, "Human Migration: A Historical Overview," in William H. McNeill and Ruth S. Adams, eds., *Human Migrations: Patterns and Policies* (Bloomington, IN, 1978), 7–9.

35. Robin Law, "Ethnicity and the Slave Trade: 'Lucumi' and 'Nago' as Ethnonyms in West Africa," *History in Africa* 24 (1997): 205–19.

36. Eltis, *Rise of African Slavery*, 9–11; id., "Atlantic History in Global Perspective," *Itinerario: A Journal of European Overseas Expansion* 23 (1999): 141–61.

37. Russell R. Menard, "Migration, Ethnicity, and the Rise of an Atlantic Economy: The Repeopling of British America, 1600–1700," in Rudolph J. Vecoli and Suzanne M. Sinke, eds., *A Century of European Migrations, 1830–1930* (Urbana, IL, 1991), relies more on the demographic approach and thus captures net migration. Aaron S. Fogleman, "From Slaves, Convicts, and Servants to Free Passengers: The Transformation of Immigration in the Era of the American Revolution," *JAH* 85 (1998): 43–76, generally prefers counts of migrants and at times combines net and gross migra-

tion estimates. For the most recent and refined estimates for British North America, see James Horn and Philip D. Morgan, "Settlers and Slaves: European and African Migrations to Early Modern British America," in Elizabeth Mancke and Carole Shammas, eds., *The Creation of the British Atlantic World* (Baltimore, forthcoming).

38. Developed in Henry A. Gemery, "Emigration from the British Isles to the New World, 1630–1700: Inferences from Colonial Populations," *Research in Economic History* 5 (1980): 179–232; Galenson, *White Servitude*, app. H.

39. Voyage mortality from Europe is set at 3 percent for the seventeenth and eighteenth centuries and 2 percent for the nineteenth. Mortality for free migrants and indentured servants is assumed to have been the same. Data for prisoners, convicts, and slaves is normally derived for those departing rather than those arriving so that a mortality adjustment is unnecessary.

40. Eltis et al., *The Transatlantic Slave Trade*; for detailed derivations see Eltis, "The Volume and Direction of the Transatlantic Slave Trade," 17–46, though some additional data have been added since the publication of this essay.

41. Including the 111,211 German immigrants to the Americas before 1776 charted by Marianne Wokeck, *Trade in Strangers: The Beginnings of Mass Migration to North America* (University Park, PA, 1999), 45–46, 240–76.

42. "European Immigration to North America, 1700–1820: Numbers and Quasi-Numbers," *Perspectives in American History* 1 (1984): 315. Panel B in the table totals 419,600 (not the 428,600 shown in the table), which divided by 0.97 to accommodate shipboard mortality, yields 433,000.

43. The most recent attempt to assess migration to the British North American mainland, Fogleman, "From Slaves, Convicts, and Servants to Free Passengers," has used the more traditional approach of counting national groups of migrants. Fogleman does not engage with the specifics of the demographic issues so it is difficult to evaluate his own estimates of 273,000 gross arrivals relative to Gemery's estimates of net migration, which are preferred here.

44. Hubert Charbonneau et al., "The Population of the St. Lawrence Valley, 1608–1760," in Michael R. Haines and Richard H. Steckel, eds., *A Population History of North America* (Cambridge, 2000), 108.

45. Ibid., 106; for voyage mortality see 111; Peter Moogk, "Manon Lascaut's Countrymen: Emigration to France from North America before 1763," in Nicholas Canny, ed., *Europeans on the Move: Studies on European Migration, 1500–1800* (Oxford, 1994), 253–54.

46. Ibid., 255.

47. Vitorino Magalhaes-Godinho, "L'émigration portuguaise du XVéme

siècle á nos jours: Histoire d'une constante structurale," in *Conjoncture économique-structures sociale: Hommage à Ernest Labrousse* (Paris, 1974), 254–55. This subsequently appeared with small changes as "L'Émigration Portuguaises XV–XX siécles—une constante structurale et les résponses aux changements du monde," *Revista de História Económica e Social* 1 (1978); and as "Portuguese Emigration from the Fifteenth to the Twentieth Century: Constants and Changes," in Pieter C. Emmer and Magnus Mörner, eds., *European Expansion and Migration* (New York, 1992), 13–45. See, more recently, the survey in Stanley L. Engerman and João Cesar das Nevas, "The Bricks of Empire, 1415–1999: 585 Years of Portuguese Emigration," *Journal of European History* 26 (1997): 471–510.

48. Magalhaes-Godinho, "L'émigration portuguaise," 256.

49. See, for example, Nicolás Sánchez-Albornoz, *The Population of Latin America: A History*, trans. W. A. R. Richardson (Berkeley, 1974), 124–25. For a survey of population estimates and vital rates in Latin America in this period that suggests a very modest role for immigration, see 86–129.

50. See the literature cited by Robert Louis Stein, "The Free Men of Colour and the Revolution of St. Domingue, 1789–1792," in *Histoire Sociale/Social History* 14 (1981): 2–4.

51. Peter D. McClelland and Richard J. Zeckhauser, *Demographic Dimensions of the New Republic: American Interregional Migration, Vital Statistics, and Manumissions, 1800–1860* (Cambridge, 1982), 113.

52. Slicher van Bath, "The Absence of White Contract Labour in Spanish America during the Colonial Period," 19–32. Many Portuguese migrants went to Spanish America. These are included in the Portuguese estimates rather than in the Spanish estimates in panels 1 to 3 of table 1.

53. Galenson, *White Servitude*, 11–12.

54. Menard, "British Migration to the Chesapeake," 121.

55. See the discussion in Fogleman, "From Slaves, Convicts, and Servants to Free Passengers," 67–68, based on the work of Richard S. Dunn and Virginia DeJohn Anderson which is accepted here.

56. Russell R. Menard, "British Migration to the Chesapeake Colonies in the Seventeenth Century," in Philip D. Morgan et al., eds., *Colonial Chesapeake Society* (Chapel Hill, NC, 1988), 121; James Horn, "'To parts beyond the Seas': Free Emigration to the Chesapeake in the Seventeenth Century," in Altman and Horn, eds., *"To make America,"* 90–91. The ratio is calculated from David Eltis and Ingrid Stott, "Coldham's Emigrants from England, 1640–1699: A Database" (unpub. but available from the author). The major source of Coldham's data is the record of registrations of indentured servants at Bristol on which historians have already drawn, but other sources containing data on both servant and non-servant migrants contribute over half the Coldham sample. The compilation from Coldham's work thus offers much new data. See Peter Wilson Coldham, *The Complete Book of Emigrants, 1607–1660* (Baltimore, 1988), and *The*

Complete Book of Emigrants, 1661–1699 (Baltimore, 1990). For discussion of the data—particularly their representativeness in the light of various published estimates of transatlantic migration in the seventeenth century English Atlantic—see Ingrid Stott, "Emigration from England, 1640–1680" (MA thesis, Dept. of History, Queen's Univ., 1993).

57. Calculated from Eltis and Stott, "Coldham's Emigrants from England."

58. Moogk, "Manon Lascaut's Countrymen," based on the work of Gabriel Debien and Christian Huertz de Lemps.

59. Boogart, "The Servant Migration to New Netherland, 1624–1664," in Emmer, *Colonialism and Migration*, 61.

60. Wokeck, *Trade in Strangers*, 177–78, 233. The ratio of one-third for German-speaking migrants derives from taking one half of arrivals 1751–60 and one-quarter of arrivals before 1751, and expressing the sum as a share of total German migration.

61. Of the 226,000 migrants on British vessels, an estimated 96,000 were German speaking, 35,000 were Irish, and 95,000 were English, Welsh, and Scottish. A weighted average of 0.333, 0.67 and 0.6 for German, Irish, and British respectively, yields an overall servant ratio of 0.5.

62. Farley Grubb, "The End of European Immigrant Servitude in the United States," 818–19. Overall ratio computed from app. table 1.

63. For 1761–76, 14,612 from Wokeck, *Trade in Strangers*, 45–46; for 1776–1819, 34,700 from Fogleman, "From Slaves, Convicts, and Servants," 74–76, based on the work of Rodney Attwood and Hans-Jurgen Grabbe.

64. See the discussion in Steinfeld, *Invention of Free Labor*, 122–52.

65. As Fogleman assumes was the case ("From Slaves, Convicts, and Servants," 73–74). Marianne Wokeck, *Trade in Strangers*, 188, 213, records a sharp drop in the Irish servant share of immigration to the Delaware valley in the course of the eighteenth century—to one quarter in the 1770s.

66. B. W. Higman, "The Chinese in Trinidad, 1806–1838," *Caribbean Studies* 12 (1972): 21–44.

67. David Northrup, *Indentured Labor in the Age of Imperialism* (Cambridge, 1995), 154–55.

68. A recent example of this genre is Peter Wilson Coldham, *Emigrants in Chains: A Social History of Forced Emigration to the Americas of Felons, Destitute Children, Political and Religious Non-Conformists, Vagabonds, Beggars and Other Undesirables* (Baltimore, 1992).

69. Fogleman estimates 2,300 for the seventeenth century English North American mainland alone ("From Slaves, Convicts, and Servants," 68).

70. Timothy Joel Coates, *Convicts and Orphans: Forced and State-Sponsored Colonization in the Portuguese Empire, 1550–1755* (Stanford, 2001), and personal communications, June 6 and 9, 2001. It should be

noted that if in the early French records it is sometimes difficult to distinguish between engagé and convict, in the early Iberian world the hard distinction is more often between degredado and volunteer soldier.

71. Peter Boyd-Bowman, "Patterns of Spanish Emigration to the Indies until 1600," *Hispanic-American Historical Review* 56 (1976): 580–604; Ruth Pike, *Penal Servitude in Early Modern Spain* (Madison, WI, 1983), 3–26.

72. For early transportation see John M. Beattie, *Crime and the Courts in England, 1660–1800* (Princeton, 1986), 470–83.

73. Eltis and Stott, "Coldham's Emigrants from England."

74. Fogleman, "From Slaves, Convicts, and Servants," 68. Abbot Emerson Smith, "The Transportation of Convicts to the American Colonies in the Seventeenth Century," *AHR* 39 (1933–34): 238, counted 4,451 between 1655 and 1688. See Andrea Button, "Commodities of the State: The Trade in Convict Labour to the West Indies During the Interregnum," *Australian Humanities Review*, forthcoming, for background material that supports these larger estimates.

75. Charles Frostin, "Du Peuplement pénal de l'Amérique française aux XVIIe et XVIIIe siècles: hésitations et contradictions du pouvoir royal en matière de déportation," *Annales de Bretagne* 85 (1978): 67–94.

76. Fogleman, "From Slaves, Convicts, and Servants," 71. This figure constitutes a slightly adjusted total derived from A. Roger Ekirch, *Bound for America: The Transportation of British Convicts to the Colonies, 1718–1775* (Oxford, 1987), 21–27.

77. This ratio is calculated from the figure in Ekirch, *Bound for America*, 23, which presents data for London and the Home Counties only. The ratio is then applied to the aggregate for Great Britain and Ireland.

78. Charbonneau et al., "The Population of the St. Lawrence Valley, 1608–1760," 108, 110; Glenn R. Conrad, ed., *Immigration and War, Louisiana, 1718–21* (Lafayette, LA, 1970), 51; id., "Emigration Forcée: A French Attempt to Populate Louisiana, 1716–1720," in *Proceedings of the French Colonial Historical Society* (Washington, DC, 1979), 57–66.

79. Charles Frostin, *Les révoltes blanches à Saint-Domingue aux XVIIe et XVIIIe siècles (Haiti avant 1789)* (Paris, 1975), 166–265.

80. See chap. 9.

CHAPTER 2

For useful comments and discussion, I should like to thank Michael Les Benedict, Seymour Drescher, Robert Steinfeld, and John Thompson in addition to the conference participants and the editor of the volume.

1. There is obviously extensive literature on migration and its legal and economic aspects. Particularly useful for the discussions in this chapter have been Richard Plender, *International Migration Law* (Leiden, 1972); J. M. Evans, *Immigration Law* (London, 1976); E. P. Hutchinson, *Legislative History of American Immigration Policy, 1798–1965* (Philadelphia,

1981); Alan Dowty, *Closed Borders: The Contemporary Assault on Freedom of Movement* (New Haven, CT, 1987); John Torpey, *The Invention of the Passport: Surveillance, Citizenship and the State* (Cambridge, 2000); Robin Cohen, ed., *The Cambridge Survey of World Migration* (Cambridge, 1995); Imre Ferenczi and Walter F. Willcox, *International Migrations*, 2 vols. (New York, 1929, 1931); Maurice R. Davie, *World Immigration: With Special Reference to the United States* (New York, 1936); J. W. Brown, *World Migration and Labour* (Amsterdam, 1926); Philip Taylor, *The Distant Magnet: European Emigration to the U.S.A.* (New York, 1971); Saskia Sassen, *Guests and Aliens* (New York, 1999); George J. Borjas, *Heaven's Door: Immigration Policy and the American Economy* (Princeton, NJ, 1999); Nicholas Canny, ed., *Europeans on the Move: Studies on European Migration, 1500–1800* (Oxford, 1994); P. C. Emmer and M. Mörner, eds., *European Expansion and Migration: Essays on the Intercontinental Migration from Africa, Asia, and Europe* (New York, 1992); Ida Altman and James Horn, eds., *"To Make America": European Emigration in the Early Modern Period* (Berkeley, 1991); Leslie Page Moch, *Moving Europeans: Migration in Western Europe Since 1650* (Bloomington, IN, 1992).

2. See Henri Pirenne, *Medieval Cities* (Princeton, NJ, 1925), and Henri Pirenne, *Early Democracies in the Low Countries: Urban Society and Political Conflict in the Middle Ages and the Renaissance* (New York, 1971).

3. Distinctions between internal and external migrations, particularly in regard to colonial empires with their commonwealths and territories, are often complex. In some cases the colonies were treated as extensions of the metropolis in that free mobility was permitted, while in others they were regarded as foreign areas, with migration restricted. In the case of the granting of independence to the Philippine Islands by the United States, one important factor was the desire to limit in-migration to the US, made possible by the independence of the Philippines, which could then be subject to quotas. See Bill Ong Hing, *Making and Remaking Asian America Through Immigration Policy 1850–1990* (Stanford, 1993), as well as Hutchinson, *Legislative History*. For the British treatment of commonwealth migration in the twentieth century, see Colin Holmes, *John Bull's Island: Immigration and British Society, 1871–1971* (London, 1988).

4. A rather dramatic example of such interdependence is seen in the United States in the twentieth century, where the decline of European immigration, due to World War I and the subsequent restrictive legislation, led to a movement of blacks from the south to northern states. In the mid-nineteenth century Brazil's slave population relocated from north to south, not generally by the direct migration of slaves, but by redirection of the ongoing international slave trade from northern to southern Brazil. US slave redistribution in the nineteenth century, on the other hand, required direct interregional movement. See US Bureau of the Census, *Historical Statistics of the United States, Colonial Times to 1970* (Washington,

1975), and David Eltis, *Economic Growth and the Ending of the Transatlantic Slave Trade* (New York, 1987).

5. See Robert A. Huttenback, *Racism and Empire: White Settlers and Colored Immigrants in the British Self-Governing Colonies, 1830–1910* (Ithaca, NY, 1976). and Hing, *Making and Remaking.*

6. The benefits and costs of immigration are influenced by policies changing the immediate costs of migrating as well as those that affect the expected long-run gains of the migrant after arrival. The concern of this chapter is individual, family, or group migration for purposes of settlement, rather than organized group colonization, which usually implies, in addition, capital flow and land ownership. Nevertheless, some of the same basic principles will generally apply to both forms of movement. Subsidies were provided, at times, to individual settlers, as well as for group settlements.

7. There were earlier cases in which the composition of the immigration and the resident population was an important consideration, but these often reflected religious issues. Both England and France expelled Jews in the Middle Ages. The French also expelled gypsies and Huguenots, and other nations limited Jews. The immigration debates in England and the United States at the start of the twentieth century were basically started by Jewish inflows from Russia and England. See W. Cunningham, *Alien Immigrants to England*, 2d ed. (London, 1969); Jon Butler, *The Huguenots in America: A Refugee People in New World Society* (Cambridge, MA, 1992); Stephen Castles and Mark J. Miller, *The Age of Migration: International Population Movements in the Modern World* (New York, 1993); and Great Britain, House of Commons, *Royal Commission on Alien Immigration Report* (London, 1903).

8. Thus it is quite probable that an extension of voting rights to the working classes led to more extensive attempts to restrict immigration than when that decision had been made primarily by businessmen and ruling elites. These groups also had their own reasons to be against immigration on social and cultural, if not economic, grounds. For an analysis of changing US immigration policy, see Claudia Goldin, "The Political Economy of Immigration Restriction in the United States, 1890–1921," in Claudia Goldin and Gary D. Libecap, eds., *The Regulated Economy: A Historical Approach to Political Economy* (Chicago, 1994).

9. Views as to prospective economic change, population growth, and resource and technology discoveries (whether or not they are exogenously introduced or were themselves influenced by population levels) influence policy discussions and these are frequently debated, but not often agreed upon, questions. It is argued, for example, that the shifting nature of migration restrictions from the nineteenth to the twentieth centuries reflects the change from a belief in national underpopulation, which made less emigration and more immigration desired, to the presumption of Malthusian overpopulation, making emigration desirable and immigration less desired. For a discussion of the economic effects of immigration,

see Julian L. Simon, *The Economic Consequences of Immigration* (Oxford, 1989).

10. Net marginal product is gross marginal product less "necessary" consumption, presumably at subsistence levels. Gross national output could be the nation's goal if there was support for those producing less than subsistence provided by those with surplus incomes. The desired population would be larger in this case than if the concern was with maximizing net product with a better ability to meet military needs.

11. Even in the nineteenth century emigration was restricted for those of military age or those who had not yet undertaken military service. Soldiers were often migrants attracted from elsewhere for specified time periods or, as in case of the Swiss, as permanent out-migrants. For one example, see John McGurk, "Wild Geese: The Irish in European Armies (Sixteenth to Eighteenth Centuries)," in Patrick O'Sullivan, ed. *The Irish World Wide: History, Heritage, Identity*, vol. 1, *Patterns of Migration* (Leicester, 1992), 36–62.

12. For a discussion of relations between foreign policy and immigration policy, see Michael S. Teitelbaum and Myron Weiner, eds., *Threatened Peoples, Threatened Borders: World Migration and U.S. Policy* (New York, 1995).

13. See Francis A. Walker, "Immigration and Degradation," *Forum* 11 (1891): 637–44; and for later discussions see William Peterson, *Population*, 3d ed. (New York, 1975) 284–85; Ferenczi and Willcox, *Migration* 2:93–103; and Richard A. Easterlin, *Population, Labor Force, and Long Swings in Economic Growth* (New York, 1968), 77–110.

14. See Thomas Robert Malthus, *An Essay on the Principle of Population*, 2d ed. (London, 1803). For discussions of this episode, see Patricia James, *Population Malthus: His Life and Times* (London, 1979); and B. W. Higman, "Slavery and the Development of Demographic Theory in the Age of the Industrial Revolution," in James Walvin, ed., *Slavery and British Society, 1776–1846* (London, 1982), 164–94.

15. For a rather explicit evaluation of the costs of the "White Australia" policy ending the use of Kanaka contract labor in the production of sugar, and substituting for them white producers operating with tariff protection and bounty payments, see the remarks in the Australian Royal Commission Report on the Sugar Industry in 1912. They commented:

> A white community which prefers to grow its own sugar in its territory with white labor, rather than purchase from abroad sugar grown by cheap coloured labor, must face the responsibility of making good the increased cost of production under the higher standard of living and reward. Either the consumer or the taxpayer must pay. In Australia . . . the cost is paid by the consumer.

The controls on cane sugar laborers also meant that encouragement was given to the beet sugar industry in Victoria. See Parliament of the Commonwealth of Australia, *Report of the Royal Commission on the Su-*

gar Industry (1912). For discussions, see also A. T. Yarwood, *Asian Migration to Australia: The Background to Exclusion, 1896–1923* (Melbourne, 1964).

16. For early arguments, see Usselinx on Delaware (1624) and the British Privy Council (1596). See also Mary Staughton Locke, *Anti-Slavery in America: From the Introduction of African Slaves to the Prohibition of the Slave Trade (1619–1808)* (Boston, 1901); Joseph J. Mickley, "Some Account of William Usselinx and Peter Minuit," in *Papers of the Historical Society of Delaware* 3 (1881): 5–26; and *Acts of the Privy Council of England*, n.s. 26, A.D. 1596–97 (London, 1902). A related example is the initial post-emancipation constitution of Haiti, which aimed at restricting the entry of whites by not allowing them to either own or rent land.

17. Thus "White Australia" was introduced when non-whites (other than aborigines) were less than 2 percent of the Australian population. Since over 90 percent were male, the future national increase of this population was constrained. Chinese exclusion from the US was primarily a state matter. The Chinese were less than 1 percent of the US population in 1880, but an obviously larger share of California's population (8.6 percent) and labor force.

18. For a pre-World War II discussion of the refugee problem, see Sir John Hope Simpson, *The Refugee Problem: Report of a Survey* (London, 1939). From its initially strict political definition, the grounds for asylum have been expanded to include spousal abuse, female genital mutilation, and related activities.

19. For discussions of the reasons for limiting emigration, see Charles Emil Stangeland, *Pre-Malthusian Doctrines of Population: A Study in the History of Economy Theory* (New York, 1966; first pub. 1904); Joseph J. Spengler, *French Predecessors of Malthus: A Study in Eighteenth Century Wage and Population Theory* (Durham, NC, 1942); and E. P. Hutchinson, *The Population Debate: The Development of Conflicting Theories up to 1900* (Boston, 1967).

20. In the past, as at present, some limitations on emigration are based on working conditions for the migrants. This action reflects the continued concerns of the metropolis with its native population. Regulation of outflows of indentured labor by China led to the ending of this movement to Cuba and elsewhere in the Caribbean; in another example, Italy closed emigration to Brazil in 1902 because of the presumed terrible working conditions. On the ending of Chinese migration to Cuba, see Denise Helly, ed., *The Cuba Commission Report: A Hidden History of the Chinese in Cuba, The Original English Language Text of 1876* (Baltimore, 1993).

21. For references to the legal ending of emigration restrictions in Europe and discussions of emigration policy, see among many sources: Mack Walker, *Germany and the Emigration, 1816–1885* (Cambridge, MA, 1964); D. V. Glass, *Population Policies and Movements in Europe* (Oxford, 1940); International Labour Office, *Emigration and Immigration: Legisla-*

tion and Treaties (Geneva, 1922); United States, Emigration and Immigration, *Reports of the Consular Offices of the United States* (Washington, 1887); Dirk Hoerder and Jörg Nagler, eds., *People in Transit: German Migration in Comparative Perspective, 1820–1930* (Cambridge, 1995); Caroline B. Bretell, *Men Who Migrate, Women Who Wait: Population and History in a Portuguese Parish* (Princeton, NJ, 1986); Robert F. Foerster, *The Italian Emigration of Our Time* (Cambridge, MA, 1924); Ingrid Schöber, "Emigration Policy in Germany and Immigration Policy in the United States," in Günter Moltmann, ed., *Germans to America: 300 Years of Immigration, 1683–1983* (Stuttgart, 1982), 36–45; Kristian Hvidt, *Flight to America: The Social Background of 300,000 Danish Emigrants* (New York, 1975); Marcus Lee Hansen, *The Atlantic Migration, 1607–1860: A History of the Continuing Settlement of the United States* (Cambridge, MA, 1940); Harald Runblom and Hans Norman, eds., *From Sweden to America: A History of the Migration* (Minneapolis, 1976); Agnes Bretting, "Organizing German Immigration: The Role of State Authorities in Germany and the United States," in Frank Trommler and Joseph McVeigh, eds., *America and the Germans: An Assessment of a Three-Hundred Year History*, vol. 1, *Immigration, Language, Ethnicity* (Philadelphia, 1985), 25–38; John Duncan Brite, *The Attitude of European States toward Emigration to the American Colonies and the United States, 1607–1820* (Chicago, 1939); Dirk Hoerder and Diethelm Knauf, eds., *Fame, Fortune, and Sweet Liberty: The Great European Emigration* (Bremen, 1992); Walter D. Kamphoefner et al., eds., *News from the Land of Freedom: German Immigrants Write Home* (Ithaca, NY, 1988); Jose C. Moya, *Cousins and Strangers: Spanish Immigrants in Buenos Aires, 1850–1930* (Berkeley, CA, 1998); Carl A. Auerbach, "Freedom of Movement in International Law and United States Policy," in William H. McNeill and Ruth S. Adams, eds., *Human Migrations: Patterns and Policies* (Bloomington, IN, 1978), 317–35. The ending of restrictions in Europe generally came in the nineteenth century. The range of years includes Sweden and Norway c. 1850, the German states throughout the century, and others, within this time span. There were also stringent laws against migration until the last decades of the nineteenth century in China and Japan, with the penalty in Japan being beheading. See Victor Purcell, *The Chinese in Southeast Asia*, 2d ed. (Oxford, 1965); Virginia Yans-McLaughlin, ed., *Immigration Reconsidered: History, Sociology, and Politics* (New York, 1990); and Rupert Emerson, *Malaysia: A Study in Direct and Indirect Rule* (Kuala Lampur, 1964, first pub. 1937).

22. On the British "pauper" emigration, see Stanley C. Johnson, *A History of Emigration from the United Kingdom to North America, 1763–1912* (London, 1913); H. J. M. Johnston, *British Emigration Policy, 1815–1830: "Shoveling out Paupers"* (Oxford, 1972); Robin F. Haines, *Emigration and the Labouring Poor: Australian Recruitment in Britain and Ireland, 1831–1860* (New York, 1997); David Cressy, *Coming Over: Migration and Communication Between England and New England in the Sev-*

enteenth Century (Cambridge, 1987); Dudley Baines, *Migration in a Mature Economy: Emigration and Internal Migration in England and Wales, 1861–1900* (Cambridge, 1985); J. Matthew Gallman, *Receiving Erin's Children: Philadelphia, Liverpool, and the Irish Famine Migration, 1845–1855* (Chapel Hill, NC, 2000).

23. See K. Onewuke Dike, *Trade and Politics in the Niger Delta, 1830–1865* (Oxford, 1956). On the ending of slavery in nineteenth- and twentieth-century Africa, see Suzanne Miers and Richard Roberts, eds., *The End of Slavery in Africa* (Madison, WI, 1988).

24. In some cases such as the French, the relocation decisions were made by the metropolis, generally due to the underpopulated nature of French penal colonies. See chap. 9 below.

25. The Chesapeake colonies in the US had various constraints on migrants, particularly Irish. They had ended convict labor shipments before 1700, but these then resumed for several decades in the eighteenth century. The final ending came with the success of the Revolution although one or two ships were used in an attempt to reinstate the trade, a rather unsuccessful mission. For discussions of colonial immigration in the thirteen colonies, see Marilyn C. Baseler, *"Asylum for Mankind," America, 1607–1800* (Ithaca, NY, 1998); Marianne S. Wokeck, *Trade in Strangers: The Beginnings of Mass Migration to North America* (University Park, PA, 1999); A. Roger Erkich, *Bound for America: The Transportation of British Convicts to the Colonies* (Oxford, 1987); Abbot Emerson Smith, *Colonists in Bondage: White Servitude and Convict Labor in America, 1607–1776* (Chapel Hill, NC, 1947); Aaron Spencer Fogleman, *Hopeful Journeys: German Immigration, Settlement, and Political Culture in Colonial America, 1717–1775* (Philadelphia, 1996); Erna Risch, "Encouragement of Immigration as Revealed in Colonial Legislation," *Virginia Magazine of History and Biography* 45 (1937): 1–10; Roy L. Garis, *Immigration Restriction: A Study of the Opposition to and Regulation of Immigration into the United States* (New York, 1927); David W. Galenson, *White Servitude in Colonial America: An Economic Analysis* (Cambridge, 1981); and Emberson Edward Proper, *Colonial Immigration Laws: A Study of the Regulation of Immigration by the English Colonies in America* (New York, 1900). This attempt to limit the inflow of convict labor was made because convicts were believed to be an undesirable basis for a labor force. There was apparently some discussion of substituting white convicts for black slaves, but this was not a particularly successful policy attempt.

26. In the first half of the nineteenth century, Australia made legal distinctions between convicts, time-expired convicts, and free migrants. See David Neal, *The Rule of Law in a Penal Colony: Law and Power in Early New South Wales* (Cambridge, 1991).

27. The recent U.S. elections will no doubt lead to some modifications of these long-standing policies in the United States, in Britain, and elsewhere.

28. See, for example, Samuel Pufendorf, *De Jure Naturae et Gentium*

Libri Octo 2 (trans. Oxford, 1934; original first pub. 1688) with its critique of Grotius on state versus individual rights in regard to emigration.

29. As seen in the case of national quotas for the US after 1920, the means of determining the basis of the allocation among different groups will depend upon the particular years used to measure national representation. Thus the choice of years had been a major source of political controversy. The initial use of the nationality breakdown from 1910 led to too many from "new immigrant" countries. To lower this amount, the breakdown in the 1890 census was then utilized.

30. The range of restrictions could also apply to the period of time for which in-migration is possible, and the conditions under which return to the country of origin is possible. Many countries wish to separate the attraction of labor for a limited period of time from policies leading to the permanent expansion of the local population and have established categories such as guest workers, braceros, etc. And, as with late nineteenth-century indentured labor, return might or might not be subsidized under varying sets of conditions. For recent examples of the use of guest workers, see John Bendix, *Importing Foreign Workers: A Comparison of German and American Policy* (New York, 1990). For the Russian state-contracted movement of labor from Germany to Russia at the end of the eighteenth century, see Roger P. Bartlett, *Human Capital: The Settlement of Foreigners in Russia, 1762–1804* (Cambridge, 1979).

31. See Donald Greer, *The Incidence of the Emigration During the French Revolution* (Cambridge, MA, 1951), and Cunningham, *Alien Immigrants*, 254–60, for discussions of the restrictions on French migration into Britain during the French Revolution. The treatment of such migration was discussed by the British into the 1830s. Similar restrictions existed in the twentieth-century wars with Germany.

32. See the discussion of the case of the Scottish legislation in 1803 by Peter Dunkley, "Emigration and the State, 1803–1842: The Nineteenth Century Revolution in Government Reconsidered," *HJ* 23 (1980): 353–80. See also Thomas W. Page, "The Transportation of Immigrants and Reception Arrangements in the Nineteenth Century," *Journal of Political Economy* 19 (1911): 732–39.

33. There have been considerable differences not only in rates of return migration but also in the number of immigrants who elect to become naturalized citizens. At the end of the nineteenth century, for example, the US ratio of naturalization to immigration was about 50 percent, while that for Argentina was about 10 percent even with the Argentine provision of extended period of exemption from military service. Low rates are also found for much migration into European nations, even today. For discussions of citizenship requirements and times to qualify, see Frank George Franklin, *The Legislative History of Naturalization in the United States from the Revolutionary War to 1861* (Chicago, 1906). See also William J. Bromwell, *History of Immigration to the United States* (New York, 1856); T. Alexander Aleinikoff and Douglas Klusmeyer, eds., *From Migrants to*

Citizens: Membership in a Changing World (Washington, 2000); and James H. Kettner, *The Development of American Citizenship, 1608–1870* (Chapel Hill, NC, 1978).

34. Several states in the US still have restrictions against immigrant ownership of land and other assets within the states, a residue of a more extended set of past regulations. See Fred L. Morrison, "Limitations on Alien Investment in American Real Estate," *Minnesota Law Review* 60 (1976): 621–68; Keith Aoki, "No Right to Own?: The Early Twentieth Century 'Alien Land Laws' as a Prelude to Internment," *Boston College Law Review* 40 (1988): 37–72; Mark Shapiro, "The Dormant Commerce Clause: A Limit on 'Alien Land Laws,'" *Brooklyn Journal of International Law* 20 (1993): 217–73; and Ronald L. Bell and Jonathan D. Savage, "Our Land Is Your Land: Ineffective State Restriction of Alien Land Ownership and the Need for Federal Legislation," *John Marshall Law Review* 13 (1979): 679–715. References from Robert Steinfeld.

35. For a description of rules on internal migration for poor relief, see A. L. Beier, *Masterless Men: The Vagrancy Problem in England 1560–1640* (London, 1985), and George R. Boyer, *An Economic History of the English Poor Law, 1750–1850* (Cambridge, 1990) on Britain. For similar policies elsewhere, see Douglas Lamar Jones, "The Transformation of the Law of Poverty in Eighteenth Century Massachusetts," in Colonial Society of Massachusetts, ed., *Law in Colonial Massachusetts, 1630–1800* (Boston, 1984) 153–90; Robert Jütte, *Poverty and Deviance in Early European History* (Cambridge, 1994); Sheilagh Ogilvie, *State Corporations and Proto-Industry: The Württemberg Black Forest, 1580–1797* (Cambridge, 1997); and more recently, see Sophia Woodman, "China's Dirty Clean-Up," *New York Review of Books* 47 (May 11, 2000): 50–52.

36. The direct costs of hiring illegal immigrants and the presumed legal responsibility for their presence may, in effect, be borne either by employers or by workers, depending on the terms of the legislation. On undocumented migration more generally, see Frank D. Bean et al., eds., *Undocumented Migration to the United States: IRCA and the Experience of the 1980s* (Washington, 1990).

37. For Russian nineteenth-century constraints on eastern settlement, see Barbara A. Anderson, *Internal Migration During Modernization in Late Nineteenth Century Russia* (Princeton, NJ, 1980).

38. In regard to the aborigines in Australia, see John Chesterman and Brian Galligan, *Citizens Without Rights: Aborigines and Australian Citizenship* (Cambridge, 1997).

39. On trade and immigration restrictions in the nineteenth century, see Kevin O'Rourke and Jeffrey G. Williamson, *Globalization and History: The Evolution of a Nineteenth Century Atlantic Economy* (Cambridge, MA, 1999).

CHAPTER 3

1. William H. McNeill, "Human Migration: Historical Overview," in William H. McNeill and Ruth Adams, eds., *Human Migration: Patterns and Policies* (Bloomington, IN, 1976), 11–19.

2. See P. D. Curtin, *The Image of Africa: British Ideas and Action, 1770–1850* (Madison, WI, 1964) for the intersection of medicine and thought about race in early nineteenth-century Britain.

3. For examples of the genre, see James A. B. Horton, *The Medical Topography of the West Coast of Africa, with Sketches of its Botany* (London, 1859); and Jean C. M. F. J. Boutin, *Essai de géographie médicale ou étude sur les lois qui préside à la distribution géographique des maladies, ansi qu'à leurs rapports topograhiques entre elles. Lois de coincidence et d'antagonisme* (Paris, 1843).

4. See P. D. Curtin, *Death by Migration: Europe's Encounter with the Tropical World in the Nineteenth Century* (New York, 1989), 1–12.

5. United States Army, *Statistical Report on the Sickness and Mortality in the Army of the United States, from January 1819 to January 1839* (Washington, 1839).

6. Great Britain, Army Medical Service, *Reports*, annual series with slightly different titles beginning in 1859 as a series of annual volumes, also printed for Parliament in the series *Parliamentary Papers*. The other most valuable series for the epidemiology of migration is the French series begun in 1862 as France, Ministère de Guerre, *Statistiques médicale de l'armée metropolitaine et de l'armée coloniale*. Among imperial powers, a similar Portuguese series began in 1870–71 and a Spanish series in 1884. They and other national reports on health of the armies, however, were mainly concerned with troops stationed in Europe. Germany began to report annually on colonial troops only in 1903–4 with Kolonialamt, *Medizinal-Berichte über die Deutschen Schutzgebeiten*. The Netherlands, however, published annual medical statistics on its East India army beginning in 1848 in *Colonial Verslag*, later continued in more detail in Nederlands, Centraal Bureau voor de Statistiek, *Statistisch Overzicht der Behandelde Zieken van het Nerderlanissch-Indisch Lager* (Batavia, annual series). The major powers and the United States soon followed with similar, but separate, annual series on the health of the navy.

7. Curtin, *Death by Migration*, 40–42.

8. For smallpox in Africa see Donald R. Hopkins, *Princes and Peasants: Smallpox in History* (Chicago, 1983), 164–203.

9. P. D. Curtin, "African Health at Home and Abroad," *Social Science History* 10 (1986): 369–98, esp. 371–82.

10. P. D. Curtin, *Disease and Empire: The Health of European Troops in the Conquest of Africa* (New York, 1998), 78–82; Prosper Léonard Keisser, *Souvenirs médicaux de quatre campagnes du transport a la côte occidentale d'Afrique (Sénégal et Gabon), Seudre et Arièges* (Bordeaux, thesis no. 31, 1885), 41–42.

11. Based on a sample of several thousand Europeans and islanders, and about six hundred Africans, *Colonial Verslag* for 1853, 20.

12. Tom W. Shick, "A Quantitative Analysis of Liberian Colonization from 1820 to 1843 with Special Reference to Mortality," *Journal of African History* 12 (1971): 45–59.

13. Ralph Shlomowitz and Lance Brennan, "Mortality and Migrant Labour en route to Assam, 1863–1924," *The Indian Economic and Social History Review* 27 (1990): 313–30.

14. Ralph Shlomowitz and Lance Brennan, "Epidemiology and Indian Labor Migration at Home and Abroad," *Journal of World History* 5 (1994): 47–67, 56–58; Shlomowitz, "Differential Mortality of Asians and Pacific Islanders in the Pacific Labour Trade," *Journal of the Australian Population Association* 7 (1990): 116–27.

15. For recent discussions of part of this literature see Dane Kennedy, "The Perils of the Midday Sun: Climate and Anxieties in the Colonial Tropics," in John M. MacKenzie, ed., *Imperialism and the Natural World* (Manchester, 1990), 118–40; and Warick Anderson, "Climates of Opinion: Acclimatization in Nineteenth-Century France and England," *Victorian Studies*, Winter 1992, 135–57.

16. Curtin, *Death by Migration*, 46–47, 109–11.

17. Curtin, *Disease and Empire*, 135–38.

18. Curtin, *Death by Migration*, 99–103.

19. See Curtin, "African Health"; id., "Malarial Immunities in Nineteenth-Century West Africa and the Caribbean," *Parassitologia* 36 (1994): 69–82.

20. Curtin, "African Health," 394.

21. Farley Grubb, "Morbidity and Mortality on the North Atlantic Passage: Eighteenth-Century German Immigration," *Journal of Interdisciplinary History* 17 (1987): 565–85, esp. 578–82.

22. Watt Stewart, *Chinese Bondage in Peru: A History of the Chinese Coolie in Peru, 1849–1874* (Durham, NC, 1951). For the Chinese migration to the Caribbean, see Walton Look Lai, *Indentured Labor, Caribbean Sugar: Chinese and Indian Migrants to the British West Indies, 1838–1918* (Baltimore, MD, 1993) and *The Chinese in the West Indies, 1806–1995: A Documentary History* (Mona, Jamaica, 1998).

CHAPTER 4

1. Sources on European migration to the Chesapeake include Russell R. Menard, "Immigrants and Their Increase: The Process of Population Growth in Early Colonial Maryland," in Aubrey C. Land et al., eds., *Law, Society, and Politics in Early Maryland* (Baltimore, 1977), 88–110; Menard, "British Migration to the Chesapeake Colonies in the Seventeenth Century," in Lois Green Carr et al., eds., *Colonial Chesapeake Society* (Chapel Hill, NC, 1988), 99–132; John J. McCusker and Russell R. Menard, *The Economy of British America, 1607–1789* (Chapel Hill, NC,

1985), chaps. 6 and 10; James Horn, "'To Parts Beyond the Seas': Free Emigration to the Chesapeake in the Seventeenth Century," in Ida Altman and James Horn, eds., *"To Make America": European Emigration in the Early Modern Period* (Berkeley, 1991), 85–130; Horn, *Adapting to a New World: English Society in the Seventeenth-Century Chesapeake* (Chapel Hill, NC, 1994), chaps. 1 and 3. More general treatments include Henry A. Gemery, "Emigration from the British Isles to the New World, 1630–1700: Inferences from Colonial Populations," *Research in Economic History* 5 (1980): 179–217; Russell R. Menard, "Migration, Ethnicity, and the Rise of an Atlantic Economy: The Re-Peopling of British America, 1600–1790," in Rudolph J. Vecoli and Suzanne M. Sinke, eds., *A Century of European Migrations, 1830–1930* (Urbana, IL, 1991), 58–77; Nicholas Canny, "British Migration into and across the Atlantic during the Seventeenth and Eighteenth Centuries," in Nicholas Canny, ed., *Europeans on the Move: Studies on European Migration, 1500–1800* (Oxford, 1994), 39–75; Anthony McFarlane, *The British in the Americas, 1480–1815* (London, 1994), 56–91, 163–67, 175–79, 230–34; and Aaron S. Fogleman, "From Slaves, Convicts, and Servants to Free Passengers: The Transformation of Immigration in the Era of the American Revolution," *JAH* 85 (1998): 43–76.

2. For the seventeenth-century free migrants see Menard, "Immigrants and Their Increase"; Menard, "British Migration to the Chesapeake Colonies;" Horn, "'To Parts Beyond the Seas;'" and Horn, *Adapting to a New World*, chap. 1.

3. Menard, "British Migration to the Chesapeake Colonies," 120.

4. On indentured servant migration see Abbot Emerson Smith, *Colonists in Bondage: White Servitude and Convict Labor in America, 1607–1776* (Gloucester, MA, 1965); James Horn, "Servant Emigration to the Chesapeake in the Seventeenth Century," in Thad W. Tate and David L. Ammerman, eds., *The Chesapeake in the Seventeenth Century: Essays on Anglo-American Society* (Chapel Hill, NC, 1979), 51–95; Lorena S. Walsh, "Servitude and Opportunity in Charles County, Maryland, 1658–1705," in Land et al., *Law, Society and Politics*, 111–33; David W. Galenson, *White Servitude in Colonial America: An Economic Analysis* (Cambridge, 1981); David Souden, "'Rogues, whores and vagabonds'? Indentured servant emigrants to North America, and the case of mid-seventeenth-century Bristol," *Social History* 3 (1978): 23–41; Margaret M. R. Kellow, "Indentured Servitude in Eighteenth-Century Maryland," *Histoire sociale-Social History* 17 (1984): 229–55; John Wareing, "Migration to London and transatlantic migration of indentured servants, 1683–1775," *Journal of Historical Geography* 7, 4 (1981): 356–78; Bernard Bailyn, *Voyagers to the West: A Passage in the Peopling of America on the Eve of the Revolution* (New York, 1986), 177; and Henry A. Gemery, "Markets for Migrants: English Indentured Servitude and Emigration in the Seventeenth and Eighteenth Centuries," in P. C. Emmer, ed., *Colonialism and Migration: Indentured Labour Before and After Slavery* (Dordrecht, 1986), 33–54.

5. David Eltis and Stanley L. Engerman, "Was the Slave Trade Domi-

nated by Men?", *Journal of Interdisciplinary History* 23 (1992): 237–57; id., "Fluctuations in Sex and Age Ratios in the Transatlantic Slave Trade, 1663–1864," *Economic History Review* 46 (1993): 308–23.

6. Douglas B. Chambers, "The Transatlantic Slave Trade to Virginia in Comparative Historical Perspective, 1698–1778," in John Saillant, ed., *Afro-Virginian History and Culture* (New York, 1999), 13–19; and Maryland data collected by Lorena S. Walsh.

7. Menard, "British Migration to the Chesapeake Colonies," 120; Bailyn, *Voyagers to the West*, 127–29; Eltis and Engerman, "Was the Slave Trade Dominated by Men?", 243.

8. Galenson, *White Servitude in Colonial America*, 26–33.

9. Children under age fifteen seem seldom to have contracted formal indentures in England, so rarely appear on lists of emigrant servants. On the other hand, servant buyers in the Chesapeake had a financial incentive to bring young servants without indentures to court to have their ages judged, because they could thereby extract additional years of service from these youths, most of whom arrived between the ages of ten and fourteen. Masters had no such incentive for recording the ages of undisputably adult servants. Consequently among all servants without indentures a range of 15 to 20 percent below age fifteen seems likely across the seventeenth century. By the early eighteenth century the transportation of bound European children was largely abandoned. Lorena S. Walsh, "Charles County, Maryland, 1658–1705: A Study of Chesapeake Social and Political Structure" (Ph.D. diss., Michigan State Univ., 1977), 156–62. Cf. Bailyn, *Voyagers to the West*, 135.

10. See note 6.

11. For orphans see Walsh, "Charles County, Maryland," 106–41, and Lois Green Carr, "The Development of the Maryland Orphan's Court, 1654–1715," in Land et al., *Law, Society, and Politics*, 41–62. The high proportion of enslaved African children has been noted in Philip Morgan and Michael L. Nicholls, "Slaves in Piedmont Virginia, 1720–1790," *WMQ*, 3d ser., 46 (1989): 211–51, and in Douglas Brent Chambers, "'He Gwine Sing He Country': Africans, Afro-Virginians, and the Development of Slave Culture in Virginia, 1690–1810" (Ph.D. diss., Univ. of Virginia, 1996), chap. 4.

12. Lorena S. Walsh and Russell R. Menard, "Death in the Chesapeake: Two Life Tables for Men in Early Colonial Maryland," *Maryland Historical Magazine* 69 (1974): 211–27; Russell R. Menard and Lorena S. Walsh, "The Demography of Somerset County, Maryland: A Progress Report," *Newberry Papers in Family and Community History* 81, 2 (1981); Daniel Blake Smith, "Mortality and Family in the Colonial Chesapeake," *Journal of Interdisciplinary History* 8 (1977–78): 403–27; Darrett B. Rutman and Anita H. Rutman, "'Now-Wives and Sons-in-Law': Parental Death in a Seventeenth-Century Virginia County," in Tate and Ammerman, eds., *The Chesapeake in the Seventeenth Century*, 153–82; Darrett B. Rutman and Anita H. Rutman, "'Of Agues and Fevers': Malaria in the Early

Chesapeake," *WMQ*, 3d ser., 33 (1976): 31–60; Darrett B. Rutman, Charles Wetherell, and Anita H. Rutman, "Rhythms of Life: Black and White Seasonality in the Early Chesapeake," *Journal of Interdisciplinary History* 11 (1980): 29–53; Carville V. Earle, "Environment, Disease, and Mortality in Early Virginia," in Tate and Ammerman, eds., *The Chesapeake in the Seventeenth Century*, 96–125; Allan Kulikoff, "A 'Prolifick' People: Black Population Growth in the Chesapeake Colonies, 1700–1790," *Southern Studies* 16 (1977): 391–428; id., *Tobacco and Slaves: The Development of Southern Cultures in the Chesapeake, 1680–1800* (Chapel Hill, NC, 1986), 66–70; Menard, "Immigrants and Their Increase."

13. For Europeans see Edmund S. Morgan, *American Slavery, American Freedom: The Ordeal of Colonial Virginia* (New York, 1975); Lorena S. Walsh, "'Till Death Us Do Part': Marriage and Family in Seventeenth-Century Maryland," in Tate and Ammerman, eds., *The Chesapeake in the Seventeenth Century*, 126–52;. Rutman and Rutman, "'Now-Wives and Sons-in-Law'"; Menard, "Immigrants and Their Increase"; and Horn, *Adapting to a New World*, chap. 5. For Africans see Russell R. Menard, "The Maryland Slave Population, 1658–1730: A Demographic Profile of Blacks in Four Counties," *WMQ*, 3d ser., 32 (1975): 29–54; Allan Kulikoff, "The Beginnings of the Afro-American Family in Maryland," in Land et al., *Law, Society, and Politics in Early Maryland*, 171–96; and Kulikoff, *Tobacco and Slaves*, chap. 8.

14. Russell R. Menard, "Economy and Society in Early Colonial Maryland" (Ph.D. diss., University of Iowa, 1975); Russell R. Menard and Lois Green Carr, "The Lords Baltimore and the Colonization of Maryland," in David B. Quinn, ed., *Early Maryland in a Wider World* (Detroit, 1982), 167–215; Lois Green Carr et al., *Robert Cole's World: Agriculture and Society in Early Maryland* (Chapel Hill, NC, 1991), chaps. 1 and 5; Nicholas Canny, "The Permissive Frontier: Social Control in English Settlements in Ireland and Virginia, 1550–1650," in K. R. Andrews, N. P. Canny, and P. E. H. Hair, eds., *The Westward Enterprise: English Activities in Ireland, the Atlantic, and America, 1480–1650* (Liverpool, 1978), 17–44.

15. Russell R. Menard, "From Servant to Freeholder: Status Mobility and Property Accumulation in Seventeenth-Century Maryland," *WMQ*, 3d ser., 30 (1973): 37–64; Farley Grubb and Tony Stitt, "The Liverpool Emigrant Servant Trade and the Transition to Slave Labor in the Chesapeake, 1697–1707: Market Adjustments to War," *Explorations in Economic History* 31 (1994): 376–405; Menard, "Immigrants and Their Increase"; Menard, "British Migration to the Chesapeake Colonies"; Walsh, "Servitude and Opportunity"; Carr et al., *Robert Cole's World*, chap. 6.

16. Russell R. Menard, "From Servants to Slaves: The Transformation of the Chesapeake Labor System," *Southern Studies* 16 (1977): 355–90; Grubb and Stitt, "The Liverpool Emigrant Servant Trade"; David W. Galenson, "Economic Aspects of the Growth of Slavery in the Seventeenth Century Chesapeake," in Barbara L. Solow, ed., *Slavery and the Rise of the Atlantic System* (Cambridge, 1991), 265–340. Quotation from a 1664 let-

ter of Charles Calvert to Lord Baltimore, *The Calvert Papers*, Maryland Historical Society Peabody Publication Fund, no. 28 (Baltimore, 1889), 249.

17. The seventeenth century estimate of 20,000 comes from Galenson, *White Servitude in Colonial America*, 212–17, who estimated decennial net migration as a residual of a colony's population not due to estimated natural increase or decrease. This figure is considerably higher than the number of imported slaves that can be documented (or inferred) from extant shipping records. For estimates based on shipping records see David Eltis, "The British Transatlantic Slave Trade before 1714: Annual Estimates of Volume and Direction," in Robert L. Paquette and Stanley L. Engerman, eds., *The Lesser Antilles in the Age of European Expansion* (Gainesville, FL, 1996), 182–205. Almost all historians have emphasized the much lower numbers that are documented and have failed to ask how a total black population in 1700 of as many as 20,000 could realistically have been achieved. The marked increase in the number of slaves appearing in Chesapeake probate inventories and in headrights used to patent land in Virginia in the 1680s suggests that Galenson's estimate of a net black migration between 1680 and 1690 almost as large as the much better documented surge in the 1690s is correct. Cf. Wesley Frank Craven, *White, Red, and Black: The Seventeenth-Century Virginian* (New York, 1971), 71–109; and Susan Westbury, "Slaves of Colonial Virginia: Where They Came From," *WMQ*, 3d ser., 42 (1985): 228–37.

18. Lois Green Carr and Lorena S. Walsh, "Economic Diversification and Labor Organization in the Chesapeake, 1650–1820," in Stephen B. Innes, ed., *Work and Labor in Early America* (Chapel Hill, NC, 1988), 144–88.

19. Farley Grubb, "The Statutory Regulation of Colonial Servitude: An Incomplete-Contract Approach," *Explorations in Economic History* 37 (2000): 42–75.

20. William Byrd II to the Earl of Egmont, July 12, 1736, in Marion Tinling, ed., *The Correspondence of the Three William Byrds of Westover, Virginia, 1684–1776* (3 vols., Charlottesville, VA, 1977), 2:488.

21. Menard, "Economy and Society in Early Colonial Maryland"; Carr et al., *Robert Cole's World*, chaps. 5 and 6; Kulikoff, *Tobacco and Slaves*, chap. 2; Darrett B. Rutman and Anita H. Rutman, *A Place in Time: Middlesex County, Virginia, 1650–1750* (New York, 1984), chap. 6; Lorena S. Walsh, "Staying Put or Getting Out: Findings for Charles County, Maryland, 1650–1720," *WMQ*, 3d ser., 44 (1987): 89–103.

22. Menard, "Immigrants and Their Increase"; Carr et al., *Robert Cole's World*, chaps. 5 and 6; Horn, *Adapting to A New World*, chaps. 3 and 5; Kulikoff, *Tobacco and Slaves*, chap. 1; Darrett B. Rutman and Anita H. Rutman, "'More True and Perfect Lists': The Reconstruction of Censuses for Middlesex County, Virginia, 1668–1704," *Virginia Magazine of History and Biography* 88 (1980): 37–74.

23. Walsh, "Staying Put or Getting Out"; J. P. Horn, "Moving On in the

New World: Migration and Out-Migration in the Seventeenth-Century Chesapeake," in Peter Clark and David Souden, eds., *Migration and Society in Early Modern England* (London, 1987), 172–212.

24. Horn, *Adapting to a New World*, chap. 10; Lois Green Carr, "The Foundations of Social Order: Local Government in Colonial Maryland," in Bruce C. Daniels, ed., *Town and County: Essays on the Structure of Local Government in the American Colonies* (Middletown, CT, 1978), 72–110; Warren M. Billings, "The Transfer of English Law to Virginia," in Andrews et al., eds., *The Westward Enterprise*, 215–44.

25. Ira Berlin, "From Creole to African: Atlantic Creoles and the Origins of African-American Society in Mainland North America," *WMQ*, 3d ser., 53 (1996): 251–88; id., *Many Thousands Gone: The First Two Centuries of Slavery in North America* (Cambridge, MA, 1998), chaps. 1 and 5.

26. Berlin, *Many Thousands Gone*, 29, 100–108, 109–12.

27. There do not appear to have been major changes in the sources of slaves between 1680 and 1730, and London merchants continued to be the predominant traders. A shift of the center of the trade from London to Bristol and then Liverpool, and corresponding changes in African places of trade did not occur until after the Chesapeake plantation regime and slave codes had been fully developed. (David Richardson, "The British Empire and the Atlantic Slave Trade, 1660–1807," in P. J. Marshall, ed., *The Oxford History of the British Empire*, vol. 2, *The Eighteenth Century* [Oxford, 1998], 440–86.) For proportions from the West Indies see Lorena S. Walsh, "The Chesapeake Slave Trade: Regional Patterns, African Origins, and Some Implications," *WMQ*, 3d ser., 58 (2001): 139–70.

28. Horn, "'To Parts Beyond the Seas,'" 96–101; Horn, *Adapting to a New World*, chap. 1; Wareing, "Migration to London and Transatlantic Migration of Indentured Servants"; David Hackett Fischer, *Albion's Seed: Four British Folkways in America* (New York, 1989), 207–418.

29. Menard, "British Migration to the Chesapeake Colonies."

30. Henry A. Gemery, "European Emigration to North America, 1700–1820: Numbers and Quasi-Numbers," *Perspectives in American History*, n.s. 1 (1984): 283–342; James Horn, "British Diaspora: Emigration from Britain, 1680–1815," in P. J. Marshall, ed., *The Oxford History of the British Empire* 2:28–51; Marianne S. Wokeck, *Trade in Strangers: The Beginnings of Mass Migration to North America* (University Park, PA, 1999); Galenson, *White Servitude in Colonial America*, 212–17; Menard, "Migration, Ethnicity, and the Rise of an Atlantic Economy;" Fogleman, "From Slaves, Convicts, and Servants to Free Passengers"; Bailyn, *Voyagers to the West*.

31. A. Roger Ekirch, *Bound for America: The Transportation of British Convicts to the Colonies, 1718–1775* (Oxford, 1987), chaps. 4 and 5; Kenneth Morgan, "The Organization of the Convict Trade to Maryland: Stevenson, Randolph, and Cheston, 1768–1775," *WMQ*, 3d ser., 42 (1985): 201–27.

32. Herbert S. Klein, *The Atlantic Slave Trade* (Cambridge, 1999), 174.

33. Menard, "British Migration to the Chesapeake Colonies," 100–103.

34. For population estimates see McCusker and Menard, *The Economy of British America*, 222; and Berlin, *Many Thousands Gone*, 369–71.

35. Walsh, "The Chesapeake Slave Trade." This article includes data for the period 1698–1774 only. I have compiled a database of slave voyages to Maryland in the seventeenth century and am doing further work on the seventeenth century Virginia slave trade and on the migration from Barbados to southern Maryland.

36. Ibid.

37. Ibid.; Lorena S. Walsh, *From Calabar to Carter's Grove: The History of a Virginia Slave Community* (Charlottesville, VA, 1997), chap. 1; Stephen D. Behrendt, "Markets, Transaction Cycles, and Profits: Merchant Decision Making in the British Slave Trade," *WMQ*, 3d ser., 58 (2001): 171–204.

38. Horn, *Adapting to a New World*, 432–36.

39. Walsh, *From Calabar to Carter's Grove*, chap. 3; Patricia Samford, "'Strong Is the Bond of Kinship:' West African-Style Ancestor Shrines and Subfloor Pits on African American Quarters," paper presented at the Fourth World Archaeological Conference, Capetown, South Africa, January, 1999. Samford has subsequently identified additional artifacts from the lower peninsula of Virginia with possible Igbo associations (letter of Sept. 14, 1999).

40. Philip D. Curtin, *Economic Change in Precolonial Africa: Senegambia in the Era of the Slave Trade* (Madison, WI, 1975); Boubacar Barry, *Senegambia and the Atlantic Slave Trade* (Paris, 1988; Eng. trans., Cambridge, 1998); Walter Rodney, "Upper Guinea and the Significance of the Origins of Africans Enslaved in the New World," *Journal of Negro History* 54 (1969): 327–45. John K. Thornton has supplied overviews in *Africa and Africans in the Making of the Atlantic World, 1400–1800*, 2d ed. (Cambridge, 1998), chap. 7, and in "The African Background to American Colonization," in Stanley L. Engerman and Robert E. Gallman, eds., *The Cambridge Economic History of the United States*, vol. 1, *The Colonial Era* (Cambridge, 1996), 53–94. See also the discussions of regional differences in David Eltis, *The Rise of African Slavery in the Americas* (Cambridge, 2000), chap. 7. P. E. H. Hair, "Ethnolinguistic Continuity on the Guinea Coast," *Journal of African History* 8 (1967): 247–68, discusses the historical continuity of coastal languages, but does not address the issue of degrees of mutual intelligibility.

41. C. Wondji, "The States and Cultures of the Upper Guinean Coast," in B. A. Ogot, ed., *UNESCO General History of Africa*, vol. 5, *Africa from the Sixteenth to the Eighteenth Century* (Berkeley, 1992), 368–98; Michael A. Gomez, *Exchanging Our Country Marks: The Transformation of African Identities in the Colonial and Antebellum South* (Chapel Hill, NC, 1998), chap. 5; Walter Hawthorne, "The Production of Slaves where there was no State: The Guinea-Bissau Region, 1450–1815," *Slavery and Abolition* 20 (1999): 97–124.

42. A. A. Boahen, "The State and Cultures of the Lower Guinean Coast," in *UNESCO General History of Africa* 5:399–433; Stephanie Ellen Smallwood, "Salt-Water Slaves: African Enslavement, Forced Migration, and Settlement in the Anglo-Atlantic World, 1660–1700" (Ph. D. diss., Duke Univ., 1999); Gomez, *Exchanging Our Country Marks*, chap. 5.

43. Philip D. Curtin, *The Atlantic Slave Trade: A Census* (Madison, WI, 1969), 152–53, 185 discusses some of the ambiguities, as does Gomez, *Exchanging Our Country Marks*, 27, 103, 304 n. 45. The three regions are tabulated separately in Curtin, *The Atlantic Slave Trade*; the proportion assigned to the Windward Coast is a conjectural distribution. Eltis lumped the three regions together in "The Volume and African Origins of the British Slave Trade before 1714," *Cahiers d'études Africaines* 35 (1995): 620, and uses lumped, individual, and a combination of two regions in different tabulations in *The Rise of African Slavery*, 166, 181, 245. Richardson, "The British Empire and the Atlantic Slave Trade," and Gomez, *Exchanging Our Country Marks*, group Sierra Leone and the Windward Coast together. I counted the Gold and Windward Coasts as a single region because a number of the vessels were recorded as trading in both places and because Chesapeake newspapers often advertised ships as arriving with an unspecified mix of Windward and Gold Coast slaves. It is likely that most of these captives in fact came from the Gold Coast.

44. Richardson, "The British Empire and the Atlantic Slave Trade," 450. On European trading patterns in these areas, see Thornton, *Africa and Africans*, 192–95; Eltis, *The Rise of African Slavery*, 176–77; and Smallwood, "Salt-Water Slaves," 63.

45. Thornton, *Africa and Africans*, 186–92. Cf. Eltis, *The Rise of African Slavery in the Americas*, 253–57.

46. For the Bight of Biafra see Chambers, "'He Gwine Sing He Country,'" chap. 2; Walsh, *From Calabar to Carter's Grove*, chap. 2; Thornton, *Africa and Africans*, 189–90; and Gomez, *Exchanging Our Country Marks*, chap. 6. David Northrup, "Igbo and Myth Igbo: Culture and Ethnicity in the Atlantic World, 1600–1850," *Slavery and Abolition* 21 (2000): 1–20, argues that there was more linguistic and cultural diversity in the area than these scholars have posited, and that slaves from linguistic and cultural groups other than and differing from the Ibo were exported from this region.

47. J. Vansina, "The Kongo Kingdom and Its Neighbors," in *UNESCO General History of Africa* 5: 546–87; Thornton, *Africa and Africans*, 190–92; and Gomez, *Exchanging Our Country Marks*, chap. 6. Joseph C. Miller, *Way of Death: Merchant Capitalism and the Angolan Slave Trade, 1730–1830* (Madison, WI, 1988), chap. 1, places somewhat more emphasis on diversity.

48. Walsh, "The Chesapeake Slave Trade."

49. For general discussions of sex ratios see Eltis and Engerman, "Was the Slave Trade Dominated by Men?"; Eltis and Engerman, "Fluctuations in Sex and Age Ratios"; and David Geggus, "Sex Ratio, Age and Ethnicity

in the Atlantic Slave Trade: Data From French Shipping and Plantation Records," *Journal of African History* 30 (1989): 23–44. For sources for sex ratios of slaves brought from Senegambia see note 6.

50. Sylviane A. Diouf, *Servants of Allah: African Muslims Enslaved in the Americas* (New York, 1998), 179–80.

51. Eltis and Engerman, "Fluctuations in Sex and Age Ratios," 310. For Chesapeake sex ratios of slaves from the Bight of Biafra see note 6.

52. Kathleen M. Brown, *Good Wives, Nasty Wenches, and Anxious Patriarchs: Gender, Race, and Power in Colonial Virginia* (Chapel Hill, NC, 1966), chap. 3; quotation, 80.

53. Ibid.

54. Lois Green Carr and Russell R. Menard, "Immigration and Opportunity: The Freedman in Early Colonial Maryland," in Tate and Ammerman, eds., *The Chesapeake in the Seventeenth Century*, 206–42.

55. Lois Green Carr and Lorena S. Walsh, "The Planter's Wife: The Experience of White Women in Seventeenth-Century Maryland," *WMQ*, 3d ser., 34 (1977): 542–71; Brown, *Good Wives, Nasty Wenches, and Anxious Patriarchs*, chap. 3; Rutman and Rutman, "Of Agues and Fevers."

56. Contracts of indenture made in England only rarely included clauses exempting female servants from working in the ground, perhaps because there was no English precedent for so employing women. Those serving according to the custom of the country were clearly not exempted. Rather tellingly it was immigrant women who entered into second work contracts or the parents (by will or by contracts negotiated by widows) or guardians of native-born orphans who made agreements specifically exempting them from tending tobacco or pounding at the mortar.

57. Gloria L. Main, *Tobacco Colony: Life in Early Maryland, 1650–1720* (Princeton, NJ, 1982), 175–82; Carr and Walsh, "Economic Diversification and Labor Organization in the Chesapeake"; Brown, *Good Wives, Nasty Wenches, and Anxious Patriarchs*, chap. 3; Horn, *Adapting to a New World*, chap. 6.

58. Carole Shammas, "Black Women's Work and the Evolution of Plantation Society in Virginia," *Labor History* 26 (1985): 5–28; Carr and Walsh, "Economic Diversification and Labor Organization in the Chesapeake"; Brown, *Good Wives, Nasty Wenches, and Anxious Patriarchs*, chap. 4.

59. Ibid. Cf. Judith Carney, "Rice Milling, Gender and Slave Labour in Colonial South Carolina," *Past and Present* 153 (1996): 108–34.

60. Walsh, *From Calabar to Carter's Grove*, chap 3.

61. Brown, *Good Wives, Nasty Wenches, and Anxious Patriarchs*, chaps. 4 and 6; Philip D. Morgan, *Slave Counterpoint: Black Culture in the Eighteenth-Century Chesapeake and Lowcountry* (Chapel Hill, NC, 1998), 498–511. The positive value infants and young children commanded in the market was of little comfort to planters whose primary concern was short-run profits. It is unlikely that purchasers could be found for unweaned infants who would probably not survive separation

from their mothers, nor could maximum production be wrung from distraught mothers if their young children were routinely sold off.

62. Brown, *Good Wives, Nasty Wenches, and Anxious Patriarchs,* chaps. 3 and 4.

63. Carr and Walsh, "The Planter's Wife"; Horn, *Adapting to a New World,* 222–34.

64. Lorena S. Walsh, "Community Networks in the Early Chesapeake," in Carr et al., eds., *Colonial Chesapeake Society,* 200–241; Horn, *Adapting to a New World,* 234–50; Rutman and Rutman, *A Place in Time,* 21–30; James R. Perry, *The Formation of a Society on Virginia's Eastern Shore, 1615–1655* (Chapel Hill, NC, 1990); Kulikoff, *Tobacco and Slaves,* chap. 6.

65. Walsh, "Community Networks."

66. Ibid.; Horn, *Adapting to a New World,* 234–50; Carr et al., *Robert Cole's World,* chaps. 5 and 6.

67. Ibid. and Walsh, *From Calabar to Carter's Grove,* 32–33. Quotation from a letter of Governor Nicholson to the Board of Trade, Aug. 20, 1698, in William Hand Browne et al., eds., *Archives of Maryland* (72 vols. Baltimore, 1883–1972), 23:498.

68. Michael Graham, "Meetinghouse and Chapel: Religion and Community in Seventeenth-Century Maryland," in Carr et al., eds., *Colonial Chesapeake Society,* 242–74.

69. Berlin, *Many Thousands Gone,* chap. 1 (quotation, 46).

70. Walsh, *From Calabar to Carter's Grove,* 33, 273.

71. Menard, "The Maryland Slave Population," 37–38; Thornton, *Africa and Africans,* 228.

72. Walsh, *From Calabar to Carter's Grove,* 104–7; Morgan, *Slave Counterpoint,* 640–44; Thornton, *Africa and Africans,* 263.

73. Samford, "'Strong is the Bond of Kinship.'"

74. The presence of African "nations" in the New World was first advanced by Thornton, *Africa and Africans,* 183–92, 196–204, 227–28, 263, 321–31. Two other recent studies addressing this issue are Eltis, *The Rise of African Slavery,* chap. 9; and Douglas Chambers, "The Transatlantic Slave Trade and the Creation of Diasporic African 'Nations': Toward a Theory of Historical Creolization," *Slavery and Abolition* (forthcoming). Recent critiques that question the existence in the colonial Americas of historical African ethnolinguistic identities include Northrup, "Igbo and Myth Igbo," and Philip D. Morgan, "The Cultural Implications of the Atlantic Slave Trade: African Regional Origins, American Destinations, and New World Developments," in David Eltis and David Richardson, eds., *Routes to Slavery: Direction, Ethnicity and Mortality in the Atlantic Slave Trade* (Portland, OR, 1997), 122–45.

75. Kulikoff, *Tobacco and Slaves,* 329–30; Morgan, *Slave Counterpoint,* 563–64.

76. James Horn, "Adapting to a New World: A Comparative Study of

Local Society in England and Maryland, 1650–1700," in Carr et al., eds., *Colonial Chesapeake Society*, 164–74.

77. Horn, *Adapting to a New World*, 234–50; id., "To Parts Beyond the Seas," 109–11.

78. Thornton, *Africa and Africans*, 218–19, 324; Kulikoff, *Tobacco and Slaves*, chaps. 8 and 9.

79. Carr et al., *Robert Cole's World*, chap. 6.

80. Walsh, *From Calabar to Carter's Grove*, chaps. 1, 5, and 7; Thornton, *Africa and Africans*, 329–30.

81. William Waller Hening, ed., *The Statutes at Large: Being a Collection of All the Laws of Virginia, From the First Session of the Legislature, in 1619* (13 vols.; Richmond, 1819–23; repr., Charlottesville, 1969), 4: 126–34; 5:16–17, 19, 22–23; 6:40–42, 421–22; 7:519–20. On night time travel see Nicholson to the Board of Trade, Aug. 20, 1698, *Archives of Maryland* 23:498–99, and Morgan, *Slave Counterpoint*, 524–25. I am aware of no descriptions of what actually went on at what officials considered "unlawful meetings." After the 1670s depositions in court cases, which for earlier years provide information on mixed race gatherings, are less frequently recorded. Starting in the 1730s planter correspondence and runaway advertisements begin to supply evidence about what slave owners thought their slaves were doing. For the years between 1680 and 1730 there is little to go on aside from laws and official proclamations which are indeed problematic sources.

82. Walsh, *From Calabar to Carter's Grove*, chaps. 1, 5, and 7; Thornton, *Africa and Africans*, 328–30.

83. Sensbach, "Charting a Course in Early African-American History," *WMQ*, 3d ser., 50 (1993): 403.

84. Jack P. Greene, *Pursuits of Happiness: The Social Development of Early Modern British Colonies and the Formation of American Culture* (Chapel Hill, NC, 1988), chaps. 1 through 4.

CHAPTER 5

1. In every discussion of German-speaking settlers in eighteenth-century America the awkward task arises of finding an appropriate label for these people. Clearly the twentieth-century terms of "German" and "Swiss" are inappropriate to apply to an era in which inhabitants had strong political and cultural ties to a particular region, with little sense of a cultural nationality, and no identification with a political nation-state. If emigrants from Württemberg and Basel land were keenly aware of how they differed from each other in language and customs, they seemed equally foreign to the English-speaking settlers in the American colonies, who called them quite indiscriminately in *pars-pro-toto* fashion "Dutch" (for *deitsch* [in dialect]/*deutsch* [in high German] or German), "Palatines," or "Switzers." Following this English-centered usage and because of the absence of an alternative, convenient, correct, and comprehensive term for

the descriptive but cumbersome expression "German-speaking settlers," in the present discussion German and all the other inadequate names will be used synonymously for the sake of brevity and variation. Always, however, there must be the understanding that each term encompasses a mix of emigrants from continental Europe that is roughly bounded in the North by the Hanseatic city of Hamburg, in the South by the canton of Zurich, in the West by Alsace, and in the East by Saxony.

In an analogous fashion voyagers who left from ports on the Irish isle are labeled "Irish," although many were Scots in origin who had migrated to Ulster (labeled variably Scotch-Irish, Scots-Irish, or Ulster Scots). Similarly, "Ireland" is to be understood as a geographical, not political term.

2. For estimates of German immigrants to the American colonies and the Delaware Valley, see Marianne S. Wokeck, *Trade in Strangers: The Beginnings of Mass Migration to North America* (University Park, PA, 1999), table 2; for estimates of German immigrants to the new republic, see Hans-Jürgen Grabbe, "European Immigration to the United States in the Early National Period," *Proceedings of the American Philosophical Society* 133, 2 (June 1989): 190–222; Grabbe, ed., "Before the Great Tidal Waves: Patterns of Transatlantic Migration at the Beginning of the Nineteenth Century," *Amerikastudien/American Studies* 42, 3 (1997): 377–89. For estimates of Irish migrants to the Delaware Valley, see Wokeck, *Trade*, table 4; for estimates of Irish immigrants to all of the American colonies, see Maurice Bric, "Ireland, Irishmen, and the Broadening of the Late Eighteenth-Century Philadelphia Polity" (Ph.D. diss., Johns Hopkins Univ., 1990); id., "Irish Emigration to America, 1783–1800," International Seminar on the History of the Atlantic World, 1500–1800, Harvard University, 1996 (www.fas.harvard.edu/~atlantic); Louis M. Cullen, "The Irish Diaspora in the Seventeenth and Eighteenth Centuries," in Nicholas Canny, ed., *Europeans on the Move: Studies on European Migration, 1500–1800* (Oxford, 1994); Robert J. Dickson, *Ulster Emigration to Colonial America, 1718–1775* (1966; repr. with a new intro., London, 1988); David N. Doyle, *Ireland, Irishmen, and Revolutionary America, 1760–1820* (Dublin, 1982); Roger A. Ekirch, *Bound for America: The Transportation of Convicts to the Colonies* (Oxford, 1987); Patrick Fitzpatrick, "A Sentence to Sail: the Transportation of Irish Convicts and Vagrants to Colonial America in the Eighteenth Century," International Seminar on the History of the Atlantic World, 1500–1800, Harvard University, 1996; Aaron Spencer Fogleman, "Migration to the Thirteen British North American Colonies, 1700–1775: New Estimates," *Journal of Interdisciplinary History* 12 (Spring 1992): 691–709; id., "From Slaves, Convicts, and Servants to Free Passengers: The Transformation of Immigration in the Era of the American Revolution," *JAH* 85, 1 (June 1998): 43–76; P. M. G. Harris, *The History of Human Populations*, vol. 2, *Movements in Births, Death, and Migration* (New York, forthcoming); Audrey Lockhart, *Some Aspects of Emigration from Ireland to the North American Colonies Between 1660 and 1775* (New York, 1976); Kerby A. Miller, *Emigrants*

and Exiles: Ireland and the Irish Exodus to North America (Oxford, 1985); Thomas M. Truxes, *Irish American Trade, 1660–1783* (Cambridge, 1988).

3. The same division occurred among emigrants in the stream from Great Britain in the decade before the American Revolution, which Bernard Bailyn presented as one of the major findings in *Voyagers to the West: A Passage in the Peopling of America on the Eve of the Revolution* (New York, 1986).

4. Cullen, "Irish Diaspora," 113–14, 139–40, 143–49.

5. For a map showing the areas from which German-speaking emigrants left for the American colonies, see Georg Fertig, *Lokales Leben, atlantische Welt: Die Entscheidung zur Auswanderung vom Rhein nach Nordamerika im 18. Jahrhundert* (Osnabrück, 2000), 139; for Ulster, see Dickson, *Ulster Emigration*.

6. For a breakdown of religious affiliations among emigrants from Irish ports, see Doyle, *Ireland*. The evidence for German-speaking immigrants is scattered and not systematic for the migration as a whole. See Andreas Blocher, *Die Eigenart der Zürcher Auswanderer nach Amerika* (Zurich, 1976); Aaron Spencer Fogleman, *Hopeful Journeys: German Immigration, Settlement, and Political Culture in Colonial America, 1717–1775* (Philadelphia, 1996), chap. 4 (on the Moravians); Richard K. MacMaster, *Land, Piety, Peoplehood: The Establishment of Mennonite Communities in America* (Scottdale, PA, 1985); Hans Ulrich Pfister, *Die Auswanderung aus dem Knonauer Amt, 1648–1750* (Zurich 1987); A. G. Roeber, *Palatines, Liberty, and Property: German Lutherans in British Colonial America* (Baltimore, 1993); Leo Schelbert, "On Becoming Emigrants: A Structural View of Eighteenth- and Nineteenth-Century Swiss Data," *Perspectives in American History* 7 (1971): 439–95.

7. Unless immigrants acted as scouts for their families, settlers often waited before they reported about their experience in the new country. After having overcome the difficulties of the voyage and the harsh challenges of new beginnings, many then conveyed obvious pride in their achievement, thereby encouraging others to follow suit. For a listing of immigrant letters in the selected bibliography, see Wokeck, *Trade*, 277–310.

8. Most migrants out of Ireland headed for England and France (Cullen, "Irish Diaspora"); about 90 percent of German-speaking migrants turned eastward in their search for a decent living (Georg Fertig, "Transatlantic Migration from the German-Speaking Parts of Central Europe, 1600–1800: Proportions, Structures, and Explanations," in Nicholas Canny, ed., *Europeans on the Move: Studies on European Migration, 1500–1800* [Oxford, 1994]).

9. For developments that affected areas of out-migration in Ireland, see Louis M. Cullen, "Economic Development, 1691–1750" and "Economic Development, 1750–1800"; and John Leslie McCracken, "The Social Structure and Social Life, 1714–1760," all in T. W. Moody and W. E. Vaughn, eds., *A New History of Ireland*, vol. 4, *Eighteenth-Century Ire-*

land (Oxford, 1986); for examples of German territories with considerable migration, see Andreas Brinck, *Die deutsche Auswanderungswelle in die britischen Kolonien Nordamerikas um die Mitte des 18. Jahrhunderts* (Stuttgart, 1993); Fertig, "Transatlantic Migration"; Fogleman, *Journeys*; Mark Häberlein, "German Migrants in Colonial Pennsylvania: Resources, Opportunities, and Experience," *WMQ*, 3d ser., 50 (1991): 555–74; id., *Vom Oberrhein zum Susquehanna. Studien zur Auswanderung nach Pennsylvania im 18. Jahrhundert* (Stuttgart, 1993); and Roeber, *Palatines*.

10. Wokeck, *Trade*, tables 2 and 4; appendix listings in Lockhart, *Emigration*, and Dickson, *Ulster Emigration*.

11. For maps that depict the expansion of European settlement before the American Revolution, see Bailyn, *Voyagers*, 9, 22.

12. See, for example, the hinterland for the sales of indentured servants and convicts in the Chesapeake Bay colonies (Bailyn, *Voyagers*, 347).

13. James Kettner, *The Development of American Citizenship, 1608–1870* (Chapel Hill, NC, 1978). See also chap. 2 in this volume.

14. For examples of Irish networks, Thomas Doerflinger, *A Vigorous Spirit of Enterprise: Merchants and Economic Development in Revolutionary Philadelphia* (Chapel Hill, NC, 1986), 12, 14, 15, 20, 44, 55–57, 59, 73, 76, 101, 104, 107, 121, 148–49, 152, 155–57, 173, 185–88, 219, 237, 240–41, 253–55, 261, 277–78, 335, 337; Truxes, *Trade*, 38, 61, 73, 76–78, 86–87, 106–8, 117–21; see also Joseph S. Foster, *The Pursuit of Equal Liberty: George Bryan and the Revolution in Philadelphia* (University Park, PA, 1994), where the focus is on one prominent Presbyterian Irish merchant in Philadelphia; for Quaker connections, see Audrey Lockhart, "The Quakers and Emigration from Ireland to the North American Colonies," *Quaker History* 77 (1988): 67–92. Roeber, *Palatines*, is a testimony to the overlapping networks—regional, religious, and philanthropic—among Palatine Lutherans and Halle Pietists.

15. One such example is the group of emigrants from Zurich traveling under the leadership of the Reformed minister Moritz Götschi (Hans Ulrich Pfister, *Zürcher Auswanderung nach America 1734/35. Die Reisegruppe um Pfarrer Götschi* [Zurich, 1985]); another is the group of Schwenkfelders on the *Pennsylvania Merchant* (Samuel Kriebel Brecht, *The Genealogical Record of the Schwenkfelder Families: Seekers of Religious Liberty Who Fled from Silesia to Saxony and Thence to Pennsylvania in the Years 1731–1737*, 2 vols. [New York, 1923]). Evidence of chain migration is revealed in the work of Annette Kunselman Burgert, who has traced thousands of German-speaking families from their homelands to the American colonies. See, for example, her *Eighteenth-Century Emigrants*, vol. 1, *The Northern Kraichgau* (Breiningsville, PA, 1983); vol. 2, *The Western Palatinate* (Birdsboro, PA, 1985).

16. In early America, the term "cultural broker" most often describes the role of men and women who negotiated successfully between peoples of different cultures in the borderlands of European settlement.

17. Christopher Sauer, a radical pietist immigrant to early Pennsylvania

who became publisher of an influential German-language newspaper (usually short-titled *Pennsylvanische Berichte*), provides a prominent example (Donald F. Durnbaugh, "Christopher Sauer, Pennsylvania-German Printer: His Youth in Germany and Later Relationship with Europe," *Pennsylvania Magazine for History and Biography* 82 [1958]: 316–39).

18. On the network of known newlanders and recruiting agents operating in German territories, Georg Fertig, "Migration," 203 [map]; William T. O'Reilley, "'A Paragon of Wickedness': Newlanders and Agents in Eighteenth-Century German Migration," International Seminar for the History of the Atlantic World, Harvard University, 1996.

19. See, for example, the case of Johann Heinrich Christian von Stümpel as described in Selig, "Emigration, Fraud, Humanitarianism"; and Samuel Waldo's efforts to recruit settlers for his patent in Kennebec, Maine (Heinrich Armin Rattermann, "Geschichte des deutschen Elements im Staate Maine," *Der deutsche Pionier: Erinnerungen aus dem Pionier-Leben der Deutschen in Amerika* 14–16 [1882–1884]).

20. Wokeck, *Trade*, figure 2 shows the annual flow of German immigrants to North America (1683–1775); figure 3 the annual flow of Irish immigrants to the Delaware Valley (1730–1774).

21. It bears remembering, however, that the ship lists that yield data for the composition of the German migration are comparatively much more detailed than those from Ireland. Ralph B. Strassburger, *Pennsylvania German Pioneers: A Publication of the Original Lists of Arrivals in the Port of Philadelphia from 1727 to 1808*, ed. by William John Hinke, 3 vols. (1934; repr. ed. Baltimore, 1966); Wokeck, *Trade*, app.; "Passenger List, with Duties, 29 August 1768–13 August 1772," Historical Society of Pennsylvania, Philadelphia, PA.

22. For details about servants among Irish immigrants to the Delaware Valley and about the role of servitude among German immigrants to Philadelphia, see Wokeck, *Trade*, 99–101, 155–63, 175–78, 210–13.

23. Appendix listings in Lockhart, *Emigration*; Wokeck, *Trade*, 176–78, 211–12.

24. Wokeck, *Trade*, table 4.

25. Stuart Daultry, David Dickson, and Cormac O'Grada, "Eighteenth-Century Irish Population: New Perspectives from Old Sources," *JEH* 41 (1981): 601–28.

26. The maps and commentaries pertaining to the eighteenth century in the historical atlas of the Palatinate provide striking examples (Willi Alter, ed., *Pfalzatlas* [Speyer, 1963–1979]).

27. Wokeck, *Trade*, 52.

28. Robert Selig, "The Idea and Practice of the *ius emigrandi* in the Holy Roman Empire from the Reformation to the French Revolution," *Yearbook of German-American Studies* 27 (1992): 15–22.

29. There was little of the returning home that featured prominently in later transatlantic migrations.

30. For details on the ordeal of relocation, see Wokeck, *Trade*, chap. 4.

31. Wokeck, *Trade*, 118 (price of voyage for German-speaking migrants), 203 (price of voyage for emigrants from Irish ports).

32. Ekirch, *Convicts*, estimated that about 13,000 convicts were transported from Ireland to the American colonies, of whom less than 1,000 were landed in Philadelphia (25, 46, 83–85, 114–15); more recently, Fitzgerald, "Convicts and Vagrants," estimated that the number was even larger (2–4); see also David W. Galenson, *White Servitude in Colonial America* (Cambridge, 1981); Farley Grubb, "Immigrant Servant Labor: Their Occupational and Geographic Distribution in the Late Eighteenth-Century Mid-Atlantic Economy," *Social Science History* 9 (Summer 1985): 249–75; id., "The Market for Indentured Servants: Evidence on the Efficiency of Forward Labor Contracting in Philadelphia, 1745–1773," *JEH* 45 (1985): 855–68.

33. James T. Lemon, *The Best Poor Man's Country: A Geographical Study of Early Southeastern Pennsylvania* (Baltimore, 1972); Robert D. Mitchell, *Commercialism and Frontier: Perspectives on the Early Shenandoah Valley* (Charlottesville, NC, 1977); Klaus Wust, *The Virginia Germans* (Charlottesville, VA, 1969).

34. Historians of early America have long recognized the importance of culture in building communities, organizing societies, and shaping identities, even though the focus has been primarily on immigrants from England and their transformation into Americans. Timothy H. Breen, "Creative Adaptations: Peoples and Cultures," in Jack P. Greene and J. R. Pole, eds., *Colonial British America: Essays in the New History of the Early Modern Era* (Baltimore, 1984), 195–232; David Hackett Fischer, *Albion's Seed: Four British Folkways in America* (New York 1989); Jack P. Greene, *Pursuits of Happiness: The Social Development of Early Modern British Colonies and the Formation of American Culture* (Chapel Hill, NC, 1988). See also Jack P. Greene, "Mastery and the Definition of Cultural Space in Early America," *Imperatives, Behaviors, and Identities: Essays in Early American Cultural History* (Charlottesville, VA, 1992), 1–12.

Historians of nineteenth- and twentieth-century immigration and ethnicity have produced a large literature on the formation of ethnic groups and on competition among different groups and the dominant society. The following articles serve as introduction to that discussion: Kathleen Neils Conzen et al., "The Invention of Ethnicity: A Perspective from the U.S.A.," *Journal of American Ethnic History* 11, 1 (Fall 1992): 3–41 [also in: *Altreitalie, International Review of Studies on the Peoples of Italian Origin in the World* 3 (April 1990)]; Russell A. Kazal, "Revisiting Assimilation: The Rise, Fall, and Reappraisal of a Concept in American Ethnic History," *AHR* 100, 2 (Apr. 1995): 437–71; Ewa Morawska, "In Defense of the Assimilation Model," *Journal of American Ethnic History* 13, 2 (Winter 1994): 76–87; Werner Sollors, ed., *The Invention of Ethnicity* (New York, 1989); Virginia Yans-McLaughlin, ed., *Immigration Reconsidered: History, Sociology, and Politics* (New York, 1990).

35. Francis G. James, "Irish Colonial Trade in the Eighteenth Century,"

WMQ, 3d ser., 20 (1963): 574–84; R. C. Nash, "Irish Atlantic Trade in the Seventeenth and Eighteenth Centuries," *WMQ*, 3d ser., 42 (1985): 329–56; Truxes, *Trade*.

36. Doyle, *Ireland*, 22, 39–40; see also the references to Irish migration networks in note 15 above.

37. For a detailed discussion of the organization of the German immigrant trade, see Wokeck, *Trade*, chap. 3.

38. Charles Tilly, "Transplanted Networks," in Virginia Yans-McLaughlin, ed., *Immigration Reconsidered: History, Sociology, and Politics* (New York, 1994), 79–95, especially 84–85.

39. Roeber, *Palatines*, is a telling portrayal of this case.

40. Stephanie Grauman Wolf in *Urban Village: Population, Community, and Family Structure in Germantown, Pennsylvania, 1638–1800* (Princeton, NJ, 1976) showed the impact of these mechanisms on the character of one community over the course of the eighteenth century.

41. Instead English migration to colonial America flowed at a fairly steady rate from the late seventeenth century until the American Revolution, to a total of English immigrants that outnumbered all other migratory flows from Europe combined. Harris, *Populations* 2, chap. 4 (text to figure "Some Estimates of Migrations from England and from Europe between the 1630s and the 1850s").

42. Marianne S. Wokeck, "Immigrant Kin and Indentured Servants: Fuel for Economic Growth in the Middle Colonies," in Jean R. Soderlund and Catherine S. Parzynki, eds., *Backcountry Crucibles: The Lehigh Valley from Settlement to Steel* (Bethlehem, PA, forthcoming), chap. 3.

43. For more details, see Wokeck, *Trade*, 27–31; 116–17.

44. Winthrop P. Bell, *The "Foreign Protestants" and the Settlement of Nova Scotia* (Toronto, 1961); Rattermann, "Deutsches Element."

45. Wokeck, *Trade*, tables 1 and 2, app.

46. Rattermann, "Deutsches Element," portrays the different layers of communication that came into play in the recruitment of Germans for Maine around the middle of the eighteenth century; Dickson describes this overlap of communication and trade in the recruitment of passengers for the American colonies in the 1770s. On the complex structure of local leadership, the minister and those who derived their influence from economic power and social standing, in German villages, see David Sabean, *Power in the Blood: Popular Culture and Village Discourse in Early Modern Germany* (Cambridge, 1984); in the American colonies before 1750, see A. G. Roeber, "'The Origin of Whatever Is Not English among Us': The Dutch-speaking and German-speaking Peoples of Colonial British America," in Bernard Bailyn and Philip D. Morgan, eds., *Strangers within the Realm: Cultural Margins of the First British Empire* (Chapel Hill, NC, 1991), 265.

47. The extraordinarily high costs to emigrants, many of whom did not even survive, let alone succeed, is one of the themes in Marilyn C. Baseler, *"Asylum for Mankind": America, 1607–1800* (Ithaca, NY, 1999).

48. See Brinck, *Auswanderungswelle*; Selig, "Emigration"; and O'Reilley, "Newlanders and Agents" for many detailed examples of different kinds of recruiters.

49. Fogleman, *Journeys* (table 2.1), shows how much local patterns of emigration varied within one region.

50. Studies usually follow the emigrants across the Atlantic and do not explore the kinds of rearrangements that occurred to make up for their loss in the local economy and social structure of their homelands.

51. This kind of rhetoric underlies the calls for restricting emigration in Ireland and Germany. For details, see Wokeck, *Trade*, 21–23; Dickson, *Ulster Emigration*.

52. For details, see Wokeck, *Trade*, 18–23.

53. Leo Schelbert, "Swiss Migration to America: The Swiss Mennonites" (Ph.D. diss., Columbia Univ., 1966), 156.

54. David Häberle, *Auswanderung und Koloniegründungen der Pfälzer im 18. Jahrhundert* (Kaiserslautern, 1909), 92.

55. About 10 percent of the settlers from the electoral Palatinate east of the Rhine sought to settle their inheritances; the proportion in Baden was 2 to 3 percent (Roeber, *Palatines*, 92–97; Häberlein, *Vom Oberrhein zum Susquehannah*, 173–77).

56. The best documented cases are Samuel Waldo's efforts to settle Germans in Maine and John Dick's scheme to recruit foreign Protestants for Nova Scotia (Rattermann, "Deutsches Element"; Bell, *Nova Scotia*).

57. Gabrielle Lanier, "Ethnic Perceptions," paper delivered at the Philadelphia Center for Early American Studies, 1997.

58. Scholars who focus on issues of culture generally make three points: culture is constructed and reconstructed over time; participation in the cultural discourse is often unequal; and communities create their own cultures. Their view contrasts with that of some historians who consider culture as an immutable "template against which to *judge* the preservation of 'pure' Old World patterns and the divergence from it in the New and over time" (Kathleen Neils Conzen, "Mainstreams and Side Channels: The Localization of Immigrant Cultures," *Journal of American Ethnic History* 11 [1991]: 12). To enshrine things German or Irish this way is unrealistic and limiting because by creating such a static and idealized standard historians miss the changes that occurred on both sides of the Atlantic. Instead, immigrants invent culture to suit and make sense of their new situation, not circumstances they left behind. Labels about who people were in the Old World did not readily carry over into the New; and immigrants often have to confront new classifications of themselves. Stressing the process of adjustment redirects attention away from any one category such as "the Germans" or "the Scots-Irish" to the variety of places and types of settlement in which people actually established their new lives, usually interacting with diverse neighbors. Inquiries that deal inclusively with all participants in the "cultural conversation" in particular localities can best examine how cultural space is defined, negotiated,

and dominated (Breen, "Adaptations," 198, who adds the important point that not all voices in this conversation are heard or carry equal weight). See also Kazal, "Assimilation," 462–63; Conzen, "Mainstreams," 15.

59. For details on the workings of the redemptioner system in Pennsylvania, see Wokeck, *Trade*, 150–64, 187–89, 200–202, 210–13, 230; also, Wokeck, "Servant Migration and the Transfer of Culture from the Old World to the New," International Seminar of the History of the Atlantic World, Harvard University, 1996.

60. Galenson, *Servitude*; James Horn, "Servant Emigration to the Chesapeake in the Seventeenth Century," in Thad W. Tate and David L. Ammerman, eds., *The Chesapeake in the Seventeenth Century: Essays in Anglo-American Society* (Chapel Hill, NC, 1979).

61. Susan E. Klepp and Billy G. Smith, eds., *The Infortunate: The Voyage and Adventures of William Moraley, an Indentured Servant* (University Park, PA, 1992). Sharon V. Salinger, *"To Serve Well and Faithfully": Labor and Indentured Servants in Pennsylvania, 1682–1800* (Cambridge, 1982); Billy G. Smith, *The "Lower Sort": Philadelphia's Laboring People, 1750–1800* (Ithaca, NY, 1990); and Richard Schlecht's portfolio of portraits of runaway indentured servants in Bailyn, *Voyagers* (between pages 352 and 355), are four very different attempts to depict the life of indentured servants in colonial America. Kurt Aland, ed., *Die Korrespondenz Heinrich Melchior Mühlenbergs aus der Anfangszeit des deutschen Luthertums in Nordamerika*, 5 vols. (Berlin, 1986–96), 1:486, 3:334–36, 646, 4/10; see also Gottlieb Mittelberger, *Journey to Pennsylvania, 1756*, ed. Oscar Handlin and trans. John Clive (Cambridge, MA, 1960), 18.

CHAPTER 6

1. See, for example, Introduction and chap. 1, above.

2. Sigmund Freud, "Address to the Society of B'nai Brith" [1926] in *Works* 20 (standard ed. London, 1959): 273. For the history of the idea of identity see Philip Gleason, "Identifying Identity: A Semantic History," *JAH* 69 (1983): 910–31. For analysis of this concept see Richard Handler, "Is 'Identity' a Useful Cross-Cultural Concept?" in John R. Gillis, ed., *Commemorations: The Politics of National Identity* (Princeton, NJ, 1994), 27–40. For wide-ranging use of the idea see Michael Zuckerman, "Identity in British America: Unease in Zion," in Nicholas Canny and Anthony Pagden, eds., *Colonial Identity in the Atlantic World 1500–1800* (Princeton, NJ, 1987), 115–57.

3. Erik Erikson suggests that the words describing his Jewish identity might be better translated as "a deep commonality known only to those who shared in it, and only expressible in words more mythical than conceptual." This, however, seems to reflect Erikson's own sense of what it was to be Jewish (mythical), not Freud's. Erik H. Erikson, *Identity: Youth and Crisis* (New York, 1968), 20–21.

4. Leon Grinberg and Rebecca Grinberg, *Psychoanalytic Perspectives on Migration and Exile* (New Haven, CT, 1989), 21.

5. Ibid., 20. For contemporary views of "home" see Becky Thompson and Sangeeta Tygi, *Names We Call Home: Autobiography On Racial Identity* (New York, 1996).

6. John R. Gillis, "From Ritual to Romance: Toward an Alternative History of Love," in Carol Z. Stearns and Peter N. Stearns, eds., *Emotion and Social Change: Toward a New Psychohistory* (New York, 1988), 95–96; David Warren Sabean, *Power in the Blood: Popular Culture and Village Discourse in Early Modern Germany* (Cambridge, 1984), 35; Patricia Meyer Spacks, *Imagining a Self: Autobiography and Novel in Eighteenth-Century England* (Baltimore, 1989), 8–9; John Beattie, "Representations of the Self in Traditional Africa," *Africa* 50 (1980): 313–20; Brian Morris, *Anthropology of the Self: The Individual in Cultural Perspective* (London, 1993), 118–47.

7. For an extended discussion of this issue see Mechal Sobel, *Teach Me Dreams: The Search for Self in the Revolutionary Era* (Princeton, NJ, 2000); and Joyce Appleby, *Inheriting the Revolution: The First Generation of Americans* (Cambridge, MA, 2000).

8. John Bunyan, *Grace Abounding to Sinners* (1666) and *The Pilgrim's Progress* (1678), repr. in *The Complete Works of John Bunyan*, ed. Henry Stebbing, 4 vols. (London, 1994), 1:1–42, 2:9–135, 4:445–58.

9. Stephen Greenblatt, *Renaissance Self-Fashioning: From More to Shakespeare* (Chicago, 1980), 9. See also Gary S. Gregg, *Self-Representation: Life Narrative Studies in Identity and Ideology* (New York, 1991), 47.

10. Robert V. Wells, *Revolutions in American Lives: A Demographic Perspective on the History of Americans, Their Families, and Their Society* (Westport, CT, 1982), 23.

11. See Sobel, *Teach Me Dreams*, 3, 14, 26, 27, 110, 242.

12. John Harrower, *The Journal of John Harrower: An Indentured Servant in the Colony of Virginia, 1773–1776,* ed. Edward M. Riley (New York, 1963), 18, 59, 63, 150–51.

13. Ibid., 76.

14. Ibid., 130.

15. Ibid., 54.

16. Ibid., 116.

17. William Lee, *The True and Interesting Travels of William Lee* (London, 1808).

18. Ibid., 30.

19. John Robert Shaw, *A Narrative of the Life and Times of John Robert Shaw, the Well Digger* (Lexington, KY, 1807), 7.

20. "Magdalene Beulah Brockden," in Katherine M. Faull, *Moravian Women's Memoirs: Their Related Lives, 1750–1820* (Syracuse, NY, 1997), 77–78. Andrew's autobiography is reprinted in Daniel B. Thorp, "Chattel

with a Soul: The Autobiography of a Moravian Slave," *Pennsylvania Magazine of History and Biography* 112 (1988): 433–51. See also Katherine Faull Eze, "Self-Encounters: Two Eighteenth Century African Memoirs from Moravian Bethlehem," in David McBride et al., eds., *Crosscurrents: African Americans, Africa, and Germany in the Modern World* (Columbia, SC, 1998), 29–52.

21. Ibid., 449–50.

22. Ibid., 451. On Zinzendorf and the Moravians in America, and on the changing Moravian attitudes toward Africans, see Jon M. Sensbach, *A Separate Canaan: The Making of an Afro-Moravian World in North Carolina, 1763–1840* (Chapel Hill, NC, 1998).

23. See Beverly Prior Smaby, *The Transformation of Moravian Bethlehem: From Communal Mission to Family Economy* (Philadelphia, 1988).

24. Eze, "Self-Encounters," 39, 51 n.36.

25. Sensbach, *Separate Canaan*, 271–97.

26. Charles Brockden, who sent Beulah/Magdalena to Bethlehem, did not record any African name on the manumission document he signed in March of 1752, but he did note she had been born in Angola. The deed of manumission is reprinted in *The Pennsylvania Magazine* 29 (May 1905): 364–65. Faull, *Moravian Women's Memoirs*, 77, cites Little Popo, on the Guinea Coast, as her birthplace.

27. "Magdalene Beulah Brockden," in Faull, *Moravian Women's Memoirs*, 78.

28. During the lifetimes of Magdalena and Andrew the community was required to move toward family order for married people, but everyone remained under strict control. See Katherine M. Faull, "The American Lebenslauf: Women's Autobiography in Eighteenth-Century Moravian Bethlehem," *Yearbook of German-American Studies* 27(1992): 23–48; Smaby, *The Transformation of Moravian Bethlehem*.

29. Venture Smith, *A Narrative of the Life and Adventures of Venture: A Resident of Africa, but Resident Above Sixty Years in the United States of America* (Haddam, CT, [1798] 1896), 6. See also Robert E. Desrochers Jr., "'Not Fade Away': The Narrative of Venture Smith, An African American in the Early Republic," *The JAH* 84 (1997–98): 40–66.

30. Smith, *Narrative*, 24.

31. Ibid.

32. William Otter, *History of My Own Times. A Series of Events and Musical Incidents Altogether Original* (Emmetsburg, MD, 1835). See Richard B. Stott, "Commentary: William Otter and the Society of Jolly Fellows in the Early Republic," in the reprint of William Otter, *History of My Own Times*, ed. Richard B. Stott (Ithaca, NY, 1995), 181–224.

33. K. White, *A Narrative* (Schenectady, NY, 1809).

34. Ibid., 34.

35. Michael Martin, *Life of Michael Martin, Who Was Executed* (Boston, 1821).

36. John Binns, *Recollections of the Life of John Binns: Twenty-Nine*

Years in Europe and Fifty-Three in the United States (Philadelphia, 1854), 338. For a discussion of Binns and his community see David A. Wilson, *United Irishmen, United States: Immigrant Radicals in the Early Republic* (Ithaca, NY, 1998).

37. See Paul Watzlawick, John Weakland, and Richard Fisch, *Change: Principles of Problem Formation and Problem Resolution* (New York, 1974).

38. Grinberg and Grinberg, *Psychoanalytic Perspectives*, 9.

39. Sarah Beckhouse Hamilton, *A Narrative* (Greenwich, CT, 1806).

40. Elizabeth Ashbridge, *Some Account of the Early Part of the Life of Elizabeth Ashbridge* (Concord, NH, 1810). See also Cristine Levenduski, *Peculiar Power: A Quaker Women Preacher in Eighteenth Century America* (Washington, DC, 1996).

41. Olaudah Equiano, *The Interesting Narrative of the Life of Olaudah Equiano, Gustavus Vassa, the African, Written by Himself*, 8th ed. (London, 1794); "Narrative of the Life of Olaudah Equiano" repr. in Henry Louis Gates Jr. and William Andrews, eds., *Pioneers of the Black Atlantic: Five Slave Narratives From the Enlightenment, 1772–1815* (Washington, DC, 1998), 208.

42. Ibid., 185–86, 209.

43. Catherine Acholonu believes that she has met with descendants of Equiano's family, some reputedly over 150 years of age, and reports that they have preserved oral memories of his having been sold into slavery. See Catherine Acholonu, "The Home of Olaudah Equiano—A Linguistic and Anthropological Search," *The Journal of Commonwealth Literature* 22 (1987): 5–16; Acholonu, *The Igbo Roots of Olauda Equiano* (Owerri, Nigeria, 1989).

44. Vincent Carretta, "Three West Indian Writers of the 1780s Revisited and Revised," *Research in African Literatures* 29, 4 (1998): 86, citing the archival research for Olaudah Equiano, *The Interesting Narrative and Other Writing*, ed. Vincent Carretta (London, 1995), 282 n.485, which uncovered the musters for the *Racehorse* in which it is noted that a Gustavus Weston "joined the expedition on 17 May [1773] and is identified as being an able seaman, aged 28, born in South Carolina. Gustavus Weston was almost certainly Gustavaus Vassa." In 1996 Carretta had noted "I accept Equiano's assertion of his African identity as true, in part because I want it to be," a view I have shared as well. See Vincent Carretta, "Introduction," *Unchained Voices: An Anthology of Black Authors in the English-Speaking World of the Eighteenth Century* (Lexington, KY, 1996), 16 n.13. Carretta has continued to research this issue and has identified the records of ships that might well have brought Equiano from Africa to Barbados and on to Virginia (although these journeys were some two years before the dates given in the narrative), but he continues to regard other evidence as supporting his birth in America. He now concludes that "The evidence regarding his place and date of birth is clearly contradictory and will probably remain tantalizingly so." See Carretta, "Olaudah Eqiano or Gustavus

Vassa? New Light on an Eighteenth-Century Question of Identity," *Slavery & Abolition* 20, 3 (1999): 96–105.

45. Elizabeth Isichei, who had accepted Equiano's account of his childhood, has now also re-evaluated it and concludes that he "fused his own recollections with details obtained from other Igbo into a single version." Isichei, "The Life of Olauda Equiano or Gustavas Vassa the African," *Journal of African History* 33 (1992): 164–65.

46. Equiano, *Narrative*, ed. Carretta, notes. See also Paul Edwards, notes and "Introduction," *The Life of Olaudah Equiano* (London, 1988).

47. Harrower, born in 1734, left home in 1773. Equiano sailed to the Orkneys in 1757. Equiano, *Narrative*, ed. Gates, 230.

48. Ibid., 356–60.

49. Paul Edwards and Rosalind Shaw, "The Invisible CHI in Equiano's *Interesting Narrative*," *Journal of Religion in Africa* 19 (1989): 149.

50. Chinua Achebe, *Morning Yet on Creation Day* (Garden City, NJ, 1976), 131.

51. Ibid., 144.

52. Edwards and Shaw, "Invisible CHI," 152–53.

53. See Katalin Orban, "Dominant or Submerged Discourses in the Life of Olaudah Equiano (Or Gustavus Vassa)," *African-American Reviews* 27 (1993): 655–64.

54. Equiano, *Narrative*, ed. Gates, 206. The autobiography of William Alfred, who was born in New York City in 1922, suggests how such an identity can be created. Alfred was brought up in New York City by his grandmother, Anna Maria Gavin Egan, who had left Ireland as a young adult in 1866 or 1867. Egan spent her life in America living out of a trunk and she "taught her children to do the same." "I myself," Alfred wrote, "till well on in my twenties, felt that Ireland, which I had never seen, was my true country." William Alfred, cited by George Henderson and Thompson Olasiji, *Migrants, Immigrants, and Slaves* (Lanham, MD, 1995), 66–70.

55. Equiano, *Narrative*, ed. Gates, 293.

56. Ibid., 327.

57. Ibid., 338.

58. On the identity of the next generation see Joycelyn Moody, "Self-effacement and Collective Identity in Five Black Women's Autobiographies, 1835–1879" (Ph.D. diss., Univ. of Kansas, 1997).

59. See Introduction above.

60. I am including Equiano among the four enslaved, as either he or his mother was brought from abroad.

61. Rudolph J. Vecoli, "The Significance of Immigration in the Formation of an American Identity," *The History Teacher* 30 (1996): 9–27.

62. Shmuel Noah Eisenstadt, "Modernity and the Construction of Collective Identities," *International Journal of Comparative Sociology* 39 (1998): 140, 148–49. The word "white" has been added to the citation. See also Shmuel Noah Eisenstadt and Bernhard Giesen, "The Construction of Collective Identity," *European Journal of Sociology* 36 (1995): 72–102.

63. For an analysis of Italian American and Jewish American collective identities and values see Virginia Yans-McLaughlin, "Metaphors of Self in History: Subjectivity, Oral Narratives, and Immigration Studies," in Yans-McLaughlin, *Immigration Reconsidered: History, Sociology, and Politics* (New York, 1990), 254–89.

64. For an analysis of the role of conflict and exclusion in the formation of collective identities see Joshua Gamon, "Messages of Exclusion: Gender Movements and Symbolic Boundaries," *Gender and Society* 11 (1997): 178–99.

65. Homi Bhabha interviewed by Paul Thompson, "Between Identities," in Rina Benmayer and Andor Skones, eds., *Migration and Identity* (Oxford, 1994), 192–93.

66. Toni Morrison, *Playing in the Dark: Whiteness and the Literary Imagination* (New York. 1993), 38.

67. Ibid. See also Greenblatt, *Renaissance Self-Fashioning*, 9; and Gregg, *Self-Representation*, 47.

CHAPTER 7

I gratefully acknowledge the support of Boston College and the National Endowment for the Humanities in this research and the helpful comments on its presentation by my co-authors—especially David Eltis.

1. Hugh Tinker, *A New System of Slavery: The Export of Indian Labour Overseas, 1830–1920* (London, 1974).

2. Robert J. Steinfeld and Stanley L. Engerman, "Labor-Free or Coerced? A Historical Reassessment of Differences and Similarities," in Tom Brass and Marcel van der Linden, eds., *Free and Unfree Labour: The Debate Continues* (Bern, 1997), 107–26, quote 108; Robert J. Steinfeld, "Changing Legal Conceptions of Free Labor," in Stanley L. Engerman, ed., *Terms of Labor: Slavery, Serfdom, and Free Labor* (Stanford, 1999), 135–67; see also Steinfeld's *The Invention of Free Labor: The Employment Relation in English and American Law and Culture, 1350–1870* (Chapel Hill, NC, 1991).

3. The global history of the identured labor experiences is reviewed by David Northrup, *Indentured Labor in the Age of Imperialism*, 1834–1922 (Cambridge, 1995).

4. "Introduction," in *Slavery in Africa: Historical and Anthropological Perspectives*, ed. Suzanne Miers and Igor Kopytoff (Madison, WI, 1977), 17.

5. Northrup, *Indentured Labor*, 45–48.

6. Denise Bouche, *Les villages de liberté en Afrique noire française* (Paris, 1968).

7. François Renault, *Libération d'esclaves et nouvelle servitude: Les rachats de captifs africains pour le compte des colonies françaises après l'abolition de l'esclavage* (Abidjan, 1976), 30–33, 43–46, 93–96, quote 31.

8. Monica Schuler, "African Immigration to French Guiana: The *Cinq Frères* Group, 1854–1860," *Bulletin of the African Studies Association of the West Indies* 4 (1971): 62–78; id., "Kru Emigration to British and French

Guiana, 1841–1857," in Paul E. Lovejoy, ed., *Africans in Bondage: Studies in Slavery and the Slave Trade* (Madison, WI, 1986), 155–201.

9. Renault, *Libération d'esclaves*, 45.

10. PP 1857–58 lxi [2443–1] Slave Trade, Correspondence (Class B), no. 167, Earl of Clarendon to Earl Cowley (British Ambassador to France), FO, Oct. 19, 1857.

11. PP 1857–58 lxi [2443–1] Ambassador Cowley, Memorandum of a conversation with Count Walewski, French Minister of Foreign Affairs, Nov. 1857, enclosure in no. 173, Cowley to Clarendon, Paris, Nov. 29, 1857.

12. Renault, *Libération d'esclaves*, 30–33, 43–46, 67–71, 93–94.

13. Northrup, *Indentured Labor*, Table A.6.

14. Renault, *Libération d'esclaves*, 95–96.

15. Ibid., 29; David Eltis, *Economic Growth and the Ending of the Transatlantic Slave Trade* (New York, 1987), 246; W. G. Clarence-Smith, "Emigration from Western Africa, 1807–1940," *Itinerario* 14 (1990): 46; Paul Lovejoy, *Transformations in Slavery: A History of Slavery in Africa* (Cambridge, 1983), 156; Schuler, "Kru Emigration," 155, and "African Immigration," 71. During discussion at the Freedom and Migration conference Philip D. Curtin added his endorsement to this position.

16. Eltis, *Economic Growth*, 98.

17. Lovejoy, *Transformations in Slavery*, 255–61; Robert O. Collins, "The Nilotic Slave Trade: Past and Present," *Slavery and Abolition* 13 (1992): 140–61; William Finnegan, "A Reporter at Large: The Invisible War," *The New Yorker*, Jan. 25, 1999, 50–73.

18. PP 1859 xxxiv [2569] no. 138, Commodore Wise to the Secretary of the Admiralty, Loanda, Sept. 9, 1858, 190; PP 1862 lxi [2959] no. 72, Commodore W. Edmonstone to Rear-Admiral Sir H. Keppel, Sierra Leone, Mar. 24, 1861 (extract of a report on the Slave Trade on the West Coast of Africa from July to Dec. 1960), 153; Huntington, HM 30206, Letterbook of Thomas Dornin, Captain of the San Jacinto," Oct. 20, 1860, 62. Thanks to David Eltis for the last reference.

19. Wise to Admiralty, Sept. 9, 1858, 190.

20. PP 1859 xxxiv [2569] enclosure 6 in no. 147, Commander Hunt to Commodore Wise, off Solyman River, Nov. 6, 1958, 205, and no. 148, Commander Hunt to the Admiralty, Dec. 1, 1858.

21. PP 1860 lxx [2749-I] Correspondence Class B, African (Consular) Bight of Benin no. 2, Consul B. Campbell to the Earl of Malmesbury, Lagos, Mar. 4, 1859.

22. Hope Masterton Waddell, *Twenty-Nine Years in the West Indies and Central Africa*, 2d ed. (London, 1970), 434–35; Kannan K. Nair, *Politics and Society in South Eastern Nigeria, 1841–1906* (London, 1972), 46–51.

23. Renault, *Libération d'esclaves*, 63.

24. PP 1859 xxxiv [2569] enclosure in no. 147, Commander Hunt to

Commodore Wise, Nov. 6, 1858, 205, citing the testimony of knowledgeable headmen.

25. FO84/1054/55–60, William Lawless to FO, Apr. 29 1858; PP 1863 lxxi [3159] no. 124, Commodore Edmonstone to Rear-Admiral Sir B. Walker, Sierra Leone, Oct. 22, 1862, quoting the report of Commander Smith.

26. Cowley, Memorandum, Nov. 1857.

27. ANSOM, Martinique 131/1194. F. Lamouroux, Agent d'Emigration, au Ministre de la Marine et des Colonies, Calcutta, Dec. 3, 1875.

28. David Northrup, "Indentured Indians in the French Caribbean," *Revue française d'histoire d'outre-mer* 87 (2000): 250–52; compare P. C. Emmer, "The Great Escape: The Migration of Female Indentures Servants from British India to Surinam, 1873–1916," in *Abolition and Its Aftermath: The Historical Context, 1790–1916*, ed. David Richardson (London, 1985), 245–66.

29. Schuler, "Kru Emigration," 181.

30. FO84/1054/8–22, Lawless to FO, Feb. 28, 1858, no. 1.

31. For example, FO27/2347, Lawless to FO, St. Pierre, June 8 and Nov. 26, 1878; FO27/2477, Lawless to FO, St. Pierre, June 10, 1880.

32. 100 francs = £4 = $20 = 40 rupees.

33. Steinfeld, *Invention of Free Labor*, 147–72.

34. ANSOM, Guadeloupe 180/1118, Gouverneur-General Lucien Baffer au Gouverneur de la Guadeloupe, July 9, 1864. Chinese convictions were still higher, 15 out of 365 or 41 per thousand.

35. ANSOM, Martinique 130/1170, Etat de situation des immigrants, Dec. 31, 1859; FO27/2893, William Lawless to FO, St. Pierre, Sept. 6, 1887, no. 20, Report on Martinique, 78.

36. IO, P/1171, F. Wooldridge, Report on the treatment and condition of Indian immigrants in French Guiana during the year 1873; P/693, F. Wooldridge, Report on the treatment and condition of coolies in French Guiana—year 1873.

37. Schuler, "Kru Emigration," 179–83, table 8.3.

38. ANSOM, Guadeloupe 56/399, Hugueniz, Rapport sur arrondissement de Basse Terre, July 8, 1859; Martinique 130/1170, Situation indicante le nombre de rengagements d'Indiens dans la Colonie depuis le mois de juin 1858 au 1 octobre 1862.

39. Northrup, "Indentured Indians," 259–63.

40. FO27/3167, Surgeon-Major D. W. D. Comins to Government of Bengal, Calcutta, June 14, 1891.

41. ANSOM, Martinique 32/276, Etat nominatif des habitations et situation de leur effectif au 30 juin 1885.

42. Lawless, Report on Martinique, 88.

43. FO27/2657, Decomis, Report on the general condition and treatment of Indian immigrants in French Guiana during the years 1880, 1881, and 1882, Cayenne, May 15, 1883, enclosed in Decomis to FO, Cayenne,

May 23, 1883, no. 4; and FO27/2943, William Wyndham, Consul, Cayenne and Surinam, to FO, Paramaribo, No. 61, Oct. 23, 1888, and Consular Agent, Pondichéry and Karikal, to Government of Madras, Jan. 12, 1888, no. 31, in Government of Madras Public, no. 229–230, Mar. 2, 1888, enclosed in India Office to FO, Aug. 4, 1888, J&P 932.

44. FO27/2612, Decomis, Report on the condition and treatment of the Indian immigrants on the "Ilet Portal" (Maroni River), Cayenne Mar. 15, 1882, enclosed in Decomis to FO, Cayenne, Mar. 15, 1882, Slave Trade no. 5.

CHAPTER 8

1. Walton Look Lai, *Indentured Labor, Caribbean Sugar: Chinese and Indian Migrants to the British West Indies, 1838–1918* (Baltimore, 1993), 265. P. C. Emmer, ed., *Colonialism and Migration: Indentured Labor before and after Slavery* (Dordrecht, the Netherlands, 1986).

2. W. Arthur Lewis, *The Evolution of the International Economic Order* (Princeton, NJ, 1978), 14.

3. Lewis stated erroneously that most were indentured laborers.

4. Prakash C. Jain, "Emigration and Settlement of Indians Abroad," *Sociological Bulletin* 38, 1 (Mar. 1989): 157, citing Kingsley Davis, *The Population of India and Pakistan* (Princeton, NJ, 1968).

5. David Northrup, *Indentured Labor in the Age of Imperialism, 1834–1922* (Cambridge, 1995), 61.

6. See David Northrup, *Indentured Labor*; Kay Saunders, ed., *Indentured Labor in the British Empire, 1834–1920* (London, 1984); Emmer, ed., *Colonialism and Migration*. See also *Itinerario* 21, 1 (1997).

7. Hugh Tinker, *A New System of Slavery: The Export of Indian Labor Overseas, 1830–1920* (Oxford, 1974). See also PP 1910, XXVII (Cd.5192–94). Report of the Committee on Emigration from India to the Crown Colonies and Protectorates (Sanderson Commission).

8. Joan M. Jensen, *Passage from India: Asian Indian Immigrants in North America* (New Haven, CT, 1988). Roger Daniels, "The Indian Diaspora in the United States," in Judith M. Brown and Rosemary Foot, eds., *Migration, the Asian experience* (New York, 1994).

9. Also Burma, where small numbers of Chinese traders went, often via Southeast Asia.

10. Wang Gungwu, "Patterns of Chinese Migration in Historical Perspective," chap. 1 of *China and the Chinese Overseas* (Singapore, 1991), 15. Lynn Pan, ed., *The Encyclopedia of the Chinese Overseas* (Singapore and Cambridge, MA, 1998), 36–38.

11. Hugh Tinker, *A New System of Slavery*, 274; Walton Look Lai, *Indentured Labor, Caribbean Sugar*, 148–51. I. M. Cumpston, *Indians Overseas in British Territories, 1834–1854* (Oxford, 1953), 43–45; Jaime Sarusky, "The East Indian Community in Cuba," in Frank Birbalsingh, ed., *Indenture and Exile: Selected Papers from the York University Indo-Caribbean Studies Conference, July 1988* (Toronto, 1989), 73–78.

12. Lucy Cohen, *The Chinese in the Post-Civil War South* (Louisiana, 1984), 48–49.

13. Persia Campbell, *Chinese Coolie Emigration to Countries within the British Empire* (London, 1971).

14. Denise Helly, *Ideologie et Ethnicite: les Chinois Macao a Cuba, 1847–1886* (Montreal, 1979); Denise Helly, ed., *The Cuba Commission Report: A Hidden History of the Chinese in Cuba. The Original English Language Text of 1876* (Baltimore, 1993); Humberto Rodriguez Pastor, *Hijos del Celeste Imperio en el Peru, 1850–1900: Migracion, Agricultura, Mentalidad y Explotacion* (Lima, 1989); Ronald Takaki, *Pau Hana: Plantation Life and Labor in Hawaii, 1835–1920* (Honolulu, 1983).

15. Cohen, *Chinese in the Post-Civil War South*; Jeffrey Lesser, *Negotiating National Identity: Immigrants, Minorities, and the Struggle for Ethnicity in Brazil* (Durham, NC, 1999), chap. 2.

16. Cohen, *Chinese in the Post-Civil War South*, chap. 3; James W. Loewen, *The Mississippi Chinese: Between Black and White* (Cambridge, MA, 1971).

17. For indentured migration statistics, see David Northrup, *Indentured Labor*, 156–61.

18. Chinese brokers often transferred or sold their debt arrangements and their charges to local employers in Southeast Asia (and even in North America) in search of quasi-contract labor.

19. Maistry in Burma.

20. Malaya employed Indians (mainly Tamils) as indentureds in the sugar and coffee sectors between 1840 and 1910 and recruited them under the kangani system for the rubber plantations from 1910 to 1938.

21. Walton Look Lai, *Indentured Labor, Caribbean Sugar*, 227.

22. See United States, National Archives and Records Administration. Index to 'Chinese Exclusion' Case Files of the New York District Office of the U.S. Immigration and Naturalization Service, ca. 1882–1960. New York: National Archives and Records Administration—Northeast Region (New York).

23. Cohen, *Chinese in the Post-Civil War South*, chap. 3.

24. Ta Chen, *Chinese Migrations. With Special Reference to Labor Conditions* (Washington, 1923; repr. Taipei, Taiwan, 1967); Lynn Pan, *Sons of the Yellow Emperor: A History of the Chinese Diaspora* (New York, 1994).

25. See Ta Chen, *Chinese Migrations*, chap. 1, on the early colonization of Formosa (Taiwan) and the Pescadores islands. In the fourth century A.D., the Buddhist monk Faxian of the Jin dynasty, returning from a pilgrimage to India through about 30 countries, recorded in his *Records of the Buddhist Country* encounters with several overseas Chinese communities. For the coastal and maritime tradition between the tenth and fifteenth centuries A.D., see Wang Gungwu, *The Chinese Overseas* (Cambridge, MA, 2000), chap. 1.

26. Hugh Tinker, *A New System of Slavery*, 44–46.

27. Ibid., 39–43; Dirk Kolff, "The Historical Context of the Indian Diaspora," paper presented at *Conference on Challenge and Change: The Indian Diaspora in its Historical and Contemporary Contexts*, Univ. of the West Indies, Trinidad, August 1995.

28. Romesh Dutt, *The Economic History of India under Early British Rule* (New Delhi, 1970); Neil Charlesworth, *British Rule and the Indian Economy, 1800–1914* (London, 1982); Dharma Kumar, ed., *Cambridge Economic History of India* 2 (Cambridge, 1984).

29. Pan, ed., *The Encyclopedia of the Chinese Overseas*, 30–43.

30. As late as the 1950s Fujianese constituted 50 percent of the Chinese population of Indonesia, 40 percent of that of Malaysia, and as much as 82 percent of that of the Phillipines. By contrast, more than 90 percent of the pan-American and Hawaii Chinese before the 1970s were Cantonese. According to the recently published *Encyclopedia of Chinese Overseas,* up to the 1950s Guangdongese (northeast and southern) constituted 68 percent of the world's overseas Chinese communities.

31. The Siyi (Four Districts) were Taishan, Xinhui, Kaiping, and Enping. The Sanyi (Three Districts), just south of Guangzhou (Canton), were Nanhai, Panyu, and Shunde.

32. Look Lai, *Indentured Labor, Caribbean Sugar*, 41–44.

33. H. P. Sharma, "Perspectives on Indians Abroad," *Sociological Bulletin* 38, 1 (Mar. 1989): 3.

34. PP 1874, XLVII (314). Report by J. Geoghegan on Emigration from India. George Grierson, *Report on Colonial Emigration from the Bengal Presidency* (Calcutta, 1883).

35. John Hill, "Crucible of the Diaspora: Politics and Community in the Bhojpuri and Adjacent Regions, 1880–1910," paper presented at *Conference on Challenge and Change: The Indian Diaspora in Its Historical and Contemporary Contexts,* Univ. of the West Indies, Trinidad, August 1995.

36. PP 1910, XXVII (Cd. 5192). Report of the Committee on Emigration from India to the Crown Colonies and Protectorates (Sanderson Commission), paragraphs 68 and 77.

37. Steven Vertovec, *Hindu Trinidad* (London, 1992), 90.

38. Raymond Smith, "Some Social Characteristics of Indian Immigrants to British Guiana," *Population Studies* 13, 1 (1959): 39.

39. P. C. Emmer, "Caribbean Plantations and Indentured Labor, 1640–1917," *Itinerario* 21, 1 (1997): 79.

40. See J. Geoghegan on Emigration from India.

41. A number of the Indians who migrated to Jamaica later found themselves relocating to Cuba along with other Jamaican migrant workers around the turn of the century, mainly to work on American-owned sugar plantations, but these numbers were small and not related to our current discussion. There were 2,000 between 1905 and 1916, according to Jaime Sarusky, "The East Indian Community in Cuba." Frank Birbalsingh, ed.,

Indenture and Exile: The Indo-Caribbean Experience: Selected Papers from the York University Indo-Caribbean Studies Conference, July 1988 (Toronto, 1989), 73–78.

42. Walton Look Lai, *The Chinese in the West Indies, 1806–1995: A Documentary History* (Mona, 1998), 92–96. Arnold Meagher, "The Introduction of Chinese Laborers to Latin America: The 'Coolie Trade,' 1847–1874" (Ph.D. diss., Univ. Calif., Davis, 1975), 201 and app. 6, lists 68 mutinies in the same period, most Cuba- and Peru-bound.

43. PP 1871, XX (C.393). Report of the Commissioners appointed to enquire into the treatment of immigrants in British Guiana.

44. Chief Justice Beaumont's report to the visiting commission of enquiry had to be published independently, because the commission refused to incorporate its criticisms into their final report.

45. See Trevor Sue-a-Quan, *Cane Reapers* (Vancouver, 1999), for excerpts from the *Royal Gazette*.

46. Denise Helly, ed., *The Cuba Commission Report: A Hidden History of the Chinese in Cuba. The Original English Language Text of 1876* (Baltimore, 1993), 88–89.

47. See Look Lai, *The Chinese in the West Indies*, chap. 7, for excerpts from these critiques.

48. Penal sanctions for work offenses also existed in nineteenth-century Britain, under an act of 1823 which amended older master-servant legislation, but they were ended in the 1870s, whereas colonial indenture penal sanctions continued until the demise of indenture in 1917. See Sir William Holdsworth, *A History of English Law* 15 (London, 1956): 19–20. For a discussion on the thin line between free and coerced labor in different traditions, especially Britain and the US, see Robert Steinfeld and Stanley Engerman, "Labor—Free or Coerced? A Historical Reassessment of Differences and Similarities," in Tom Brass and Marcel van der Linden, eds., *Free and Unfree Labour: The Debate Continues* (Bern, 1997), 107–26.

49. The Indians moreover often complained about the abuse of women and nonrecognition of religious mores.

50. Look Lai, *Indentured Labor, Caribbean Sugar*, 58–60.

51. All these communities, especially Cuba's, experienced declines in the late twentieth century (post-1960s), for reasons which are not relevant to this discussion.

52. Though there has been a small renewed inflow since the late 1980s into several of the older territories, and even a few new ones, migration from the East has generally played a small role in the life of this community since the 1950s.

53. With the exception of those metropolitan countries at the turn of the century which had explicitly adopted anti-immigration laws.

54. A miniscule migration of Sindhi and Gujerati merchants to the West Indies in the 1930s and 1940s is discussed in Peter Hanoomansingh,

"Beyond Profit and Capital: A study of the Sindhis and Gujeratis of Barbados," in Rhoda Reddock, ed., *Ethnic Minorities in Caribbean Society* (Trinidad, 1996), 272–342.

55. Look Lai, *Indentured Labor, Caribbean Sugar*, 37.

56. Evelyn Hu-de Hart, "Immigrants to a Developing Society: The Chinese in Northern Mexico, 1875–1932," *Journal of Arizona History* 21 (1980): 49–86; Leo M. D. Jacques., "The Anti-Chinese Campaign in Sonora, Mexico, 1900–1931" (Ph.D. diss., Univ. of Ariz., 1974).

57. Edgar Wickberg. "Relations: Ethnicity," *The Encyclopedia of the Chinese Overseas*, 114.

58. Until the formation of Singapore in 1965 (and not counting Hong Kong).

59. Persia Campbell, *Chinese Coolie Emigration*, 7.

60. Steinfeld and Engerman, "Labor—Free or Coerced? A Historical Reassessment of Differences and Similarities," 107–26.

61. Persia Campbell, *Chinese Coolie Emigration*, chap. 1.

62. See Gunther Barth, *Bitter Strength: A History of the Chinese in the United States: 1850–1870* (Cambridge, MA, 1964), 55–58; Patricia Cloud and David Galenson, "Chinese Immigration and Contract Labor in the Late Ninteenth Century," *Explorations in Economic History* 24, 1 (1987): 22–42.

63. See Herbert Klein and Stanley Engerman, "The Transition from Slave to Free Labor: Notes on a Comparative Economic Model," in Manuel Moreno Fraginals et al., eds., *Between Slavery and Free Labor: The Spanish-speaking Caribbean in the Nineteenth Century* (Baltimore, 1985), 254–77.

CHAPTER 9

1. Britain also transported several thousand convicts and military prisoners to its colonies in the Caribbean during the seventeenth and eighteenth centuries. As a work force for fortifications, 9,000 convicts were sent to Bermuda between 1824 and 1863, and 8,000 to Gibralter between 1842 and 1875. No residence was intended for the convicts in Bermuda and Gibralter, and those who survived were repatriated, apart from several hundred who were sent from Bermuda to Australia.

2. Aaron S. Fogleman, "From Slaves, Convicts, and Servants to Free Passengers: The Transformation of Immigration in the Era of the American Revolution," *JAH* 85 (June 1998): 44.

3. Albert Emerson Smith, *Colonists in Bondage: White Servitude and Convict Labor in America 1607–1776* (Chapel Hill, NC, 1947), 98–99.

4. J. M. Beattie, *Crime and the Courts in England* (Princeton, NJ, 1986), 468–78.

5. J. A. Sharpe, *Judicial Punishment in England* (London, 1990), 40.

6. Quoted in Beattie, *Crime and the Courts*, 479.

7. Ibid., 485, 493.

8. Ibid., 502–3.
9. 4 Geo. I, c. 11 (1718).
10. Smith, *Colonists in Bondage*, 110 ff.
11. Beattie, *Crime and the Courts*, 507.
12. Ibid., 519.
13. Fogleman, "From Slaves, Convicts and Servants," 44.
14. Beattie, *Crime and the Courts*, 251–52.
15. A. Roger Ekirch, *Bound for America: The Transportation of British Convicts to the Colonies 1718–1775* (Oxford, 1987), 5 and 31.
16. Ibid., 104–5.
17. Ibid., 124–25. For a more detailed discussion of the prices of convicts and indentured servants, see Farley Grubb, "The Transatlantic Market for British Convict Labor," *JEH* 60, 1 (Mar. 2000): 94–122.
18. Ekirch, *Bound for America*, 166. This measure of density relates to the white population only. Blacks were about 40 percent of the population in the Chesapeake as a whole in 1755. See Stanley L. Engerman and Robert E. Gallman, eds., *The Cambridge Economic History of the United States*, vol. 1, *The Colonial Era* (Cambridge, 1996), 173.
19. Smith, *Colonists in Bondage*, 128–29.
20. Ekirch, *Bound for America*, 150.
21. Bernard Bailyn, *The Peopling of the British Peripheries in the Eighteenth Century* (Canberra, 1988), 19. The reference to Australia is from the title of a book by Robert Hughes, *The Fatal Shore* (London, 1987).
22. Ekirch, *Bound for America*, 194–95, 206–9.
23. For the opinions of contemporaries, see e.g. Smith, *Colonists in Bondage*, 129–30. Smith and a number of other historians agree with the contemporaries. See e.g. Richard B. Morris, *Government and Labor in Early America* (New York, 1965), 327–33.
24. 4 Geo. I, c. 11(1718).
25. David W. Galenson, *White Servitude in Colonial America: An Economic Analysis* (Cambridge, 1981), 178–79.
26. Sheila Lambert, ed., *House of Commons Sessional Papers of the Eighteenth Century* 9 (Wilmington, DE, 1975): 357–67.
27. 16 Geo. III, c. 43 (1776).
28. The alternative of penitentiaries was considered but rejected.
29. 24 Geo. III, c. 56 (1784). Ireland and Scotland followed with similar provisions.
30. See, e.g., Alan Frost, "Towards Australia: The Coming of the Europeans 1400 to 1788," chap. 19 in *Australians to 1788* (Sydney, 1987). For an opposing view, Mollie Gillen, "The Botany Bay Decision, 1786; Convicts not Empire," *English Historical Review* 97 (1982): 740–66.
31. *Parliamentary Register* 21 (1787): 2.
32. A. G. L. Shaw, *Convicts and the Colonies: A Study of Penal Transportation from Great Britain and Ireland to Australia and Other Parts of the British Empire* (Melbourne, 1966), 149.
33. Raymond L. Cohn, "Maritime Mortality in the Eighteenth and

Nineteenth Centuries: A Survey," *International Journal of Maritime History* 1 (June 1989): 189. Drawing on several sources, Cohn gives mortality figures for convicts per month of voyage: to America 1719–36, 65.5; 1770–75, 14.1; to Australia 1788–1814, 11.3; 1815–68, 2.4.

34. L. L. Robson, *The Convict Settlers of Australia* (Melbourne, 1965), 182, 184.

35. Shaw, *Convicts and the Colonies*, 150–54.

36. C. M. H. Clark, *A History of Australia* 1 (Melbourne, 1962); Robson, *The Convict Settlers*; Shaw, *Convicts and the Colonies*.

37. Clark, *A History*, 94.

38. Shaw, *Convicts and the Colonies*, 164–65.

39. Robson, *The Convict Settlers*, 176–77, 185. No information concerning previous offenses was obtained for about two-fifths of the sample.

40. Stephen Nicholas and Peter R. Shergold, "Unshackling the Past," in Stephen Nicholas, ed., *Convict Workers: Reinterpreting Australia's Past* (Cambridge, 1988), 7, 46. For discussion of these issues, see John Hirst, "Convicts and Crime," *Overland* 113 (1988): 81–83.

41. Stephen Nicholas and Peter R. Shergold, "Convicts as Migrants," in Nicholas, ed., *Convict Workers*, 46.

42. N. G. Butlin, *Forming a Colonial Economy, Australia, 1810–1850* (Cambridge, 1994), 39–43.

43. Stephen Nicholas and Peter R. Shergold, "Convicts as Workers," in Nicholas, ed., *Convict Workers*, 75.

44. Ibid., 63–74.

45. Ralph Shlomowitz, "Convict Workers: A Review Article," *Australian Economic History Review* 30, 2 (Sept. 1990): 70–74.

46. Shaw, *Convicts and the Colonies*, 228.

47. *Historical Records of Australia*, ser. 1, vol. 19 (1923), 653–54.

48. Ibid.

49. Stephen Nicholas, "The Care and Feeding of the Convicts," in Nicholas, ed., *Convict Workers*, 181.

50. Shaw, *Convicts and the Colonies*, 230.

51. Nicholas, "Care and Feeding," 187.

52. The flow of 9,643 convicts into Western Australia did not stop until 1868. They provided a much-needed labor force for the faltering settlement.

53. Butlin, *Forming a Colonial Economy*, pt. 3.

54. See e.g. David Neal, *The Rule of Law in a Penal Colony: Law and Power in Early New South Wales* (Cambridge, 1991), chap. 1.

55. John B. Hirst, *Convict Society and Its Enemies* (Sydney, 1983), 89.

56. Shaw, *Convicts and the Colonies*, 227–28. The figure of 2,087 persons convicted appears to be a misprint for 2,807.

57. Ibid., 216; Hirst, *Convict Society*, 72.

58. Memorandum by Sir Richard Bourke to Lord John Russell, Dec. 26, 1838, in Irish University Press, Series of British Parliamentary Papers, *Transportation*, vol. 6, 1810–41, 749.

59. Hirst, *Convict Society*, 81.

60. Shaw, *Convicts and the Colonies*, 229.

61. Gustave de Beaumont and Alexis de Tocqueville, *Du système pénitentiaire aux États-Unis, et de son application en France; suivi d'un appendice sur les colonies pénales et de notes statistiques* (Paris, 1833).

62. *Moniteur*, Nov. 13, 1850, 3246.

63. Gordon Wright, *Between the Guillotine and Liberty: Two Centuries of the Crime Problem in France* (New York, 1983), 93.

64. The background to France's decision to begin transportation is set out in Colin Forster, *France and Botany Bay: The Lure of a Penal Colony* (Melbourne, 1996).

65. Centre des Archives d'Outre-Mer, *Terres de bagne* (Aix-en-Provence, 1990), 19.

66. Michel Pierre, "La transportation (1848–1938)," in Jacques-Guy Petit et al., *Histoire des galères, bagnes et prisons, XIIIe.–XXe. siècles* (Toulouse, 1991), 240.

67. Isobelle Merle, *Expériences coloniales: La Nouvelle-Calédonie (1853–1920)* (Paris, 1995), 62–69.

68. Pierre, "La transportation," 242.

69. Figures for the categories of prisoners are taken from Centre des Archives, *Terres de bagne* (1990), 39, 63.

70. Ibid., 41–42. The law required mandatory sentencing, and this was related to the seriousness of the offenses and their number; see H. Donnedieu de Vabres, *Traité élémentaire de droit criminel et de législation pénale comparée* (Paris, 1943), 273–79. In fact, magistrates found ways to soften the application of the law.

71. Centre des Archives, *Terres de bagne*, 60.

72. Merle, *Expériences coloniales*, 121, 125–26, 136.

73. Centre des Archives, *Terres de bagne*, 63.

74. Merle, *Expériences coloniales*, 144.

75. Centre des Archives, *Terres de bagnes*, 78.

76. Merle, *Expériences coloniales*, 146.

77. Bernard Quris, *Les portes de l'enfer* (Paris, 1975), 276–77.

78. Early on, convicts in prisons in France took a rosy view of life in New Caledonia and committed serious offenses in prison so that they could be sent there. Their number was sufficient for a law in 1880 requiring the new sentences of these convicts to be served in France. Donnedieu de Vabres, *Traité élémentaire*, 263–65.

79. Merle, *Expériences coloniales*, 337.

80. Centre des Archives, *Terres de bagnes*, 75.

81. Ibid., 39.

82. Michel Pierre, *La terre de la grande punition* (Paris, 1984), 41.

83. Michel Pierre, *Le dernier exil: histoire des bagnes et des forcats* (Paris, 1989), 111.

84. Pierre, "La transportation," 251.

85. Ibid.

86. Centre Des Archives, *Terres de bagnes*, 45.
87. Pierre, *La terre*, 262.
88. Quris, *Les portes*, 316.
89. C. Péan, *The Conquest of Devil's Island* (London, 1953), 171. Pierre, *Le dernier exil*, 126.
90. Centre des Archives, *Terres de bagnes*, 82.
91. Hughes, *Fatal Shore*, 586.

CHAPTER 10

1. V. P. Alekseev, *Proiskhozhdenie narodov Vostochnoi Evropy (Kraneologicheskoe issledovanie)* (Moscow, 1969), 10, 206–7. Osteologically, the contemporary Great Russian people are 95 percent Czech/Bohemian and 5 percent Finnic. Important recent publications on Russian migration and colonization are M. K. Liubavskii's *Obzor istorii russkoi kolonizatsii* (Moscow, 1996), written decades ago but only now published, and V. A. Aleksandrov et al., *Russkie: Etnoterritoriia, rasselenie, chislennost', istoricheskie sud'by (XII-XX vv.)* (Moscow, 1995).

2. See also Arcadius Kahan, *The Plow, the Hammer, and the Knout* (Chicago, 1985), 16 *et passim*.

3. *AMG* 1, nos. 210 and 297; 2, nos. 423 and 1073.

4. See, for example, *Dopolneniia k aktam istoricheskim* 3 (1848): 243–49, no. 67. An English-language translation of this document under the title "Working Orders to Olonets Governor Vasilii Aleksandrovich Choglokov on the Exercise of His Duties as Governor, 1649" is available in various editions of my *Readings for Introduction to Russian Civilization*. The *Ulozhenie* of 1649 noted that Russians regularly crossed the frontiers with Sweden and the Rzechpospolita and got married (Richard Hellie, trans. and ed., *The Muscovite Law Code [Ulozhenie] of 1649* [Irvine, CA, 1988], 94, chap. 11 art. 34). Hellie, "The Impact of the Southern and Eastern Frontiers of Muscovy on the *Ulozhenie* of 1649 Compared with the Impact of the Western Frontier," *Russian History* 19 (1992): 75–96 argues that half of the law code was motivated to one or another extent by frontier concerns, which in turn were migration concerns.

5. *Istoriia Sibiri s drevneishikh vremën do nashikh dnei v piati tomakh*, 5 vols., ed. by A. P. Okladnikov et al. (Moscow, 1968–69), 2:25–352.

6. This has provoked dreams among Turkish "nationalists" down to the present day about a greater Turkey/Turania which would involve uniting Turkey with Azerbaijan and the Turkish regions across the Caspian in Central Asia and beyond.

7. The material in this chapter on the Turkic and Mongol peoples along the southern frontier has benefited from my reading Michael Khodarkovsky's book manuscript *From Frontier to Empire: The Russian Empire in the Southern Steppe, 1480–1800* and especially his article "Taming the 'Wild Steppe': Muscovy's Southern Frontier, 1480–1600" summarizing

Muscovite relations with the Tatars, Nogais, and Kazakhs, in *Russian History* 26, 3 (Fall 1999): 241–97.

8. The Muscovite conquest of Astrakhan' in 1556 reminds the historian of the conquest of Khazariia in 965 by Sviatoslav, which gave the Pechenegs full access to the Black Sea steppe. The consequences for the Eastern Slavs were not the same, however. At the end of the tenth century Vladimir, the "Christianizer of Rus'," built fortified lines along the rivers south of Kiev flowing into the Dnepr, which generally kept the Turkish nomads out of the forest zone and away from Kiev (except when they were invited to participate in East Slavic civil wars), just as Muscovite fortified lines ultimately protected Moscow. The Kievans, however, did not have the resources to move their lines further out into the steppe, as the Muscovites did, with the consequence that the Slavs in the Kievan and Mongol periods had to abandon hopes of farming the steppe and the farmers were forced to withdraw entirely into the forest zone.

9. I have told this story in much greater detail in my documentary collection *Muscovite Society* (Chicago, 1967 and 1970) and monograph *Enserfment and Military in Muscovy* (Chicago, 1971). Those who might think my comparison is excessively fanciful should ponder the fact that today Russia accounts for only 0.6 percent of the world economy.

10. N. A. Rozhkov, *Sel'skoe khoziaistvo Moskovskoi Rusi v XVI veke* (Moscow, 1899), 305–17; V. D. Koroliuk, *Livonskaia voina* (Moscow, 1954); S. B. Veselovskii, *Issledovaniia po istorii oprichniny* (Moscow, 1963). The number of works on the Oprichnina is legion, but I summarized the issues in my article "What Happened? How Did He Get Away With It? Ivan Groznyi's Paranoia and the Problem of Institutional Restraints," *Russian History* 15, 1–4(1987): 199–224.

11. The account by John Stow of the firestorm in Moscow on May 24, 1571, is one of the more terrifying accounts in all of Russian history (Hakluyt Society, *Early Voyages and Travels to Russia and Persia, by Anthony Jenkinson and Other Englishmen*, ed. E. Delman Morgan and C. H. Coote [2 vols., London, 1886], 2:338–40). This account alleged that the Crimeans attacked with 120,000 men and that more than 200,000 Russians perished.

12. These documents, the most interesting collective first-person narratives issuing from Muscovy, are translated in Hellie, *Muscovite Society*, 167–205.

13. This is available in English in my translation, *The Muscovite Law Code (Ulozhenie) of 1649*. The legal history of the document can be found in my "Russian Law from Oleg to Peter the Great," in *The Laws of Rus'—Tenth to Fifteenth Centuries*, trans. and ed. Daniel H. Kaiser (Salt Lake City, 1992), xi–xii.

14. A. G. Man'kov claimed that the 52-article decree of March 2, 1683, to the state's fugitive serf and slave hunters was the most important legislative document of the second half of the seventeenth century (*RZ* 4:79).

15. This subject will be discussed further below.

16. See chap. 11 art. 30 and chap. 15 art. 3 which permit estate owners to set free or move around their peasants, "rights" which are forbidden to holders of service landholdings because subsequent servicemen holding such lands had the right to get back any peasants so moved or manumitted.

17. *RZ* 4:102–3. The law further provided that if no sum was mentioned, then a tax of 30 kopeks per person should be collected. Interestingly, the 1688 decree noted that the service land chancellery was supposed to handle such transactions, not the slavery chancellery. Thus the distinction between serfs and slaves was being juridically preserved, even though it was fast becoming a fiction. Man'kov pointed out in his recently published monograph that for a time until 1675 transactions ceding hereditary estate peasants without land were registered in the slavery chancellery (*Zakonodatel'stvo*, 85). Obviously the government in 1675 was not willing to countenance the fact that its seignorial serfs were de facto close to slaves.

18. *PRP* 8:246–54.

19. *RZ* 5:19–21.

20. The text of this decree can be found in Basil Dmytryshyn, ed., *Imperial Russia. A Source Book, 1700–1917* (Hinsdale, IL, 1974), 126–27.

21. A. A. Novosel'skii, "Pobegi krest'ian i kholopov i ikh sysk v Moskovskom gosudarstve vtoroi poloviny XVII veka," *Trudy Instituta istorii RANION* 1 (1926): 325–54.

22. A. A. Titov, ed., *Kungurskie akty XVII veka (1668–1699)* (St. Petersburg, 1888), 32–33, no. 15.

23. *Novgorodskie pistsovye knigi, izdannye Arkheograficheskoiu komissieiu* (6 vols. + index; St. Petersburg, 1859–1915).

24. In 1556 the government required all owners of *votchina* land to render military service more or less equally with holders of *pomest'e* landholdings, but the former retained a mystique which the latter never had: possession just is never the same as ownership.

25. See the court cases in A. I. Iakovlev, *Kholopstvo i kholopy v Moskovskom gosudarstve XVII v.* (Moscow-Leningrad, 1943). All of these cases are summarized in my *Slavery in Russia 1450–1725* (Chicago, 1982).

26. See also my comprehensive essay "The Stratification of Muscovite Society: The Townsmen," *Russian History* 6, no. 2 (1979): 119–75. Chapter 19 of the *Ulozhenie* deals with the issue of the townsmen, their binding to their towns, and the consequences thereof (especially what is to happen when fugitives marry). This document and the documents leading up to it are translated in my *Muscovite Society*, 33–62.

27. These were the last major invasions of Russia across the western frontier until the ill-fated attempted invasions of Charles XII in 1709 and Napoleon in 1812. Between 1709 and 1812 Russia's wars were fought primarily outside the country with a corresponding diminution of demographic losses.

28. See AMG 1, no. 651, for a 1634 petition by Russian troops asking

the government to overturn its edict that they could not keep military captives. Their request was granted.

29. A. A. Novosel'skii, *Bor'ba moskovskogo gosudarstva s tatarami v pervoi polovine XVII veka* (Moscow-Leningrad, 1948).

30. This was somewhat different from the African slave raiding system. Africans initially went on slave raids to capture women and children for lineage expansion. Men of other tribes were slaughtered because they might resist enslavement, could not be incorporated in a lineage, were of little labor utility in a system where most agricultural work was done by women, and might organize to try to recover their family members if left alive. The organization of the overseas slave trade changed this equation because adult males could be sold abroad, rather than slaughtered. See my article "Slavery," *The New Encyclopaedia Britannica*, 15th ed. (1989) 27:285–98.

31. Michael Khodarkovsky, *Where Two Worlds Met. The Russian State the Kalmyk Nomads, 1600–1771* (Ithaca, NY, 1992).

32. N. A. Zhukovskaia, "Kalmyki," *Narody Rossii. Entsiklopediia*, ed. Valerii A. Tishkov (Moscow, 1994), 179.

33. V. P. Zagorovskii, *Belgorodskaia cherta* (Voronezh, 1969). The most impressive, informative description of the building of a section of the Belgorod Line is Brian Davies's magisterial "The Role of the Town Governors in the Defense and Military Colonization of Muscovy's Southern Frontier: The Case of Kozlov, 1635–1638" (2 vols.; Ph.D. diss., Univ. of Chicago, 1983).

34. V. P. Zagorovskii, *Iziumskaia cherta* (Voronezh: Izd–vo Voronezhskogo Un-ta, 1980).

35. Alan W. Fisher, *The Russian Annexation of Crimea 1772–1783* (Cambridge, 1970).

36. The enserfment decrees typically were annulled for such areas (Hellie, *Enserfment*, 250–51).

37. See 1649 *Ulozhenie* 20:74, 97–99, 117–18.

38. W. F. Reddaway, ed., "The Instructions to the Commissioners for Composing a New Code of Laws," in *Documents of Catherine the Great* (Cambridge, 1931), 257, chap. 12, art. 265. Her legislative commission failed primarily, in my opinion, because no Odoevskii commission had prepared a draft for discussion, as had been the case of the great *Ulozhenie* of 1649. Others have advanced other reasons, such as irreconcilable differences among the various social estates represented at the legislative commission. The fact is, however, that, had there been a draft text, the areas of discord could have been isolated and either resolved or let be, while the main issue, a workable law code, could have been effected.

39. V. M. Kabuzan, *Emigratsiia i reemigratsiia v Rossii v XVIII-nachale XX veka* (Moscow, 1998), 14.

40. See my "Patterns of Instability in Russian and Soviet History. Part 1, 750 to 1917," *The Chicago Review of International Affairs* 1, 3 (Autumn 1989): 3–34. The theme of violence and neurobiology is the sub-

ject of my paper currently in press in Kiev in a Festschrift for Jaroslaw Pelenski. Violence is a central theme in Georg Bernhard Michels's work on the Russian church schism (*Raskol*) and other religious dissent (most of it unrelated to the schism) of the 1650s–80s (*At War with the Church: Religious Dissent in Seventeenth-Century Russia* [Stanford, 1999]).

41. The period of the collapse of the Soviet Union in 1991 and subsequent years has been the first time in Russian history when major disruptions did not result in deurbanization and a return to the farms. The Soviets firmly urbanized much of the population to the point that many people had no farms to return to. As urbanites had no farms to return to while conditions throughout Russia were uniformly dreadful, the major option for Russians has been to emigrate abroad. This option has had its limits because most countries will accept only the most skilled former Soviets.

42. I. I. Polosin, "Pomestnoe pravo i krest'ianskaia krepost'," in *Sotsial'no–politicheskaia istoriia Rossii XVI-nachala XVII v. Sbornik statei* (Moscow, 1963), 47–49; Iu. V. Got'e and M. G. Roginskii, "Poslanie Ioganna Taube i Elberta Kruze," *Russkii istoricheskii zhurnal* 8(1922): 36.

43. See Michels, *At War with the Church*; and Chester S. L. Dunning, *Russia's First Civil War. The Time of Troubles and the Founding of the Romanov Dynasty* (University Park, PA, 2001).

44. These decrees are all discussed in detail in A. G. Man'kov, *Zakonodatel'stvo i pravo Rossii vtoroi poloviny XVII v.* (St. Petersburg, 1998), 116–21. See my review of this important book in *Kritika. Explorations in Russian and Eurasian History* 1, 3 (Summer 2000): 571–77. See the laws themselves in PRP 7:297 (Mar. 5, 1677, permitting Spasskii Monastery peasants to remain in Iaroslavl'); 298 (Dec. 17, 1684, permitting peasants to remain in Moscow who had migrated there earlier); 299–300 (Aug. 7, 1685, all peasants permitted to remain in any town to which they had migrated earlier); 300–301 (Oct. 19, 1688, peasants can stay in towns who arrived there between *Ulozhenie* and Dec. 17, 1684). This trend continued: see ibid., 302 (Nov. 24, 1699, peasants and others in urban occupations could remain there if willing to join urban tax rolls; otherwise, they had to be returned to their landholding masters). The Oct. 19, 1688, document is reproduced in *RZ* 4:146–47.

45. See my *The Economy and Material Culture of Russia 1600–1725* (Chicago, 1999), 435, citing *Akty otnos. k istorii Voiska donskogo, sob. General-maiorom A. A. Lishinym* (3 vols.; Novocherkassk, 1891–94), passim.

46. A. A. Vvedenskii, *Dom Stroganovykh v XVI-XVII vv.* (Moscow, 1962).

47. The great Soviet historian M. N. Tikhomirov, the dean of historians of Old Rus' between the death of B. D. Grekov in 1953 and his own demise in 1965, observed that there was something "not fully intelligible but miraculous in the settlement of the steppes, which were subjected to constant Tatar raids" (*Rossiia v XVI stoletii* [Moscow, 1962], 418). Tikhomi-

rov attributed the push into the steppe to a rapid growth of the population after the curtailment of civil wars and an increased demand for agricultural products (ibid., 419). The problem with this argument is the timing: the increase in population prior to the 1560s has been observed, but population movement into the steppes became a serious matter really after the 1570s.

48. The best account of town building in the 1590s remains P. P. Smirnov's *Posadskie liudi i ikh klassovaia bor'ba do serediny XVII veka*, 2 vols. (Moscow-Leningrad, 1947–48).

49. The *Ulozhenie* of 1649 permitted an unmarried woman or widow who fled to the frontier and married a serviceman to remain there and not to be returned if someone (presumably her husband) would pay for her. For peasant women the sum was 10 rubles, for slave women it was 50 rubles (*Ulozhenie*, 169, 20:27). This contradicted one of the oldest principles of Russian slavery, that anyone who himself or herself married a slave thereby also became a slave (ibid., 171, 20:31). For the government, populating the frontier was of higher priority than the property rights of serfholders and slaveowners. The price for a serf woman probably was "fair," that for a slave woman unquestionably was punitive.

50. In light of the poor conditions for servicemen on the frontiers, it is not at all surprising that a number of the uprisings in the summer of 1648 that forced the government to convoke the Odoevskii Commission to compile the *Ulozhenie* were in southern frontier towns (E. V. Chistiakova, *Gorodskie vosstaniia v Rossii v pervoi polovine XVII veka: [30–40-e gody]* [Voronezh, 1975]).

51. The evolution of landholding south of the Oka is detailed by Man'kov in *Zakonodatel'stvo*, 34 *et seq*. A successful 1650 claim by three impoverished provincial cavalrymen for a steppe land is in AMG 2, no. 431.

52. N. I. Nikitin, *Sluzhilye liudi v Zapadnoi Sibiri XVII veka* (Novosibirsk, 1988).

53. *Akty khoziaistva boiarina B. I. Morozova*, ed. A. I. Iakovlev (2 vols., Moscow-Leningrad, 1940, 1945), 1, nos. 26, 27, 30, 33–36, 45; Hellie, *Muscovite Society*, 209–13; D. I. Petrikeev, *Krupnoe krepostnoe khoziaistvo XVII v. Po materialam votchiny boiarina B. I. Morozova* (Leningrad, 1967), 172–75.

54. Man'kov, *Zakonodatel'stvo*, 89–90.

55. *RZ* 5:496–98. Exile of a husband by decrees of 1720, 1753, and 1767 dissolved a marriage and permitted the wife to remarry (N. A. Minenko, "O vliianii ssylki na semeinuiu zhizn' russkikh krest'ian," in *Ssylka i obshchestvenno-politicheskaia zhizn' v Sibiri* [Novosibirsk, 1978], 283).

56. *RZ* 5:502.

57. This certainly was true for Moscow in the 1960s, when exile 100 kilometers away from the Kirov Street post office for almost any offense involving violence made the capital one of the safest cities in the world;

purportedly Aleksandrovo, 101 kilometers distant, was a cesspool of violence. Almost certainly this measure would be effective in any large urban concentration in the world plagued by violence.

58. Terry Martin, "The Empire's New Frontiers: New Russia's Path from Frontier to Okraina 1774–1920," *Russian History* 19 (1992): 181–201; Kabuzan, *Emigratsiia*, 46–47.

59. The potato had little impact in Russia until the 1840s. See Alison Smith, "Cabbage and Cuisine: Food in Russia before the Great Reforms" (Ph.D. diss, Univ. of Chicago, 2000). For evidence that crop yields did not improve in the period of this chapter, see A. V. Dulov, *Geograficheskaia sreda i istoriia Rossii konets XV-seredina XIX v.* (Moscow, 1983), 56.

60. Arcadius Kahan, "Natural Calamities and Their Effect upon the Food Supply in Russia," *Jahrbücher für Geschichte Osteuropas* 16 (1968): 353–77. See also his *Plow*, 14. The two centuries 1551–1750 were especially bad, with 47 famines (Dulov, *Geograficheskaia sreda*, 15).

61. Kabuzan, *Emigratsiia*, 46.

62. E. I. Vainberg studied the migration of hundreds of peasants on the southern frontier and found none who moved back to old Muscovy proper ("Bor'ba krest'ian protiv krepostnichestva na iuzhnoi okraine Russkogo gosudarstva v pervoi polovine XVII v.," in *Novoe o proshlom nashei strany* [Moscow, 1967], 259–61).

CHAPTER 11

1. See D. Moon, *The Russian Peasantry 1600–1930: The World the Peasants Made* (London, 1999), 69, 84, 97–108; M. Matthews, *The Passport Society: Controlling Movement in Russia and the USSR* (Boulder, CO, 1993).

2. See W. M. Pintner, "The Burden of Defense in Imperial Russia, 1725–1914," *Russian Review* 43 (1984): 250–55; E. K. Wirtschafter, *From Serf to Russian Soldier* (Princeton, NJ, 1990), 3–25.

3. See E. N. Anuchin, "Issledovaniya o protsente soslannykh v Sibir' v period 1827–1846 gg.," *Zapiski Imperatorskogo Russkogo Geograficheskogo obshchestva po otdeleniyu statistiki* 3 (1873): 65–73.

4. See V. I. Semevskii, *Krest'yane v tsarstvovanie Imperatoritsy Ekateriny II*, 2 vols. (St Petersburg, 1901–3), 1:139–90; A. Kahan, *The Plow, the Hammer and the Knout: An Economic History of Eighteenth-Century Russia* (Chicago, 1985), 145–49; I. I. Ignatovich, *Pomeshchich'i krest'yane nakanune osvobozhdeniya*, 3d ed. (Leningrad, 1925), 36–45, 246–79; I. de Madariaga, "Catherine II and the Serfs," in id., *Politics and Culture in Eighteenth-Century Russia* (London, 1998), 129–37.

5. E. V. Anisimov, *The Reforms of Peter the Great*, trans. J. T. Alexander (Armonk, NY, 1993), 60–61, 81–82, 176; Kahan, *Plow*, 140–44; N. Petrovich, "Prinuditel'nọe pereselenie bobletskikh krest'yan," *Arkhiv istorii truda v Rossii*, bks. 11–12 (1924), 149–63; Madariaga, "Catherine II,"

129–30; D. Moon, "Peasant Migration and the Settlement of Russia's Frontiers 1550–1897," *HJ* 30 (1997): 887–88.

6. See Moon, "Peasant Migration and Settlement."

7. See chap. 10 above. (See also R. Hellie, *Enserfment and Military Change in Muscovy* [Chicago, 1971], 1–147.) Church peasants became part of the state peasantry in 1762, and court peasants were redesignated appanage peasants in 1797.

8. *PSZ*, 1st ser., 5:748–50 (esp. 750), no. 3445 (Oct. 30, 1719); 6:638–40 (esp. 639), no. 3939 (Apr. 6, 1722); 7:310–18 (esp. 315–16), no. 4533 (June 26, 1724). See also Anisimov, *Reforms*, 160–62, 226–35; B. N. Kazantsev, "Zakonodatel'stvo russkogo tsarisma po regulirovaniyu krest'yanskogo otkhoda v XVII-XIX vv.," *Voprosy istorii* (1970), no. 6, 22–23. On the revisions of the tax census, see V. M. Kabuzan, *Narodonaselenie Rossii v XVIII-pervoi polovine XIX v. (Po materialam revizii)* (Moscow, 1963).

9. See H. W. Dewey, "Russia's Debt to the Mongols in Suretyship and Collective Responsibility," *Comparative Studies in Society and History* 30 (1988): 249–70; Semevskii, *Krest'yane* 1:259–60; Ignatovich, *Pomeshchich'i krest'yane*, 188.

10. *SZ* 14, *SUPB*.

11. *SZ* (1857), 14, *SUPB*. In the following section, citations to articles (*stat'i*) are given in brackets in the text. Regulations concerning population movement are also to be found in other volumes of the *Digest of Laws*, and, where appropriate, are cited in the notes.

12. *SZ* (1857), 9, *Zakony o Sostoyaniyakh*, 206, art. 1037, 211, art. 1058.

13. See also *SZ* (1857), 9, *Zakony o Sostoyaniyakh*, 211, art. 1059.

14. For examples of estate owners' instructions on permits, see V. A. Aleksandrov, *Sel'skaya obshchina v Rossii (XVII-nachalo XIX v.)* (Moscow, 1976), 70–75; L. S. Prokof'eva, *Krest'yanskaya obshchina v Rossii vo vtoroi polovine XVIII-pervoi polovine XIX v.: na materialakh votchin Sheremetevykh* (Leningrad, 1981), 183.

15. V. I. Neupokoev, *Gosudarstvennye povinnosti krest'yan Evropeiskoi Rossii v kontse XVIII-nachale XIX v.* (Moscow, 1987), 34–35.

16. See I. D. Koval'chenko and L. V. Milov, "Ob intensivnosti obrochnoi ekspluatatsii krest'yan tsentral'noi Rossii v kontse XVIII-pervoi polovine XIX v.," *Istoriya SSSR* (1966), no. 4, 55–80; B. G. Litvak, *Russkaya derevnya v reforme 1861 goda: Chernozemnyi tsentr, 1861–1895 gg.* (Moscow, 1972), 115–27.

17. V. A. Fedorov, *Pomeshchich'i krest'yane tsentral'no-promyshlennogo raiona Rossii kontsa XVIII-pervoi poloviny XIX v.* (Moscow, 1974), 176–84; Anon., "Ocherki Tambovskoi gubernii v statisticheskom otnoshenii," *ZhMVD*, pt. 31 (1858), sect. 3, 55.

18. See Kazantsev, "Zakonodatel'stvo," 28.

19. See D. Moon, *Russian Peasants and Tsarist Legislation on the Eve of Reform: Interaction between Peasants and Officialdom, 1825–1855* (Basingstoke and London, 1992), 26, 38–39, 55.

20. See also *SZ* (1857), 9, *Zakony o Sostoyaniyakh*, 206–7, arts. 1040–41.

21. For more detailed summaries, see P. Kolchin, "After Serfdom: Russian Emancipation in Comparative Perspective," in Stanley L. Engerman, ed., *Terms of Labor: Slavery, Serfdom, and Free Labor* (Stanford, 1999) 91–94; D. Moon, *The Abolition of Serfdom in Russia, 1762–1907* (Harlow, 2000), chap. 6. Most of the Statutes were reprinted in O. I. Chistyakov, ed., *Rossiiskoe zakonodatel'stvo X-XX vekov*, 7, *Dokumenty krest'yanskoi reformy* (Moscow, 1989). In the following section, citations are to the relevant Statute and the article (*stat'ya*).

22. Most historians have stressed the barriers to leaving, rather than the new right. See A. Gerschenkron, "Agrarian Policies and Industrialization: Russia, 1861–1917," *Cambridge Economic History of Europe* 6, pt. 2 (Cambridge, 1965): 752–54; G. T. Robinson, *Rural Russia under the Old Regime* (Berkeley, 1960), 75–76.

23. See also Chistyakov, *Dokumenty*, 102–3, 164, 176.

24. See A. Kaufman, "Pereseleniya," in *Entsiklopedicheskii Slovar'*, 82+4 vols. (St. Petersburg, 1890–1907), 23 (1898): 269.

25. N. N. Leshchenko, "Vvedenie," in A. Z. Baraboi et al., eds., *Otmena krepostnogo prava na Ukraine: Sbornik dokumentov i materialov* (Kiev, 1961), 20, 25.

26. N. M. Druzhinin, *Gosudarstvennye krest'yane i reforma P. D. Kiseleva*, 2 vols. (Moscow and Leningrad, 1946–58); G. I. Bogatnikova, "Reforma 26 iyunya 1863 g. v udel'noi derevne," *Istoricheskie Zapiski* 63 (1958): 82–123; L. R. Gorlanov, *Udel'nye krest'yane Rossii, 1797–1865 gg.* (Smolensk, 1986).

27. The 1890 edition of the *Digest of Regulations concerning Passports and Fugitives* made no distinction between the former categories of peasants. On the separate regulations for state peasants from the late 1830s to the 1860s, see *SZ* (1857), 2, pt. 1, *Obshchee Gubernskoe Uchrezhdenie*, 313, arts. 1406–9, 623–24, art. 3077, 649–50, arts. 3212–17, 908–11, arts. 4722–40, 975–76, arts. 5136–44, 990–91, arts. 5238–45.

28. For a summary of the reasons for the origins of serfdom, see chap. 10 above. See also D. Moon, "Reassessing Russian Serfdom," *European History Quarterly* 26 (1996): 483–526.

29. B. V. Anan'ich, "Iz istorii zakonodatel'stva o krest'yanakh (vtoraya polovina XIX v.)," in V. V. Mavrodin, ed., *Voprosy istorii Rossii: XIX-nachala XX v.* (Leningrad, 1983), 34.

30. See J. Blum, *Lord and Peasant in Russia from the Ninth to the Nineteenth Century* (Princeton, NJ, 1961), 161, 228–35, 250, 253–54, 269–70, 427–28, 463–64; Hellie, *Enserfment*, 3, 8, 10, 16, 87, 122, 141–45.

31. See S. L. Hoch, "The Serf Economy and the Social Order in Russia," in M. L. Bush, ed., *Serfdom and Slavery: Studies in Legal Bondage* (London, 1996), 312; Moon, *Russian Peasantry*, 88–93.

32. R. M. Vvedenskii, "Pasportnaya politika russkogo Tsarizma i ee vliyanie na krest'yanskii otkhod," in V. T. Pashuto, ed., *Sotsial'no-politi-*

cheskoe i pravovoe polozhenie krest'yanstva v dorevolyutsionnoi Rossii (Voronezh, 1983), 167–68; Fedorov, *Pomeshchich'i krest'yane*, 205; Anan'ich, "Iz istorii zakonodatel'stva," 34–35.

33. *SZ* (1857), 14, *SUPB*, 25, art. 123, 31, art. 154, 33, arts. 164–66, 39, arts. 199–200; 2, *Obshee Gubernskoe Uchrezhdenie*, 909, art. 4726; 4, *Ustavy o Povinnostyakh*, I *Ustavy Rekrutskie*, 115–16, art. 433.

34. General Statute, art. 130, clause 2 (Chistyakov, *Dokumenty*, 64).

35. *SZ* (1857), 14, *SUPB*, 123, art. 583, 126–27, art. 597, 599, 130, art. 616; *Ustavy o Povinnostyakh*, I *Ustavy Rekrutskie*, 243–45, art. 969.

36. D. Atkinson, *The End of the Russian Land Commune, 1905–1930* (Stanford, 1983), 22–23; Gerschenkron, "Agrarian Policies," 710–11; Kolchin, "After Serfdom," 90.

37. L. G. Zakharova, *Samoderzhavie i otmena krepostnogo prava v Rossii, 1856–1861* (Moscow, 1984), 120–24.

38. Anan'ich, "Iz istorii zakonodatel'stva," 35.

39. See W. M. Pintner, *Russian Economic Policy under Nicholas I* (New York, 1967), 91–111, 235–37; E. Kingston-Mann, "In the Light and Shadow of the West: The Impact of Western Economics in Pre-Emancipation Russia," *Comparative Studies in Society and History* 33 (1991): 86–105.

40. O. Crisp, "Labour and Industrialization in Russia," in P. Mathias and M. M. Postan, eds., *Cambridge Economic History of Europe* 7, pt. 2 (Cambridge, 1978): 313.

41. Kazantsev, "Zakonodatel'stvo," 28–30; Vvedenskii, "Pasportnaya politika," 162–72.

42. See P. R. Gregory, *Before Command: An Economic History of Russia from Emancipation to the First Five-Year Plan* (Princeton, NJ, 1994), 55–80.

43. See J. Pallot and D. J. B. Shaw, *Landscape and Settlement in Romanov Russia, 1613–1917* (Oxford, 1990), 14–26; S. A. Chekmenev, *Sotsial'no-ekonomicheskoe razvitie Stavropol'ya i Kubani v kontse XVIII i v pervoi polovine XIX v.* (Pyatigorsk, 1967), 22–76; E. I. Druzhinina, *Severnoe Prichernomor'e v 1775–1800 gg.* (Moscow, 1959).

44. See Moon, "Peasant Migration and Settlement," 887–88; Yu. M. Tarasov, *Russkaya krest'yanskaya kolonizatsiya Yuzhnogo Urala: Vtoraya polovina XVIII-pervaya polovina XIX v.* (Moscow, 1984); W. Sunderland, "Peasants on the Move: State Peasant Resettlement in Imperial Russia, 1805–1830s," *Russian Review* 52 (1993): 472–85.

45. Druzhinin, *Gosudarstvennye krest'yane* 2:189–95.

46. Hellie, *Enserfment*, 129–31; Druzhinina, *Severnoe Prichernomor'e*, 261; Moon, *Russian Peasants and Tsarist Legislation*, 29–32.

47. See Chekmenev, *Sotsial'no-ekonomicheskoe razvitie*, 39–41 (North Caucasus); D. W. Treadgold, *The Great Siberian Migration: Government and Peasant in Resettlement from Emancipation to the First World War* (Princeton, NJ, 1957), 74.

48. *PSZ*, 3d ser., 9:535–38, no. 6198 (June 13, 1889).

49. Treadgold, *Great Siberian Migration*, 73–81, 120–30; A. Kaufman,

"Pereselencheskaya politika," in *Entsiklopedicheskii slovar'*, 7th ed., 57 vols. (Moscow, 1910–36) [repr., Moscow, 1993–], 31, cols. 531–48; S. M. Dubrovskii, *Stolypinskaya zemel'naya reforma* (Moscow, 1963), 383–402.

50. J. L. H. Keep, *Soldiers of the Tsar: Army and Society in Russia, 1462–1874* (Oxford, 1985), 375–78.

51. N. I. Anan'ich, "K istorii otmeny podushnoi podati v Rossii," *Istoricheskie zapiski* 94 (1974): 183–212; L. Bowman, "Russia's First Income Taxes: The Effects of Modernized Taxes on Commerce and Industry, 1885–1914," *Slavic Review* 52 (1993): 256–82.

52. M. S. Simonova, "Otmena krugovoi poruki," *Istoricheskie zapiski* 83 (1969): 158–95.

53. See V. A. Fedorov, ed., *Konets krepostnichestva v Rossii: Dokumenty, pis'ma, memuary, stat'i* (Moscow, 1994), 463–64.

54. Atkinson, *End of the Russian Land Commune*, 41–100.

55. *PSZ*, 3d ser., 14:347–56 (1st pagination), 284–94 (2d pagination), no. 10879 (June 3, 1894); Anan'ich, "Iz istorii zakonodatel'stva," 39–35.

56. *Sbornik deistvuyushchikh postanovlenii, izdannykh v poryadke stat'i 87 osnovnykh gosudarstvennykh zakonov* (St. Petersburg, 1913), 12–17. On the restrictions abolished, see *SZ* 9, *Osoboe prilozhenie k zakonam o sostoyaniyakh* (St. Petersburg, 1902), 47–48, art. 208.

57. A. A. Dobrovol'skii, *Svod Zakonov... dopolnennyi po Prodolzheniyam 1906, 1908, 1909, 1910 gg i pozdeishim uzakoneniyam 1911 i 1912 gg.*, 16 vols. in 4 bks. (St. Petersburg, 1913), bk. 1, col. 9, art. 76.

58. See Kaufman, "Pereseleniya," 265.

59. See D. J. M. Hooson, "The Geographical Setting," in R. Auty and D. Obolensky, eds., *An Introduction to Russian History* (Cambridge, 1976), 1–48; B. N. Mironov, *Vnutrennii rynok Rossii vo vtoroi polovine XVIII-pervoi polovine XIX v.* (Leningrad, 1981).

60. See B. G. Plyushchevskii, "Krest'yanskii otkhozhie promysli na territorii evropeiskoi Rossii v posledne-predreformennye desyatiletiya (1830–1850 gg.)" (doc. diss. *Institut Istorii, AN SSSR* Leningrad, 1974), 43–70, 88–98, 126–38, 150–247; Fedorov, *Pomeshchich'i krest'yane*, 210–18; J. Bradley, *Muzhik and Muscovite: Urbanization in Late Imperial Russia* (Berkeley, 1985), 70–99; E. G. Economakis, *From Peasant to Petersburger* (New York, 1998), 16–25, 102–13.

61. See Plyushchevskii, "Krest'yanskii otkhozhie promysli," 70–87, 98–113; E. I. Druzhinina, *Yuzhnaya Ukraina v period krizisa feodalizma 1825–1860 gg.* (Moscow, 1981), 26–28; T. Mixter, "The Hiring Market as Workers' Turf: Migrant Agricultural Laborers and the Mobilization of Collective Action in the Steppe Grainbelt of European Russia, 1853–1913," in E. Kingston-Mann and T. Mixter, eds., *Peasant Economy, Culture, and Politics of European Russia, 1800–1921* (Princeton, NJ, 1991), 294–340.

62. T. H. Friedgut, *Iuzovka and Revolution: Life and Work in Russia's Donbass, 1869–1924* (Princeton, NJ, 1989), 193–258; J. L. Schecter, ed., *Khrushchev Remembers: The Glasnost Tapes* (Boston, MA, 1990), 4.

63. See V. I. Snezhnevskii, "K istorii pobegov krepostnykh v poslednei

chetverti XVIII i v XIX stoletiyakh," *Nizhegorodskii sbornik* 10 (Nizhnii Novgorod, 1890): 517–95.

64. See S. A. Chekmenev, "Razvitie khutorskogo khozyaistva na Kubani i Stavropol'e v kontse XVIII-pervoi polovine XIX v.," *Ezhegodnik po agrarnoi istorii Vostochnoi Evropy 1966 g.* (Tallinn, 1971), 298–309; S. O'Rourke, *Warriors and Peasants: The Don Cossacks in Late Imperial Russia* (New York, 2000), 38–40.

65. A. V. Predtechenskii, ed., *Krest'yanskoe dvizhenie v Rossii v 1826–1849 gg.: Sbornik dokumentov* (Moscow, 1961), 559–77, 799.

66. Fedorov, *Pomeshchich'i krest'yane*, 187–89; Plushchevskii, "Krest'yanskie otkhozhie promysly," 325–39; Kahan, *Plow*, 147; M. Tugan-Baranovskii, *Russkaya fabrika v proshlom i nastoyashchem*, 3d ed. (Moscow, 1922), 75–77; Bohac, "Agricultural Structure and the Origins of Migration in Central Russia, 1810–1850," in G. Grantham and C. Leonard, eds., *Agrarian Organization in the Century of Industrialization: Europe, Russia, and North America, Research in Economic History*, supp. 5, pt. B (Greenwich, CT, 1989), 374–80.

67. J. Burds, *Peasant Dreams and Market Politics: Labor Migration and the Russian Village, 1861–1905* (Pittsburgh, PA, 1998), 38.

68. Ibid., esp. 28–141. See also Local Statute on the abolition of serfdom in Great Russia, arts. 168–77 (Chistyakov, *Dokumenty krest'yanskoi reformy*, 289–93).

69. B. V. Tikhonov, *Pereseleniya v Rossii vo vtoroi polovine XIX v.: po materialam perepisi 1897 g. i pasportnoi statistiki* (Moscow, 1978), 161.

70. See Bradley, *Muzhik and Muscovite*; Burds, *Peasant Dreams*; Economakis, *Peasant and Petersburger*; B. A. Engel, *Between the Fields and the City: Women, Work and Family in Russia 1861–1914* (Cambridge, 1994); R. E. Johnson, *Peasant and Proletarian: The Working Class of Moscow in the Late Nineteenth Century* (New Brunswick, NJ, 1979).

71. Fedorov, *Pomeshchich'i krest'yane*, 198–205, 210, 297–306; V. M. Kabuzan, *Izmeneniya v razmeshchenii naseleniya Rossii v XVIII-pervoi polovine XIX v. (Po materialam revizii)* (Moscow, 1971) 167, 175.

72. Calculated from "Ocherki Tambovskoi gubernii," *ZhMVD*, pt. 31 (1858), 19–21, 52–55.

73. Fedorov, *Pomeshchich'i krest'yane*, 297; Blum, *Lord and Peasant*, 452.

74. See Fedorov, *Pomeshchich'i krest'yane*, 199–204.

75. B. N. Mironov, *Sotsial'naya istoriya Rossii perioda imperii*, 2 vols. (St. Petersburg, 1999), 1:466.

76. Mironov, *Sotsial'naya istoriya* 1:180–81, 247–48, 466. Cf. Burds, *Peasant Dreams*, 24.

77. Anon., "O chisle passportov, vydavaemykh v Yaroslavskoi gubernii," *ZhMVD*, pt. 29 (1858), sec. 3, 20; "Ocherki Tambovskoi gubernii," 64.

78. Mironov, *Sotsial'naya istoriya* 1:244.

79. See Engel, *Between the Fields and the City*.

80. Tikhonov, *Pereseleniya*, 116.

81. A. G. Rashin, *Naselenie Rossii za 100 let: Statisticheskie ocherki* (Moscow, 1956), 86.

82. M. F. Hamm, "Introduction," in Hamm, ed., *The City in Late Imperial Russia* (Bloomington, IN, 1986), 2. For data on the European part of the empire, excluding Poland, see Rashin, *Naselenie*, 87.

83. Rashin, *Naselenie*, 89–91, 93.

84. D. R. Brower, "Urban Revolution in the Late Russian Empire," in Hamm, ed., *City*, 326–28. For data on St. Petersburg and Moscow, see Rashin, *Naselenie*, 113, 116.

85. See J. H. Bater, "Transience, Residential Persistence, and Mobility in Moscow and St. Petersburg, 1900–1914," *Slavic Review* 39 (1980): 239–54.

86. Mironov, *Sotsial'naya istoriya* 1:341; R. B. McKean, *St Petersburg Between the Revolutions: Workers and Revolutionaries June 1907–February 1917* (New Haven, CT, 1990), 16. See also Moon, "Estimating the Peasant Population of Late Imperial Russia from the 1897 Census," *Europe-Asia Studies* 48 (1996): 141–53.

87. B. A. Anderson, *Internal Migration during Modernization in Late Nineteenth-Century Russia* (Princeton, NJ, 1980), 90–120; Economakis, *Peasant and Petersburger*, esp. 11–50; Tikhonov, *Pereseleniya*, 159–60 and app. 1.

88. Anderson, *Internal Migration*, 121–53; Treadgold, *Great Siberian Migration*, 88–92; Tikhonov, *Pereseleniya*, 148–52.

89. For a fuller discussion, see Moon, "Peasant Migration and Settlement."

90. See ibid., 862–70; S. I. Bruk and V. M. Kabuzan, "Migratsiya naseleniya v Rossii v XVIII-nachale XX veka," *Istoriya SSSR* no. 4 (1984): 41–59.

91. See, for example, Predtechenskii, *Krest'yanskoe dvizhenie ... 1826–1849*, 223–27, 330–32, 579–80, 817; S. B. Okun', ed., *Krest'yanskoe dvizhenie v Rossii v 1850–1856 gg.: Sbornik dokumentov* (Moscow, 1962), 76–87, 574–93. See also Moon, *Russian Peasantry*, 254–62.

92. M. Gorbachev, *Memoirs* (London, 1996), 19. See also Moon, *Russian Peasants and Tsarist Legislation*, 44.

93. Kaufman, "Pereseleniya," 269.

94. See Moon, *Russian Peasants and Tsarist Legislation*, 23–61.

95. Treadgold, *Great Siberian Migration*, 80.

96. Kaufman, "Pereseleniya," 269.

97. See Treadgold, *Great Siberian Migration*, 34.

98. See Burds, *Peasant Dreams*, 15.

99. See Ya. E. Vodarskii, *Naselenie Rossii v kontse XVII-nachale XVIII veka* (Moscow, 1977), 153–56; Bruk and Kabuzan, "Migratsiya," 52; N. A. Yakimenko, "Agrarnye migratsii v Rossii (1861–1917 gg.)," *Voprosy istorii* (1983), no. 3, 19–20.

100. See K. V. Chistov, *Russkie narodnye sotsial'no-utopicheskie legendy XVII-XIX vv.* (Moscow, 1967); N. A. Yakimenko, "Sovetskaya istoriografiya pereseleniya krest'yan v Sibir' i na Dal'nyi Vostok (1861–1917)," *Istoriya SSSR* (1980), no. 5, 95.

101. See Moon, *Russian Peasantry*, 49–54, 254–60; Treadgold, *Great Siberian Migration*, 83–84, 95.

102. I. Stebelsky, "Agriculture and Soil Erosion in the European Forest-steppe," in J. H. Bater and R. A. French, eds., *Studies in Russian Historical Geography*, 2 vols. (London, 1983), 1:45–63.

103. S. I. Bruk and V. M. Kabuzan, "Dinamika chislennosti i rasselenie Russkogo etnosa (1678–1917 gg.)," *Sovetskaya etnografiya* (1982), no. 4, 14. The figures quoted are for all ethnic groups in the empire. On the proportion of peasants, see Moon, "Estimating."

104. See Rashin, *Naselenie*, 76–79.

105. Mironov, *Sotsial'naya istoriya* 1:246.

106. P. Gatrell, *The Tsarist Economy 1850–1917* (London, 1986), 112–15.

107. See Pallot and Shaw, *Landscape and Settlement*, 116–31.

108. Kaufman, "Pereseleniya," 265–66; id., "Pereseleniya i pereselencheskii vopros," cols. 508–9.

109. See Robinson, *Rural Russia*, 109–10; Yakimenko, "Sovetskaya istoriografiya pereseleniya," 96.

110. S. G. Wheatcroft, "Crises and the Condition of the Peasantry in Late Imperial Russia," in Kingston-Mann and Mixter, *Peasant Economy*, 128–72. See also S. L. Hoch, "On Good Numbers and Bad: Malthus, Population Trends and Peasant Standard of Living in Late Imperial Russia," *Slavic Review* 53 (1994): 41–75.

111. See Kaufman, "Pereseleniya," 267–68; id., "Pereseleniya i pereselencheskii vopros," cols. 511–13; N. A. Yakimenko, "O sotsial'nom sostave krest'yan-pereselentsev v Rossii 80–kh godov XIX-nachala XX veka," *Otechestvennaya Istoriya* (1993), no. 1, 174–82.

112. See, for example, Moon, *Russian Peasants and Tsarist Legislation*, 41–45.

113. S. G. Wheatcroft, "The 1891–92 Famine in Russia," in L. Edmondson and P. Waldron, eds., *Economy and Society in Russia and the Soviet Union, 1860–1930* (Basingstoke and London, 1992), 44–64.

114. Yakimenko, "Agrarnye migratsii," 25–26.

115. See A. Kahan, "Natural Calamities and their Effect on the Food Supply in Russia," *Jahrbuecher fuer Geschichte Osteuropas* 16 (1968): 353–77; Moon, *Russian Peasantry*, 28–33.

116. H. Rogger, *Russia in the Age of Modernisation and Revolution, 1881–1917* (London, 1983), 105.

117. S. G. Marks, *Road to Power: The Trans-Siberian Railroad and the Colonization of Asian Russia, 1850–1917* (Ithaca, NY, 1991), esp. 153–69.

118. See Treadgold, *Great Siberian Migration*, 81, 96–97.

119. Burds, *Peasant Dreams*, 143–70; O. Semyonova Tian-Shanskaia, *Village Life in Late Tsarist Russia*, D. L. Ransel, ed., trans. M. Levine (Bloomington, IN, 1993), 55.

120. B. G. Litvak, *Perevorot 1861 goda v Rossii* (Moscow, 1991), 152–70; P. A. Zaionchkovskii, *Otmena krepostnogo prava v Rossii*, 3d ed. (Moscow, 1968), 232–45.

121. Litvak, *Perevorot*, 171–75; Zaionchkovskii, *Otmena*, 245–46.

122. Yu. E. Yanson, *Opyt statisticheskogo issledovaniya o krest'yanskikh nadelakh i platezhakh* (St. Petersburg, 1877), cited in Z. Deal, review article, *Kritika*, 1980, no. 1, 48.

123. Zaionchkovskii, *Otmena*, 134.

124. Litvak, *Perevorot*, 173–74.

125. Ibid., 179; Hoch, "On Good Numbers," 71–72.

126. See Moon, *Russian Peasantry*, 113–15.

127. See Yakimenko, "Agrarnye migratsii," 21. On Ukrainian peasants' "well developed propensity" to migrate, see D. Saunders, "Russia's Ukrainian Policy (1847–1905): A Demographic Approach," *European History Quarterly* 25 (1995): 191.

128. Yakimenko, "Agrarnye migratsii," 21.

129. See N. M. Druzhinin, *Russkaya derevnya na perelome, 1861–1880 gg.* (Moscow, 1978), 87, 109, 116–17.

130. Kaufman, "Pereseleniya," 267.

131. Rashin, *Naselenie*, 66–67.

132. See Bruk and Kabuzan, "Migratsiya," 41–42; Tarasov, *Russkaya Krest'yanskaya*, 88–89, 171; Vodarskii, *Naselenie Rossii v kontse XVII*, 197; Yakimemko, "Sovetskaya istoriografiya pereseleniya," 104. Cf. A. Donnelly, "The Mobile Steppe Frontier: The Russian Conquest and Colonization of Bashkiria and Kazakhstan to 1850," in M. Rywkin, ed., *Russian Colonial Expansion to 1917* (London, 1988), 197, 202; Marks, *Road*, 141, 153–56.

133. Kaufman, "Pereseleniya," 269.

134. Quoted in Anan'ich, "Iz istorii zakonodatel'stva," 39. My emphasis, DM.

135. N. Lenskii, quoted in Treadgold, *Great Siberian Migration*, 80–81.

Index

In this index an "f" after a number indicates a separate reference on the next page, and an "ff" indicates separate references on the next two pages. A continuous discussion over two or more pages is indicated by a span of page numbers, e.g., "57–59." *Passim* is used for a cluster of references in close but not consecutive sequence.